The Gun Digest® Book of

THE AR-15

ARMALITE INC.
GENESEO, IL

FIRE

SAFE

PATRICK SWEENEY

©2005 Krause Publications

Published by

Gun Digest Books

An imprint of F+W Publications

700 East State Street • Iola, WI 54990-0001

715-445-2214 • 888-457-2873

www.gunlistonline.com

Our toll-free number to place an order or obtain
a free catalog is (800) 258-0929.

Library of Congress Catalog Number: 2005922945

ISBN 13-digit: 978-0-87349-947-7

ISBN 10-digit: 0-87349-947-6

Designed by Kara Grundman

Edited by Kevin Michalowski

Printed in the United States of America

ACKNOWLEDGMENTS

First, let me thank the manufacturers who sent me their product in the hopes I would praise them to the skies, and like them so much I'd actually want to buy them, thus saving their shipping department the hassle of re-entering it in the bound book. Seriously, manufacturers take a leap of faith in sending out guns.

So I'd like to thank them all for sending a rifle or rifles. In particular, Walt Kulek of Fulton Armory, who practically had rifles here before I finished the cup of coffee I'd been sipping when we discussed the project. Tom Spithaler, of Olympic, who kindly answered my questions about how ARs are made and what goes into them. Mark Westrom and the whole crew at Armalite, for allowing me to wander the plant for a day and take photos and pester them with endless questions. Jeff Hoffman of Black Hills, who did his best once again to bury me in ammunition.

And most of all, thanks to Felicia, for her support, encouragement, and for listening to me prattle on about the latest tidbits of AR lore that I might have found each day, and not letting on that I was boring her to tears. Without her help in the beginning, I never would have gotten this far.

For those of us tuned into guns, a firearm represents a time, place, incident or age. If you see someone in a suit, holding a Thompson, you immediately think "Roaring Twenties." The same image, but with Winston Churchill instead of an anonymous person, and you think "WWII." If you see a tri-corner hat and a smooth-bore musket, you think "American Revolution." (with apologies to my international readers, who may think of some other fracas)

The M-16 brings up a plethora of images, each with a particular time and place. A triangular handguard and a plain green uniform brings recollections of Vietnam. Round handguards and woodland camouflage brings photographs from Central America to mind, or to someone stationed in Europe, Germany, Italy, Belgium or Turkey. And an M-4 and tan/desert uniforms bring to mind Afghanistan, Iraq and whatever else the current situation brings us.

The ubiquity of the AR-15/M-16 rifle is due to exposure and time. While you or I might only have a single drawing of the American Revolution to fix that image in our memories, we have a constant repetition of images of modern rifles, courtesy the modern news media. As an example, several friends of mine, when they see an AK-47, cannot escape the visceral reaction of "there is something terribly wrong here" while my first reaction on seeing one is to think of the news photo of an AK being held aloft at Wounded Knee. (As far as I know, no one was ever prosecuted for owning or handling that firearm. Never mind that at that time there was no such thing as a semi-automatic only AK, and thus it had to be a select-fire rifle.) They were a few years older, there in the jungle, and I was reading the newspapers at home.

The AR-15 has been with us now for over 40 years. Longer than the '03 Springfield was a front-line rifle, longer than the M-1 Garand, and far longer than the M-14. (Despite the M-14 still being used in many tasks, it isn't a front-line, general-issue weapon.) Despite the struggles of the 30-caliber crowd, the AR has supplanted 30-caliber rifles as the winner in target competitions. It is now being accepted as a law enforcement tool, and is embraced by many as an entirely suitable defensive firearm. There are still some who feel it isn't powerful enough, but "powerful enough" is not a valid question. If it were, we'd still be using rifles with designations that start in "5" or "6" as only those calibers can be depended on to stop miscreants reliably. As in 50- caliber or bigger, although there were instances in the American Civil War of combatants who were shot with .58 caliber Minie balls who kept on fighting. Indeed, there were reports over a century ago coming back from the Indian Frontier about the adoption of a smaller caliber. From British Officers, complaining that the new .303 round did not stop the natives as well as the old .45 had.

The AR is deceptive: It is both the easiest rifle to home-gunsmith, and can be the most maddening to get properly assembled and reliably functioning. When I was a practicing professional gunsmith, during the height of the first (there will be more to come, I'm sure) wave of home-assembled kits, I did a good business finishing the assembly and ensuring proper function of home-assembled AR kits that the owners had gotten almost finished. Sometimes they needed a special tool to finish, something too expensive to buy for a one-time build. Or in other cases they needed special knowledge to figure out the real problem, and apply the correct fix, not the "obvious" and wrong one.

The AR doesn't need any specialized stock work, no sanding, oil-finished wood, or complicated glass bedding. It doesn't need (in most cases) a free-floated barrel or special bedding methods. The triggers are simple, and with a little work or the right parts can be quite livable. And the recoil is soft, encouraging practice, practice and more practice. Where you can beat yourself into a flinch in an afternoon with a 30-caliber rifle, you can burn out an AR barrel on a weekend with no fear of a dreaded flinch.

And for the gadget buffs there is perhaps no rifle on the face of the planet for which you can buy more gear, accessories, add-ons, improvements and just plain "stuff." You could easily take a 6-pound AR and turn it into a 12-pound AR by bolting on "essential additions." Indeed, target shooters add plain old lead weights to bring their ARs up past 15 pounds, to make them more stable for long shots.

Those who have read my earlier books know my methods in these matters. In order to properly address the field of AR-15 rifles, I needed rifles to test. It would not be suitable to simply photograph and write about my own rifles. For the most part, they are not stock. And they have all been fussed over until they can be depended on for reliable function. And it would not be acceptable to simply digest and re-write the press handouts of various manufacturers and wholesalers. Not that they would lie, but the whole idea of marketing is to remove dispassionate analysis and replace it with lust. So, I needed rifles. But what to cover? There are a host of parts suppliers, and gunsmiths who are at least basically competent to build an AR. Many are more than just competent, and turn out marvels of reliability and accuracy. How to decide which guns, options, accessories and custom features for the first book? I settled on two tests, both of which a manufacturer had to meet, or I would not give a full test and review: They had to manufacturer or assemble complete rifles. And they had to have their name on the receiver. Bob Smith of "Bob Smiths Gunsmithing" may build excellent ARs for his SWAT and competition customers. But if it didn't say "Bob Smith Armory" on the receiver, he'd have to wait for the second book. Assembly was also a requirement. If a firm offered complete kits, but not assembled rifles, they too would wait. I inquired with all the manufacturers I could find. In the process of writing the book, I found even more than had known of. I figured I'd be lucky to locate a dozen makers. I ended up with over 30 rifles. And, I re-discovered the world of marketing. A world where some makers are much better than others.

As you read this there are no doubt makers who have yet to send the promised rifle or rifles. I asked everyone I could find, and in this regard the internet is quite useful. I found makers who had a rifle to me by the end of that week. I found makers who took six months to get me a rifle. I found makers who promised and didn't deliver. And others who were more than happy to sell me a rifle, but had none to loan. For the readers who are still under the illusion that all gun writers get to "keep the goodies" I have news for you: the local FedEx office knows me on sight. Rifles go back. There are some writers who keep everything that is sent to them. They are well-known in the industry and receive a very few rifles for testing. (Some of my problems in getting test rifles may be due to unfortunate experiences on the part of the manufacturer with those other writers.) Let me repeat this for those who feel I may have slighted their favorite rifle: I asked everyone I could track down. I tested all rifles that were sent to me. If a rifle did not meet my expectations, I inquired with the maker for a solution. If the problem was solved, I did not make a fuss over it. If it didn't return, or was never satisfactorily fixed, it did not make it into the book.

I also needed ammo. I cannot say enough good things about Jeff Hoffman at Black Hills, and the staff at Hornady. My delivery driver staggered under the load of ammo shipped. There was nothing I asked for that I didn't receive at least some amount. Some of the ammo, like the Mk 262 Mod 1, so highly sought-after in Iraq and Afghanistan, was scarce enough in the pipeline that I only got enough to test the rifles for accuracy. Fair enough, the guys overseas have a more-pressing need for it than I do.

So, if there is a rifle you were curious about, but I don't list, there is a reason. I left out none of the ones I received that worked. Good or indifferent, the performance of each was noted. The really bad ones will have to try harder for Volume 2. Some were so good I really, really considered buying rather than sending back. But what is a man to do with a dozen AR-15s?

The AR-15 is presently in a resurgence. There are more manufacturers than there have ever been. The armed forces are using more of them than they have in more than a generation. (You thought everyone in the Army or Marine Corps spent all their time on the range, wearing out rifles? You poor, mislead taxpayer!) They are also looking to replace it with more fervor than they ever have. However, the latest rounds are not trying to replace it with an "all dancing, all singing" electronic rifle. Yes, we can currently have a PDA that is also a cell phone, digital camera, GPS unit and MP3 player. But rifles aren't consumer electronics. Rifles launch bullets, and nothing in the digital revolution so far (except CNC machining stations) has changed how rifles work or are used. But the next decade or so promises to be very entertaining in the regard of attempts to replace the AR.

As for the next volume, that will be out soon, and there we'll dive headfirst into modifications, basic gunsmithing and maintenance (beyond cleaning) and accessories galore. We'll also cover the guns that didn't arrive in time, or took a lot of work to struggle up to satisfactory performance. Use this book to select and purchase a basic gun. Then, when you encounter the second volume, you'll have had a good time shooting your gun and planning the modifications, upgrades and improvements.

CONTENTS

History Of The AR-15 And How It Is Made

I am not going to give you a detailed, blow-by-blow history of the trials, tribulations, acceptance and use of the AR-15/M-16. There are a number of books out there in which you can find out the exact date some such memo or another was written, authorizing this or squashing that. If you want historical minutia (which some of us do) then try those other titles. My intent here is to point out some of the highs and lows, and illustrate how they created the rifle we now use, build, wear out and invest so much passion in.

The history of the AR-15/M-16 is actually a four-part story so far. First, there is the story of the change in how a rifle was viewed and used, from the adoption of a modern service rifle in the late 19th century to the middle 20th. Then, the acceptance and adoption of the M-16 by the U.S. Department of Defense. Third, the improvements made to it, and the acceptance of the AR by civilian shooters. And finally, the culmination of the M-16 into the M-4, and the acceptance (so far) by the Armed Forces that the digital revolution was not going to come to small arms anytime soon.

Just to keep us all from going crazy, and to make my editor's job easier, I will as of this moment stop using the clumsy construction of "AR-15/M-16." When I'm talking about the rifle system in general, I'll simply use "AR-15." When I mean the select-fire or burst-fire basic system, I'll call it "M-16." And when I'm talking about a specific rifle or model, I'll use its exact designation, like M-4, XM-177, etc. Otherwise you'd be faced with the prospect of seeing the clumsy construction a couple of thousand times. (And I'd have to type it, making us all a bit cranky.) And as the rifle was known as the AR-15 even for a while after it was made as a select-fire weapon (I've seen a bunch of military select-fire rifles marked "AR-15", made by Colt) it is correct to call them all that. Be aware that Colt owns the rights and trademark to "AR-15" and no rifle not made by Colt can be properly or legally called that. Now that we've gotten all cozy with a comfortable agreement, let me upset some of you:

Eugene Stoner did not invent the gas impingement system that is the heart of the AR-15. In 1942, Sweden adopted the Ljungman rifle in 6.5 caliber. They did not replace all the bolt-action rifles in use, but simply added the Ljungman to each squad of riflemen as a means of increasing firepower. After the war, Sweden managed to entice the Danish armed forces into adopting a modified Ljungman, and even sold Egypt tooling and technical help in setting up their own manufacturing facilities. The armed forces of Egypt were at least sharp enough to insist in changing the rifle to 7.92 Mauser from the 6.5X55 of the Swedish model. The Ljungman was unique in having the direct-impingement gas system, which Stoner either copied or designed anew not knowing it existed. The Ljungman is still unique in the hazard it poses to users. When I was new to the gun business, I worked at a gun shop that specialized in surplus and collectible firearms. We'd see Ljungmans passing through the shop now and then, and my first exposure was to watch it being handled without touching it. You see, the bolt and carrier of the Ljungman are triangular in cross section, and there are no safety guards. You open

The AR now is not the same as the M-16. In the early days, it was often called both by its manufacturer, Colt.

(U.S. Air Force photo by Airman 1st Class Heather Forrest)

Once the machinegun was invented, infantry tactics soon came to revolve around, and support, the machinegun. This is a West German MG-3, basically a WWII MG-42 rechambered in 7.62 NATO.

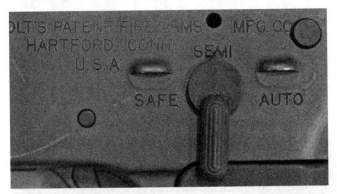

The M-16 in all its variations is a select-fire rifle. You can select Safe, Semi, Auto or Burst, depending on what version you have.

the bolt by pushing the safety lever to "ON" (I forget after all this time if that is to the left or right) grasping the cover and pushing it forward. At the forward end of its travel it locks onto the bolt, and retracts the bolt with it when you pull the whole bolt and cover assembly rearward.

If there is a loaded magazine in place, when the bolt gets to the rear of its travel it snaps forward, chambering a round. If it is empty the bolt will stay back. If you go to close the bolt on an empty chamber, it snaps forward even faster. As there is nothing in the way of a dust cover or guard, if your hand or fingers are in the way, they'll get snapped up too. You can get an "M-1 Thumb" from a Garand, but you can lose a fingernail or even finger tip in a Ljungman.

The operation of the mechanism is simple, and familiar to any user of the AR-15: the gas is vented out of a port in the barrel, and travels directly down a tube to the face of the bolt carrier. There, the carrier is blown back, unlocking and taking the bolt with it. The design is simple, and uses fewer intricate and moving parts than other systems, save perhaps the Vorgrimmler delayed roller lock of the CETME and H-K systems.

The first section of the story begins in the late 19th century. The adoption of smokeless powder brings several revolutions: high velocity, greater firepower, and a lack of smoke. The result is that infantry can control more ground than before. The greater range allows a unit to project rifle fire to greater distances, and the lack of smoke allows for continued fire. In the years before the wholesale adoption of machineguns, infantry worked out methods of controlling and directing fire by units to impressive distances. The U.S. Army training manual of 1909 lays out the Army qualification process, with firing to 900 yards on moving targets. Target competition, which had always been a long-range sport with black powder rifles, stayed long with smokeless. The standard course for the National Matches requires firing at 200, 300, 500 and 600 yards. Other matches called for shooting to 1,000 yards or more.

At the end of WWII, many armed forces wished to upgrade their equipment. While it was prudent to continue using old gear during a war and not interrupt current manufacture and supply, once a war is over, no one wants to be stuck with "the last war's tools." Contrary to that, the accountants will look at warehouses full of perfectly serviceable weapons, ammunition and support equipment, and ask "What's the advantage?" The advantage, hopefully, is to win the next war. However, you have to be fighting the right kind of war. What the Germans and Soviets found, and what the experts in the United States Army were not willing to admit, was that most combat took place at close range. While the rifles and machineguns used in WWII were designed and built to allow long-range

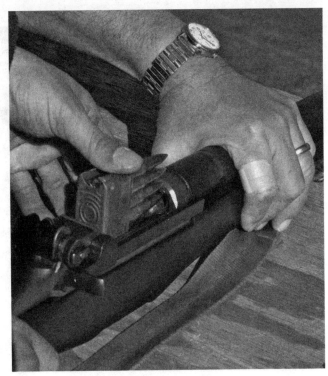

The M-1 Garand, accurate and powerful, was the rifle all replacements were compared to. Except combat didn't need a thousand-yard rifle any more.

The M-1 Carbine filled the same role the M-16 was first bought for. And also shared its history of insufficient development.

engagements, well past 300 yards, experience showed that most combat was well within 300 yards. In fact, most of it was within less than 100 yards. S.L.A. Marshall debriefed units involved in the Korean War (Marshall has some critics, and there is much discussion of the validity of his data) and found that long-range rifle fire alone was not enough to stop Chinese units from maneuvering in the open. While all others armies were looking to develop rifles that would be best used within the close distances of actual combat, the U.S. Army insisted on the performance of the .30-06 cartridge. With the improvements of ball powder, they were able to shorten the cartridge and thus the .308 Winchester was born. We then forced the new cartridge onto our NATO allies, creating the 7.62X51, or "7.62 NATO" cartridge, a .308 designed for the rigors of combat.

Any company or designer who wanted to sell rifles to the Army had to do so with designs that used the new 7.62 cartridge. So that is what the new Armalite company and Eugene Stoner did. The design took advantage of "something old and something new, something borrowed and" ..... well, there wasn't anything blue in the AR-10. The something old was the Johnson eight-lugged bolt. Back when the Garand was struggling to be adopted, Melvin Johnson had a rifle and light machinegun that he thought was better. (I've owned and shot both, Melvin was wrong.) It used (and he patented) an eight-lugged bolt that locked into the back of the barrel. By using the barrel or a barrel extension as the locking location, the new rifle did not need a large, heavy steel receiver to take the stress of the cartridge pressure on firing. The something new was the gas impingement system, taken from the Ljungman. With the gas directed back via a small tube, there was no need for a long heavy operating rod or handle. By these two design changes alone, the Armalite rifle could be several pounds lighter than other designs. The something new was the use of new aluminum alloys as the receiver component. With new alloys, forged and machined, a receiver could be even lighter than a steel one, even one designed without the need to take the firing stresses, as a Garand receiver was designed to. And in the early years, the Garand was the comparator, as the AR-10 was new enough to be a design competitor to the M-14 and FAL.

To further reduce weight, Stoner and George Sullivan, in charge of ideas at Armalite, experimented with thin barrels that had aluminum jackets for stiffening and to aid in cooling the barrel. To reduce the felt recoil of the stout 7.62 cartridge

When the Army adopted the M-16, it already had the wretched M-60. It took almost 30 years, but the awful M-60 got replaced by the M-240, which is really the FN MAG-58. (Yes, 30 years to replace a bad design with one that was already in existence when we adopted the M-60.) The AR shows no signs of slowing down.

The rest of the world went with the FN-FAL in one form or another.

We adopted the M-14, an improved M-1 Garand in many respects, but still a rifle designed for long-range shooting.

The Germans adopted the CETME, and built a company, H-K, to build their new rifle, the G3 in the 1950s.

in a light rifle (the prototypes weighed less than 7 pounds!) he designed muzzle brakes made of Titanium. However, newer is not always better, and even if it is, it isn't always early enough. By the time the Armalite company and Stoner had worked the bugs out, and produced enough rifles to demonstrate they had "something" the Army had already adopted the M-14. And our NATO allies had almost without exception adopted the FAL. The AR-10 found itself in a bad spot: Armalite had a manufacturer in Artillerie-Inrichtingen in Holland, and a few countries interested in buying it. But with the big players already committed to either the M-14 or the FAL, there were not many sales of the AR-10. A few hundred here, a few thousand there, not enough to keep the doors open, and production ceased in 1960. By that time, design changes and real-world requirements of durability had brought the weight up just past ten pounds, offering little advantage over the M-14 or FAL.

Eugene Stoner by then had taken a step back and started over again.

The government's 30-caliber lightweight rifle program had been formal, ponderous and bureaucratic. The result was a rifle that satisfied no one except those in the program. (Hey, I love the M-14/M-1A platform, but given the choice between it and a bunch of other 30-caliber rifles with which to fight, I'll take them.) Meanwhile, beneath the surface, there were other programs at work. One such program was in direct response to the lessons learned in WWII. To wit: High volumes of short-range fire were preferable to long-range fire. As a result, the Small Caliber High Velocity study produced the suggestion that a cartridge smaller than 7.62 could do the job. One result was the ill-fated SPIW program, which used flechettes as the projectiles. Trying to drive the firearms equivalent of a finishing nail to 4,000 feet per second or more proved technically impossible. But tests with M-1 carbines rebarreled to various .22 caliber wildcats proved promising. The SCHV program led to a requirement for a test rifle in .22 which was select-fire, 6 pounds in weight with at least 20 rounds of ammo in the magazine, and could penetrate a steel helmet or 10-gauge steel plate (.135") with a trajectory equal or better than the M-1, wounding as well as the M-1

Carbine, out to 300 yards. Not bad, eh? Unfortunately, as the requirements wound their way to Procurement, the range increased. First to 400 yards, then 500.

The result was a great deal of fussing over bullet weights and designs, and an increase in pressure to meet the new, excessive range requirements.

Stoner and Armalite had produced a scaled-down AR-10, chambered in .222 Remington. A brief aside here, on the nature of recoil. Newtonian physics tells us that you will have opposite and equal reactions to any force applied. Launching a bullet generates recoil. If the point of resistance of the impacted mass (that is, you) is below the center of mass of the recoiling object (that is, the rifle) the created lever pivots the rifle. The muzzle rises. If the point of resistance on the impacted mass is not on line with its center of mass the impacted mass will pivot. Thus, full-auto fire in a shoulder weapon causes the muzzle to rise and move to the right. You can fight it, but Sir Isaac Newton is working against you. Now, back to the Armalite prototype. Chambered in .222, with little recoil, and with the center of the bore straight through the stock, the minimal muzzle rise created was a sensation. Armalite had a request for more almost on the spot. They quickly produced rifles that the Army distributed for test and evaluation.

Meanwhile, Winchester was also working in a .22 rifle. Imagine a scaled-up M-1 Carbine, and you'd be on the right track. What killed the Winchester was the behind the scenes increase in the range requirement. While the AR-15 prototypes could be done in a cartridge (the ".222 Special") that could make the range, the Winchester couldn't. They had the unenviable choice of either submitting a rifle that couldn't make the range requirements, or using ammo that blew primers trying.

The SCHV tests in 1958 improved the design of the AR-15. In testing in the worst possible conditions the AR-15 prototypes produced stoppages at a third of the rate of pre-production .30 caliber rifles. But the fix was in, and a promising contender had to be scuttled or the Army might not get a new rifle at all. By 1958, we weren't in any wars, and if the pronouncements of the U.S. Air Force and SAC were to be believed, all future wars would be nuclear, decided in our favor, and require only the equivalent of police and military police to restore order in the (glowing, radiation-saturated, barely habitable remnants) recently-devastated enemy territory. The AR was elbowed out, and the M-14 proceeded.

But the AR didn't die, it simply went on tour. Armalite teamed up with Colt for further production of the AR-15. And the whole thing very nearly didn't happen. You see, Colt back than was on life support. In 1959 there hadn't been any new tooling installed in the 20th century except for wartime production. And none of that had been state-of-the-art when installed. Colt was strapped for money, and made old designs on old machines. They did manage to scrape up $75,000 to buy the rights to the AR-10 and AR-15 from Armalite, and even cut Armalite in for 4.5 percent of the profits of future sales. The tour was a success, especially the Southeast Asia stops. Many governments were interested in a rifle that was reliable, accurate, powerful, and better-suited to their short-statured troops than the M-1 Garands and BAR's the U.S. government was interested in selling them. But the fly in the ointment was, the Armalite/Colt wasn't in the U.S. arsenal, so no funding from defense loans could be used to buy them.

The solution came from the Air Force, beginning story Two. Each base needed security forces. The SAC bases, as they were our front line in the Cold War (just ask them) needed greater security. I don't argue that a base with nuclear weapons stored in the bunkers needs tight security. Despite separating it self from the Army, the Air Force still used the weapons the Army had. The new M-14 was deemed too large and bulky, which left many base security personnel with M-1 and M-2 Carbines. Which the Army had phased out, and no longer had spare parts or support for. The "end run" was to get the U.S. Air Force to adopt the AR-15, which got it into the supply line, and thus could be sold overseas.

Night combat does not require a long-range rifle. Most daytime combat doesn't either. These Marines are training for what actually happens, not theoretical target-range shooting.

The Army insisted on the forward assist. The Air Force insisted on not having it. Since they bought more, the Army won.

The original sights were plenty good enough for combat. You can adjust the sight to zero it, but not fiddle with it on the target range.

The selector points towards the hole for the autosear pivot pin, which as been removed in this rifle. Removing it removes the ability to fire full-auto, but does not change the rifles legal definition: machinegun.

(Is this starting to sound like a Monty Python sketch to you, too?) The method? The same one arms makers had used for centuries: get the gun in the hands of someone who could approve a purchase. As arms makers went straight to President Lincoln in the Civil War, Armalite managed to get General Curtis LeMay to a party, where he fired an AR-15 and immediately wanted it to replace his SAC bases M-1 Carbines. Once the Air Force was on board, however, things spiraled out of control. Forced to consider the AR-15, the Army found itself in a quandary: if they cooked the books again (as they had the first time around) the AR-15 supporters would raise a huge fuss. And they'd be publicly screwing the Air Force on their prized new small arm. If they didn't, the M-14 would suffer by comparison. As all this was happening, Defense Secretary McNamara was receiving conflicting reports as to which rifle was superior, just as he was reorganizing the Ordnance Department along the lines of what he considered an efficient procurement system to be. As part of the process, he eventually closed Springfield Arsenal, and was determined to depend on outside, civilian manufacturing for the development of small arms. The idea was that rather than have hidebound military officers trying to develop new weapons, he'd let industry do it, and select the best of the contenders after extensive testing.

McNamara, a brilliant man, had a great deal of faith in the ability of brilliant people. However, brilliant people without a solid base of experience can go astray much faster than less-brilliant people. The Department of Defense forced the Army into a "one-time buy" of AR-15 rifles until the real solution, the SPIW, could be perfected. The SPIW used flechettes, and would be the high-tech solution to everyone's problems. (We're still waiting.) But then the "whiz kids" made a mistake: they failed to look deeply into the matters of rifles, how they are made and how they are used. The whole messy problem can be summed up in two sentences: The demo rifle used on the Southeast Asia tour never failed. And

no development engineering had been done since Stoners first efforts. The staff who were now doing the job that had been that of the Ordnance Department wanted more testing, development and engineering. The "whiz kids" kept insisting that the Stoner rifle was perfect, needed no extra engineering, and felt the Ordnance types just wanted to get in and mess things up. They probably also looked at the M-14 program, which took a decade, spent millions of dollars, and produced a rifle marginally better than the rifle it replaced, the M-1 Garand.

This time the Ordnance types were right. And so, a mere 20 years after the M-1 Carbine was rushed into production without testing and engineering study, we did the same thing with the AR-15.

And problems surfaced with embarrassing regularity. The

The Swiss waited a long time to adopt the 5.56mm, for they actually did have a need for long-range accurate fire, and weren't going to give up their 7.62mm rifles until the 5.56 could deliver at 300 meters. This Sig 552 is capable of first-shot hits at 300 meters.

rifle slam-fired, requiring a fix, which ended up being a simple process: make the firing pin lighter. The accuracy was sometimes not very good. That was traced to the rifling twist, a source of controversy to this day. The original twist rate was one turn in 14 inches (marked or denoted as "1/14") the 1/14 twist was fine for a .222 Remington. But in the newly-designated .223 Remington, with a slightly heavier bullet at a higher velocity, it was marginal. So marginal that in Arctic weather the extra density of the cold air was enough to cause accuracy problems. Accuracy problems is perhaps understating things: in cold weather, a slightly worn rifle with a 1/14 barrel can't keep all its shot on a man-sized target at 100 yards. Volume is good, but there has to be some accuracy, or volume is for naught. The solution was to speed up the rate to 12 inches (1/12) but then the "buzzsaw" on impact effect apparently disappeared. Or didn't, depending on who you talk to.

The ammunition also came in for development and controversy. The original ".222 Special" specifications hadn't been changed (nor worked on) since 1958, but in 1963 when the AR-15 was being adopted the whiz kids again deemed it perfection, since Stoner had personally designed it. Despite this "perfection" there was a scramble to perfect bullet shapes for the best "long-range" performance (long-range for the AR-15 being deemed 500 yards) and for a suitable powder to drive it. One fateful change that was made was in the powder. Since DuPont could not supply the IMR powder needed to load the new .223 Remington in the kind of volume a shooting war requires, the whiz kids at DoD approved the use of Ball powder. The two problems with the ball powder selected were that its burning rate differed from the IMR powder, and no one bothered to check the formulation of the flash suppressant.

Any gas-powered firearm needs to use powder with a certain burning rate. Just like an automobile (for a cartridge is a specialized internal combustion engine) you have to give it what it needs. If you do not, the rifle will suffer. This was known even in 1963, for if you fed an M-1 Garand ammo loaded with the wrong powder you could bend the operating rod. A fired cartridge reaches a peak pressure quickly, and the powder then burns and expands down the bore, pushing the bullet ahead of it. A "progressive" powder does not reach as high a peak as quickly, and keeps pushing (retains residual pressure at a higher level) the bullet. Ball powders of the time were more progressive than the IMR powder selected for the AR-15. A progressive powder thus has the bullet passing the gas port with a higher pressure behind it, feeding more gas to the system. In the AR-15, that meant a higher impulse delivered to the bolt carrier. Colt could not deliver rifles within mil-spec using ammunition loaded with the selected ball powder. The cyclic rate allowed by spec was approximately 750 rpm. Firing ammunition loaded with ball powder, M-16s would run at 900 rpm. To "solve" the problem, the spec was temporarily re-written to allow up to 900 rpm in full-auto fire.

We still see today that the AR is powder-sensitive. If you reload, and use a powder that burns too quickly (a "fast powder" in the parlance) the rifle will short-stroke, and fail to function. Using a powder that burns too slowly will push the pressure curve down the bore, increase port pressure, and work the action too hard. You want the firearms equivalent of the middle bowl of porridge.

As for the flash suppressant, military use calls for a powder that offers less muzzle flash than other applications. As a result, the 7.62 NATO round was loaded with powder that had 2 percent of calcium carbonate in the mixture. The AR-15, with the gas blown back into the receiver, couldn't work for long with 2 percent. But it wasn't until soldiers were dying in a place called Vietnam that anyone thought to check that little detail. Then, we found out the .223 was relatively non-flashing, and the AR-15 reliable, with half a percent of calcium carbonate. The fouling and high cyclic rate were compounded by the history of the AR; it had been touted as the "rifle that didn't need cleaning." Something GIs would believe, since when the rifles arrived in Vietnam there were no government .22 caliber cleaning rods in the system. With few rods, few

chamber brushes, fouling cartridges and the high-humidity Vietnam environment; the miracle isn't that so many rifles malfunctioned, but that so few did.

So, we started Vietnam with two rifles: a 7.62 long-range rifle unsuited for use in the jungle, and a small-caliber bullet hose that wasn't reliable unless you kept it clean, fed it good ammo, and tested your magazines. So guess what happened? When it came time for volume production, we went with the bullet hose, but didn't bother cleaning it, getting good ammo, or good magazines. At least not for the first couple of years. So much for the brilliant "whiz kids."

Vietnam

There are two groups of Vietnam vets: those who had reliable M-16s, and those who didn't. Without casting aspersion on either group, generally the former were those who kept their rifle clean, and the latter were not. But not all M-16s worked even when clean. And not all dirty ones failed. Such was the appalling lack of development that went into the M-16.

The "standard" M-16 of the Vietnam War was the M-16 or the M-16A1. It had a solid stock, 20-inch, skinny barrel with a 1/12 twist, and triangular handguards. I've seen, handled and shot a bunch of them. The only ones that failed me did so because someone earlier in the ownership stream had neglected maintenance. But then, I never dragged them

A Colt Commando the result of letting the end-user design a weapon: light, handy, and kept clean, plenty reliable for jungle combat. Just don't expect much terminal effect past 200 meters.

Armalite is making the AR-180 again, with some updates. In some ways it is better than the AR-15, in other ways not.

The new AR-180 uses AR-15 magazines without the need to modify the mag tube, as was the case with the old AR-18 and AR-180.

through swamps, either. The standard cartridge was the M-193, a 55-grain boat-tail bullet at something over 3,100 fps. Many hate it for its failure to stop bad people from doing bad things. Others found no fault with it. I've had more than one combat vet tell me he never saw the M-16 fail to put an enemy soldier down. "Everyone I ever saw shot with an M-16 dropped, and was DRT." (Dead Right There.) Is a commonly-recited experience.

But the little 55-grain bullet had shortcomings. One, it failed to penetrate chance obstacles except at close range. And it lacked long-range accuracy. So once the war was over, and things got more or less back to normal (except for gas shortages, stagflation and disco) the various branches of our armed forces looked to improve the M-16. And we got the M-16A2.

While that was going on, Armalite found themselves out of the market: they'd sold the rights to Colt, and the AR-15 took off. So they went back to the drawing boards (Armalite then being an idea company, not a manufacturer) and came up with the "anti-AR" the AR-18. Instead of aluminum forgings, it used sheet metal steel stampings. Instead of direct gas impingement, it used a captured operating/gas rod. It used the same rotary bolt, and the magazines were similar enough that with a single machine cut you could use AR-15 magazines in your AR-18. But no one was buying. On top of

all the mechanical and material advantages of the M-16, a foreign government could buy M-16s cheap, and with loaned money. They could do neither with AR-18s.

AR-18 manufacture went through three different makers as the civilian-legal, semiautomatic only AR-180, before the tooling ended up in the Philippines and disappeared when the Marcos regime fell.

Progress, Of Sorts

Story three begins with the Marine Corps who in particular were not happy with the M-16A1. Rifle qualification courses call for firing out to 500 meters. Connecting with an M-16 at that distance is not something entirely under the control of even the best marksman. And the rear sight was part of the problem. So, with much pushing, prodding, encouragement and who knows what, the Corps steered the M-16A2 to what they wanted. What came out had a heavier barrel, a slightly

One advance the M-16 brought about was the dual-use weapon, the M-16 with an M-203 grenade launcher under the barrel. At a cost in bulk and weight, the grenadier can still have a rifle when he needs one.

longer stock, a rear sight click-adjustable to 800 yards, and most importantly, a faster-twist barrel to use heavier bullets. The new twist was one turn in 7 inches. Why? I've heard a number of "reasons" but the only one that makes any sense at all is the tracer requirement. The new cartridge, teamed with the new rifle, was the M-855. It was a clone of the NATO SS-109, 62 grains in weight, with a small steel penetrator tip in the core. To go along with it, the M-856 Tracer round was developed. The tracer was required to show a "trace", a visible burn, past 700 meters. (700 meters, while long for a rifle, is not long for a light machinegun in the support role. It does no good to load tracers in the belt, if they can't burn the full distance you'll need them.) To pack enough compound into the bullet it had to be made similar to a tiny little stub of a brass #2 pencil. To keep the bullet stable (and thus on

target) past 700 meters required a fast twist.

The new rifle was all everyone wanted it to be. And more than needed for the job of a rifle in combat: light, handy, fast to use, easy to carry, and reliable. The A2 was reliable, but for everything else, it was what it was; a target rifle.

The new heavyweight fast-twist barrel brought complaints: it wasn't accurate with 55-grain ammo (untrue) it wore out too fast due to the fast twist (untrue) it was heavy (perhaps) and it was too long (perhaps). What it was, was more than what was needed. One thing it did not improve, though was terminal ballistics. Sometimes. The faster twist, when coupled with the old 55-grain bullets, worked as well as before. Sometimes better, if the bullet jacket was thin or fragile. But the new twist, with the new bullet, created puncture wounds, simple channels through the intended target. Some

The old A1 sight wasn't good enough for the Marines, who wanted a sight that let them score well on the 500 yard line of their qualification course. The A1, with two springs and three moving parts, became the A2 sight, with four springs and five moving parts.

In the not-so-old days, you could have bare receivers in a plethora of names, to be built to your own specs or needs. Here, an Olympic before they were Olympic.

PacWestArms made excellent receivers, and no rifles. We finished assembly of dozens back in the 1980s, when home gunsmiths got in too deep.

targets were not impressed. So what else was new? (The best comment I ever heard on the subject was this: "Out there, somewhere, there is a GI who can tell you about the guy who needed a second burst of .50 before he went down." Nothing is perfect, nor should we expect it to be.)

The M-16A2 turned out to be a great rifle for shooting high scores on the qualification course, but not the best rifle for shooting people. Not the first time we've made that mistake. The AR-15, with a little more development in bullets, suddenly swept the 7.62mm rifles off the competition courses. At 600 yards, an 80- or 90-grain .224-inch bullet has less wind drift than a 7.62mm bullet does. And the recoil is markedly less, too. Combined with the more-durable (in target rifle mode) design of the AR-15, the competition shooters on the rifle ranges suddenly found themselves in a predicament

familiar to IPSC shooters: keeping up with the equipment race. If you wanted to be competitive you had to leave your tuned M-14 in the rack, with its heavy recoil, and get an AR-15 racegun or Service Rifle for competition. Back in the Vietnam War years, Colt worked on a shortened version of what was already a carbine. The XM-177, XM-177E1 and XM-177E2 were variations of shortened AR-15s. With a shorter barrel came a more ferocious muzzle blast. So Colt developed a flash hider that actually worked to some small degree as a silencer. (Moderator, suppressor, "can", whatever you want to call it.) While it wouldn't pass muster as an actual sound suppressor, it did cut the muzzle blast by a few decibels. Which became Colt's problem later. You see, the U.S. State Department clamped down on the export of suppressors. Colt had a popular model that they couldn't sell with the flash hider. Not the first time Colt has been stymied.

Meanwhile, a cottage industry was building in the AR-15 market. You had two choices in the early 1980s: you could buy a Colt, who offered a paltry one or two models of the AR-15, or you could dream about what Colt might build if they paid any attention to the market. With suppliers and subcontractors able to make parts, the only critical parts were uppers and lowers. And uppers could be had military-surplus. Which left lowers. The forge companies found themselves being approached by would-be AR makers. And for enough money, you could buy forged lowers and do the machining or contract with a machine company to machine forgings to your specs, with your name on them. I saw a number of lowers back then machined from billets of aluminum, as well as machined from forgings or castings. As the market grew, the quality improved. There are many brands of lowers from those days still in use: PWA (PacWestArms) SGW, the early name for Olympic, E.A. Co, Essential Arms, there are bunches of them. And few were made as complete rifles. Almost all were assembled, either in basements by aspiring gunsmiths and shooters, or by gunsmiths finishing the job started by home gunsmiths. For a few years during one of the "home assembly" waves I did a good business finishing guns others had started, and cleaning up the mistakes, errors and "oops" they'd done. Why all this activity? Simple, Colt made good rifles, but they didn't offer much variety. And they had no customer service to speak of. You could send them an AR in need of service, and get it back months later. Maybe even repaired. Getting a new barrel installed simply wasn't worth the wait. So shooters built, repaired, modified and altered their own.

Story Four comes when the various programs to replace the aging M-16 came up empty-handed. The Advanced Combat Rifle, various resurrected flechette programs, the caseless ammo dead-end, the "smart ammo" problems, all left the armed forces facing a simple fact: nothing they had come up with could replace the M-16, even though no one was happy with the M-16. Then, in the mid-1980s, Colt resurrected the idea of a carbine as a compact rifle for support troops, supply and logistics, etc. The idea was to make a compact rifle that would be less hassle to carry, but still capable of being used as a weapon. By the time Colt was done refining, improving, testing, proving and upgrading the rifle, the users on the sharp end had had enough of long heavy rifles. They wanted compact rifles. But they didn't want the emasculated little "PDW" (Personal Defense Weapon) that the pointy-headed experts back in the testing labs came up with. They wanted real rifles in real calibers, at least "real" by 20th century fin de siecle standards. By the mid-1990s, "the" rifle to have for any unit that was front-line ready was the M-4. And Colt had spent a great deal of time, effort, money and engineering expertise at their own expense in making the M-4 much more than just a shorty AR-15/M-16. Colt defended it against others. When FN won the contract to make M-16 rifles, they did not get to make M-4s. The M-4 is a trademarked designation and model, owned by Colt. The Technical Data Package of the M-16 is government property, and anyone who wins a bid to produce M-16s for the government can have access to the package. But the M-4 was developed by Colt, with their own money, and only Colt can make it.

The result of the work, first on the "A2" and then the M-4, was to do the engineering work on the AR-15/M-16 (oops, sorry about that) that should have been done in the first place. Instead of the McNamara "Whiz Kids" and the slavish adoption of the Stoner system with all its good and bad points, the improvements were done by engineers who knew firearms, and approved by military officers and NCOs who understood what a rifle was supposed to do. Not that there weren't problems, but in due time things were ironed out.

But some things we can't engineer away. The rifle is still two halves held together by a pair of steel pins through aluminum parts. You can't use it as a baseball bat, it will break. It can withstand a certain amount of bayonet work, but it wasn't designed to be an impromptu pike. The gas

Full circle. The M-1 Carbine, in 1941, and the M-4 Carbine, in 2005.

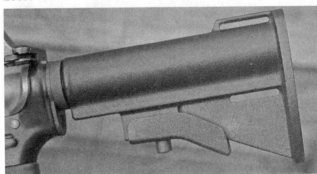

The answer to the question of "Can you own this stock?" depends on where and when you asked it.

system is dirty, and if you want it to work you have to spend time keeping it clean. And the magazines suck. The new H-K magazines show promise, but if the past history of H-K is any guide, their magazines will be available only to the government and law enforcement, be ferociously expensive, and require a special tool and a days instruction to disassemble and clean.

(U.S. Army photo by Sgt. Jeremiah Johnson)

The M-14 has not gone away, it just has a new job. Instead of being a general-issue long range rifle, it is now a medium range, powerful, sniper rifle. This trooper can probably engage a target at 900 yards, but most of his work will be done from 200 to 400.

Story Four also happens during the spate of gun-control legislation devoted to "Semi-automatic Assault Weapons." Forget for the moment that an "assault rifle" is by definition a select-fire rifle. Various government entities (State and Federal) decided that some rifles were "bad" and should be controlled. Colt, always sensitive to the political winds, was back and forth about rifles and options. Yes, they'd sell on the civilian market. No they wouldn't. Yes, but they won't offer tele-stocks. The changes got so dizzying that many just threw up their hands and started buying from other makers. Or building what they wanted. (Sound familiar?) Pretty soon there were so many makers out there that you needed a scorecard just to keep track of them. The AWB/94 is history now, and for the time being we can make pretty much what we want (check the chapter on "Legalities" for more info) with some state restrictions. But building from a collection of parts can bring its own problems.

One aspect of weapons design that trips up even the cleverest is the multi-use rifle. We saw it with the M-14. It was not only going to replace the M-1 Garand, it was going to also replace the M-3 Grease gun submachinegun, the M-1 Carbine and the BAR. One rifle could do it all. And the accountants and bureaucrats, who knew nothing of rifles but had the authority to approve the project, bought into the idea. The "real replacement" for the M-14 and M-16 was going to be the SPIW. The Special Purpose Individual Weapon was both a flechette and grenade launcher. One rifle would do all. The British, when they adopted the egregious SA-80, also tried to make one rifle do it all. They made their bullpup, the new Enfield not just in the standard model, but also a squad support weapon. Neither works particularly well. If anyone ever tells you that one rifle can do it all, hold onto your wallet.

Nothing is everything. No object can do all things. And the more you try, the more you pay. The idea of a "Swiss Army Rifle" similar to the knives we all own is illusory. You can't have it all without paying for it all.

The Future

Who knows? The Stoner system does not show any signs of expiring from old age. It also does not show any signs of being replaced by something better. There has not been a shortage of would-be successors. Back in the 1980s, the West German G-11 made by H-K was going to replace the M-16 before the 21st century. Ultra-reliable, with caseless ammo and a built-in optical sight, it was going to be everything the M-16 wasn't. When the Berlin Wall fell, the suddenly unified Germany found they; a) had no need to defend themselves against the no longer extant East Germany, and b) had no money for new weapons, as they suddenly had millions of new, and poor, relatives to take care of.

The Offensive Individual Combat Weapon was going to be the new wonderweapon: a grenade launcher, rifle, optical-sighted weapon that could do everything but brew coffee and call for a medic. At 18 pounds and $10,000 each, with grenade ammunition that cost $25 a shot, and voracious for batteries, it never got past the testing stage. Along the way, H-K, which had always been in competition with Colt and the M-16 for military contracts, upgraded and redesigned the G-3. Where the G-3 was all-steel and used a delayed roller-lock system, the G-36 uses polymer, and a gas system to drive it. Unfortunately, they over-engineered it, and the result is clunky, hard to aim (it has an included optical sight that I personally find a real pain to use) and has no advantages over the M-16.

The FN P-90, a Personal Defense Weapon. The potential market for the PDW is being eaten away by the volume of issued M-4 carbines.

The FN 2000, a potential candidate to replace the M-16/M-4 when it has run out of steam. (Hasn't happened yet.)

We now see the H-K XM-8, which is better in every way than the M-16 (just ask, H-K will tell you) but in every way just a little bit better. New weapon systems are not funded and fielded just because they are "a little bit better" unless it is being built in some Senator's home state. Unlike a new jet fighter, you can't make a rifle in two-dozen states, so its future is not bright.

Two interesting shifts in the M-16 are the adoption of the flat-top, and shorter barrels. When warfare is conducted in wide-open spaces, with iron sights, a long barrel and long sight radius are useful. Especially if optics are fragile and not up to the rigors of combat, which has been the case until recently. With the improvement of optics, iron sights have become less and less a requirement, and more a back-up. If an optical sight can stand up to military use, and you have to deal with opponents in the open, then not using optics is a bad choice. The wide-open spaces are not only fewer and fewer (even in Iraq) but even when you're in an open space, you probably arrived there in a vehicle. Hence the attraction of short rifles or carbines. A flat-top rifle gives you the option

of irons or optics, where a standard-handle M-16A2 does not. (At least not easily.) The change has been so marked that the Marine Corps announced during the writing of this book that they would only consider rifles with flat-top uppers in current and future purchases.

The shorter barrels also come as an aspect of the increased engagement of combatants in urban areas. Doors, windows, holes in walls, vehicles, all make a 20-inch barrel a real hassle. The 14.5-inch barrel of the M-4 is a real asset, and desired despite the decreased effectiveness of the shorter barrel in terminal ballistics. (The velocity loss can be offset by careful bullet and load selection.) In tight quarters, even the shortest rifle/carbine can be too bulky, and we see many of our soldiers and Marines in Iraq with sidearms. When the distance is "hard off the muzzle" or closer, a handgun has many advantages over even the Colt Commando, with an 11.5-inch barrel.

Another new feature, so new it is still being worked out, is the Squad Designated Marksman. Begun by the Marine Corps, and lately adopted by the Army, the SDM fills the

The H-K XM8, their candidate to replace the M-16/M-4.

The H-K G-36, the replacement for the German G3, and what came along instead of the caseless G-11.

The Cavalry Arms synthetic lower is one piece, and may be the future of the AR system.

But flat-top rifles need back up iron sights.

gap between the squad and unit snipers. The best use of a school-trained and experienced sniper is not in tagging along with a squad on patrol. He is often under the command of a larger unit, with a higher command. (If a Captain needs a sniper, he asks the Major or Lieutenant Colonel who is in charge of assigning snipers.) The sniper is looking past the squad. So what does the squad do when they are faced with a predicament that could be solved one of two ways: Much maneuvering and the application of large amounts of force (like air support) or a precise shot? One example would be a rooftop team of a light machinegun with an RPG at 300 meters. Yes, the squad could get in a firefight, but while they're trying to suppress the machinegun, the RPG gunner is merrily launching rockets at the squads machinegunners. With an SDM, while the firefight is getting started, the optic-equipped SDM is taking precise shots to drop the RPG gunner, then the opposing machinegunner and anyone rash enough to take their places, while the rest of the squad weighs in, and the platoon leader plans where the squad will maneuver next

to take the building.

A refinement of the rifle used by the SDM is the Special Purpose Rifle. Built as a medium- to long-range sniper M-16 (although the 5.56 at long range is not very robust in terminal ballistics, it is better than nothing) it features some kind of free-floated barrel, optics and other refinements. (There have been two so far, the Mk 12 Mod 0, and the Mk 12, Mod 1.) The idea is to provide a medium- to long-range accurate rifle that sniper-trained soldiers or Marines could use that utilized the same ammunition and magazines as the M-16 or M-4. It also bridges the gap between the long-range, bolt-action 7.62mm rifle-equipped snipers who are

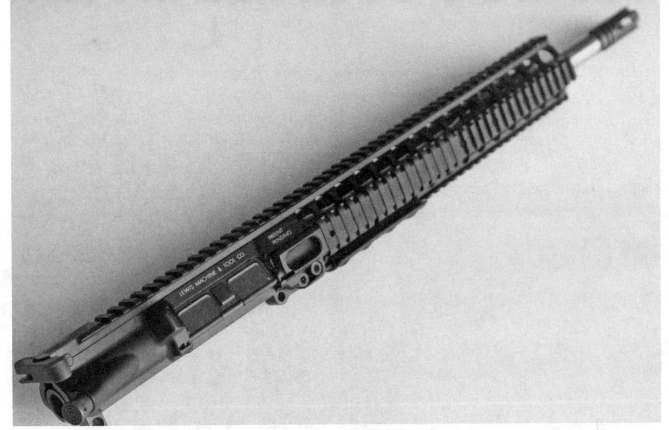

The LMT has the ability to quickly swap barrel lengths, a maintenance boon.

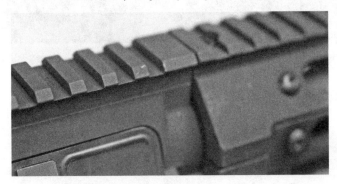

Makers can design tactical forearms that continue the flat-top.

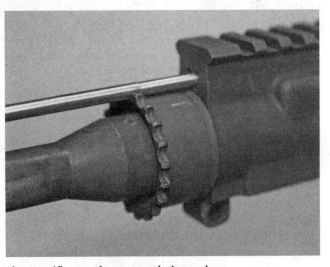

Flat-top rifles are the current design and rage.

usually working for higher authority. If a sniper is tasked from a higher unit (Battalion, Brigade, etc) and answers to a Lieutenant Colonel, he usually doesn't have time to deal with a mere Captain's problems. And breaking cover or revealing a good "hide" to do so will get him a thorough chewing-out from the LTC.

Which brings us, curiously, to the situation of the M-16 now being a rifle that "does it all." From compact interior, CQB work, to general duty, to medium sniper, and if you're willing to trash a rifle, short-term SAW use, the M-16 seems to have finally become accepted.

Who'd a thunk it?

Lessons Learned

The AR-15/M-16/M-4/SPR isn't perfect. The Stoner system runs dirty. It requires ammunition of a higher quality, and within stricter tolerances, than say an AK-47. It must be cleaned and inspected on a more frequent basis. But if you give it the care it needs, it will work for quite a long time. Longer than you need it to, even.

The Lewis Machine & Tool monolithic upper is the culmination of the flat-top upper, with the tactical forend built-in.

The Stoner rifle, the AR, is now approaching the status of ubiquitous. From close-in VIP protection, to medium-range sniper rifle, one version or another can do it all.

But reliability comes at a price, and the price tag for the AR-15 is simple: good ammo, regular cleaning, dependable magazines and quality parts. Get cheap on anything, and it can come back and bite you.

Making The AR-15/M-16

The process is complex, involved, and exacting. Rifles before the AR were made one of two ways, the old and the new. The old way was to take a steel forging and machine away everything that wasn't a rifle. As the forging (the receiver) was going to take the brunt of the firing pressure, it had to be strong. To work, it was complex. The barrel was simply screwed into it, and the stock and firing mechanism parts were hung onto it. Done. The new-old method was to make the receiver from steel stampings. The original rifle made this way were the variants of the Stg-43-44-45 made by the Germans at the end of WWII. The AK-47 was also made this way, and also the AR-18 that came about after the original Armalite rifles. The steel stampings were simply housings to hold the mechanism, and the receiver was reduced to a block that held the locking lugs for the bolt.

The AR-15 is different. The locking lugs are on the barrel extension, and the upper and lower housings simply guide the moving parts and keep them in the proper relationship to each other. The upper and lower don't take any real load, so they needn't be as strong as old receivers. Thus, they are made of aluminum.

The upper and lowers are made of an alloy referred to as "7075 T6." Metal standards are covered or defined by the ANSI, the American National Standards Institute, with some covered by SAE, the Society of Automotive Engineers. The numerical designation, such as "4140" for steel tells you what components of alloying materials are in the steel, with further standards defining crystal size, heat-treat, etc. The "7075" tells you what is in this aluminum alloy, and the "T6" refers to the heat treat the mix gets. The cookbook numbers for 7075 are; 5.6 percent Zinc, 2.5 percent Manganese, 1.6 percent Copper and .23 percent Chromium added to the aluminum. But knowing the numbers doesn't tell the whole tale. To make 7075, you need to know just what temperature you need to have your initial aluminum melt at, what order you introduce the alloying metals, the stirring/agitation method and time, etc. Alcoa will not tell you all that. No one who makes it will. If you want 7075, you place an order for as many tons as you need, and specify what shape. Does alloy matter? You bet. The earliest production guns were made with the uppers and lowers fabricated from 6061 alloy, which uses magnesium and silicon as alloying agents. In the field testing they received (AKA, the Vietnam War) end-users discovered a curious thing: that particular alloy seriously corroded in certain conditions. Combine sweat, heat, high humidity and constant handling, and the alloy used could corrode at a high rate, to the point where receivers could be weakened or eaten through. Switching to 7075 prevented that small problem.

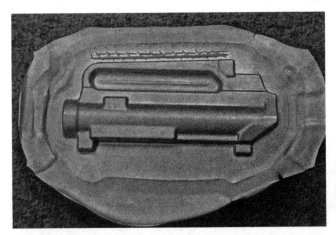

The forged platter, that the uppers and lowers are cut from.

A rollmarked lower, ready to begin the machining odyssey.

AR makers get their 7075 in rods of a specified diameter. Each rod is cut to a certain length (I'm not trying to be coy here, the makers don't go blabbing their production secrets) and heated to a specified temperature. Each section is then fed into a forge, where it is whacked by a set of dies machined to each side of the upper or lower. I use the term "whacked" in the strictest technical sense: many tons of hydraulically-moved steel slam against the rods to form the "pancakes." The forged pancakes are then "blanked" where the excess aluminum from the forged platter is shorn off.

They then get their heat-treat, where the pieces are run through a "temper-quench cycle." Each material in the ANSI or SAE standards has a particular cycle. Every manufacturer has minor differences. Once the forged lumps have gone through the heat and quench cycle, they are "T6" material.

The uppers and lowers arrive at the machining stations cool and covered with a protective film of lubricant or preservative. From here their paths differ slightly. Although they are all shipped to the manufacturer who is going to machine them, what happens to each varies a bit.

Manufacturers have bins of parts, all of which they have to keep track of.

Yowza! The 7-foot, $10,000 bar goes screaming through the lower forging, broaching the magazine well.

Lowers, The Real Gun

First, the blank is rollmarked. While we all use the term "rollmark" the markings are not always rolled on. Mostly it is just a hammer forge that hits the blank once, when it is cool, and that's it. A sophisticated operation will have an auto-advance die counter and marker, that automatically advances the serial number die one digit each impact. Why roll mark and serial number first? That way the force used to impress the markings doesn't distort a machined product. If something goes wrong later, the serial number can be marked in the books as "scrapped in production" and thus accounted for. It also avoids the prickly legal question of having machined but as-yet unmarked receivers lying about, a situation possible with a shop flow-plan of "machine then serial number."

Some lowers are not rollmarked, but engraved. An engraved lower tells you one of two things; the maker has a lot of CNC machines and can afford to engrave them, or the makers name on it is not the company that machined it. Some machine shops make lowers (and uppers) for other companies. If you are making lowers for a dozen people, each with their own logo and company name, then machining the logos and serial numbers in the CNC machine is a lot easier than rollmarking them. It also makes inventory problems easier: if you need to shift production to another maker, or you have a production run volume change, you can adjust by stopping the CNC mill, changing some programming parameters, and going on. If you roll-marked receivers, you'd risk real headaches in keeping logos, serial number blocks, and production rates properly juggled. The CNC engraver simply uses a small-diameter ball end cutting tool, and "writes" out the logo, name and serial number on the receiver side. Engraved logos and serial numbers can happen at any time in the CNC process, where rollmarking must be done first.

The lower goes into a CNC machining station and gets the rear plate, buffer tube threads, and top deck machined to final dimension. The magazine well also gets roughed out in this step. Then it goes into probably the oldest machine in the shop, certainly the oldest one in design. The magazine well is broached. That is, instead of a rotating cutting tool going down into the receiver and cutting away metal, a single, non-rotating cutter is pushed or pulled through the opening. A typical magazine well broach is 7 feet long, and has hundreds of cutting teeth on each of its four sides. Each cutting tooth is a fraction taller or wider than the previous one. The last cutting teeth are the exact size and shape of the desired magazine well opening. The Lower is placed into the holding fixture, the tongue of the broach is pressed through the milled opening, and the hydraulic ram locks onto the broach. Then, in a few seconds, the broach gets pulled through by the multi-ton hydraulic ram, cutting the magazine well to final dimension in one pass. Broaching magazine wells can happen at the rate of two a minute, with most of that time spent getting the finished lower out, the rough-cut one in, and shuttling the bar back and forth. The actual cutting takes less than 10 seconds.

The broach, at 7 feet long and made of hardened steel, can take a couple of weeks to fabricate (they are made by specialty machining shops, not the AR manufacturer), and can cost well over 10 grand.

Once the lower is broached, then the receiver goes back into a CNC machine, and the rest of the cuts are made: the fire control well, bolt hold open slots, magazine catch, the trigger guard and the pistol grip base are all machined. Once machined and inspected, the lower goes off to be anodized. Anodizing is an electrochemical process that hardens the surface of the aluminum. Type 1 is the least strong, but can be done in colors. Type II is harder and more durable. Type IIA is the toughest and the only one to meet mil-spec. The cost differences in volume production are minimal, so if you have a decent-quality receiver chances are it was done with a Type IIA anodizing.

After anodizing, the lower can then be assembled. The various parts that go into the lower are either steel (fire control parts) that is case-hardened, spring steel (the springs and roll pins) or plain old machineable steel, like the pistol grip screw. The buffer tube can be 7075-T6 like the receiver, or it can be a "60" series aluminum, also known as "aircraft" aluminum. Machinists prefer the "70" series as it cuts a bit

A lower with the top deck and buffer tube machining cut, and mag well broached.

Bins of machined parts, to be sent to the next step.

cleaner (I've had experienced machinists refer to the "60" series as "gummy" and "grabby") than aircraft.

The Upper

The upper also comes as a forging. Once the billet is forged and the platter blanked, the forgings go into the CNC machine for deep drilling and milling. The carrier tunnel is drilled and bored, and then the lower clearance slot for the hammer and magazine is milled. Twice. You see, the forging has residual stresses in it. The forged part has been squeezed. The drilling bores out the center, and when the clearance slot is machined the uppers spring inwards a bit. A smart company will ream and mill the tunnel and slot on a second pass, to bring it them to their proper dimensions once the stresses have been relieved. Some flat-top receivers are forged with the handle in place, and raised ribs where the rail will be machined. Why? It is easier for some companies to simply machine existing forge dies to add a small raised rail than engineer new dies for flat-tops, with a different heat-treat, forge impact speeds, etc. And many machining setups use the handles as locating points. It is just simpler to alter existing dies, then make some changes in cutter path programming, and then as one of the last cutting paths cut off the handle and machine the top deck of the flat top. Still other companies have separate dies for regular and flat-top receivers.

Then the rest of the dimensions are machined: the operating handle slot, forward assist tunnel, gas tube hole, barrel nut threads, and the roll pin hole for the forward assist and dust cover pin are drilled. Then the uppers go off to the anodizer.

The other parts get fed as blanks or partially-processed blanks (like barrels) into various CNC lathes and mills. The barrel blanks go into CNC lathes that turn them down to diameter, and the blanks get threaded and chambered. If the barrels are to be hard-chrome plated the machined blanks go off to the plater before they are then assembled into barrels. The buffer weights are turned, deep-drilled and anodized. Various small parts like sight assemblies for flat-top rifles are machined on CNC mills and sent out in bins for anodizing before assembly.

Front sight assemblies come as either forgings or castings, and are machined to take the barrel diameter being made for the current production batch, then topped, drilled and threaded for the front sight post.

Many small parts are simply purchased from subcontractors. After all that was one of the designed-in points of the M-16. Instead of using retaining pins of an odd and particular size, or screws that are unique in thread pitch, size and head shape,

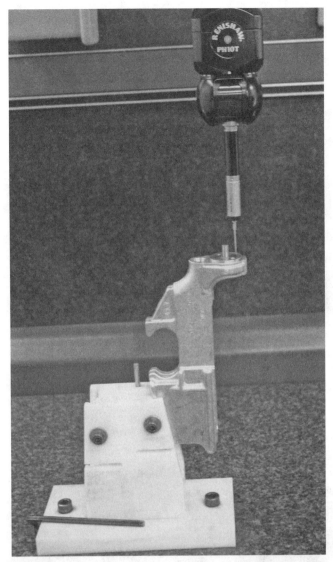

In a good manufacturer (and Armalite is one of the best) parts are regularly checked for quality and dimensional stability

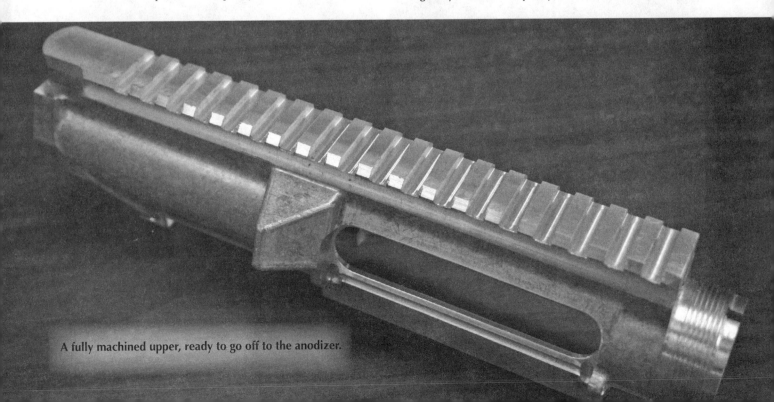

A fully machined upper, ready to go off to the anodizer.

Assemblers start with bins of parts, and end up with assembled rifles.

Match rifles have their parts kept together from the start, so there is no question of fit and function.

the AR was designed to use common industrial fasteners. Why then would an arms maker install and run machines to make roll pins, when they can literally buy them by the ton in any size needed from a company that makes them? Even the biggest makers buy small parts, and some buy many parts.

The makers of AR-15s fall into three categories: Assemblers, custom machinists, and manufacturers. The assemblers simply have their receivers made by someone else, with the assemblers logo on the lower. They then buy all the components from specialty manufacturers, subcontractors or custom shops, and assemble the rifles as needed. Being an assembly shop is not a slam. Not everyone with the knowledge or skill to assemble a first-class AR has the money to invest in a CNC machine to machine forgings. Nor the desire to run a company big enough to warrant the investment

in such machines. The custom machinist category is a lot more varied. You can have someone who buys everything but barrels. Call them the Barrel Specialist. The Barrel Specialist then buys barrel blanks, turns them to diameter, chambers, fits and installs the barrel as they assemble the rifle. If I wanted a super-accurate long range AR, I'd probably have it built by a Barrel Specialist. You can also have the Tactical Specialist. The tactical specialist has contacts for trick gear that makes a rifle really efficient at CQB. They are more than simply an assembler, as the Tactical Specialist is likely to have greater knowledge, and do a lot of test-firing before shipping.

The manufacturer is the company that does their own machining out of forgings. Even a manufacturer would not make every single part that goes into an AR. All parts manufacturing or production is decided after finding the

All rifles are test-fired.

At Armalite, a high-speed video camera captures the function of each shot, to ensure function is within defined limits.

answer to two questions: Does it cost more to buy than make? Can we get the volume we need when we need it? If the cost is less to buy, then buy. But, if the maker of that part doesn't have production capacity to manage all their customers' needs, then why find yourself at a bottleneck because the subcontractor got swamped by someone else's big order? You'll find there are differences between manufacturers, too. Companies like Colt, Armalite and Olympic machine forgings only for their own use. Colt does not make lowers for other companies. (They may sell production over-runs of uppers, but then again they may not. The AR community is very closed-mouth about such things.) Then there are dual-maker companies like Lewis Machine & Tool, and L.A.R. Grizzly, who make uppers and lowers both with their name on them, and the names of assemblers who buy machined uppers and lowers from LMT and Grizzly. Then there are wholesaler-only manufacturers like Continental Machine, who make uppers and lowers only for assemblers and manufacturers. You'll never see a lower marked "Continental" for they do not retail them. If you want to buy product from CMT, you'd better have a manufacturer's license, and be prepared to purchase in lots of hundreds or thousands of uppers and lowers. If you meet both, you can have your production lot marked with any kind of logo and maker's name you want, provided it isn't already in use, and doesn't offend the production staff.

As I've mentioned before, forging is a specialty operation. No one who machines receivers, or assembles rifles, does both the forging and the machining. (At least none I've talked to, and doing both would definitely be a situation to be bragging about.)

Many makers get smaller parts, and specialized parts from sub-contractors. The forge code on this front sight housing lets you know who made it, if you know the code.

Cast vs. Forged: What's The Big Deal?

Part of the appeal of a cast receiver was economic. To make a forged receiver (upper or lower) you needed either a forging operation, with the huge forges, the ovens and quenching baths, or a forge that will sell you blanked platters. Then the fun begins. Each lower requires at least two dozen machine operations before it can be sent off for anodizing. More, depending on what kind of setup the machine shop has. The most efficient way to machine uppers and lowers is with a computer-controlled mill and multiple cutters. A CNC machine, back even in the early 1990s, was ferociously expensive. A million-dollar machine was a small one. CNC machines were so expensive that those companies that could afford them usually didn't buy them, but leased them. And kept them working 24 hours a days, 7 days a week, to pay off the lease cost.

Casting was less expensive. Yes, the casting machinery was expensive, and the moulds were too. Casting in the firearms business is the "investment cast" or "lost wax" process. A caster uses a mould to make a wax impression of the part. (The mould designer takes into account the shrinkage and warping on cooling, and the material used, to design a mould that produces a correctly-dimensioned part.) The wax parts are assembled on a "tree" of wax. The tree is then dipped in a ceramic slurry until it is strong enough to be handled. The dipped tree is fired in a kiln to harden the ceramic and burn out the wax. Then the molten metal is poured into the hot tree. Once it is cool, the ceramic is broken off, the parts cut away, and the final machine cuts are performed.

A cast AR-15 lower cut from the tree is ready to go except for a few small things: the spring tunnels have to be drilled, and fire control parts detent and pivot pin holes, too. In all, a cast receiver can be ready for anodizing with as few as five holes drilled, and the threads cleaned with a tap.

Faced with the high costs of a CNC machine, or the few steps to finish a cast receiver, there were a bunch of cast receivers made in the 1980s. Cast receivers appear rougher, and are viewed by many as being not as good as forged/machined receivers. That may be the case, but I've built and used a bunch of cast- receiver guns through the decades, and found the ones I worked on to be satisfactory. What changed, to cause cast to disappear from the market? One, CNC machines became relatively cheap. When the older machines could no longer be leased, they were sold by the leasing company. By the exacting standards of the machine tool world, they were worn out. The ultra-precise ones were so worn they could no longer guarantee cutting to a tolerance of .00001" or less. (That's a ten-thousandth of an inch) but the buyers of the "worn out" machines didn't care. .00001" was a whole lot less than the .0001" that was way more than accurate enough. Two, as forged receivers became more common on the market the price came down, and the cast ones lost their cost advantage. Three, with the price difference decreased, and general availability up, why consider cast?

Anodizing: What's The Big Deal?

Anodizing is a surface treatment for aluminum, to harden the surface, provide corrosion protection and some small amount of structural stiffness. Anodizing produces a clear (in many alloys) surface, and what we think of as "anodizing" is the dyed finish applied as part of the anodizing process. One problem with anodizing at least in the older mil-spec (the Mil-A-8625 Type 1 protective finish) was the use of Chromic acid in the process. The EPA views Chromic acid as a near-plutonium substitute as an evil environmental by-products. In this case, unlike other products, they are correct. The new standards are Mil-A8625, Type 2, Class 1 and 2. The difference is, Class 1 uses a dichromate solution as a protective sealant in the finish. Bad for the environment, but

not as bad as Chromic acid. The result is black. Class 2 can only be applied to some alloys (and not 7075) but allows for colors other than black.

An anodizer who offers their product as Mil-A-8652, Type 2, Class 1, must comply with a rigid set of inspections, tests and certifications. All of which add cost. An AR maker who says (and can back up) that their parts meet that standard have paid more for it, and rightly charge more for it. You can sometimes find receivers offered that have a finish that "meets mil-spec standards" or some such claim. They may well be right. If the anodizer went through the identical production process, but simply failed to do the inspections, tests and certifications, the receivers may well be just as good. But no one in the chain of supply can be certain.

As with all other things, you usually get what you pay for.

As with forging, anodizing is a specialized operation, and manufacturers of ARs ship their machined forgings off to be anodized.

The Future Of AR Manufacturing

One of the newest fronts of AR manufacturing is the use of polymers. Once you've paid for the mould, making polymer-framed firearms is dirt-cheap. Ask Glock. (Well, they won't tell you, but its true.) Back when I went through the armorer's class, the armorers replacement cost of a frame was on the order of $20. Yes, a slide went $150, but a frame was twenty bucks. Making an AR upper and lower of polymer has great potential, but there are many engineering challenges to be solved. Too hard, and it is brittle. Too flexible, and it won't hold its shape under duress. But there are more makers looking into it all the time.

The other frontier is the monolithic upper. The military has this burning desire for interchangeable barrels. (I can think of one good, and several superfluous reasons for the interest.) By making one or another design of monolithic upper, manufacturers can offer quick-change barrels, requiring (depending on the particular design) just hands, or a few simple tools, to change barrels. If it catches on, and which one becomes ascendant, will be a matter of what passes military tests, and what the commercial market accepts in volume.

We'll see what the future holds, and bring you the news, in Volume 2 if we know then, and in future updates of these volumes. I don't see the AR platform going away anytime soon. It may not last long enough to be issued to Marines on space-borne vehicles, but it isn't going to disappear in our lifetimes.

A properly-assembled AR, built with decent parts, will last a long time. You can expect, depending on your use/abuse and accuracy requirements, 5,000 to 15,000 rounds use out of a barrel. You can use a bolt for two or three barrels. The rest of the parts except springs, experience so little wear they'll last a really long time. With proper care and investment in quality parts, your AR can last a lifetime.

How It Works

(DoD Photo)

The basic AR-15/M-16 platform has worked so well for so long that the firearm has become the weapon of choice for most of the free world's armed forces. The same flexibility of the design allows units and soldiers to optimize performance.

Many books and manuals explain in sketchy detail how the AR-15/M-16 works. Some include charts showing which malfunctions are caused by what problems, and potential solutions. All are short, skimpy on mechanics and background, and only a minimal guide. If all you do is read this chapter, pay close attention to the information, and stop now and then to mentally construct a three-dimensional model that you then move through its steps, you'll be far ahead of many courses you could pay good money for. To cover completely the intricacies, dimensions, tools and techniques for working on the AR-15/M-16 would require this entire volume. (And will probably come to pass in the future.) What I'll do here is give you a thorough explanation of what happens, so you can understand the rifles I'm testing in Volume 1. And then when we go into more detail of working on modifications and accessories in Volume 2, you'll know exactly what's going on.

As far as explaining how the AR-15 works, we can break it down into two areas: The Gas System, Bolt, Carrier and Buffer, and The Fire Control Mechanism. The two parts are perceived differently by many shooters: For the most part the gas system is mysterious and complicated, while the fire control system is viewed as a simple thing. Ahem. In fact, the gas system is simplicity itself (at least in concept and function) while the fire control system can be a snakepit of small, mysterious functions that have to be tuned by knowledge and experience of the AR-15, and not by previous experience with other firearms. So, we'll take the mystery out of the gas system first.

The direct-impingement gas system was not invented by Stoner. As mentioned earlier, it was in relatively wide use prior to the AR system, in the Ljungman rifles and the French MAS 44 and 49. In function, it is quite simple: instead of the gas port in the barrel directing gas to the head of the operating

The carrier key rides over the gas tube, where the tube sticks into the upper receiver.

The cam pin pivots to the side, turning the bolt. That's why that square lump is there, on the left side of your upper.

rod, as in the M-1 Garand, or a short piston, as in the M-1 Carbine or M-14, the gas in the AR-15 is directed straight back to the bolt carrier. There is nothing in the tube you see on top of your barrel except empty tube. No pistons, no valves, nothing. The end of the gas tube inside the front sight housing is sealed. There is a hole short of the end of the gas tube that lines up with the clearance hole through the front sight housing, where it rests snugly around the barrel and the gas port. At the other end, the gas tube has a small raised lip. That lip rides inside the key on the carrier.

The bolt rides inside and on the centerline of, the carrier. There is a hole through it, and the cam pin sticks through the hole. (The firing pin passes through a hole in the cam pin, in the hole in the bolt. Sort of like a Chinese puzzle.) The carrier has a slot in it that the cam pin sticks through. The carrier slot is crooked. Behind the carrier are the buffer and the buffer spring.

Lets start the sequence from firing. The firing pin strikes the primer and the powder burns. The bullet is pushed forward

through the barrel (and this is the entire reason for the existence of all these parts) and out of the muzzle. When the bullet passes the gas port, the gas expands into the gas tube. (That is what gas does; expand into the available volume.) The gas tube is almost instantly pressurized to the same level as the bore, and remains at the same pressure as the bore until the bullet leaves the muzzle. The name for this time period is "gas dwell time." The pressurized gas exerts force on all the walls containing it. The only one that can move is the carrier, pressurized by way of the carrier key, with the gases expanding into the key, rear of the bolt and interior of the carrier. Movement of the carrier is not instantaneous, as the gas must first overcome the inertia of the carrier and buffer weight. Then it must begin working against the power of the buffer spring. The bolt has not moved by the time the bullet has left the muzzle, and only begins to move once the carrier inertia has been overcome. The term for the time gap here is "mechanical dwell time."

Once the carrier begins to move, it does not stop until it either has delivered all of its recently-acquired energy into compressing the buffer spring, or the entire assembly bottoms out in the rear of the buffer tube.

The moving carrier pulls off of the bolt. The crooked cam pin slot forces the cam pin to move from the side (where it rests at closing) to the center of the carrier. In so doing it rotates the bolt. The seven lugs of the bolt (the eighth lug would be where the extractor rests) are turned out of engagement with their corresponding locking lugs in the barrel extension. The mechanical dwell time has allowed the case pressure to vent through the bore. And the mechanical spring of the flexing case under pressure has had time to work, partially or completely breaking the frictional bond between case and chamber wall. Rotation of the case (even partially) completes breaking of the frictional bond between case and chamber wall. All rotating bolt mechanisms perform the partial rotation of the case to one degree or another. The rotation aids in extraction, as the case friction to the chamber is diminished. H-K firearms do not have this "primary extraction" that breaks the frictional bond. They must therefore depend on a fluted chamber to diminish frictional forces prior to bolt extraction. The lack of primary extraction is the root cause of the family of H-K rifles having fluted chambers, extreme ejection distances, and severe recoil. (The recoil and ejection distance both come from the high bolt velocity needed to ensure absolute reliably when dealing with a lack of primary extraction.)

Once unlocked, the bolt is not done. It is dragged back by the carrier, and will retain (hopefully) the fired case as it moves. The bolt extractor has the case rim hooked on the right side (from the shooter's viewpoint, left side in a Stag Arms lefty rifle) while the ejector maintains continual pressure on the left side of the case head, via its spring. Once the case clears the chamber, the ejector spring pivots it out of the way.

A brief aside to consider the path of the brass. The brass pivots out of the bolt face, into the open air. It takes a considerable amount of heat with it, something firearms engineers plan for. One of the problems the German Army and H-K had with the caseless G-11 they were working on when the Berlin Wall fell was just that: what to do with the heat generated by the burning powder, if there is no case to remove much of it in the cycling stroke? But back to the AR-15/M-16. The case flips out into the air, hopefully to fall unobstructed to the ground. Left-handed shooters know that it is entirely likely that if they shoot a "slickside" AR, one of the original M-16s or M-16A1s, a Colt SP1, or something built to resemble them, they could be in trouble. You see, the typical ejection path of brass from a 20-inch slickside rifle is back at a sharp angle. A left-handed shooter quite often gets pelted with hot brass. The later models incorporated a brass deflector, or lump, on the side of the upper receiver. It is possible to do some diagnosing of an ARs problems by observing which direction, and how far, the brass goes.

On deflector-equipped rifles, the case has only enough time to exit the port before it (still traveling rearwards, due to inertia) it strikes the deflector. The result in a 20-inch rifle is to direct the brass 90 degrees to the side. On shorter-barreled rifles, the brass goes forward at a 45-degree angle.

In all cases it bounces off the exterior of the rifle, leaving brass marks. The brass marks aren't too bad, but the hot brass on your arm or shoulder is.

Back to the bolt and carrier. The brass ejected, the carrier continues its travel until all of its energy has been converted into either potential energy stored in the spring, or potential energy and heat produced by the impact as the column of parts bottoms out in the end of the buffer tube.

If there is no more ammunition in the magazine (and the magazine is in good repair) the rear of the follower lifts up, pressing on the bolt hold-open, and blocks the bolts forward progress. The bolt "locks back" and you are thus signaled that you are out of ammunition. (Which, by the way, is Farnam's First law of Gunfights: the number-one malfunction encountered in shootouts is running out of bullets.) If the magazine is not empty, as soon as the carrier uncovers the magazine the top round is pressed upwards and to the feed lip by the magazine spring.

The carrier, having delivered all of its energy to the buffer and spring, now receives it again, converting that potential energy back into kinetic energy. The spring drives the buffer and carrier forward. One of the two bottom lugs of the bolt engage the rear of a cartridge, and drive it forward. The round strips out of the magazine and up the ramp to the chamber. The cartridge rides forward of the bolt until it is centered in the chamber (but not fully seated) and only at that point does the cartridge base line up with the recessed bolt face. The bolt, pushing the cartridge ahead of it, continues forward until the cartridge bottoms out in the chamber. The bolt stops, and as its last function of

chambering the extractor snaps over the cartridge rim.

With the bolt stopped, the carrier continues forward, pushed by the buffer and spring. The carrier now shoves the cam pin, via the cam pin slot, rotating the bolt. The bolt lugs slide under the locking lugs of the barrel extension. Once the carrier is completely forward, the action is closed but not quite ready to fire. You may have noticed when handling the buffer that there is something moving inside of it. When the carrier crashes against the barrel extension on closing, it will bounce. Steel striking steel will always bounce, the collision is (in the technical sense) completely elastic. The free-sliding weights in the buffer act as a dead-blow hammer. In a dead-blow hammer used for construction, the weight inside the hammer moves back during the acceleration, and then when

The buffer has free-sliding weights, to act as a dead-blow hammer when closing.

Only bullets in good condition will feed and chamber. Don't expect dented softpoints to find their way.

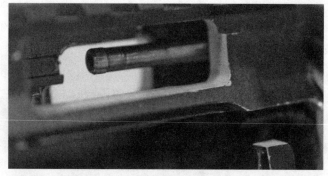

When the bolt and carrier are back, the gas tube is all by itself in the upper. It must be correctly aligned, or the wear of firing will eventually cause a loss of gas pressure seal.

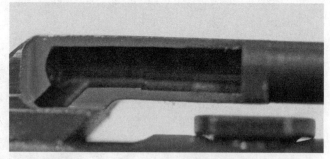

The carrier key is hollow, and the gas builds up in the carrier behind the bolt.

The front sight is part of the gas system, holding the gas tube and lining it up with the barrel port.

Adjustable gas blocks allow you to throttle down the gas flow, restricting pressure and volume.

the hammer stops, hurls forward inside the hammer to strike the inside front face just as the hammer would otherwise be bouncing off the struck object. The bouncing carrier proved to be problematic in full-auto fire. If the hammer happened to fall just as the carrier was bouncing away from the barrel extension, the hammer could not strike the firing pin properly. You'd be in mid-burst and have the hammer suddenly down on an unfired cartridge. Most embarrassing. By adding the dead-blow weights to the buffer, the designers dampened the bounces of the carrier on closing. Once the buffer weights have crashed forward, the rifle is ready to fire.

With the basics of the mechanism laid out, now let us look into the intricacies of, and occasional problems in, the upper and gas system.

Gas Tube High Points

The gas tube is merely a conduit for the gas, from the barrel gas port to the carrier key. Your only control over gas flow comes from either the load selected, or a variable gas port gas block. High-end custom guns will often have an adjustable gas port. The adjustment screw acts to block excess gas from entering the tube. Load selection comes from the selection of one or another powder. The burn rate of the powder the case is loaded with can have an affect on gas port pressure.

A fast-burning powder will have entirely combusted before the bullet moves from the case. The time/pressure curve of the powder will have a sharp peak, then taper off as the bullet moves down the bore. To consider the gas port, think of the curve chart as having a "window" at the distance of the gas port. The window is the acceptable high and low gas port pressure. The curve of the powder being used has to pass through the window. A fast-burning powder may have the tail of the curve taper off too fast, the curve comes under the window, and the port pressure is too low to cycle the action. Why not use more powder? Because the cartridge and rifle have an acceptable chamber peak pressure. The fast-burning powder reaches that peak before the tail of the curve has risen enough to pass through the window.

With low port pressure, the gas tube cannot deliver enough gas to the carrier to both overcome its inertia, and deliver enough additional energy to the carrier to fully cycle the rifle. And the rifle ends up short-stroking, either closing up on an empty chamber, or moving back just far enough to let the top round tip up but not lift up.

Slow-burning powders have the opposite problem. Slow burning powders (also known as "progressive" or "magnum") have a burn curve that does not taper off as quickly as a fast-burning powder. They continue burning longer (relatively speaking) than fast powders, continuing to accelerate the bullet. The curve has its peak later than the fast-burning powder, and the tail does not taper off as quickly. In mechanics and statistics, we learned very early that "work is the area under the curve." The more you can stretch the curve out, the more work is done. In this case, accelerate the bullet. Thus, progressive or magnum powders deliver more velocity. As with everything else in life, the velocity gain is not free. You gain velocity by using more powder, which has to funnel through the case neck and chamber throat, increasing barrel wear in the throat. You also have a louder muzzle blast. Your bullet arrives at the muzzle with a column of powder gases behind it that are at a higher pressure than it would have with the fast-burning powder all that powder creates more noise when released to the air.

And similarly, it arrives at the gas port with a column of gases at a higher pressure. In some cases, higher than the window you are aiming for. Using a slow-burning powder can over-pressure the gas tube. Why is this a problem? Remember the gas dwell time? While the bullet is continuing to the muzzle, the gases are acting on the carrier. If the pressure is too high, the gas tube delivers too much gas to the carrier. The carrier inertia is overcome sooner and faster, and the higher unlocking speed shortens the mechanical dwell time. Thus the carrier moves, and attempts to turn the bolt and extract the empty, much earlier than it otherwise would and with greater force. The case is still stuck firmly to the chamber wall. The extractor either slips off the case, or rips through the rim.

An adjustable gas block allows you to restrict the opening, slowing the rate of gas flow, and offsetting the too-great gas port pressure. However, if you use a slow powder and adjust the gas port to allow normal function, the rifle will short-stroke when fed ammunition loaded with the typical powder used in .223 Remington/5.56 NATO ammunition.

All of the explanation is simply preface to the nearly universal admonition: There is no problem you can solve by drilling out the gas port. Do not drill the gas port! If your rifle is malfunctioning, find the problem, do not mask it by delivering more gas to the system and over-riding the problem.

Can gas tubes get clogged? Some say yes, but I've never seen it. After all, you're pressurizing that tube with 14,000 psi of hot abrasive gases every time you fire it. What will stick? Can they wear out? Yes. If the spigot in the upper is misaligned, the key will bang into it and flex it straight each time the action closes. The tube seals when it is centered in the key, pressurizing the carrier. With a non-straight tube you'll have higher friction on one side, which can wear the tube. Once the tube wears down enough, the tube stops flexing, and you do not have a gas seal. To check a new rifle, remove the bolt assembly from the upper and remove the bolt from the carrier. Then gently slide the carrier (with the operating handle in the upper) into the upper and over the tube. If the tube is misaligned you'll feel the carrier drag, and flex the tube, before coming to rest. How can tubes be bent? If the barrel nut is not perfectly timed when tightened, the tube has to snake past the top notch and into the upper. It is then tilted as seen by the carrier key. Use a large screwdriver

to bend the gas tube end until it lines up and slides into the key without binding.

Carrier Essentials

The carrier key must be tight. While most rifles have keys that are tight and will stay tight, some will come loose. A loose key allows gas to blow out of the interior, causing short stroking. The problem is not insufficient gas, but gas leakage. Remove the key, scrub everything clean (even run a tap down in the threads if you have one) and then Loctite and re-stake.

Occasionally, I see keys where the screw head has been broken. The key can stay on and tight with only one screw, but consider it only an emergency-use situation. The trick is to remove the screw that is left, and once the stub of the broken screw is uncovered you can usually remove it with a pair of vise grips as your wrench. When you replace the key, use new screws. The existing one may have been taking the entire brunt of the gas flow for some time, and may be ready to break.

Keep the carbon scrubbed out of the interior with the Mark Brown tool.

Lubricate the entire carrier to keep the carbon soft. The only bearing surfaces are the "rails" you see on either side of the key, and the ones down near the bottom. They ride on the interior of the upper. Periodically, check your carrier for cracks. While rare, the usual place is in the upper front, from the front face to the cam slot for the cam pin. Less common are cracks on the sides, where the carrier is thinnest for the hammer clearance area. If you have an M-16 carrier that has been ground or machined to something approximating the AR-15 configuration, check the ground area now and then. The grinding may have overheated the area, or created sharp edges that could act as stress risers. If your carrier is cracked, the only thing you can do is replace it.

Bolt Essentials

Your bolt must be kept clean and free of carbon. You must have three gas rings, and they should be in good condition. To check, work one out. To remove a gas ring, get the tip of a knife or a safety pin into the gas ring slot and hook one ring near its gap. Lift the end out, and then run the tip around the bolt, lifting the ring out. (Yes, just like you'd treat a tire.) If you try to pull it out at once you'll over-flex it, damage it, and make it useless. Check the thickness of the ring at the hooked end. If the ring is half or less thick at the narrowest part, compared to a new ring, replace them. Gas rings are cheap. If you have to replace one, do them all.

Check the extractor. The hook must be sharp and complete. Worn, chipped or damaged extractors must be replaced. If the spring lacks a buffer, install one. If up to that point the rifle has been extracting and ejecting just fine, re-use the old spring. If not, put in a new spring along with the little buffer. The extractor spring rests in a lipped hole drilled into the extractor. You cannot simply lift it out. Again use your knife point and hook the spring at one point. Then lift and turn to work the spring out. Replace the spring by starting one side under the lip, and then running the knifepoint around the edge to compress the base coil into the recess.

Extractors on the AR are weak. There just isn't a lot of room in there, so you can only get so much extractor lip and spring to work with. Thus, the internal buffer thingies. The older ones will be weaker, and be tan, green or red. The newer ones will be blue or black. If your extractor lacks one, install one. Additionally, you can add an external booster. The first one I learned of, and found it worked well enough to not bother experimenting further, is the "D-Fender" from Mack Gwinn. Shaped like a "D" it slips over the extractor spring with the flat toward the chamber. It adds extractor tension to the assembly, and increases the likelihood that the brass will be extracted as it is supposed to be. Since then, others have come out with similar products. You can't just use a small rubber "O" ring, for the environment of lubricants, solvents and abrasive powder residue may dissolve polymers not formulated to take the work. But if an AR maker offers one, it is probably made of tough enough stuff.

The ejector is spring-loaded. To remove it you should use the Sinclair bolt tool. Compress the ejector, drift the pin out, then unscrew the tool. Often, the ejector spring will be stuck in the tunnel by a combination of carbon and old oil. You may have to tap it against a table or the vise to move it. If that doesn't work, a pin or needle can be used as a pry bar to lever it out. Don't get the bright idea of using compressed air to move it. The spring will travel quite a distance, probably not to be found. (The record so far, at least of found springs, is 32 feet.) Sometimes the ejector and spring will come out along with a pile of brass shavings. Always a bad sign, it usually means that you're either using ammunition with soft cases, or you are reloading your ammo too hot. The shearing mechanism works this way: when the round is fired, the case expands in all directions. The case head expands back against the ejector. Since the ejector is spring-loaded, it can allow the case head to expand past the surface level of the breechface. Then, when the bolt turns, the now-raised brass at the ejector is either burnished flat (leaving a bright spot) or burnished and some of it is shorn off. That little bit of brass shaving has to go somewhere. Often it simply clings to the bolt. It can easily get sucked into the ejector tunnel as the ejector cycles. When enough build up, the ejector binds and fails to eject the empty just fired. Other times it builds up enough to bind chambering, preventing the bolt from closing, or constricting headspace enough to cause function problems.

Rarely, the brass-shaving problem is caused by the ejector not having been beveled on the top. The sharp edge can shave brass more efficiently, leading to a quick stoppage. A sharp-edged ejector used in combination with soft brass can bring a rifle to a stop in a couple of magazines of firing.

Headspace

Headspace is this mysterious property that all firearms have. Mysterious in that no one ever explains it properly. Here goes: headspace is the chamber room. Too little and the bolt can't compress the case enough to close. Too much and the case will stretch when firing. (Remember, the case expands when fired, and given enough room it will stretch until it breaks) Some stretch reduces useful case life. Too much stretch breaks the case on firing.

Cartridges are made to maximum and minimum dimensions. The minimum is the shortest length and diameter that will allow for a useful case life and good accuracy. (American ammunition makers long ago realized their customers would be reloading, so useful case life is an important part of dimensioning a production lot.) The maximum case dimensions are still less than the minimum chamber dimensions. The minimum chamber dimensions are large enough to safely chamber the largest case allowed by the cartridge specifications. And the maximum chamber dimension is the largest size that the smallest case can be fired in, be safe, and have a useful case life.

The important thing to remember is that all things are relative. As an example, a benchrest shooter will have his chamber neck cut to a size barely a thousandth of an inch larger than his case neck. Since he is hand-turning his case necks, he measures each one, and he'll have 20 or 30 cases (total!) that he uses, his max/min dimensions are different than yours. He does not have to have a rifle that can use any factory ammo, or surplus that he gets at a bargain. His rifle is safe with his ammo, as the two are tuned to each other. You cannot have the chamber on your AR cut to his dimensions, and still be able to safely use factory or surplus ammo. Some will have necks too thick for your tight-neck chamber.

Headspace can be adjusted in some rifles. Those with chrome-plated chambers and bores cannot have the headspace adjusted by reaming the chamber. They can be adjusted only by fitting a new bolt, one with the lugs and breechface cut to fit that particular chamber. A mil-spec rifle will have all the parts held to very close tolerances, where the bolt can be exchanged between rifles, because they will all fall within the limits of proper headspace. Rifles with carbon or stainless steel barrels can have headspace increased by reaming the chamber. All rifles can have the headspace decreased only by replacing the bolt with one that closes to a smaller headspace. Theoretically, you could decrease headspace by removing the barrel from the barrel extension, lathe-turning its shoulder back a thread, re-installing it, and thus take up excess headspace. I say "theoretical" because there are now going to be all kinds of problems since the front sight housing sits a thread farther back, the gas tube does as well, and then there is the little matter of getting the handguards to fit in the shortened space. At first glance, this traditional gunsmithing method of shortening excess headspace seems like it will work. But the more you think about it, the less attractive it becomes.

The Lower:
What Goes On In There?

The easy part of the lower is the buffer tube and its spring and weight. The tube simply holds the buffer and spring, and is the attachment point for the stock. I've seen a bunch of rifles assembled by people who were guessing about assembly, and the main problems seen are the use of a thread locker, and not getting the tube in the right position. There is one place you need use a threadlocker, and that is holding the carrier key to the carrier. Otherwise, using goo to hold stuff together is a clue the assembler either didn't know his stuff, or was taking shortcuts. Screwing the standard tube on is simple: it has a stop shoulder. Just make sure you hold the buffer retainer down against its spring while you tighten the tube. Wring it on hand-tight. For those installing a tele-stock, you have no shoulder to stop you. You must tighten the tube enough to retain the buffer retainer plunger, but not so much that you cause the buffer tube to bind against the upper when it hinges down to close.

The standard tube stays tight because the stock screw stays tight. The tele-stock tube stays tight from tightening the lock ring, and staking the lock ring and retaining plate.

Use a long buffer in a standard tube, and a short buffer in a tele-stock tube. You can't use a long in a tele-stock, there isn't enough room for the mechanism to fully cycle. Conversely, you mustn't use a shorty buffer in a standard tube. The carrier will over-cycle, or travel too far, and the key will impact the upper ring of the lower tube threads. If you're lucky you'll simply shear one or both of the key screws. If you're unlucky, you'll crack the lower, and have to buy a new one.

The Colt M-4 uses a new buffer, the "H" or the "H2" buffer. They have one or two, respectively of the internal weights of steel replaced with tungsten. The extra weight slows down the cyclic rate of the M-4 in full auto fire, and relieves the stress of any firing.

Shorty tubes should use recoil springs of 37 to 39 coils, while full-size rifles use springs of 41 to 43 coils. You can use an extra-power spring if you want, but like the 1911, if you have to in order to make the rifle work properly, that is a clue that something else is wrong and should be addressed.

Fire Control Parts

The trigger mechanism of the AR is relatively simple. The hammer has a hook on the bottom, the sear. The trigger tip rests in that notch. When you pull the trigger, you are pulling the tip of the trigger nose directly out of the hammer hook, and when they part company the hammer falls and the rifle fires. The trick is in getting the rifle to fire once, and only once. To do that, all semi-automatic rifles have a part that is called the "disconnector." It catches the hammer on the rebound, and holds it until you release the trigger to re-set the mechanism.

In the AR, the disconnector is a flat plate that rides in the middle of the trigger. When the carrier cycles, it launches the hammer back and re-cocks it. The small hook underneath the

The disconnector holds the hammer back while the action cycles. If not correctly timed, the disconnector can be the cause of many headaches and much trouble.

The hammer sear hook. Lube it, keep it clean, but do not stone it.

The disconnector rides in the middle of the trigger.

As your finger goes forward, releasing the trigger, the trigger nose rises into the path of the hammer sear.

And if correctly timed, the trigger catches the hammer as the disconnector lets go. If the trigger does not catch the hammer, the rifle will fire again. It is dangerous to have a rifle timed early enough to fire on release. Get it fixed!

As the disconnector rides off the hammer hook,

big tail of the hammer is the disconnector hook. When the carrier cycles, your finger is still holding the trigger down. The disconnector, operating on its own spring, hooks and stops the hammer. When the bolt crashes forward, the hammer is held back. Now, the tricky part: if the disconnector lets go of the hammer before the trigger rises high enough (as you release it) to catch the hammer, the hammer will swing forward and fire the chambered round. This is called "early release" or "early timing" and is bad news. What it means is you will fire two rounds, one when you pull the trigger, and one when you release. Technically, you have a machinegun. In the non technical/legal, real world, it means you have an unsafe and/or badly gunsmithed rifle.

What you want is a disconnector that releases the hammer only after the trigger rises enough to catch the hammer. It is possible to have a disconnector timed so late that it does not let go of the hammer. If the disconnector is still hooked after the trigger has risen all it will rise, the rifle won't fire. You want a disconnector timed as late as possible, while still providing 100 percent release of the hammer.

The safety is a rotating bar with a shelf cut in it. The shelf provides clearance for the tail of the trigger to rise when you pull it to shoot. Rotated so the shelf is gone and the bar blocks the trigger, the safety prevents firing. In select-fire

The rear of an AR-15 trigger is enclosed, to prevent the use of an M-16 disconnector.

AR safety levers have two detents, and the middle is solid. M-16 selectors have three detents, and the middle is radically slotted.

The hook you see on the side of some hammers is the burst-selector autosear. It means nothing, don't worry about it as long as the top of the hammer is "slick."

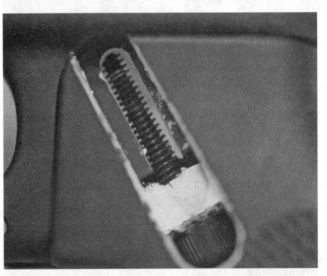

The pistol grip holds the detent and spring that hold the safety in each position.

rifles, the safety also allows the disconnector on the M-16 or M-4 to pivot up to engage the autosear. There, the trigger is held down by your trigger finger. The disconnector hooks the hammer and holds it cocked. Then, as the carrier closes the last bit, it trips the autosear, which pivots the disconnector, and the hammer gets released. As mentioned in the "Legalities" chapter, the M-16 carrier in and of itself is no big deal. It doesn't do anything by itself. But the other parts, they can get you in trouble. And they are easy to modify. So, do not keep unmodified M-16 fire control parts on hand.

Trigger Pull

In many other firearms, you improve the trigger pull by stoning the engagement surfaces of the hammer and sear. No so in the AR. The hammer and trigger are often (at least in good parts) case-hardened. That is, the surface is hardened but the internal portion of the parts are left relatively soft. Case-hardening allows a manufacturer to make parts of relatively soft steel for lower cost and greater ease of manufacture, but use the hardening process to produce parts that will last a long time and resist wear and corrosion.

The hammer spring legs must ride on top of the trigger pins, and outside of the trigger spring.

The Chambersafe allows gunhandling in a training environment secure in the knowledge that the chamber cannot hold a round.

The Chambersafe allows a rifle to be stored in a rack, with the chamber empty and a loaded magazine in place. It is a quick and easy thing to get it loaded, but not something that can be done inadvertently.

If you stone the surfaces, you risk breaking through the hardened surface and subjecting softer steel to the wear of firing. More importantly, as the trigger bears directly on the hammer, if you change the engagement surface angles you risk creating an engagement that is mechanically unable to stand the load. The angles of the trigger and hammer act to keep them together. If you change the angles, you may create a situation where the hammer cams the trigger out of the way. If it wears a bit (soft internals, remember?) the rifle could get to the point that pushing the safety to "Fire" causes it to fire without touching the trigger.

Springs

The hammer and trigger springs have to go together in a particular order. See the photo for the proper way, as in this case a picture is worth a thousand words. When you assemble the lower, pay particular care that the legs of the hammer spring go to the outside of the trigger, and rest in the notches of the trigger pivot pin. If you do not, the trigger pin can work lose, fall out of one side, tipping the trigger and leading to malfunctions.

Safety Pivot

The safety is retained and held to position by a plunger and spring held in place by the pistol grip. The pistol grip screw is sometimes an allen-head screw and not a slot-head. My friend Jeff Chudwin likes to simply cut the allen head with a hacksaw to make a dual screw that works with both. Me, I just swap the allen for a slot screw. If you do have the allen head screw, it takes a 7/64 wrench, and one long enough to reach. Standard ones won't do it. Some safety parts can be removed without loosening the pistol grip. But not all, and you can't find out which one you have without removing the pistol grip first.

Ready Conditions

The whole point of a firearm is that you think you will be needing an emergency tool (which is what a firearm is for most of us) and need it badly. By "badly" I mean you are contemplating the need to use it against another human being to defend you live or the lives of others. If you are not morally and psychologically ready for that, you shouldn't be carrying one. If you haven't prepared for the legal consequences, you definitely shouldn't be packing. If you have made the necessary preparations, then here goes:

Empty

An empty firearm is kind of like a seat belt that you plan to snap on when you see an accident coming. If you see the accident coming, your time is better spent avoiding it, rather than scrambling for the seatbelt you should already have on. But a rifle should be stored empty. Do not confuse "stored" with a ready rack you have nearby. Stored means empty, and in a safe. To store empty, remove the magazine. Retract the operating handle and look into the chamber. Look intently, and with good light. Once you know the chamber is empty, close the bolt. Point the rifle in a safe direction. Dry fire it. Check the safety. It should not move from "Fire" to "Safe." That it doesn't lets you know the hammer is down. Now put it in the safe and leave it alone. If at any time you pick up that rifle, try to move the safety. If the safety doesn't move from "Fire" then the hammer is down, the action is uncocked. You don't have to pull the trigger to see if it is loaded or cocked.

Is there any time other than in the gun safe that you need a rifle unloaded? While transporting it to and from the range or a competition. And again, you pull it out of the safe, check the safety, insert it in the case, and go. If you want to check the bore, then work the action to cock it, put the selector in "Safe" and then press the action pins to disassemble the rifle.

When you put it back together, check the action, dry fire and put it in the safe or case.

Cruiser Ready

Cruiser Ready comes from the police method of rack-storing a loaded pump shotgun in a police squad car. It starts out the same as "Empty" for storage: Remove the magazine, if present. Work the action and inspect the chamber. Once empty, close and dry fire. Here, however, things get different. For Cruiser Ready, leave the hammer down, and the safety off. Insert a loaded magazine. Stick the rifle in a secure rack, and it is ready. The rack must be secure, because anyone can snatch the rifle out of the rack at a moment's notice, operate the charging handle, and have a loaded rifle. A loaded rifle with the safety off. Where rifles must be ready, and the response to charging the chamber is almost always firing, Cruiser Ready works. In a military context, it can work. In a civilian defensive or law enforcement setting, I'm not so comfortable with it. After all, police officers point firearms at suspect and offenders a whole lot more often than they fire on those same individuals. The response to heightened tension is not always to fire (nor would I want to live in a city where the police department held that view). But, it does work. My friend John Farnam is a big proponent of Cruiser Ready. One of the advantages Empty and Cruiser Ready have, is that the ejection port cover can be kept closed, to block the entry of dust, dirt and grit.

An additional option with Cruiser Ready is to leave the hammer cocked, and have the safety to the "Safe" position. Then, chambering a round does not leave you with a hot rifle and the safety off.

The problem with both Empty and Cruiser Safe is that there is no positive way to know there isn't a round in the chamber. So the rifle resting in the rack may have a chambered round.

Chambersafe

A different step to that same end is to use some kind of a chamber block to keep the loaded magazine separate from the chamber. Some methods use a dummy cartridge, or a spring-loaded chamber flag. The problem (or advantage, if you desire such) with these methods is that removing the block also chambers a round. If you're using a dummy round, for example, you can't get the dummy out without getting a loaded round into the chamber. Working the action to extract the dummy introduces a live round. The Chambersafe is different. It sticks into the chamber, keeping a round out. If the Chambersafe can't fit in the chamber, there is something wrong. If you try to chamber a round with the Chambersafe installed, the round won't fit. The

big ring on the outside is easy to grasp, and pulling it out does not chamber a round. You can keep the rifle in a rack, knowing there cannot possibly be a round in the chamber. The method of use is to first select a safety mode: safety to "Fire" as in Cruiser Ready, or safety to "Safe." Then check the chamber, and set the rifle up as you want it. (Getting the bolt back enough to introduce the Chambersafe while in Cruiser Ready can be hard to manage.) I use mine with the action cocked and the safety set on "Safe." Then, pull the bolt back part way, insert the Chambersafe into the chamber, and ease the bolt forward. Now, insert a loaded magazine. Rack and lock (or whatever you do) and you're ready.

When you need the rifle, snatch it out of the rack. Grab the Chambersafe and snatch it free. You can drop it, let it fly, pocket it or throw it at the bad guy. It has served its purpose. Work the charging handle to chamber a round. Proceed to solve your problem.

In a training environment, the Chambersafe is a godsend. Instead of actions open, or lengths of yellow nylon rope hanging out, we just insert Chambersafes and we're all ready to talk. When it is time to shoot again, insert a magazine, yank out the Chambersafe, and chamber a round. The beauty of it is that the handling in training replicates the duty environment, and what you do in training is most likely what you'll do in an altercation. In a duty setting, the Chambersafes can be marked with the rifle serial number, officers initials or badge number, or whatever. In the car the rifles are safe. Out of the car the Chambersafe marks the general area where the officer took the first step of using deadly force. Being bright orange, it also reminds the officer what condition the rifle is in: there isn't a round in the chamber, and he'd better get one in there if he's going to deal with the problem.

If there is a shortcoming to the Chambersafe, it is that the action is slightly open, and the dust cover down, to allow entry for debris. But, since most rifles in patrol cars are on the ceiling, there isn't a whole lot of lint that can get in there. The Chambersafe isn't a "Fallujah" kind of tool: it is for training and police duty carry, not hot weapons on patrol in a military environment. But in a military training environment, it can ensure that chambers are empty, even if a magazine is inserted.

Lock And Load

Simple: insert a loaded magazine. Work the charging handle. Put the safety on Safe if it wasn't already there. Retract the charging handle just enough to see and feel that there actually is a round in the chamber. Close the action, close the dust cover, put it in the rack or sling it. Definitely a "Fallujah" kind of approach. Also, the condition of your rifle in a match, after the Range or Safety Officer gives you the command: "Load and make ready." You're carrying a loaded rifle, so you'd better be absolutely sure of where you're pointing it each and every microsecond.

Barrels

The invention of rifling some centuries ago was not the boon you'd think. The problem was, how to get the bullet to grip the rifling, to be spun, without making loading a royal hassle? Riflemen in the age of the smoothbore musket were in great danger. First, loading was very slow, so they could not stand up to a unit of musket-armed men and trade fire. In the time the riflemen could fire, and then reload, a unit of musket-armed men could close the gap, fire and then charge. Second, rifles traditionally didn't have bayonets, so when the musket-armed men charged, the riflemen had to flee or be stabbed. Why no bayonets? Because the elaborate

The result of a bullet weight/ rifling twist mis-match. If you shoot a 75-grain Match bullet out of some 1/9 twist barrels, this is what you get.

and physically-involved ramming of a bullet down a rifled bore made a mounted bayonet as much danger to the user as the intended target. Third, many musket-armed soldiers took it personally that riflemen aimed, and took great pleasure in bayoneting riflemen when they could.

The American Civil War changed much of that. The Minie ball, invented by a French Army officer, allowed for loading as fast as a smoothbore musket. Accuracy was good enough that units could be accurately fired upon at 300 yards, and individuals at 100. What transpired between old tactics and new weapons was slaughter: Units that charged across open ground, or stood their ground and traded fire, would suffer 10, 20 or even 30 percent casualties in short order. It wasn't unheard of for units in the Civil War to engage in a single attack, and suffer such casualties that they were for all military intents and purposes non-existent.

The Iron Brigade was a unit that amply demonstrated the problem. Mustered in August of 1862 with roughly a thousand men each, the "Black Hats" of the 2nd, 6th & 7th

Barrels are not made to a single, precise dimension. All production wanders in tolerances. The better the barrel, the tighter the tolerances, the higher the cost.

Wisconsin, 19th Indiana and the 24th Michigan Regiments went into the meat-grinder of the Civil War right away. Eleven months later, the 1,030 men of the 24th Michigan arrived in Gettysburg with 490 effectives. After the first day of combat, there were 99 left. The 2nd Wisconsin had the greatest percentage of losses of any unit in the war, while the 7th had the largest number killed. It was not at all unusual for a unit to suffer 10, 20, 30 percent casualties in a single engagement lasting less than an hour! And the war was fought with black powder (lots of smoke) and mostly muzzle-loading rifles. At close range.

The disparity between tactics and weaponry continued until WWI, where it reached its apex. But the legacy persisted for some time; that true riflemen needed long-range rifles to deal with their opponents at the maximum range possible. The AR-15 was one of the two weapons that changed that, the other being the AK-47. Combat is a chaotic, close-range affair, and most participants are not well-served with rifles capable of reaching long distances with great power.

But within the short (Almost always inside of 300 meters, and mostly 100 or less) distance of rifle combat, a rifle still needs to be accurate. And reliable. Lets look at what a barrel needs be, and what your AR barrel should be.

Parts Of The Barrel

As our model barrel, at least for the exterior, I'll be pointing things out on a DPMS barrel from Brownells. As a replacement barrel that you can plug in to replace one worn, abused or used up, they are one heck of a bargain. For about $150, you can have a barrel accurate enough to do you well in any match up to NRA High Power, limited only by your shooting skill. And as a chrome-moly steel, you can ream the chamber to adjust headspace if your bolt happens to produce less than minimum headspace when you first check it.

Any barrel is simply a steel tube. At the rear is the chamber, in the middle the bore, and the end is the crown. A barrel receives a cartridge, holds it for firing, launches a bullet along a known and predictable path, and does so for as long as the steel can take the work. All manufactured products must be made within specifications. Any product is made to within a maximum and minimum size. It simply isn't feasible or economically wise to make each and every part perfect, conforming exactly to the specifications drawn. So, each part will have a maximum and minimum size, with all parts falling within that spread. For example, we refer to the .223/5.56 as being a ".22" or using .224-inch bullets. Actually, the bullets can (depending on who is making them, and for what application) be any size from .2235 inches to .2245 inches

(DoD Photo)

Modern combat is often a chaotic, close-range affair. Sometimes a short-barreled rifle is useful. Sometimes the loss of velocity is a hindrance. We'll never have a "rifle for all seasons."

and the interior of the barrel, the bore, has another set of specifications. A match barrel may be held to a smaller spread, but there is still a spread. And a barrel may vary from one end to the other. Again, a Match barrel varies less, but if you were to measure a perfect barrel, and find the bore averages .22410 inches, it may vary between .22408 and .22412 inches along its length. A non-match barrel may vary from .22392 inches to .22415 inches or more. And most measuring instruments won't even register the fifth digit, so a barrel that measures between .2239 and .2241 could be quite good.

So, when we talk of a barrel being Match we simply mean the dimensions are held between a smaller spread of max and min.

Barrel Material

You'll see barrels touted as "stainless," "chromed," "match" and "G.I." And other terms as well. What they are telling you is what it is made of, how it is treated, and in some cases (as in the "GI" part) the general specifications of it.

A barrel is made of steel. Steel is iron with a small amount of carbon in it for hardness. If you want to flip through the specs, the American National Standards Institute can tell you more than you need to know about steel. There are all sorts of alloying metals that can be added. "Alloy" simply tells you that something besides iron and carbon are in there. It does not necessarily mean that it is a hard, tough or desirable steel. Some things harden it, some things make it easier to machine. Others add uniformity to the crystalline structure, making it easier to forge, heat-treat, machine or otherwise fabricate into barrels. Some alloying materials add corrosion resistance, others abrasion resistance. Carbon steel has no alloying components that reduce oxidation (rust). Stainless steel does have some, primarily chromium or nickel, or both. (A chrome steel is not the same as a chromed barrel) However, you cannot add enough of them to make a steel truly "stainless." By the time you have done so it is so soft it isn't useful as a steel, except for kitchen tableware.

A chromed barrel has either the chamber, or the chamber and bore, plated with chromium. But not bumper chrome, instead a hard, tough layer of chromium that resists corrosion, abrasion and heat. Very early M-16 barrels had nothing, then briefly they had only chamber chromed to resist corrosion and aid extraction. Once the process was refined enough, the entire bore was chromed. A chromed bore is much tougher in the long run. However, the plating is not as uniform in thickness, coverage and smoothness to make it attractive to competition shooters. At least not the long-range ones. While three-gun shooters will often gladly use a chromed bore, serious long-range shooters will only use stainless Match barrels.

As for "GI," it means whatever the maker wants it to. Now, if they were to say Mil-spec, and quote a particular military specification, then that is different. The government has exacting standards, know as Military Specifications, or Mil-spec. If someone says their (barrel, extractor, shoelaces) is "mil-spec"

then you can look up the spec cited and see just what they're claiming.

Barrel Extension

Unlike many other rifle designs, the AR-15 bolt locks to the barrel, and not the receiver. Specifically, to the barrel extension, a part that screws onto the barrel itself. In military rifles like the M-14 or the FN-FAL, even the competitor AK-47, the bolt locks against the receiver when it closes. Thus, the receiver takes the force of the bolt thrust on firing. The receiver thus must be stoutly constructed to take the stress of the cartridge firing. The AR-15 removes that stress, by having the bolt lock into the barrel extension, and thus the barrel itself. The receiver does not have to do anything more than guide the parts as they cycle back and forth. (And hold the sights, the magazine, fire control parts, etc. But you get the idea.) The barrel extension is composed of a much harder steel than the barrel. It has to be, because it takes the stress of firing, and it can be, because it is a compact part, easily fabricated. (Relatively speaking.)

The barrel extension is threaded, and screws onto the

The barrel extension is what the bolt locks into. The barrel nut is what secures the barrel to the upper receiver.

This sectioned barrel shows the barrel extension, locking lugs and the rear of the chamber.

rear of the barrel. It contains the locking lug recesses, and a locating pin on top. The locking lugs of the bolt pass between the lugs of the barrel extension, and when the bolt turns its lugs pass in front of the extension lugs, locking the two together against the thrust of the cartridge.

The cartridge has to pass through all this on its way to the chamber. To make that possible, the barrel extension has a pair of feed ramps machined into it. The original feed ramps were only as long as the sidewall thickness of the barrel extension itself. That is, the ramps did not extend down past the barrel extension diameter. Occasionally, a rifle would be reluctant to feed, if the rounds stubbed against the vertical wall of the upper receiver below the barrel extension feed ramp. Colt solved this problem with the M-4 feed ramp. The ramp extends down below the barrel extension diameter, into the receiver. You can have problems in a parts gun if you combine an M-4 upper and a non-M-4 barrel or barrel extension. There, the non-ramped extension overhangs the ramped upper receiver, and you can have feeding malfunctions. The other combinations will not cause feeding problems due to the tolerance problems. Some create "faux M-4" ramps by machining the extension and upper to create an M-4-dimension ramp. Some worry that the cut exposes un-anodized aluminum. I have several rifles where I machined the ramp to solve a rare feeding malfunction (years before Colt did this, and registered it), and those particular uppers show no ill effects from the work. One is now on its third barrel, so it apparently is durable enough even after the modification.

The M-4 extension and upper modification is a Colt-developed improvement, and a Colt-protected one.

Do you need an M-4 ramp on your rifle? Colt found they needed to do it on the short-barreled rifles they were developing, which became their M-4 Carbine. What happened, was in some rifles, when firing full-magazines bursts, the last couple of rounds of M-855 would not feed reliably. Considering that in such a use, the rounds are rattling around in the magazine tube like it is a maraca, is it any wonder the last few would refuse to feed? Colt solved the problem with the altered ramps. They do not make the ramps on their full-size rifles. Unless your rifle occasionally stubs on feeding, you don't either.

Installing barrels onto extensions is easy in the manufacturing process: fit barrels and extensions into a torquing machine, tighten, then send off for gas port drilling, sight installation, etc.

Custom AR gunsmiths will commonly machine a barrel blank to fit it to a target gun, thread the rear, and tighten a barrel extension on. Rather than depend on someone making hundreds or thousands at a time, they make one, perfect. With a large and precise lathe, you can machine the barrel and extension so they are centered and parallel to the bore. The custom gunsmith will also go to the extra trouble of "clocking" the barrel. That is, machining it so the gas port drill breaks through into the bore centered in the bottom of a groove.

The Internal Barrel Parts

The chamber is composed of four parts, chamber, neck, throat and leade. The chamber is the part we all think of as the chamber. That is, the opening in the rear of the barrel where the case resides, up to and including the case shoulder. A tight (as in narrow) chamber will hold its cases with less play side to side, adding to accuracy. It will also allow less expansion, adding case life. However, a tight chamber can create malfunctions sooner, as it gets fouled, or if something gets in there like dust, dirt or grit. Too loose, and while reliable, accuracy and case life suffer. Accuracy, due to the case moving (a small amount, admittedly) and case life due to excessive expansion of the case on firing.

You can see the feed ramps cut on this barrel extension.

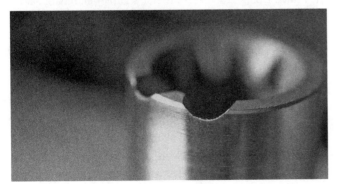

The new Colt M-4 feed ramps cut deeper into the barrel extension, and into the upper receiver.

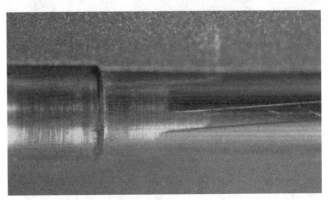

The chamber neck and leade.

What we term "headspace" is the gap between the breechface of the bolt, and the forward shoulder of the chamber, when the bolt is closed. It is independent of chamber diameter, which can be large or small regardless of headspace. Cases expand in all directions on firing. A chamber with excessive headspace reduces case life, as the case stretches on firing. When resized to bring it back to an acceptable size, the shoulder is shoved back. The next firing stretches it again. While the sizing sets the shoulder back, the stretch comes at the expense of the brass closer to the rim. After enough firings, it stretches more than it can hold, and breaks apart.

Chamber size is a delicate balance between case life and reliability. It is possible to exceed the limits in either direction. In years past it was common to advise reloaders new to the AR-15 to use "small base" dies in order to size their cases down enough to provide reliable function. We now know that small base dies simply mask the real problem, improper chamber size. If your AR proves unreliable, find out the real problem, and don't just over-work your brass to "deal" with it.

The "proper" distance between the bolt face and the forward shoulder of the chamber is a subject of much discussion. You see, headspace is not a single measurement, but a range. "More than this, but less than that" is headspace. How much is allowed by mil-spec, and commercial standards, differ.

The chamber neck is that portion of the chamber where the case neck, containing the bullet, rests. A chamber neck, as does the chamber, must be small enough to limit case expansion, but large enough to allow the rifle to operate reliably. Benchrest shooters commonly have chambers cut so tightly that their cases do not need to be resized after each firing. However, they use the same 20 cases over and over, and those cases are not just common-garden-variety cases. Each has been weighed, measured and hand-machined to be identical. The necks are all the same thickness and length, and correspond to the chamber neck thickness. They do not feed their rifle off-the-shelf ammunition. You, on the other hand, will be. Even if you reload, you will not be going to such

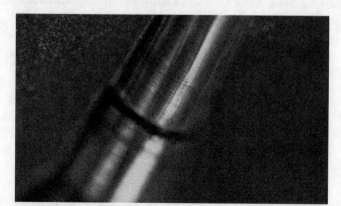

The front of the chamber neck, with the shelf of the neck-to-throat juncture visible. That shoulder is why you must make sure your brass is trimmed, if you plan to reload .223 ammo.

lengths in your brass prep. Not unless you expect to go to the range to shoot 20 rounds, and return.

The throat is a short section of cylindrical area forward of the neck, that is smaller than the diameter of the case neck but larger than the diameter of the bullet itself. (It may be, and usually is, the same diameter as the bore diameter.) The portion of the cartridge forward of the case, i.e., the bullet, rests here. The throat is the bullet space, and allows the bullet to project out of the case and aid feeding. The bullet (any bullet except a wadcutter) has a forward portion smaller than its bearing surface. This forward bullet portion, the ogive, provides for lessened drag and a flatter trajectory. The bore must be relieved to accommodate it. How much depends on the bullet weight and length, shape and proportion. A shorter throat (all other things being equal) provides greater accuracy, as the bullet has less time to shift before entering the rifling. However, a short throat increases pressure, as the bullet "stalls" when it hits the rifling, and the momentary hesitation, as the powder burns, also stalls the pressure release created by the bullets movement.

Last in the chamber is the leade. Pronounced "leed", it is the angle of the onset of the rifling. The steeper the angle (as the bullet sees it) the greater accuracy. Again, it has to do partly with how much time and movement the bullet has to shift before the rifling controls it, and the uniformity of a steep leade as opposed to a gentle one. If you have a steep leade, it is easier to keep them all the same angle. If they are shallow, it becomes more of a problem to keep them the same. The differences, however, are minor.

Target shooters pay great attention to the length of the leade. It can have a large impact on accuracy, velocity and pressure. To measure leade, you use something like (or the very thing) the Stoney Point gauge. The gauge uses a modified case and holding fixture. You insert the gauge and a test bullet into the chamber. You them press the bullet forward until it stops. Lock the holder, remove the holder and bullet, and then measure overall length of the test bullet in the locked gauge. The difference between the loaded overall length (which will feed from the magazine) and the test length is the leade, or bullet jump. Long-range target shooters will load the bullets as long as needed to get the bullet as close to but not touching the rifling. Doing so increases useful accuracy and marginally increases case capacity. Such long bullets do not fit into magazines, and must be single-loaded.

When dealing with ammo 223 Remington and 5.56 NATO, aren't the same.

The Remington, designed as a long-range varmint cartridge, has a narrower neck, shorter throat and steeper leade. The idea is that if you are using your rifle to whack varmints at 300 and 400 yards, you need all the accuracy you can get. And since varmint hunters reload, they want long case life. On the other hand, military uses are not so exacting in the accuracy department. As long as a cartridge/rifle combination retains "minute of bad guy" accuracy to 300 yards, it is plenty accurate enough. As an example, if a varmint shooter takes a shot at a prairie dog at 300 yards, and holds the crosshairs of his scope exactly on the center of the 'dog and has a perfect trigger press, he expects a hit. If the accuracy of the cartridge is only good for a 6-inch group (a lousy group, by the way, for a varmint rifle) he'll probably miss through no fault of his own. A soldier doing the same thing will have 100 percent hits on a standing man, and 50 percent hits on one attempting to hide. (People are bigger than prairie dogs.) A military rifle has to work for a long time, in harsh conditions, and has to deal with one more thing the prairie dog rifle doesn't: Tracers. In the military tracers are not just a means of giving a machinegunner feedback. Officers and NCOs will commonly have a magazine loaded with all-tracer ammo. If they see a target that the machinegunner should be dealing with, but

Some makers clearly mark the chamber their rifle gets. There's no question about this one.

the machinegunnner is otherwise busy, they'll begin shooting at the target with their rifle. As soon as the assistant gunner (or anyone nearby) sees the steady stream of tracers going out, they immediately inform the machinegunner, who shifts his fire. Tracer bullets are long. They are longer than regular bullets, to hold the burning trace compound.

The long throat and gentle leade of the 5.56mm chamber allows the long tracer bullets to be fired without causing an increase in pressure. Without it, the tracer would either have greater pressure than regular 5.56mm ammunition (which is already high) or have to be loaded to less pressure, adversely affecting trajectory.

What this means is that if you have a rifle which has the chamber cut to 223 Remington dimensions, using 5.56 ammunition in it could cause an increase in chamber pressure. The increase might not be something to worry about. However, added to other pressure-increasing factors, it can cause problems. If you are shooting a dirty rifle, on a hot day, with ammunition loaded in soft cases, you could quickly cause a malfunction from soft brass being shorn off by the ejector. Excessive pressure could cause cases to stick and the extractor then fails to extract. Changing any single factor can reduce or eliminate the problem. Yes, you can use ammo with hard brass, but you don't always have that choice. And you certainly can't change the ambient temperature. As for cleaning, well, they all start clean, but they all get dirty soon enough. Get the chamber reamed, if you can. Luckily, all manufacturers who make chromed barrels make them in 5.56mm and not .223.

These barrels can be anything the maker wants, and their quality depends on how much time and effort the maker puts into them.

The Bore

The portion of the barrel the bullet itself travels down is the bore. A rifle bore is produced in one of three methods: broaching, buttoning, or hammer-forging. The basic method is simple: the barrelmaker produces a cylinder with a hole down the center. The exact method depends on the machinery used, but it is typical to drill the cylinder halfway from each end, then ream and polish to a finished dimension. The finished dimension is the diameter of the finished barrel to the tops of the rifling.

In broaching, a hooked cutter is pulled through the barrel, to cut away the grooves of the rifling. In the very early days of rifles, the broach would be a single hook, and would have to be pulled through the barrel repeatedly, gradually cutting each groove in turn to full depth. Once steel became uniform enough, and hydraulics came into common use, broaches could be made as single units. A broach (which can cost several thousand dollars or more, depending on size and quality) has many steps, each cutting deeper, and all four, five, six or however many grooves there are. Looking like a miniature, golden, Christmas tree, it broaches the barrel in one pass.

A button barrel operates in a different method. Instead of the blank being reamed to a size that matches the tops of the rifling, the blank is reamed to a dimension in between bore and groove diameter. Then, a hardened button is pushed or pulled through the bore. The button is shaped to the dimensions the finished bore will be, and it literally squeezes the steel into the shape of a rifled bore.

Hammer-forged barrels start much larger and shorter than the finished barrel. The reamed cylinder is placed in the multi-ton forge, and a mandrel, shaped to be the bore dimensions (sometimes even including the chamber) is placed in the blank. Then, the huge hammers of the forge pound the cylinder down until it has been squeezed around the mandrel and is shaped internally into a rifled bore. Then the mandrel is pulled out, and a new blank inserted.

Which is best? There is no simple answer. All can be accurate. All can be durable. Which a barrelmaker makes depends on what equipment he has.

Chrome-lined barrels have their dimensions cut (or buttoned, or hammered) to account for the extra thickness the chrome will take up. If the chrome will plate to a thickness of .0005" (half a thousandth) then the bore and grooves have to be made a thousandth larger. (The bore is circular, the chrome plates all around, so a plating of half a thousandth makes the diameter a thousandth smaller.) You cannot have a regular bore chromed after it has left the plant. You either get a barrel that is already chromed, or you get a barrel that isn't.

Gas Ports

Forward of the chamber is the gas port. In order to work the action, the port bleeds gas back to the action. The port pressure on the Stoner system is quite high, on the order of 15,000 to nearly 20,000 psi depending on barrel length and gas port location. The gas is fed back to the carrier, where it launches the carrier back off the bolt to work the action. I've seen high-speed video of the action on an AR working, and it is impressive. At 1,000 frames a second, if the timing is right, you can see the spurt of gas that comes out of the vent holes on the side of the carrier. Apparently, if an assembler has been a bit too free with lubricant, the gases and burnt lubricant can obscure the rifle from the video camera for a few shots, until the lube gets burned off.

Gas ports are drilled to a set diameter according to the length of the barrel and the thickness of the barrel wall. All gas ports are not drilled to the same size. Almost no malfunction of the AR system can be cured by drilling the gas port to a larger diameter. The last thing I look at when a rifle is malfunctioning is the gas port diameter. Even if a rifle is being starved for gas, there are other things more likely (tipped front sight housing, pinched gas tube, worn gas tube tip) that should be checked first.

As the bullet slides past the gas port, the gas enters the front sight housing. But it also slams forward against the wall of the gas port. You can see the erosion on any barrel that has been shot more than a few hundred rounds. Gas port erosion has no discernable effect on accuracy. There may be 600-yard shooters who disagree, and feel that erosion harms accuracy. Were I in the position of vying with David

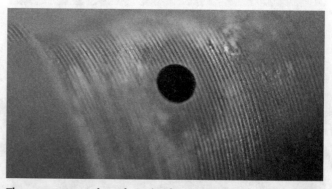

The gas port on a barrel. Resist the temptation to drill it out to a larger size to "increase reliability." There is almost no problem the AR is heir to that you solve by drilling the gas port.

The gas gets funneled out of the port, through the front sight housing, to the gas tube and thus the carrier.

Tubb for the Wimbledon Cup, I'd probably pay attention to gas port erosion. But for anything less demanding, it doesn't matter. I just had the opportunity to view a Colt M-4 barrel that has some serious mileage on it. The owner is a Sergeant with a multi-jurisdictional SWAT team, who supervises the training and deployment of an impressive number of officers. (Basically, he's in charge of a company-sized unit of SWAT cops. Think Urban Light Infantry, and you're on the right track.) His M-4 has been in use for a few years, and he's used it on raids (lots of scary stories and rounds at or on bad guys), training and competition. Despite the hard use, it is still fully capable of going 20 hits on 20 targets, out to 300 meters, on the National Guard range. The targets are a foot and a half wide, and two and a half feet tall, and Big Ed can easily drop them, using iron sights. The gas port was far beyond eroded. Instead of the simple concave erosion "tail" it had a trench eroded several gas port diameters forward of the port.

I was amazed to see it and told Ed that when he had the rifle re-barreled I wanted the old one so I could section it and photograph it. The trench was so long I couldn't even get all of it in the field of view of the borescope at once. I had to move the scope to see it all.

The threads allow you to attach a flash hider, which not only hides the threads, but protects the crown.

Muzzle

The crown of the muzzle is the last influence the barrel has on a bullet, and for good accuracy it must have as uniform an influence as possible. An uneven crown, or one worn through poor cleaning habits, allows a small puff of gas to escape on one side of the bullet as the bullet leaves. The bullet as it leaves the muzzle is in a delicate transition zone: it has to switch from barrel to air. Anything that disrupts that transition hurts accuracy.

It doesn't matter if the crown is crusty from powder residue. As long as it is even around its perimeter, the crown will not degrade accuracy.

You see, when a bullet is going down the bore, it is forced to rotate around its center of shape. Once in the air, it then transitions to rotating around its center of mass. A good bullet has the center of shape and mass very close to each other. (A perfect bullet would have them the same.) The bullet wobbles for a short distance until it "settles down." Anything that unduly influences the bullet before it settles down has a disproportionate effect on accuracy.

A perfect crown is best. To protect the crown, the military gets double-duty from the flash hider; it also acts as a crown protector.

On the muzzle, you can have a bare crown, as we saw on so many post-ban AWB/94 rifles. You can have muzzle with a flash hider, or a muzzle with a muzzle brake or compensator. All will shoot accurately.

If the crown has been nicked or dented, or mis-cut from the maker, re-cutting it can improve accuracy.

Rifling Twist

A smoothbore firearm is less accurate than a rifle because of the unstable nature of the non-rotating projectile. Basically, a shotgun slug is a knuckleball. But how much twist do you need? Sir Alfred George Greenhill, Professor of Mathematics of Woolrich, England, came up with a formula to calculate

The cutting tool is a special reamer and pilot, available from Brownells.

weight that matters. If you take two bullets, one a flat-based round-nose, and the other a sharply pointed with boat-tail, of the same weight, they will have a different stability factor when fired from the same barrel.

You cannot have a barrel precisely rifled for a particular bullet. You have to compromise. But compromise is not bad, as the stability factor for a bullet can be in a wide range and produce acceptable, even excellent, accuracy. As long as your SF is over 1.3, you'll have good groups. Faster twists can degrade accuracy, but marginally, and only at severe twist rates. But dropping off the low end, accuracy quickly goes away.

In the AR, in 223 or 5.56, we have three general ranges of twist: 1/12, 1/9, and 1/7. there are other twists, some long-range shooters use a 1/8 twist in custom barrels, and the earliest ARs had barrel with a 1/14 twist. The 1/14 was abandoned when testing disclosed a problem: in very cold air, or after a moderate amount of use, the rifles lost accuracy. The twist was so marginal with 55-grain bullets that the added density of artic air caused a loss of accuracy. As many men and officers in the early 1960s would have had clear memories of dealing with night attacks by Chinese Communist troops in Korea, a loss of accuracy in the cold could not be borne. And the loss of accuracy from a moderate amount of use simply meant higher maintenance costs, but also a loss of accuracy early in a war. Again, not good.

So, the twist was quickened to 1/12. Which provides plenty of spin to stabilize bullets up to about 60 grains. I've even had 1/12 barrels that shot the Winchester 63-grain softpoint bullets spectacularly well. But they cannot handle bullets any heavier or longer.

In testing for the M-16A2, the twist rate of 1/7 was settled on. Why? I've heard two reasons: one, that it was needed to stabilize tracer bullets. As we adopted the M-856 tracer well after settling on the 1/7 barrel, I doubt it. The other was that preliminary testing done in Europe for the SS-109 bullet used barrels with a twist as fast as 1/7. Since it worked with all lesser weights (the SS-109 tests went well beyond the 62 grains of the SS-109 and M-855, up to 100 grains) why not use the fastest twist with tested results?

So, where did the 1/9 come from? The Sierra 69-grain MatchKing bullet. When competition shooters were trying to make the AR shoot well in High Power matches, the 69 Sierra was the heaviest, and most accurate, bullet available. It needed more twist than 1/12, and 1/9 was plenty. So, custom barrel makers offered the new twist for competition shooters, and once it became the hot ticket, everyone had to have it. And why not? It still shot the 55-grain military ammo just fine, and it offered the option of more accurate, heavier bullets. And once something gets into the American shooter's mind, it takes decades to get it out.

So where does the 1/8 come in? Bullet stability. Or rather, too much of it. If you spin a bullet too fast, you can lose some accuracy. Not much, but to benchrest shooters and long-

The best makers mark their barrels. The data here tells you everything you need to know about this barrel.

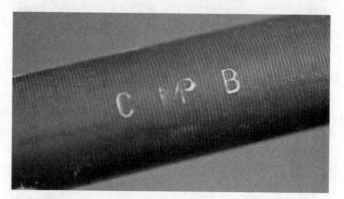

No notation of twist, which in a military barrel usually means a 1/12 twist.

range shooters, any loss is "too much." Long-range shooters also have another problem: gyroscopic stability. As a bullet noses down at the end of its trajectory, the forces of drag and gyroscopic stability compete to control orientation. Drag wants to point it down. Gyroscopic stability wants to keep the nose pointed at the same spot in the sky it was directed at from the beginning. If the bullet is too stable, from excess rotation, then the bullet lurches from angle to angle as it noses down, degrading accuracy at the end of the trajectory. What's the problem? You ask. Well, if your target happens to be out on the end of the trajectory, then loss of accuracy couldn't come at a worse time. If, as well, the bullet happens to be slowing down enough to be going subsonic when this happens, accuracy, in the exacting technical description of long-range shooters "goes to hell."

In the end, what twist you use depends on what you intend to shoot, how you'll shoot it, and how deep your wallet it. When you consider that a good barrel will last on the order of 3,000 rounds (for a varmint shooter) 5,000 (for a long-range target shooter) or 15,000 (three-gun competitor or duty rifle) the cost of the ammo itself far outweighs the cost of a barrel. Ammo costs between $90 per 1,000 rounds for reloaded ammo and $200 per 1,000 for good factory. The best can cost much more. If you take the highest normal cost, the varmint shooter will have put $600 of ammo down a barrel before accuracy may (I repeat, may) suffer. The three-gun shooter will have put $3,000 of ammo downrange. Now, many use

The "HBar" on this barrel means it is a heavyweight.

Everything you need to know: who, what chamber, what twist.

If you know the code, you know this barrel is a 5.56 chambered stainless ultra-match.

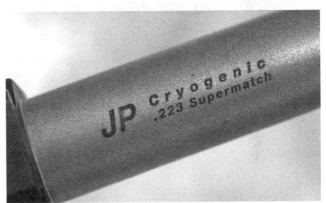

And makers who really care for their barrels don't stamp, they laser-etch. Cryogenic treatment of barrels improves their quality, but only if you start with a quality barrel

the cheaper ammo. Still, with barrels costing $150 to $300, the barrel costs less than the ammo. And the threshold of what is the end of the life of the barrel depends on the accuracy you expect: the varmint shooter wants serious sub-MOA accuracy. The long-range shooter will settle for nothing greater than one MOA, while the three-gunner is quite happy using a 2-MOA rifle, if it is rock-solid and dependable.

To increase barrel life, use a chrome-lined barrel. Also, don't overheat your barrel. Another way to look at it is time: how long will a barrel last? A varmint shooter can go through those 3,000 rounds of barrel life in a year. A long-range shooter might get two or three competition seasons out of a barrel. A three-gun shooter could likewise get two or three seasons out of a barrel. Those of you who do not shoot that much could spend a lifetime trying to wear out a barrel. Lets take as an example an officer in one of the Patrol Rifle course I teach: He goes through the three-day Operator's course, then the five-day Instructor's course. In the Operator's course he'll put 800 to 1,000 rounds through his rifle. (Or his department's rifle) In the Instructor's course, he'll do another 1,500. Then, every year as a patrol or supervisory officer until he retires, he might put as much as 100 rounds through that rifle. In 20 years on the job, the grand total will be 4,500 rounds. A SWAT officer might do more. He could do the equivalent of the Operator's and Instructor's course each year. (But don't bet on it.) At 2,500 rounds a year (a whole lot of shooting, by law enforcement standards) he'll be on the job seven years before he gets to the threshold the three-gun competition shooter thinks is reasonable.

And those who do not shoot even that much? Let's put it this way: a child born today would be eligible to run for the Presidency before your barrel is worn from shooting. But then, not all wear comes from shooting.

Barrel Externals

On the outside you'll often see the maker's marks as to twist rate, chamber type, and manufacturers name. If there are no markings, you should be suspicious. A super-match barrel made from a premium blank might not have any markings on it. Why take a hand-lapped tube and pound on the exterior with a set of stamps? But you'll know such a barrel by the quality of the machining and assembly. Be suspicious of the military-looking barrel with no markings. Why would someone make a barrel and not mark it? Some, like Colt, even mark the date of manufacture on the barrel. The M-4 Carbine Match Target they sent me had a barrel made at the same time as the rifle, marked 09/04.

You'll also see inspector's marks, proof marks, and other stamps on military, mil-spec or even "mil-spec" barrels.

The next thing to look at is the front sight housing. Is it forged or cast? A forged housing looks rougher than a cast one, but many feel they are stronger. The important thing to look for is how is it attached? The best, original, and mil-spec method is with tapered pins. At the factory, the housing is pressed on the barrel, and then with the barrel and housing held in a fixture, the taper pin holes are drilled and reamed. Then the pins are driven home. Look at he pins. One side should have a larger head than the other. If you need to remove it, drive the pins out by striking the smaller heads.

Some barrels, especially older, cheaper ones, will have the front sight held on with a pair of roll pins. Roll pins aren't as strong, but that isn't a big deal. They are not as securely held in as taper pins, another "not a big deal." But they are an indication that whoever made the barrel didn't have the proper tooling to do taper pins, and did the simpler, drill a straight hole and drive a roll pin in method.

The next two methods are controversial. Fulton Armory uses four allen-head screws to secure the front sight housing to the barrel. Armalite uses a special front sight housing where two larger screws clamp the housing around the barrel. Both use their method for a simple reason: It allows them to fine-tune the front sight housing installation so the front sight tip is "top dead center" over the barrel. They do that. However, the sight housing can tilt when struck. I worked on a rifle for a police department where the front sight housing had caught on a window when fired, and after that it was always unreliable in function. The recoil of firing, with the front sight caught on a window frame, had pulled the front sight housing forward enough to partially mis-align the gas port and front sight gas tube hole. I fussed over it quite a bit, getting the alignment correct, and securing it so it would not ever move again.

I would not have any problems using a rifle so configured, now that I'm aware of the implications. But if I was using it for duty or defense, I'd paint-in the front sight housing. With a paint witness mark, I could tell at a glance if the front sight housing had moved or tilted. If the witness mark was broken or out of alignment, I'd test the rifle before using it on duty.

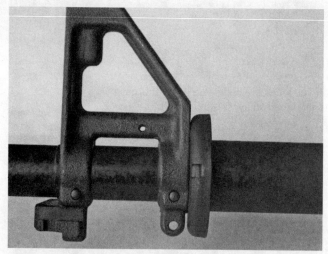

The mil-spec front sight attachment method is with a pair of taper pins.

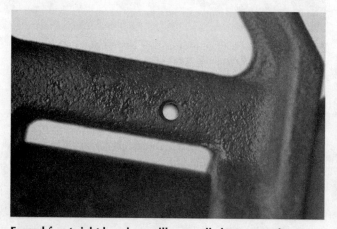

Forged front sight housings will generally have a rougher texture than cast ones.

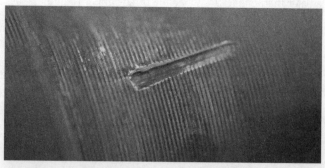

The barrel with the locking-screw front sight housing that gave my client problems has this underneath the front sight housing. It had slipped, and closed the gas port.

Some makers secure their front sight housings with four locking screws. The method works, but is not quite as durable as the original method.

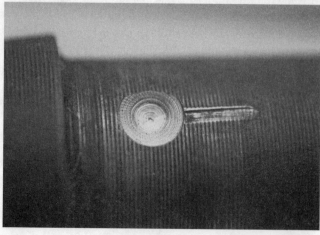

I re-secured it with a drilled dimple, and tested thoroughly before sending it back.

What Barrel Should I Buy?

A discussion of barrels alone could fill this book. The simple answer is this: Unless your requirements are extreme, most anything will do. (Provided it is a quality barrel, and not some Third-World import reject junk) For those with a need for a compact rifle, get a 16-inch barrel. Otherwise, a 20 feels a bit softer in recoil, and gives you a bit more velocity. Unless you will be in severe-use conditions, a chrome-lined bore is optional. Stainless will serve you well for anything except actual combat, overseas, or defensive use on a boat. I've gotten a good service life and excellent accuracy out of chrome-moly steel barrels. You can't go wrong with a 1/9 twist rate, as it will stabilize anything up to the 69-grain Sierra MatchKing, and even some heavier bullets.

What about the chamber? Should you get a 5.56 chamber instead of a 223? Yes, but you don't always have a choice. All the makers who produce a chrome-lined barrel offer it in the 5.56 chamber, with the longer leade. Theoretically, the longer leade of the 5.56 chamber (the extra length of the bullet jump is also called "freebore") supposedly has a negative effect on accuracy. However, you have to ask yourself "how much?" Weatherby rifles have traditionally been made with large amounts of freebore, to help control the peak of the initial chamber pressure spike on firing. Weatherby rifles have always been known as accurate, and for a long time they have come with an accuracy guarantee.

My choices, were I building particular rifles would be: for a duty or patrol carbine, I'd go with a lightweight 16-inch stainless barrel with a 1/9 twist. For an NRA High Power Service rifle, I'd get a stainless, 20-inch, 1/7 or 1/8 twist barrel, as heavy as I could get assembled. For a varmint rifle, I'd go back to a 1/9 twist, get a stainless barrel, and either a heavy for a prone, stationary varmint rifle, or a medium contour for a walking-around varmint rifle. Building an SPR, or a police marksman rifle, I'd shorten the barrel a bit to 18 inches, go with a medium contour, and 1/7 twist. The barrel would again be stainless. As you can tell, I'm partial to stainless barrels. However, if I were going to someplace dusty on a government contract, I'd be willing to give up a small and theoretical amount of accuracy for the durability of a chrome-lined barrel.

For USPSA three-gun competition, I'd have to first decide what category I'd be shooting in. A Tactical Division rifle would be a 16-inch, 1/9 stainless lightweight. Basically, a duty gun. An Open gun would be a fluted, 18-inch stainless barrel inside a carbon fiber freefloat handguard. (Think Clark Gator.) A Limited gun would, despite the name, would be more involved. It would be a medium to medium-light 20-inch barrel, with a shaved gas block, and a front sight on a housing out at the muzzle. Using only iron sights, I'd want the longest I could get.

And all of these will be built or tested in Volume 2.

Cleaning The Barrel

You can ruin a barrel from cleaning it. The typical method to ruin a barrel is simple: use a sectioned, steel, uncoated cleaning rod, with very tight patches or brushes, pushed from the chamber. Worse yet, use a patch so tight you have to hammer the rod to get it down the bore. If you want to follow the Hippocratic Oath in cleaning your barrel, "First do

In some very limited instances, a short-barreled rifle can be a useful choice. But not often, and too many law enforcement agencies select such a rifle for the "cool factor" instead of something longer.

A copper solvent will get the copper fouling out of your bore. Just don't let it sit in the bore too long, as some have been implicated in barrel etching.

The BoreSnake is great on the range, in training, or for a quick clean in the field when you don't have a lot of time. But a thorough cleaning takes more.

no harm" then use a one-piece, coated rod, a rod guide, and patches the right size.

If there is any subject in the shooting world filled with more supposition, voodoo and quasi-religious opinions, I haven't found it yet. In the old days, we'd clean our barrels until we had the powder residue out, and for those using ammo old enough, to get the corrosive primer residue gone. We didn't worry too much about jacket residue, as it was hard to see, difficult to clean, and didn't matter much. Back in the "old days" a hunter who could put three targeting shots on the target, better yet in a 2- or 3-inch cluster near the center, from the bench, at 100 yards, was good to go. Only benchrest rifles did better, and who wanted to be like them?

Today, with the improvements in rifle and ammunition quality, it is a rare bolt gun that doesn't do under 2 inches out of the box. With a little tuning and ammo selection, many will do an inch. It has become almost de rigueur to insist on a "one MOA" rifle as the minimum for any kind of serious hunting. A hunter who doesn't have such a rifle runs the risk of serious social ostracism. And so the quest for accuracy has crept into the combat rifle arena. Who wants to be using a rifle that isn't a "tackdriver" even in a tactical match? Who wants to admit they aren't serious enough about tagging that

200-yard plate to test for, ensure and keep the bore clean enough to deliver the accuracy needed?

There even used to be a school of thought that you wanted a bore fouled with a few rounds, to make sure it would be just as it was supposed to be for a second or third shot. We now know better, and the best barrels will not change their zero to any significant amount (1,000-yard competition shooters might disagree) from bare clean to the second or subsequent rounds. And proponents of the idea also wanted to avoid over-cleaning a bore, and wearing it with the brush or rod. Benchrest shooters were well known to be borderline loony about cleanliness, but when you're shooting five shots under a quarter-inch, every detail matters.

And then the idea of breaking-in a barrel sprang upon us. The idea was that you would use the bullets themselves to burnish out the microscopic burrs that machining created. Shoot a round (or two or three) and clean. Repeat to some stated number of rounds, then begin shooting groups. Repeat until the bore is broken in, or you die of boredom. I must admit that even I, Mr. Skeptic, tried it. Then I consulted my records. I found I had rifles that shot well without going through the laborious process. And I had some that were still average despite the process. Now, without a double-blind study, requiring a couple of dozen rifles, volunteer shooters, a truckload of ammo, and a year or so, I can't tell you the truth or fiction of the process. I know that some barrel makers swear by it. And others aren't so sold on it. Me, I've adopted a less laborious process. Since everyone seems to be in the throes of naming things after themselves in the early years of the 21st century, I'll call it the "Sweeney Barrel Prep." I swab a barrel clean before I shoot it. Barrel makers ship barrels with preservative oil in the bore. Many rifle makers test-fire without cleaning it out, or re-swab bores after test-firing. I figure a minute spent swabbing the dust, lint, oil, powder residue from test-firing, and anything else that might have gotten in there is time well-spent. I then test-fire the rifle, shooting groups to get it sighted-in. If it won't shoot acceptable groups, then I look into the likely problems. If it does, I then put it in the cleaning cradle when I get home and go through the following process:

1) I swab the bore clean with a powder solvent.

2) I apply a copper solvent, with brush and patch, and clean until the patches come out clean. My current solvents of choice are Shooter's Choice Copper Remover, and Hoppes Copper Remover.

3) I load up a patch with J-B Bore compound, and scrub the bore for 25 passes. I replace with a fresh, loaded, patch and repeat.

4) I use powder solvent to remove the J-B residue.

That's it. After that, bores get cleaned when I have a chance to clean them, as in after a high-volume class, or annually. My process would no-doubt make a benchrest shooter cringe, but I'm not worried about the last few .001 inches of accuracy to be had.

Peculiarities Of The AR-15

While it is a rifle, like all other rifles, the AR-15 has some differences that you should be aware of. There are a few things you should pay attention to, in order to keep yours up to snuff.

Use A Solid Rod

Always a good idea, but so many ARs come with the jointed military cleaning rods. A jointed rod has two problems: it flexes more than a solid rod, and the joints don't always match exactly. A flexing rod thus presents a sharp edge of the overlapping rod ends to the bore, with the risk of more scraping. Also, avoid using aluminum rods. The soft aluminum can pick up grit that gets embedded in the surface, and then rubs against the bore.

The Dewey coated rods, the new Hoppes carbon fiber, or other such rods will not be such a problem. They'll still flex, but they won't rub and wear.

That said, there is a way to use a military rod and risk the wear from rubbing: do it the Marine way. I learned this from a shooter who learned it in the Marines. (I don't know if it is a approved method, or just the "gotta get it done fast while the Gunny isn't watching" method) Put your brush, or patched

You need cleaning supplies to clean a rifle barrel. The rod guide (top) keeps you from wearing the leade with your rod.

tip, in the end of three or four sections of rod, without a handle on them. Holding the upper in one hand, insert the rod, unpatched end first, in through the chamber end. Let the rod fall until the patch stops it. Then pull the rod out through the muzzle. You cannot flex a pulled rod. You are cleaning in the direction the bullet travels, something some shooters feel is important. And you cannot get a patch stuck this way. If it won't go through by being pulled, tap the butt end of the rod on the floor (or a handy rock, truck bumper, etc) and it will pop free. If you try to push a rod in with a patch that is too big, you can apply more pushing force to stick it than you can pulling force to un-stick it. If that happens, you can have a real problem getting the stuck patch out.

Use A Chamber Brush First

There isn't much point in scrubbing the bore clean, then finishing the job by scrubbing the crusty chamber and pushing crud into the clean bore. Scrub the chamber first, then the bore.

Use A Bore Guide

If you are using a proper one-piece rod, you can eliminate rod wear with a bore guide. A bore guide will minimize rod wear when using a sectioned rod. Without a guide, the rod will flex under a load. The flex usually comes at the worst spot possible: the throat and leade. The guide takes the load of the flex, and feeds the rod in through its end without flex. Bore guides are simple tubes that fit inside the upper, with a bore-sized hole through them for the rod and patch. Stuff the rod guide into the upper, then shove the rod with patch through the rod guide. The best guides have a witness window where you can apply solvent just before the whole thing enters the chamber, so you aren't wasting solvent on more of the inside of the rod guide than necessary.

Don't Fret About the Gas System

I know shooters who will only clean their ARs with the upper in the upright position, to avoid getting solvent and other stuff in the gas tube. They don't want to be (for instance) blowing left-over solvent and J-B bore compound back into the action, having left it in the end of the tube. First, how much could there possibly be? Sure, if you plugged the muzzle and left the solvent standing in the bore, you'd end up with a tube full of solvent. And it would mostly drain out when you drained the bore, too. Considering how much powder residue gets blown back with each shot, in a couple of magazines you'd never notice any residue blown back from your cleaning process.

Also, you'll find military cleaning kits with pipe cleaners for cleaning the gas tube from the receiver end. As a means of keeping the D.I. happy, they are great. At any other time, they are a waste of time and effort. Now, were I stuck in a dust storm in Afghanistan or Iraq, I might be singing a different tune. But short of that (and even then, I'd wonder if it was really necessary) don't waste time. The same goes for the cute little brushes. Every class I'm at, I see something on the order of 50,000 rounds go downrange. I've never seen a rifle that was malfunctioning because someone didn't scrub the end of the gas tube.

Clean The Locking Lugs

You don't have to do them every time you clean. (Unless the D.I. or Gunny is going to be doing a white-glove inspection) Annually will do for most of us. If you live or work in a really dusty or grubby environment, then regular cleaning can be something you should tend to. But your rifle isn't going to stop working after a few hundred rounds because you failed to clean the lug recesses.

Wipe Out Of Upper And Lower

Or better yet, use a bucket full of solvent to scrub them clean. With a 5-gallon pail holding 3 or 4 gallons of mineral spirits, and a brush the right size, you can scrub the carbon out.

Avoid Lots Of Aggressive Solvents

One solvent in particular, Sweets 7.62, has a noticeable ammonia smell. It attacks copper deposits like mad. However, it has been implicated as having etched some bores when left on too long. "Too long" as in overnight or over several days. Soaking a bore for half an hour or an hour probably won't be a problem, but the risk is that you'll forget, get distracted, or be called away by someone or something. And then, a day or week later, you smack yourself on the forehead as you contemplate the remnants or your barrel. Any solvent that will dissolve copper has the potential to harm your bore, it is simply a matter of how long it takes. Many can be left in for days or weeks with no harm, but even they might cause problems if left in for a month. You think I'm kidding? I had to replace a barrel on a rifle where the owner had used rubber stoppers to plug the chamber and muzzle, and left the rifle standing with copper solvent for months after hunting season. (He wasn't happy with the accuracy he was getting, and the barrel was "obviously" inaccurate due to jacket fouling.) I don't know what it looked like before, but after it looked like a couple of miles of bad road.

Don't Worry About Jacket Fouling

Can there be too much? Yes. How much is too much? Your rifle will tell you, if you let it. Once you find a brand or load of ammo that your rifle shoots accurately, set some aside. Now and then, check the accuracy of your rifle with that load. When accuracy starts to drop off, scrub the bore down to bare bore, and check accuracy again. If it comes back to previous levels, then you had too much fouling. If it doesn't, maybe you've just worn your barrel out.

I have a loaner rifle that I take with me to classes. When there is time, I'll get in some trigger time in the drills and qual course. When someone's rifle goes down, I hand them mine and proceed to fix theirs. (That is usually why I'm there, as armorer as well as instructor.) In four years of classes with this rifle (I used another one before this one) it hasn't been cleaned much. It occasionally gets a brush or patch down the bore. The chamber gets brushed. Now and then someone squirts some lubricant in here or there. In all that time the rifle has never failed to work, and it still can shoot clean on the National Guard range computer pop-up course, with targets out to 300 meters.

If Possible, Free-Float That Barrel

Any barrel shoots better if it does not have variable external forces at work on it. Changing sling tension, hanging lights and stuff, or other abuses, can change the zero and group size of your rifle. One of the reasons the Clark Gator, the DSA and the Armalite varminter shot so well was that the barrel was simply hanging out in space, with nothing to interfere with it doing its work. If the competition allows it, get a tube handguard or a fiberglass or carbon fiber handguard, and get your barrel out there on its own.

Conclusion

Before you break the bank for a barrel that is "good enough" considers what you'll use it for, and how well you can shoot. I've shot plain, old military "pencil barrel" 20-inch, 1/12 chromed barrels that were more accurate than I was. And I've shot rifles with a barrel where the blank cost more than my rifle did, before someone got paid a lot of money to install it, that only shot as well as my rifles, with common barrels. If you aren't going for your High Master card in NRA High Power, spending a cool grand on a barrel and its installation is a waste of money. And if you're going for your Grandmaster card in USPSA Three-Gun competition, that grand is probably better spent on more practice ammo than on a barrel you'll burn up before the season is done.

In almost every case I've seen, money invested in practice ammo or lessons is better than money invested in a better barrel. If the one you have delivers, stick with it. If you've worn one out, think long and hard before you invest money moving up in barrels, unless you know for a fact that the old one just wasn't accurate enough and was holding you back.

Ammunition For The AR-15

A rifle without ammunition is a club. And in the case of the AR-15, a lightweight and clumsy club at that. You need reliable, reasonably accurate ammunition to make any rifle a hunting, target or defensive tool. Not all ammunition is the same. Ammunition, as we discussed in the Barrel chapter, is manufactured to meet a certain size package. It can't be too short or long, too skinny or wide, and the bullet can't be too short or too long (as in too short in the case or too long). If it is too far out of the design envelope, it won't work. Too-small cases will split on firing, damaging the rifle or impeding function. Too-long ammo will jam into the chamber or rifling, preventing the bolt from closing. Or if it closes,the situation will increase chamber pressure.

And then there is operating pressure. Too much and the bolt wears or breaks. Too little, and the action won't cycle properly. If the powder used is improper, the port pressure will be too high or low at the gas port, and the action will be over or under worked.

A reasonable amount of accuracy is needed, but you can have too much. Well, you can have too much if it comes from the ammunition being expensive, or specialized, or both.

And then there is cost. Good ammo is expensive. If you are going to be feeding your rifle only Federal 69-grain Match ammunition, brace yourself for the price. Something in excess (at 2004 prices) of $350 per 1,000 rounds. But you can get too cheap, too. The surplus stuff can be inexpensive,

down under $150 per 1,000, but you have to be careful. There is a reason it is cheap, and surplus. It could be that the home country wants to generate a bit of cash, and sells excess production. Or, it could be that the ammo has been improperly stored, and is beginning to fail inspections. In that case, you could be getting ammo with pressure variances due to powder breakdown from storage problems. Saving a few bucks, only to damage your rifle by using bad ammo, is hardly a bargain. Or even, the ammo sold didn't pass inspection, being too small, too large, too short or too long. Or it came from the first few production lots in a new arsenal, and they hadn't worked the bugs out. Surplus is surplus for a reason, always remember that.

What Ammo Is Available?
Weights And Styles

The lightest-weight bullet ammunition you'll likely run into will be the varmint ammo sold as .223 Remington. It will have 40-, 45- and 50-grain bullets, jacketed hollow-points of fragile construction. The bullets are fragile so they will catastrophically disintegrate at long range when striking a small, furry pest of a target. The typical application will be past 200 yards, on prairie dogs, marmots and other burrowing animals that ranchers hate. It may not be loaded with a powder suited to the gas port needs of your AR-15, and thus may not always be reliable in function. And in a

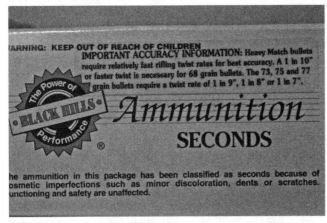

It takes a lot of ammo to test, and Jeff Hoffman of Black Hills is gracious enough to send me plenty. I don't mind the seconds, the boys in Iraq and Afghanistan need the primo stuff more than I do.

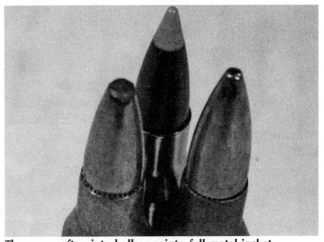

There are soft-points, hollow-points, full-metal-jacket and varmint bullets. Be sure to get the right stuff for your application.

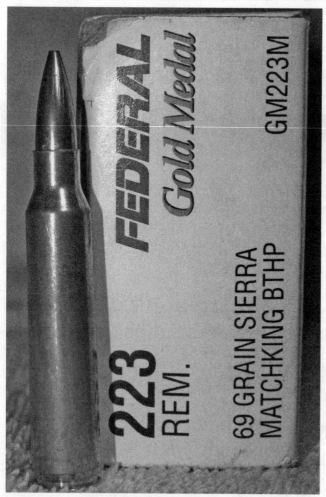

For accuracy, Federal Gold was the stuff to beat for a long time. They now have more competition, but it is still really good ammo.

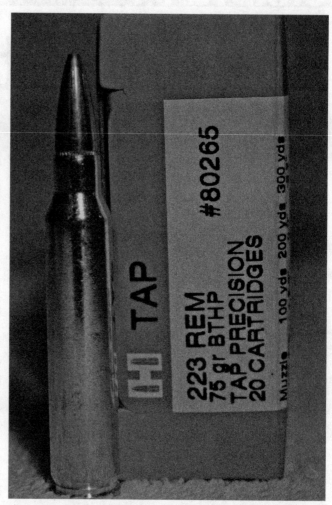

As good as this Hornady TAP ammo is, these are 75-grain bullets, and won't shoot well in 1/9 barrels.

fast-twist barrel, it may not be accurate. A 1/7 barrel may over-rotate the fragile bullets, and they have been known to spontaneously come apart downrange. I had one Chicago police officer attend an AR-15 class, with a departmental Colt Hbar and its 1/7 barrel, and using departmental-issue (for training, anyway) Winchester varmint silvertips. The bullets miraculously stayed together long enough to get him zeroed and qualified, out to 75 yards. But on the long-range targets, bullets sometimes came apart before they arrived.

The past treasurer of my gun club once got a great deal on a couple of cases of ammo loaded with varmint bullets. Out of his Colt HBar 1/7 barrel, the bullets left gray streaks in the air in their way to the targets. Sometimes he had holes in the 100 yard targets, and sometimes he didn't. Closer than that, they all had enough "oomph" to get to the targets and leave holes. Ed ended up using the ammo only in matches with targets closer than 75 yards.

Next up are the mid-weight bullets, hollow-points, soft-points and full-metal-jacket. They'll range from 52 to 55 grains. The 52-grain hollow-points are some of the most accurate bullets made. And they are strong enough to stand even fast-twist barrels. The 55-grain bullets are clones of the

military M-193 bullets, with a cannelure. The ammunition loaded with the hollow-points is meant for target shooting, and the velocities may be a bit slow. The soft-points are meant for hunting of one kind or another, and their velocities will usually be a bit more than the hollow-points. Commercial full-metal-jacket ammunition is meant for the big-bore equivalent of plinking, and quite often the velocities are a bit slower than military. Since the commercial fmj is meant to be inexpensive plinking ammo, the makers can save a small amount on powder costs, and be sure they aren't beating up customer's guns, by loading a bit light. And for practice, that's just fine.

The hot stuff is the XM-193 as loaded by Federal. I have had some production lots produce 3,250 fps out of a 20-inch barrel. Why is it "XM-193?" Well, the real M-193 is a military designation. And to call it that, Federal would have to do all the testing, and production steps, required by the mil-spec for M-193. Which would increase the price. The XM-193 they produce meets all commercial standards for size and fit, weight, velocity, pressure and function. It however, does not always meet all military standards. (Usually the waterproofing standard is skipped, or a lot fails that test.) It is perfectly safe to use, and will meet all but the most absolutely stringent user needs. Were I to be spending my time up to my waist in a hot, wet, flooded environment, I might pass on XM-193. (That pesky waterproofing standard.) But anyplace else, I would have no problem using XM-193 as my carry or duty ammo.

Heavier bullets come in a variety of options, and require a faster twist than we have needed so far in this discussion. The Black Hills 60-grain V-Max bullets are superbly accurate, and often will stabilize in a 1/12 barrel. But I've found they are more accurate in a 1/9 barrel. The Winchester 63-grain soft-point will stabilize in some 1/12 barrels, but not all. It is designed to be a hunting bullet, for jurisdictions that allow the 223 on deer. I have found it to be very accurate in rifles that tolerated it, and hopeless in those that didn't. It is right on the cusp of stability in a 1/12 barrel, and accuracy seems to be an "all or nothing" proposition. The European SS-109, also known as the US M-855, at 62-grains, is actually worse in a 1/12 barrel than the 63-grain Winchester. Stability depends on length, not just weight. The M-855 has a 10-grain steel penetrator tip, and the less massive steel insert makes the 62-grain bullet longer than the blunt, soft-point Winchester 63-grain bullet. Combined with the sharper taper, for better downrange trajectory, it means the M-855 needs at least a 1/9 barrel to stabilize.

The longer-still 69-grain Match bullet is significantly longer than the 62-grain M-855, as the weight adds length, but the hollow tip also adds length. The 69-grain bullets will stabilize in many 1/9 barrels, but not all. I think the difference is more a matter of bore quality than twist, as the 1/9 rate would seem to be fast enough, but some guns just won't shoot them. Not that groups are useless, just larger than you'd expect from an expensive Match bullet.

The longer bullets all require a 1/7 twist. The 75- and 77-grain open-tip Match bullets, tested for the Mk 262 Mod 0 and Mod 1 loads, aren't stable in slower twists. They offer more terminal performance, but only for those with fast-twist barrels.

Testing bullets takes equipment and experience. Testing bullets on barriers takes expensive test sections, and makes a mess.

What'd I tell you? A mess.

Heavier than this, you find bullets and loads that do not feed from the magazine. The 80-grain and heavier bullets are designed to be singly-loaded, crafted in premium cases and loaded to an overall length too long to fit in the magazine. They are specialty loads, meant for use in long-range target rifles with the leade reamed long to accommodate the long-loaded bullets. You can find Very Low Drag bullets (with very long points) and super-heavy Match bullets for these applications. The competition shooters using them are shooting at 600 yards and beyond, and expect sub-MOA accuracy from their ammunition and rifles.

Terminal Ballistics Of The AR-15/M-16

When discussion comes up of the AR, we're usually talking of the terminal ballistics of the .223/5.56 round. But not always, as the AR can be had in a number of calibers. If you want a scholarly volume on terminal ballistics, you can find out the mechanics of it in Duncan MacPhersons' "Bullet Penetration." And for the effects on the target, read "Gunshot Wounds" by Vincent DiMaio. But DiMaio uses photographs from autopsy reports to illustrate his book, so don't say I didn't warn you. They are no big deal if you've sat through an episode of "CSI" but for some the photos can be disturbing.

What we're concerned with here is what the AR can do to intervening obstacles, to the target itself, and how they effect the impression observers have. In many cases those observers are both ill-informed and in positions of authority. When the Chief or Sheriff says "No one in my department is going to be on the street with a machinegun" you have a problem. But in many cases the proper demonstration can change his or her mind. And for those readers who do not have a Chief or Sheriff to convince, knowledge is always useful.

The primary problem with selecting the AR-15 and the 5.56mm as a defensive round is the impression some have of it being a grossly over-penetrating cartridge. In the movie "Johnny Dangerous" Michael Keatons' character is asked why he carries an ".88 Magnum" His answer: "Because it shoots through schools." The impression many have is that the 5.56 will shoot completely through a house, and go on down the block, acting as an "innocent bystander-seeking missile."

Not true. The typical method by which the 5.56 is "proved" to be an over-penetrating round is by shooting a steel plate. The result is either a hole punched through it, or a big crater. Looking at the hole it is hard to argue that it isn't an over-penetrator. First, I'll explain how the 5.56mm does that, then how to show it is an illusion.

When a bullet strikes a hard surface, it is very quickly decelerated. Physics tells us that matter and energy cannot be destroyed, simply moved from one state to another. The sudden stop of the bullet causes its kinetic energy to be turned into heat. At a high enough velocity the heat melts the bullet and the surface of the target. The impact of the bullet creates pressure on the surface of the target. The heat and pressure act as an instantaneously-applied welding or cutting torch. The hard surface yields. The result on steel or other metals is a hole or crater. The surface of the hard target does not have the time nor flexibility to "get away" from the impact of the bullet, and is thus deformed. At lower levels of impact, the surface is not cratered. What happens is that the surface is

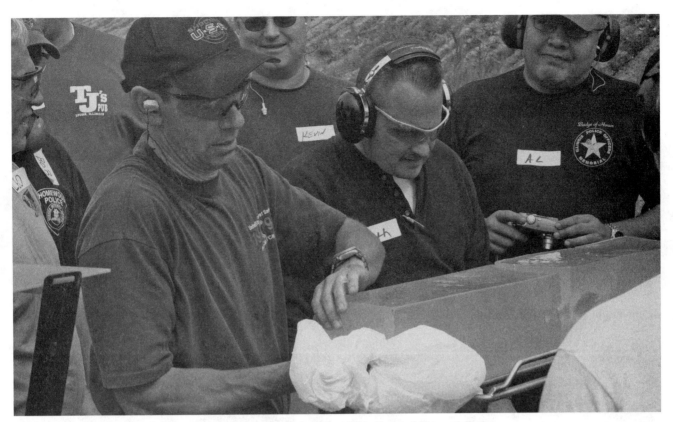

Here the finer points of ballistic gelatin testing are explained by Mitch Shore of Shore Galleries.

A .223 impact on steel seems greater than it is, due to the time frame of the impact.

You can get an entirely wrong impression of the performance of .223 by looking at what it does to steel.

slightly stretched, and work-hardened. Ever wonder why a steel plate that receives thousands of rounds of handgun bullet impacts bends away? Because of the stretch of the surface from the work-hardening done by the impacts. Hard steel doesn't bend like that because the surface is too hard to be slightly stretched at the point of impact.

Why is the impact on steel illusory? Because we see the result on the steel, but not the result on the bullet. The bullet is vaporized. If you place a recording surface behind the steel plate (like plywood, drywall or cardboard) you'll see that the recording surface receives the jet of particles at close range. Back off a short distance, and the jet disperses in the air and simply splatters the front face of the recording surface. If you focus on the steel, you fail to see the results behind it.

In an attempt at getting permission to use the .223/5.56, officers have tried to substitute soft-point or hollow-point bullets for the full-metal-jacket bullets typically found in 5.56mm ammunition. To their chagrin, the steel plate has a hole or crater blown in it only slightly smaller than that of the fmj. Why? Because the time frame of the impact on the hard target is so brief that the mechanics of the expanding bullet simply don't have time to work. In the several thousand G-forces deceleration the bullet experiences, it hardly matters if it is constructed to expand in flesh or gelatin, or is just a copper jacket around a steel core.

What about softer targets? Shouldn't a 5.56 simply slice through walls? No. The bullet is traveling too fast for it to remain intact when it strikes a soft target.

Gelatin testing also involves simulated clothing.

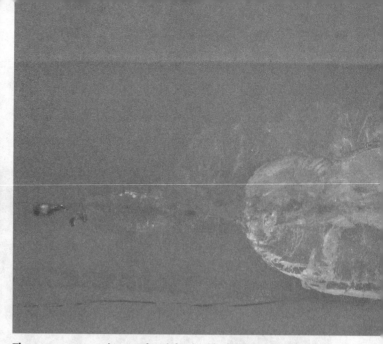

The temporary cavity, on the right, is simply the stressed part of the gelatin. It does not equate to a wound channel created by the bullet.

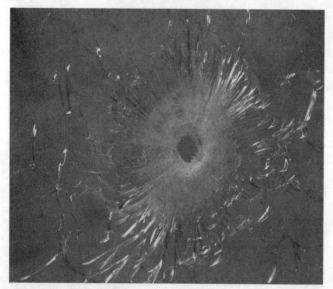

Glass is very hard on bullets. Curiously, it is very difficult to tell the caliber of the impacting bullet from the hole it leaves. Many end up very similar in size. Most .223/5.56 bullets are turned into tiny fragments by glass.

Soft Target Impacts

A rifle bullet is stabilized by the rate of twist of the barrel through which it travels. To minimize drag, bullets are made long and pointy. A long, pointy bullet has its center of mass behind its center of shape. The twist keeps it point-on, even though the forces of drag would otherwise cause it to swap ends. (See the chapter on barrels for the full discussion) That stability is good only for a single medium. A bullet traveling through water requires a different twist rate to remain stable than it does through air. (Due to the density of the medium.) A bullet encountering a medium with a greater density than air enters that medium with insufficient stability to remain traveling point-first. It will begin to yaw. (Due to the center

A good soft-point, on bare gelatin, expands like you'd expect a hunting bullet to.

of mass-center of shape mismatch) All bullets experience drag, the resistance of the medium through which it passes to its passage. When a bullet is point-on, there is no difference in drag over the surface of the bullet. As soon as the yaw is great enough, the differential drag of the medium on the bullet will cause it to turn end-for-end, or tumble. (When yaw reaches a high enough angle, the difference in drag between the tip and base, added to the center of gravity difference, causes overturning.) All bullets are subject to these forces, but not all are observed to tumble. Some simply require more target depth in which to turn than there is target. Others are so stabilized, and shaped to resist tumbling, that they do not

And recovering bullets gets messy, too. That is, if you expect to use the expensive gelatin blocks more than once.

tumble. An example of bullets highly resistant to tumbling are those made for elephant or dangerous game hunting. Typically, they are a .45 caliber, 500-grain bullet with a blunt, round nose. The rate of twist creates a very high stability factor. The center of mass is close enough to the tip that differential drag is very small, and the stability factor keeps it point-on enough to prevent differential drag from tipping and overturning it. The end result is that the bullet will travel through many feet of dangerous animal without turning over or changing course.

The same shot, taken with a lower-drag, pointy bullet results in much less penetration, bullet tumble and a stomped hunter.

What happens in the 5.56mm is that the bullet overturns, and at the moment it is going sideways the drag though the target is greater than the structural integrity of the bullet. The bullet breaks apart. In the 55-grain M-193, the break typically comes at the cannelure, the knurled recess meant to keep the bullet from setting back in the case on feeding. So in soft targets, the extended time frame (relative to the steel impact) allows the target to have as much effect on the bullet as the bullet does on the target.

Short-range impacts and bullet instability are magnified by "initial yaw" starting at the muzzle. When a bullet is fired it is shoved down the bore and forced to rotate by the rifling. It is rotated about its center of form. Even the best bullets cannot have the center of form and the center of mass exactly matching. When the bullet leaves the muzzle it yaws slightly as it transitions from rotating about its center of form, to rotating about its center of mass. When you first spin up and release a top, it wobbles and moves. Once it has settled down, it spins in one spot. A bullet is a high-speed top. If it strikes a target while still settling down, the instability of the settling-down process is added to the instability of the impact. A perfect example can be found in "Hatcher's Notebook." In testing, the .30-06 armor-piercing bullets fired at 50 yards penetrated "only" 10 inches into oak boards. The penetration path was a nearly constant arc. The same bullet, fired into the same boards from 200 yards penetrated nearly 3 feet. And on a straight line. At 50 yards the bullet had not settled down from its initial yaw. At 200 it had. In both cases the target (oak boards) were tough enough to stop the bullet, but not tough enough to cause break-up.

The new Mk 262, Mod 0 and Mod 1 bullets are demonstrations of adjustments in terminal ballistics. The 62-grain SS-109 bullet is hard, in order to penetrate. It quickly drops below its threshold of tumbling and breaking apart. By going to a heavier bullet, you do two things: you decrease stability, so the bullet is more likely to overturn at lower velocities than the 62-grain SS-109. Also, by making the bullet longer, you increase the lever arm the drag on the bullet has with which to work. That is, the increased length of the bullet gives the gelatin or tissue more ability to break the bullet at the cannelure.

Not all bullets will break, at least not at the velocities at which they are launched. The bullet from a .45 ACP or 9mm, in standard weight and full-metal-jacket construction, will not break. You could drive a 230-grain fmj .45 bullet sideways through a railroad tie and not break it. Ditto a 9mm, 115- or

A properly-expanded bullet, a rarity in the .223 world.

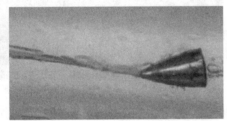

The broken-off tip of a 55-grain fmj, stopped backwards in the gelatin.

A standard gelatin block is 16 inches long, and many bullets will not stop in that length.

Vel-3204 f/s 977 m/s	Vel 3192 f/s 973 m/s	Vel-3155 f/s 962 m/s	Vel-3107 f/s 947 m/s
Vel-2650 f/s 808 m/s	Vel-2620 f/s 799 m/s	Vel-2555 f/s 779 m/s	Vel-2523 f/s 769 m/s
Vel-2395 f/s 730 m/s	Vel 2139 f/s 652 m/s	Vel-2077 f/s 633 m/s	Vel-2010 f/s 613 m/s
Vel-1996 f/s 608 m/s	Vel-1674 f/s 510 m/s	Vel-1616 f/s 493 m/s	Vel-1556 f/s 474 m/s

Bullet breakup depends on velocity. As velocity drops off due to long range or short barrel length, breakup becomes less violent and predictable.

(courtesy Dr. Fackler & IWBA.)

Barrel length has a lot to do with terminal performance. The slowest load, in the shortest bullet, may not create bullet breakup, even at close range. The hottest, in the longest, could at 200 yards.

125-grain round nose full-metal-jacket bullet. They could be spinning sideways like a top on impact, and not break or probably even deform. These bullets are too short, too stoutly-constructed, and simply not going fast enough.

Ramifications Of Tumbling

The 55-grain M-193 is in many ways superior to the "better" M-855 replacement that came on board when the M-16A1 was upgraded to the M-16A2 and later M-4. The velocity of the M-193 is so great in the best loads (3,200 fps or more) that bullet overturning and breakup is a certainty. As long as distance is taken into account. You see, bullets lose speed as they travel through air. Speed is what causes the bullet breakup. Once a bullet has slowed down enough, it will still overturn, but not break apart. At an even lower velocity, it won't even overturn, as the rotation (which slows at a much lesser pace) keeps it point-on even with impact in a denser medium. Out of a 20-inch barreled M-16, the 55-grain bullet retains its breaking threshold out to almost 200 meters. However, shorter barrels launch their bullets at lesser velocities. A short-barreled M-4, at 14.5 inches or "Commando" with an 11.5 inch barrel, may find the breakup threshold velocity ends at 100 meters.

At most defensive uses, and law enforcement needs, the velocity loss is not a problem except with the shortest of barrels. And then only when matched to ammunition with low velocity. As an example, a lot of XM-193 may deliver 3,200 fps from a 20-inch barrel. From a 16-inch barrel, it delivers 2,850, and from an 11.5-inch barrel the velocity may still be over 2,750. All exceed the break-up threshold. However, if a different load is selected, say one that starts at 3,050 fps in the 20-inch, delivers 2,775 in the 16-inch, and only 2,650 in the 11.5-inch, terminal effects may be greatly diminished.

The breakup has an effect not only on gelatin and bad

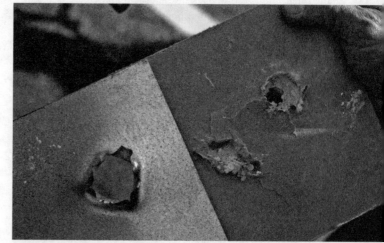

After striking thin sheet metal, one bullet didn't even have enough power to penetrate the drywall behind it. So much for over-penetration.

guys. It also greatly diminishes penetration of incidental barriers. A 55-grain bullet going 3,200 fps that strikes an interior wall of sheetrock or drywall will not act like the bullet that strikes a steel plate. However, a 55-grain fmj out of a short-barreled AR, starting out at that previously mentioned 2,650 fps, may be worse. If you miss the bad guy, and the bullet then travels 50 yards past him to strike a building, it may only be going 2,500 fps by the time it arrives. Or less. At that reduced velocity, it will (counter-intuitively) penetrate more than the same bullet that starts at 3,250 fps from a longer barrel.

The worst case would be to use a 69-grain Match bullet (for accuracy) and depend on the hollow-point to cause breakup when fired from a short-barreled rifle. The accuracy increase is meaningless at most defensive ranges. The hollow-point is a manufacturing byproduct, not meant to cause expansion. And out of a short barrel that bullet may only be going 2,350 fps, not fast enough to break up when it hits a wall.

Typical 5.56 mm FMJ Wound Profiles

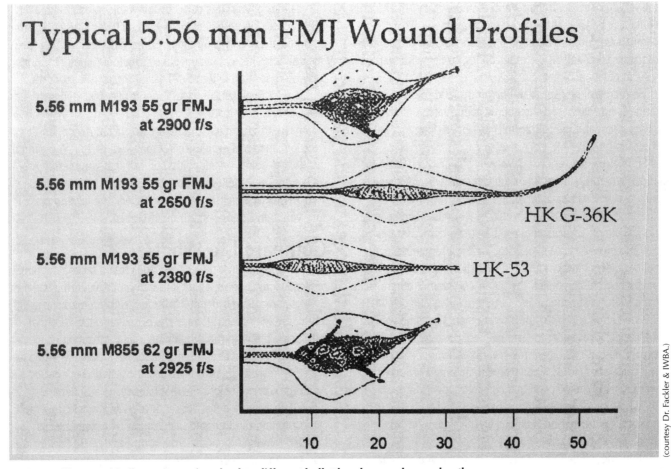

5.56 mm M193 55 gr FMJ at 2900 f/s

5.56 mm M193 55 gr FMJ at 2650 f/s — HK G-36K

5.56 mm M193 55 gr FMJ at 2380 f/s — HK-53

5.56 mm M855 62 gr FMJ at 2925 f/s

10   20   30   40   50

(courtesy Dr. Fackler & IWBA.)

Various calibers and bullet constructions lead to different bullet breakups and wound paths.

Hard Target Penetration And Incidental Barriers

At close range, velocity is king. At conversational distances, hard target penetration depends more on velocity than construction. Large differences of course, will overcome that. The all-steel core M-995 bullet will penetrate better than a super-velocity 40-grain varmint load will. But given relatively similar bullets, more velocity gains more penetration in steel, wood, glass and other hard objects.

Velocity also causes more breakup of the bullet in non-hard incidental barriers. The common one would be drywall or sheetrock. More velocity causes less penetration, as the extra velocity is used to break up the bullet.

Why the difference? Time. The bullet striking steel is decelerated at a greater rate. The vaporized bullet creates heat, the impact and vapor cloud create pressure, and the result is a bulged or burnt-through barrier. The drywall acts over a much longer time (relatively speaking) and the bullet is not broken up at a rate sufficient to create heat and a vapor cloud. All the energy is used to break up the bullet and barrier. That is why a 5.56mm bullet penetrates less in drywall than a 9mm bullet does. The 9mm bullet does not have sufficient velocity to break itself against the barrier, where the 5.56mm does.

The Geneva Convention

Use of bullets other than full-metal-jacket almost always causes someone in the discussion to bring up "the Geneva Convention." The argument is that, since "TGC" prohibits the use of soft-point, hollow-point or exploding ammunition, then the group being discussed (civilians, law enforcement, military) should use only full-metal-jacket bullets in their rifles. The argument fails on a number of fronts.

First, it was the Hague Accords of 1899, not the Geneva Conventions, that prohibits their use. (If you're going to argue technical matters, you'd better cite the correct ones.) The Hague Accords prohibit the use of small arms ammunition "designed to increase the severity of wounds, or suffering by the wounded." Which leaves out hollow-points and soft-points, and would seem to mandate full-metal-jacket bullets. Except that we have just seen that a suitably designed full-metal-jacket bullet causes greater wounding than would otherwise be the case. But since fmj is OK, then the fmj design is not considered inhumane.

Next, the Hague Accords only come into force between signatory combatants, in a declared conflict. Non-signatories don't have to abide, and if the conflict isn't a declared one, then all bets are off. Since there is no declared war between your local police department and the drug gangs in town, and neither are signatories, then the conflicts are not covered by the Hague Accords. If they were, then the rest of the accords could also be used as the Rules of Engagement: Firing on combatants without warning, prisoners held for the duration of the conflict, and all the other things that go with warfare instead of law enforcement.

How do we then get to military units, and soldiers, sailors, airmen and Marines, using hollow-point match bullets in sniper rifles, and the Mk 262, Mod 1 open-tip match bullets in their issue M4s?

Simple: the lawyers got- involved. The first step came in 1990, when the Judge Advocate Generals office declared match bullets as not covered. The reason? They were not "designed to increase the severity of wounds." The open tip was simply an artifact of the production process, and not intended to cause expansion. As a matter of fact, many police snipers have complained over the years that the typical open-tipped match bullet, the Sierra 168-grain 7.62mm lacks expansion. In shootings, and in testing in ballistic gelatin, it is no better, and sometimes worse than, the same weight full-metal-jacket bullet in terminal performance. If it doesn't expand, it can't "increase the severity of wounds." The next test came after 9/11. Since we were fighting a group who were non-signatories, and in a conflict that was undeclared, then the Hague Accords did not apply. The JAG ruling is cover enough, but further declarations on the situation made it absolutely clear.

Now, the whole thing is pretty silly when you consider the realities of war: it is perfectly allowable to deal with a fighting position with active combatants in it by dropping large amounts of explosives on them. Or napalm. Or shooting their position with heavy machineguns or light automatic cannons until there is nothing left. But heaven forbid you shoot them with a (just to pick a couple at random) Federal Hydra-shok, or a Cor-bon PowRball.

Outside of the military, there are no Hague Accords, just state law and local ordinances. It may well be that you cannot use hollow-points or soft-points. I recall that New Jersey has such a law, and there may be others. If you are going to use your AR-15 for defense, you should check the laws to make sure you aren't using something forbidden.

Compared To What?

The big dig against the .223/5.56 is that it lacks "stopping power." Compared to what? Rifles with half again the weight, twice the recoil, and the difficulties of learning marksmanship that come with recoil? One of the big advances of terminal ballistics came with the development and utilization of ballistic gelatin. As a representation of what happens when a bullet strikes a living organism, ballistic gellatin isn't perfect. As a reproducible record of what happens to a bullet and the gelatin when a bullet strikes, it is great. I was one of the earliest to join the International Wound Ballistics Association, founded (among others) by Dr. Martin Fackler. Dr. Fackler was a trauma surgeon in Vietnam, and after the war

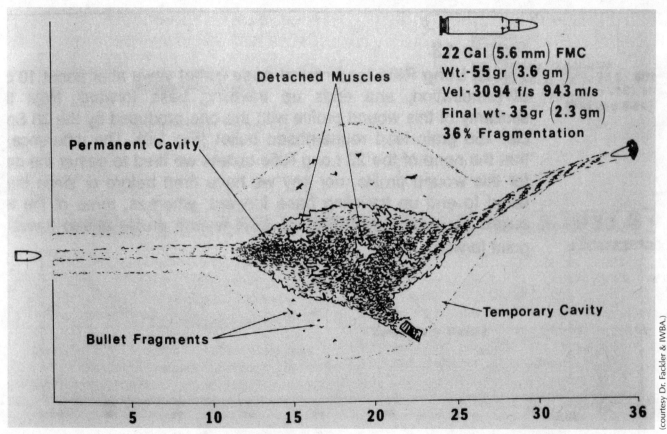

22 Cal (5.6 mm) FMC
Wt.-55 gr (3.6 gm)
Vel-3094 f/s 943 m/s
Final wt-35 gr (2.3 gm)
36% Fragmentation

Detached Muscles

Permanent Cavity

Temporary Cavity

Bullet Fragments

(courtesy Dr. Fackler & IWBA.)

The M-193 bullet breaks up in a predictable manner, even if it does not penetrate as much as larger bullets do.

The Cor-bon DPX bullet holds together even after penetrating glass.

The steel core of AK ammo doesn't break up, and rarely does the jacket come off, as it has here.

worked for the U.S. Army in wound ballistics. Ballistic gelatin, properly formulated and used, provides a reproducible record of the bullet and the gelatin.

The 5.56 round acts in a predictable manner in gelatin. So predictable that when we conduct ballistic tests we can attempt to account for bullet behavior. The 55-grain bullet from the M-193 load travels some 4 to 5 inches into the gelatin before it has overturned enough to begin breaking apart. The nose and base come apart, fragments disperse through the gelatin, and then the base and nose travel onward. The nose typically "J-hooks" or turns 90 degrees as it travels, often exiting the side of the block. The base travels further into the block, usually at a slight angle from the direction of the impact. The dispersed fragments typically stop in the next 6 inches, while the tip can travel as much as 14 to 16 inches. Some fault the M-193 for lack of penetration, citing the 4-inch depth as not being deep enough. They would prefer a round that penetrated more before overturning. However, as most people are not much more than a foot thick, how much more do you need before you risk losing the fragmentation effect?

The M-855/SS-109 is an example of that. With the longer bullet, a faster twist is needed to stabilize it. The military barrel, at 1/7 may over-stabilize it. Yes, even an overly stable bullet in air will eventually overturn in a target, but if the overturn distance is increased from 4 inches to 6, 8 or more, the 62-grain bullet can create a punctuate wound, a simple "knitting-needle" wound track. And unlike the .45 ACP, which produces such a wound its entire wound length, the M-855 bullet is only .224" in diameter, compared to the .451" of the .45 ACP.

The 5.56 is often compared to the 7.62 X39 of the AK-47. However, the AK, despite having a larger diameter, has three things working against it: light weight, low velocity, and steel bullets. The light weight of the AK bullet, a nominal 123-grains, makes it short. A shorter bullet is less likely to break apart at any given velocity. The low velocity of the AK bullet, 2,350 fps, is far short of what is needed to break apart such a short bullet. And as a final problem, the AK bullet is often a steel core, or a steel jacket over a lead core. (In some production lots, it was a soft steel jacket over a steel core, with a lead liner to keep it all together.) Steel is much tougher than copper.

As a result, the AK round will overturn in gelatin, but the bullet won't break apart, and the bullet then proceeds through the block of gelatin, to exit base-first. Due to the short bullet length, the overturn distance can be quite long, even on the far side of the target. I know personally several Vietnam vets who had been shot and wounded with AK rounds at typical distances. (Not long-range "spent bullet" hits) Their wounds were simple punctuate wounds, and one simply received a pair of adhesive bandages as "wound treatment" and stayed with his unit. The AK does its stopping by having more energy and larger frontal area.

Not all 7.62mm rifles are so meager. The larger ones are a significant step up from the 7.62X39 cartridge. The 308 Winchester, or 7.62 NATO, uses a nominal 150-grain bullet at 2,650 fps. The longer bullet overturns sooner, and with higher velocity and weight, stops significantly better than the AK round does. The old M-2 load for the .30-06 was even better, with a 150-grain bullet at 2,750 fps. But they were not the best. It turns out that the Germans, and the Swedes, had better rounds. But not by intent. Indeed, the Swedish were very vocal and negative about the "tumbling" 5.56mm bullet in Vietnam. Well, it turns out that some production lots of 7.62 NATO ammo both countries loaded used steel jackets. (Copper-plated steel, to be exact.) Since steel is stronger, they could use a thinner jacket, right? So they did. Some jackets were too thin. The bullets would tumble, as expected, then flatten, as the thin steel deformed, and finally break at the cannelure. Only after a couple of training accidents, in which soldiers were killed, and the bullets with one entrance wound produced two exit wounds, did they investigate the wound dynamics of their "more humane" ammunition.

The 5.56mm does a good enough job stopping the enemy as far as many people are concerned. Combined with the light weight, reliable function, and excellent ergonomics, and when fed appropriate bullets, the 5.56mm works well. Match your bullet to your barrel, and use the heaviest bullet your rifle will shoot accurately, and you're well on your way. In 1/12 barrels, the XM-193 is hard to beat. In 1/7, use the 75- or 77- grain M262 Mod 1. And in 1/9, use what you can shoot accurately.

Extra Penetration Desired

Not all occasions call for bullets that overturn and break apart. In many cases, you need a bullet that stays together and keeps penetrating. State Police, who deal with offenders in and around cars, for instance, need something that holds together. Sheet metal and auto glass are very hard on bullets. Yes, the M-193 loads will punch holes through, but the fragments on the other side may be so small that they do not produce significant wounds.

A deep-penetrating bullet is needed. One such is the Federal tactical round. Literally hand-made, they used to cost over a dollar each. Federal has been working on the process, and they are now around 75 cents a shot when bought in volume. The Federal round uses a core that is bonded to the jacket. Unlike traditional cup-and-jacket bullets, where a hollow copper jacket has a lead slug pounded into it, the Federal bullets have molten lead applied for the core. Federal Tactical bullets can go through a windshield (a very difficult barrier for a bullet) and still hold together well enough that what you dig out is a recognizable bullet.

Another bullet is the Cor-bon DPX. Using a hollow-point bullet constructed of a solid copper (or copper alloy, they won't give me a list of the exact constituents, obviously)

with driving relief bands machined on the bullet, the Cor-bon penetrates as well as the Federal. Sometimes the petals break off, but often they do not. The result is a deep-penetrating bullet that holds together. You can't get something for nothing, so the cost for the deep-penetrating bullet is that the wound tracks they produce in gelatin look a lot more like that of the .45 ACP than the M-193 5.56mm.

The question then comes up, how to have the deep-penetrating rounds handy when you need them? For a State trooper, the answer is easy: always. Almost everyone he (or she) will deal with will be in, on, around or behind a car. For the rest of us, the two best solutions are the Redi-mag and the Mag Cinch. In a Redi-Mag, mark the DP round magazine with a wrapping of tape, and leave the softpoint or M-193-

Even through sheet metal, the Cor-bon DPX held together. Highway Patrol Officers, pay attention.

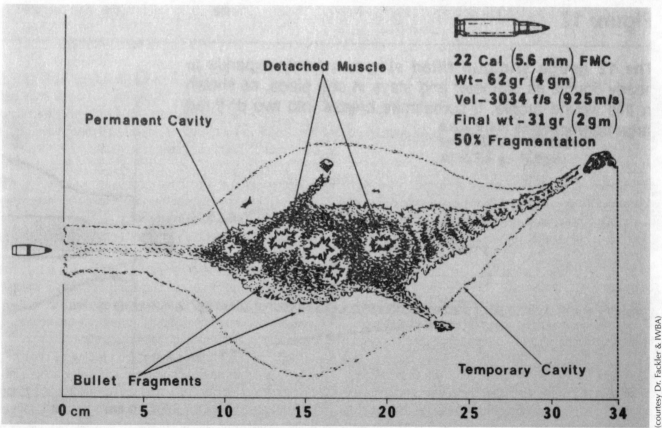

Detached Muscle

Permanent Cavity

22 Cal (5.6 mm) FMC
Wt- 62gr (4 gm)
Vel- 3034 f/s (925 m/s)
Final wt- 31gr (2 gm)
50% Fragmentation

Bullet Fragments

Temporary Cavity

0 cm   5   10   15   20   25   30   34

(courtesy Dr. Fackler & IWBA)

Experience shows the M-855 bullet can break up at close range, but the tough construction and lower velocity quickly ends the bullet breakup, and at long range it can produce punctuate wounds.

loaded magazine bare. If you find you have an immediate need of barrier-penetration, do a quick magazine swap and keep shooting. In the Mag Cinch, you can use tape or some easy to see paint. You could just load one side always with M-193 and the other always with the DP rounds. But, in a stressful situation it will be hard enough to remember anything, let alone "right is Light, and left is Heavy" or some such mnemonic. Better to have the back of the mags painted, taped, or even marked so you can read them.

Imports, Steel Case

When the AK-47 was developed, I'm sure one of the design points was the ability to utilize steel-cased ammunition. Steel is much cheaper than brass, but it has drawbacks as a cartridge case material. Despite being the material we makes springs of, steel has less "spring" when fired. An expanded brass case, provided it has not been expanded by too much pressure, will contract after firing, allowing it to release from the chamber walls. A steel case expands and contracts, but if expanded too much will not contract at all. (Or so little that it doesn't matter, firearms-wise.)

Steel also rusts, a big problem in a cartridge case. Military production has always looked for a cheaper, more available, metal than brass. In WWII, the U.S. experimented with steel cases, and even issued significant amounts of .45 ACP and .30 Carbine ammunition with steel cases. .30-06 was beyond the ability of steel cases or their fabrication, at least to the satisfaction of the U.S. ordnance experts. The Germans produced steel-cased ammunition in all calibers in WWII. During and after Vietnam, the military looked into aluminum cases in 7.62 and 5.56, but the cost savings weren't worth the operational problems.

The solution to the rusting problem in United States production was to galvanize the steel. Galvanic-plated steel is steel with a zinc plating bonded electrically to the surface of the steel. All those bright metal garbage cans you see are galvanized steel. Properly done, it is very rust-resistant. U.S. arsenals made .45 ACP and M-1 Carbine ammunition using steel cases, with a galvanized surface. The Soviet solution (I can't help but wonder if they got the information and equipment from over-run German production plants they captured. History tells us that many other captured factories were packed up and moved to Russia in their entirety.) was to use lacquer. With a proper coating, lacquer will protect the surface of the steel well enough that it won't rust before it is used.

The AK, with a heavily-tapered case, a relatively low operating pressure, and robust parts, easily adopted to use of steel cases. The later Soviet 5.45X39 also featured steel cases. Fired in an AK, I wonder if a rusted case would even be an impediment.

When the Iron Curtain was pulled back, Soviet ammunition plants found they didn't have as big a market as they had had before. They went into competition with China to sell ammunition to the United States consumer market. Selling AK ammo was no problem. Whether semi or select fire, an AK is an AK when it comes to ammo. But 5.56mm was a different beast.

Compared to the 7.62X39, the 5.56 is longer, less tapered, operates at a much higher chamber pressure, and runs in rifles with a much less robust extractor. Would AR rifles work with steel-cased ammo? There are many who would tell you no. My own experience prior to this book would have led me to believe not. However, opinions change as information is learned. Prior to this book, my exposure to steel-cased ammo was a few times at law enforcement classes when someone would show up with the ammo. Their rifle invariably failed to work with the ammo they had. In one class, we managed to choke an M-249 SAW, a belt and/or magazine fed 5.56mm light machinegun, using steel-cased ammo. Then, while shooting in the USPSA Area 5 2004 Three-Gun Championships, I ran into a shooter who was shooting in the match with steel-cased ammo. "Have any problems with that stuff?" I asked. "Not one, in thousands of rounds." He obviously felt comfortable enough with it to shoot it in a match. Later, I lucked onto a supply of Wolf .223 ammo, almost 3,000 rounds of it. Well, this called for a test. But which ones to test?

I obviously couldn't test the .308 or 9mm rifles with it. And it wouldn't be fair to test rifles whose manufacturers said not to use steel-cased ammo in. That left a few, and those got tested. (And if I forgot, and slipped someone in who does not approve, well, that's why it is a field test.)

The testing procedure was simple: at a range day, I selected some rifles to get tested with Wolf. We would do all the standard tests, running drills, plinking plates, shooting groups, etc. The idea was to get the guns a bit dirty. (A couple of hundred rounds each, minimum.) Then, at the end of the days testing, the rifles to get the steel-cased ammo were set on the gear table with instructions: Shoot nothing but Wolf, as fast or slow as you liked. Keep track of how much each rifle gets shot, and stop at 150 rounds. (With a group of shooters, each with a magazine to load, that doesn't take long.) I have to see each and every malfunction. I wanted to get the rifles hot, as the lacquer melting or burning in the chamber is cited as a cause for malfunctions.

Once each got to 150 rounds, we stopped and let them cool. I then packed them up and took them home. I looked into the chamber of each of the four (The Vulcan .223, Armalite shorty, Bushmaster shorty and the Olympic Lightweight). I could not see any evidence of scars, gouges, wear or chatter from the steel cases. I wasn't surprised, as the steel of cartridge cases is quite soft as steel goes, and it would probably take a lot more than 150 rounds to appreciably wear the chambers. What did surprise me was the lack of burnt lacquer deposits. The big knock against Wolf ammo is that the lacquer gets soft when heated, and leaves deposits on the chamber walls. I saw very little, and only in one chamber, the Vulcan. Later I took them back to the range and without cleaning, fired a couple of magazines of hot XM-193 ammo through each one. I wanted to give the crust of powder residue and (if it was present) melted lacquer time to cool and harden before trying them again. As there was no crusted lacquer, I wasn't expecting function problems.

Once all had gone through the test, I rotated them through again. The idea was to see if we could cause a malfunction through the kind of shooting an eager shooter could easily manage on a range session or two. Basically, all I did with that test was provide my eager testers with high-speed plinking ammo. So, I tried a different approach. I selected three different rifles on a subsequent test session, the Colt, the

DoubleStar M4gery and the DPMS M4gery, and gave them a different test: the testers had a magazine each, and the rifle was on the bench with a supply of 120 rounds each of Wolf. The test was simple: load and shoot as fast as you could hit the backstop. To put 120 rounds through the rifles took not much more than five minutes. The barrels were hot enough that you could not touch the barrel. I then closed the bolt on a chambered Wolf round and put them in a rack where they wouldn't be touched. (Nor could anyone walk in front of them!) We waited until they had cooled while testing other rifles, and then extracted the chambered round. There was no change in the lacquer, nor could I see any deposited on the chamber walls when peering in with the bore scope made by Gradient Lens Corp.

Editor's note: All Wolf 223 ammunition is now manufactured with a polymer coating in place of the laquer. Jacki Sagouspe, sales manager at Wolf, said the change was made because of consumer concerns of the laquer coating. "People fired thousands and thousands of rounds without problem, but for some there still was a concern. So we addressed that," said Sagouspe. "The polymer coating is bonded directly to the steel case and we have not had a single complaint. As a frequent shooter of Wolf ammunition in several calibers, I have never never experienced a single ammunition-related malfunction of any kind with either the laquer-coated rounds or the new polymer-coated cases.

Kevin Michalowski--Editor

Accuracy

"How accurate is my AR-15?" is a question asked many times. The answer is the same as for any other rifle: As accurate as your barrel and ammo. What can you expect? That depends. As a general rule, the old 1/12 "pencil" barrels are either average or brilliant. Most will shoot 2 to 3 inches at 100 yards (groups fired with iron sights, a scope brings that down some) while a few are absolute tack-drivers as my old "Trusty" was. New 1/12 "pencil" barrels (yes, they are making new ones. It's a military thing) tend to be less variable than the old ones. Partly due to the newer ones being less used, and partly that in the old days barrels were not so good as they are today.

The newer, 1/9 barrels, coming as they do from a) newer machinery, and b) not hurried-up military production as many old 1/12 barrels were, are more accurate. I've seen many that would do under 2 inches, some down to one.

Military 1/7 barrels tend to shoot the same as 1/9 do, but some are very good. What matters more than the barrel (except if you get real cheap and buy a bad barrel) are two things: the ammo, and how the barrel hangs.

Military ammunition, and full-metal-jacket plinking ammo are not made to be particularly accurate. Not that it is bad ammo, its just that the makers don't go to any extra effort to make it any more accurate than the military desires. You will often find lots that shoot much better than the specs

Steel-cased ammo is not highly thought of in the AR world. My testing has not been so negative.

call for, but not because the manufacturer tried to make it more accurate. It just worked out that way. If you want more accurate ammo, you have to use a better bullet, for one. The same ammo, loaded in the same cases, loaded with the same powder and primers, will shoot a lot better with a match hollow-point bullet than military-production 55-grain fmj. It was not unusual in years past for military rifle teams to shoot "Mexican Match" ammo. Required to use military ammo, and having no budget for commercial or reloaded ammo, they would improve the accuracy of their ammo by pulling the bullets of military ammo and replacing them with match-grade hollow-points. It worked very well if the ammunition they used was already decent or better in accuracy, with uniform case necks and powder charge weights. Bullets matched to the barrel twist will shoot better than those not. Yes, you can sometimes get good accuracy with medium-weight bullets in a 1/12 barrel, but you have much better chances if you use 52- or 55-grain bullets. And the final detail is the barrel: is it free-floating, or is it also supporting the handguards and all the stuff you've got bolted to them? A free-floated barrel will shoot more to its potential than one not free-floated.

Last, but not least, is you. If you can't shoot, then testing your rifle is not going to tell you much. You either need someone who is a better shot, or you need some sort of mechanical rest. The simplest is a set of sandbags and a rest. Get the rifle securely settled in the bags, and a lot of the variances that you introduce will be minimized. Another approach is to use the Lahti rifle rest. Instead of sandbags you suspend your rifle in the Lahti and fire it with uniform control. You can even suspend the rifle in its entirety in the rest, and fire it without touching it at all.

Calibers Of The AR

Compared to some rifles the AR-15 has pretty severe restrictions on what cartridges can be stuffed into it. If you're rebuilding a surplus Mauser bolt-action, you have a wide range. You can make it anything with a nominal .470-inch rim diameter or larger just with a new barrel. You can make it anything that fits through the receiver. You can easily turn an old 8mm into a rebuilt .308, .30-06 or other caliber. With the right machine tools and skills, you can turn an 8mm Mauser into a .375 H&H or even a .458.

The AR does not offer you such options. First, you are limited by the magazine. Unless you can find a magazine that feeds the cartridge you are considering (or can readily modify one) it is off the list. Second, you are limited by the breechface. With a good lathe you can open a bolt to a larger breechface. In the case of the Mauser you then recut the extractor to fit the new caliber. Because the AR extractor pivots, you are very limited in choices to open the breechface. If you open it too much, the extractor pivots incorrectly, and can't hold the rim. And the bolt isn't overly large anyway, so there isn't a lot of metal you can take out of the bolt.

The barrel is not such a big deal. If you can lay hands on

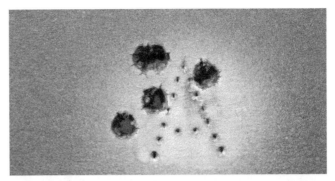

A good, solid group from Federal XM-193.

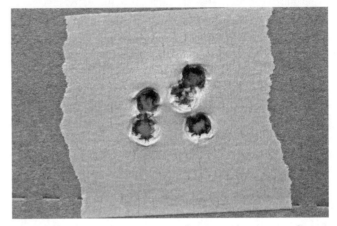

The kind of group you can expect from match ammo and a good rifle.

This group came from the Fulton Armory Accutron. I like it!

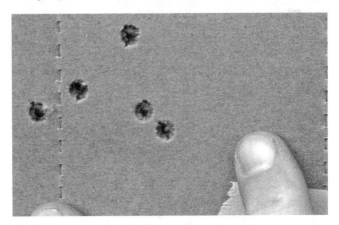

The best group of the Wolf ammo fired. Everything else was much bigger. Don't buy cheap, expecting accurate.

a barrel extension that is proper for your rifle, you need a barrel blank (Brownells has pages of barrels, and barrel extensions, too) and a lathe or a gunsmith with a lathe. Getting a barrel turned, fitted and chambered is not work that falls under the heading of R&D. It is simply paying attention to dimensions and details.

So, you have a limited number of magazines to choose from, and a limited number of breechfaces. And they are not combinations you can cross, either. That is, you can't take a bolt from a 45 ACP carbine and use it as the bolt for a 308 Win. conversion, despite their having the same breechface diameter. And you can't use a 308 upper and a 45 conversion, to produce a locked-breech 45 that lets you radically increase the pressure.

Pistol Calibers

The rimfire and center-fire pistol caliber ARs and conversions do not use the gas system of the AR. They are blowback, with the bolt unlocked. Inertia and spring force keep them closed during firing. You cannot, as a result, exceed the power specifications of these conversions or uppers by much before you exceed the strength of the system. Yes, a longer barrel (16-inch in the AR, vice 5-inch in a 9mm handgun) allows for a longer powder burn, but the system is built for a standard charge. Trying to turn a 9mm AR carbine into a 9mm Magnum just beats the gun up.

Rimfire

The conversion and dedicated uppers for the AR meant for rimfire use are set up for .22 LR. I'm sure with the development of the .17 caliber rimfires someone will make a .17 upper (if they haven't already) but you are still limited to the rimfire bolt/conversion and magazines. The entire purpose of the rimfire AR is for a cheap practice rifle, or an indoor rifle. And as rimfire ammo is so very cheap, it is a good thing. But they can be particular in function, working only with a particular brand or bullet weight of ammunition.

Can you turn a .22 LR into a .22 WMR? Perhaps. But you'd have to change barrels (the .22 LR uses a nominal .221" bore, while the Magnum uses a .224") and re-spring the bolt for the more powerful cartridge. As an experimental project it might be fun. Once done it would have marginal improvements over the LR in power, range (but not accuracy) and much higher ammunition costs. And there is the problem of magazines, as the .22 WMR does not fit into magazines made for the .22LR.

A complicating factor in the rimfire AR is that there is no "standard" conversion, and each conversion uses its own particular magazine. If you change conversions, you often have to change magazines as well.

Centerfire Blowbacks

The 9mm conversion comes one of two ways: Colt and Olympic. The Colt system uses a dedicated bolt carrier that

has a breechface machined directly into it. Instead of boring out the bar stock used to make carriers for a bolt and cam pin, the 9mm bolt/carrier has the breechface machined right on its face. The Colt also uses modified Uzi magazines. The original Uzi magazines can be made to work in Colt conversions, but they lack the hold-open tab and spine, and won't lock the gun open when empty. The Colt method thus calls for a barrel that simply has a blank rear face, and the chamber directly at the rear. For a manufacturer with a large machine base to work with, it is a simple and elegant method of making the AR something it wasn't in the first place.

The Olympic is different. Since Olympic can't dedicate machine tools and inventory to the production of specialized carriers, they went a slightly more complex route. They devised a bolt to replace the head of the standard AR bolt and carrier combo. The Olympic bolt sticks forward of the carrier. As a result, the barrel of the Olympic conversion has a conical recess in the rear, leading to the actual chamber. The Olympic conversion uses modified Sten gun magazines. A couple of decades ago, when all this was new, Sten gun mags could be had for a dollar each. (No kidding, I bought a carton of them from The Gun Parts Company, Numrich, NY, for a dollar each.) Uzi mags were not so common, and cost more.

All conversions use one of these two methods.

For the magazines, there are four approaches. You can pin a block or blocks in place, as Colt does. You can insert an adapter block that is held in place by the magazine catch, as Olympic did and Vulcan does. Or you can spot-weld an attachment adapter to the magazine tube, to fill the AR-15 magazine well. The latest approach is to use a one-piece adapter block that either stays in place via the magazine catch, or inserts from the top and uses small shoulders to keep from falling through.

Additional calibers are 40 S&W, 10mm and 45 ACP. They are mostly found from Olympic, although there are others. The 40 and 10mm use modified Uzi magazines, while the 45 conversions either use Uzi mags or M-3 Grease gun magazines.

You could make a conversion into another caliber given enough work. For instance, any pistol caliber with a rim diameter the same as the 9mm can use that bolt. If you have a lathe, you can turn barrel blanks to fit an upper and then ream the chamber. If you had a warehouse full of 7.62 Mauser/7.63 Tokarev, you could turn a .30-inch barrel blank into a barrel for a 9mm bolt. You'll then have to find a mill to modify or construct magazine well adapter blocks to hold the appropriate magazines. Or, simply turn a 9mm conversion into a 30 Luger conversion, with a .308-inch bore barrel blank. (I guess, for places where you can't own military calibers, but can own "military" rifles.)

Consider any conversion carefully before you go cutting on parts. Yes, you can make it almost anything, but what will you gain? Unless there is some big cost advantage to a particular caliber, the common ones will probably serve you well.

.223

The bolt face of the standard AR will serve for any cartridge based on the parent case diameter that you can fit into the magazine. The catch is in getting a barrel. Yes, you can theoretically build a 17 Remington AR-15, but who makes a barrel? The new 204 Ruger looks like it will become popular. You can call up Olympic and order a barrel in a host of other diameters, 6mm, 6.5, 7mm to fit your AR. If you want something really wild, call J.D. Jones and get a barrel in 300 Whisper. That cartridge (which Cor-bon loads, by the way) uses 221 Fireball cases as a starting point, then necks them up to take .308-inch bullets. Why, you ask? To put a truly quiet cartridge in a suppressed AR, with a bullet heavy enough to do the job. (Whatever the job might be.) I watched Ned Christiansen once at Second Chance using a 300 Whisper on the Light Rifle Pop and Flop racks. The rifle was so quiet that the brass hitting the ground sometimes made more noise than the sound of the shot. The bullets hitting the steel targets were noisier still.

One rare collector's piece is a Colt AR-15 in .222 Remington. Made on a contract for a country (Italy as I recall) where ownership of military calibers was forbidden, they looked like regular ARs. As there were a few extras after the contract was fulfilled, Colt sold the overage. I had a customer come into the shop wanting work done on his AR-15, newly-purchased from a gun show. The ammo he'd bought at the same time (reloads) wouldn't work. I told him I'd take a look. Sure enough, the bolt wouldn't even come close to closing. As I sat there fiddling with the rifle, mulling over the possibilities, I happened to glance at the barrel markings. Big as life, ".222 Rem" was rollmarked on the barrel. Now the dilemma arose: this was a rare collector's piece. The owner just wanted something to shoot. So, I explained the situation to him. I showed him the rollmark. I showed him the correct ammo. I showed him the price of the correct ammo. I told him how much it would cost to make his rifle shoot "regular" AR-15 ammo. Since he just wanted something to shoot like his buddies had, he was willing to trade his AR for one of ours, provided we would guarantee that it would work. No problem, step back to the test-fire drum and try a few rounds for yourself!

I forget who acquired that rifle, but there was quite a scramble amongst our collector customers to get there first and buy it. The only shortcoming from a collector's viewpoint was the fact that the customer had disposed of the box before arriving at our door.

7.62X39

When the wave of Chinese "surplus" ammunition and rifles was at its peak, everyone was trying to figure out a way to piggyback on the wave. Ruger came out with their Mini-30, but made the magazines different from AK magazines. I've heard both tales, that a) Ruger did it to make sure magazine supply and capacity remained under their control, and b) the

ATF told them not to make the Mini 30 take AK magazines, or it would be treated the same as the AK in any subsequent regulations) Me, I tend to think more from a mechanical viewpoint: If you were to try and make the Mini 30 take AK magazines you'd have a truly ugly rifle, and Ruger wasn't in the business of making ugly rifles.

The AR was easy to adapted to the 7.62X39 cartridge. There was enough room in the bolt face to take the rim. The barrels could easily be made thick enough for 7.62mm bullets. The chamber and port pressures are well within AR spec. The big stumbling block, and one never really solved, was magazines. The tapered AK round requires a curved magazine. And a fatter one than the AR can readily accept. The 7.62X39 AR is more of a five-shot hunter's rifle for places where a .224-inch bullet isn't large enough. Curiously, there are continued attempts in the armed forces to find some kind of an AR that can use both 5.56mm and 7.62X39 uppers. Supposedly, the idea is to be able to use captured supplies of magazines and ammunition in a pinch. Or, to make an AK-magazine accepting AR, so troops won't have two different sets of controls to keep track of. Maybe I'm just not paying attention, but the AK has never seemed so difficult to manage that I would want to carry all the extra gear required by these approaches. If I run out of 5.56, and there are plenty of AKs lying around with ammo, I'll just sling my AR (or M-16, M-4, whatever) pick up an AK, and get on with things.

The 7.62X39 breechface allows for such cartridges as the 502 Thunder Saber, using a rebated case rim on a .50-inch case. If you wanted, you could experiment with a blown-out 7.62X39 case, to remove the taper that makes the AK round so pesky. Why hadn't there been much experimentation done in the last decade? Magazines. In order to make the new caliber work, you have to have magazines that work. One pesky interpretation the ATF had during the AWB/94 was that you could modify existing magazines. But, if you modified a magazine such that it no longer worked in the rifle for which it was manufactured, you had produced a new (evil, nasty, verboten) high-capacity magazine. Magazines were not easy to come by, so why destroy magazines in testing? And why run the risk of committing a federal felony, by producing a magazine that might be declared a newly-manufactured one?

Now, with the sunset, we can knock ourselves out.

5.45X39

The newer Soviet round, with rifles and uppers made by Alexander Arms. Other than dirt-cheap surplus/import ammo, there isn't much reason for it. But, if you do happen to have a source for cheap ammo, any caliber is better than none.

6.8 Remington SPC

The 6.8 is still up in the air as of the writing of this volume. So much so that there are not even complete rifles available for testing. (I know, I've been promised one for seven months as of writing this sentence.) I have ammunition, but no rifle. Volume 2 will correct that. (As a matter of fact, I was told by one of the

AR makers I talked to about this, that I probably had more 6.8 ammo in one spot than anyone who wasn't either at Remington, or over in Iraq.)

The 6.8 is a modified 30 Remington case. Trimmed shorter, to 43mm, it is necked down to .270-inches, has the case blown out and the shoulder moved. Is it new? That depends on how you look at things. In the 1920s the Army developed the Garand rifle, which was to fire the .276 Pederson. It ended up firing the .30-06 because the Army Chief of Staff, General Douglas MacArthur took a look at the inventory of .30-06 still on hand, and decided that switching to a new rifle caliber was not prudent. In 1986, I took a .30 Remington case and modified it as an experimental rifle cartridge for the AR-15. At that time I did not have a lathe up to the task of modifying a bolt, else I probably would have proceeded. I'm sure many others tried similar experiments in between, and since.

The 6.8 rim is slightly larger than the 7.62X39. The 6.8 came about from the bottom up. Instead of Generals forming a panel to investigate, and a budget to research, increased stopping power, some Special Forces personnel managed to convince Remington and others to do some work for them: something bigger than the 5.56, that would only take new barrels, new bolt heads, and perhaps new magazines, to convert existing M-16s.

The result was the 6.8. Now, it isn't perfect. A 115-grain .270 bullet at 2,600 fps is not a long-range cartridge. But then, most long-range shooting is done with 7.62mm rifles and belt-fed machineguns, anyway. For typical combat ranges, under 300 yards, and mostly 100 or less, trajectory figures show it to work just fine.

308 Winchester

The original AR cartridge, and the one many have been lusting for for a long time. The trick is how to make an AR into a .308 without busting the bank. The answer is to use as many AR-15 parts as possible, and to not re-invent the wheel. The Armalite 308s use a modified M-14 magazine, which is relatively common, and certainly reliable. The Bushmaster rifle uses unmodified FN-FAL magazines, which on the current market can be had by the dumpster full for about $5 each. The bolt face is a nominal .470 inches in size, so you can use it for any cartridge short enough to fit the magazine and using the parent 308 case. If you wanted an autoloading 358 Winchester, you could have one with a barrel swap and some tuning. Or, going the other way, how about an autoloading varmint rifle in 243 Remington? All you need is a spare barrel extension, a barrel blank, a lathe and chambering reamers. (Well, and a gunsmith who knows how to put it all together, but you should be able to manage that.)

Bigger

I've seen rifles offered in some of the new Winchester short magnums, which are grossly over the 308 Winchester

Bad reloads can mean bad things. This case blew up the gun, but didn't hurt the shooter, except in his wallet. The only thing we could salvage off the upper were the sights and the handguards.

breechface size. While they are on the market, I haven't had a chance to play with one and see just what they did to make it take such a large cartridge.

Reloading For The AR

Reloading will be covered in greater detail in Volume 2. What I'll be doing here is laying out the groundwork, and pointing out the process, of loading for the AR-15. If you plan to load, you will have to learn reloading (learning first on the .223 for the AR is not for the faint of heart) and you will have to get some specialized equipment. Why reload? Surplus ammo can be cost-effective, but it can also be unavailable. And some ammo was surplused for a reason. Some of it is just plain awful. And you can't always use surplus for special applications. If you want to try your hand at NRA High Power, you will find surplus unsatisfactory. As most is loaded with 55-grain fmj bullets, accuracy and trajectory will suffer once you get past 300 yards. And surplus won't be much fun if you get invited on a varmint shoot. Reloading can save you money, but not like the savings you can get in handgun. A careful and volume-producing reloader can save about $60 per 1,000 rounds ($90 vs. $150) loading an M-193 equivalent round. You'll save more, but spend more, loading a hollow-

Another factory round. Always inspect your ammo.

point varmint bullet compared to factory varmint ammo. It may take some time recouping your reloading investment, at $60/K for ammo.

For some calibers, reloading is simple: if you have a pistol-caliber AR, you simply load what you'd load for your handgun. You can get some puzzling results, however. If you load your 9mm (as one example) with Bull's-eye powder, you might find that you get a bit more velocity out of a 16-inch AR barrel than you do your 5-inch handgun barrel. And both deliver less than a 10.5-inch barrel. Why? The Bull's-eye has finished burning between the 5- and 10-inch mark, and in the 16-inch tube the bore pressure has dropped off enough that friction can slow the bullet. If you were to load your 9mm rounds with a slower powder, say Accurate Arms #5, you'd find velocity increasing with each increase in barrel length.

Most reloaders, however, will have questions concerning loading .223/5.56. The answers are sometimes simple, and sometimes complicated.

Before you go and blame reloads, this happened on a factory round. The primer wasn't seated straight, and the round did not fire.

What Press Do I Need?

If you are willing to spend endless hours in your basement crafting ammo, a single-stage press will do. However, a progressive is not much more money, and the time savings are well worth the cost. A Dillon 550 or 650, or a Hornady Lock N Load would be good. A Dillon 650 with a case feeder, or a Hornady Lock N Load with case feeder would be better. Best is a Dillon 1050. What you get as you move up in press cost is speed. The biggest speed increase is the case feeder.

Must I Trim Brass?

Yes. Maybe not every time, but too-long brass increases pressure, and the one thing you don't want in the AR is an excess of pressure. You can keep your brass segregated by lot, and measure after you size, and then trim when needed. But in volume loading, the only choice is to invest in a Dillon power trimmer. The Dillon fits right into a toolhead, and you can trim as you size and deprime. You can't size, deprime and trim in the same operation as loading (powder drop, primer seat, bullet seat, crimp) as the vibration of the trimmer can throw off the other steps. So, you assemble a dedicated toolhead for sizing, depriming and trimming. And then all your brass is trimmed every time. If a particular piece of brass doesn't need trimming, the trimmer leaves it alone.

Should I Full-Length Resize?

Yes. Neck-sizing, and sizing to the minimum amount needed for greatest accuracy, things done with bolt guns and in benchrest shooting, have no place in an AR. You must full-length resize, and use a case gauge to check your settings, for reliable function. You do not necessarily need a small-base sizing die. Back in the old days it was fashionable to insist on using a small-base die (which sizes the brass body down under minimum diameter) for "reliable function." What we found was that it simply shortened the life of the brass, and made for more work in sizing. If a rifle wasn't reliable with brass full-length sized to proper dimensions, then there was something "off" in the chamber dimensions.

You should also be lubricating your brass. In reloading handgun ammunition, it is common to use a "carbide" die which does not require lubrication of the brass. Rifle brass is much longer, with a greater surface area. It also operates at a higher pressure. If you try to use a carbide rifle die without lubricant, you will sooner or later get it stuck. If carbide rifle dies don't negate the need for lubrication, why have them? Longevity. As I mentioned, rifle brass takes a lot of work to resize. You may never wear out a sizing die for .45 ACP, but you can wear out a .223 die. For those who plan to do really large volumes of reloading, carbide dies last longer.

Should I Crimp?

Yes, if the bullet has a cannelure. A crimped neck, pressed into the cannelure, prevents bullet setback on feeding. On bullets that lack a cannelure, you should at least crimp enough to remove the sharp edge of the trimmed case mouth. The crimp is not what keeps the bullet in place, neck tension does that. If you find you cannot keep bullets seated, your neck expander is probably too large.

What About Crimped Primers?

Military brass uses a crimp around the primer. The crimp is there to prevent blown-out primers in heavily-used machineguns. In combat conditions, rifles and machineguns that work are used even if they (usually unknowingly) have excess headspace. In a firefight, no one is going to toss away a rifle or machinegun with excess headspace (as if anyone would ever bother to measure it) as long as it was still working. The first sign of excess headspace in a combat environment is blown primers. A primer that blows out of the case, and goes rattling around inside the receiver, can stop

the weapon. To prevent that, military ammo has crimped-in primers. The military doesn't reload, so what do they care? We do, and it can be a hassle. The elegant solution is the Dillon 1050. It has a station just for swaging crimped primers.

If you don't have a 1050, or access to one, then your options are few: You can swage them yourself, using the Dillon bench tool. You can trim them. In older reloading manuals, you can read about using a pocketknife to cut the crimp. Maybe in the Fabulous Fifties, when reloaders were loading a box or two of .30-06 for a hunting rifle. I'd rather have to interview a recalcitrant anti-gun movie star, than spend my time with a pocketknife and a bucket full of 5.56 brass. My reloading/gunsmithing cabal, "The Gang of Four" and I once built an electrically-powered crimp trimmer. We used a deburring tool mounted on a motor, with a faceplate that kept us from trimming too much. We'd sit with hearing protectors on, merrily trimming the crimps off of .45, 5.56, 7.62 NATO and .30-06. Let me tell you, the thrill of the trimming speed wore off in a few minutes. The last choice is to discard crimped brass in favor of commercial or already-swaged or trimmed brass. If you buy a couple of cases of Black Hills ammo, the primer pockets are already swaged for you. If you stick with that (or other, similar) brass, you're good to go. Or, you can buy some 100 percent prepped military brass (for as long as it is available) and use that.

I know shooters who want to load specialized ammo, but who do not want to spend any more time loading than needed. They buy the 100 percent prepped brass, load it, shoot it, and then sell it to other reloaders. They then buy more 100 percent prepped brass and repeat.

Should I Worry About Case Separations?

That depends on how long you use your brass, and how you treat it in reloading. If your rifle has a chamber almost to the point of excess headspace, with the shoulder as far forward as possible without taking a NO-GO headspace gauge, your brass will stretch. The shoulder of the case will move forward on firing, to fill the chamber. If, in resizing, you set the shoulder back to the minimum length, the next time you fire it, it will stretch again. Do that a couple more times, and the case will separate at the thinning portion where it stretches.

Case separations are bad only in that they stop the rifle, which can hurt your score. (Do not use reloads for defense, for that reason.) I've had a few case separations through the years, and the only way you know it happened is that the bolt won't close. The next round tries to chamber, but the front half of the previous case is still in there. Often, when you extract the feeding round, it removes the broken half with it. If it doesn't, you need a specialty tool, a broken case extractor. Nothing else will get it out, not a chamber brush, cleaning brush or cleaning rod.

Your remedial action drills usually clear a case separation. But not always, and it is a sign of poor reloading or tired brass.

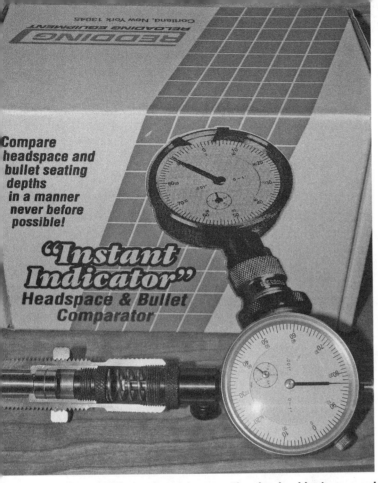

Compare headspace and bullet seating depths in a manner never before possible!

"Instant Indicator"
Headspace & Bullet Comparator

If you reload, you must take care. Size the shoulder just enough, and no more. How can you tell? You measure, of course.

How Long Will My Brass Last?

That depends on sizing, chamber size, and the load you're using. As I just mentioned about case separations, if you have a large chamber and a sizing die set to size to the minimum, you'll increase wear on the cases. If you are going to load for defense, then you want to use once-fired brass, of a known provenance (origin) and size it to the minimum. You'll also gauge each and every round.

If you are loading to stretch your practice dollars, and shoot in club matches at less cost, then you want to size your brass the least amount that will produce reliable ammunition. You also want to throttle back your loads. If your idea of the "perfect" .223/5.56 load is a 69-grain match bullet loaded to the highest possible velocity to buck the wind, then your brass isn't going to last as long as someone who is willing to give up 100 or 200 feet per second, and dial in a couple more clicks of wind value.

You can easily get three or four uses out of rifle brass. If you are careful in setting your sizing die, your chamber and sizing die are in close agreement, and you are not in the habit of loading right up to the red line, you could get 10.

Can Reloads Ammunition Be Accurate?

Usually put as: "Can ammo made on a progressive be accurate?" Carefully crafted gems of ammunition, made on single-stage presses, can be very accurate. Progressives can

equal many single stage presses in accuracy. The secrets are two: consistent sizing, and accurate bullet seating. The first is easy, as many sizing dies are now made to the standards that only benchrest-grade dies were made to 20 years ago. As CNC lathes have become common, and more accurate, precision in dies is becoming taken for granted.

Seating the bullet is the critical part. The standard method is to perch a bullet in the case neck and let it ride there as it goes up into the seating die. What I found helped greatly was a Redding Straight-Line bullet seater. Instead of perching the bullet on the case, I thumb the bullet in the port of the die. The die holds it centered, as the case rises, then aligns case neck and bullet, seating the bullet. Bullet runout (tipped bullets in case necks wobble as they are rotated. The wobble is called runout.) is greatly decreased.

By combining straight-line bullet seating with separate-station crimping, I have produced ammo that shot groups you could cover with a single paster. That is, 0.500-inch groups, center to center.

Best of all, the straight-line seater works even with cheap bullets. You don't have to use expensive match-grade bullets. Even military production run 55-grain full-metal-jacket bullets shoot more accurately when they are seated straight.

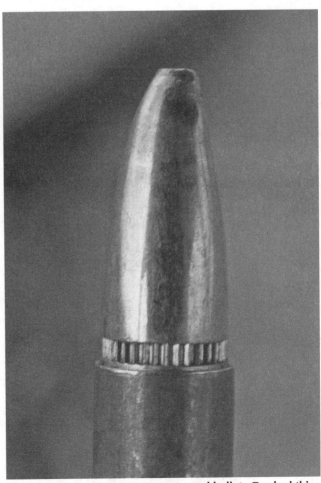

If you want accuracy, you must use good bullets. Too bad this came out of another factory box. Check your ammo!

Testing

"**T**esting. There's a process for testing?" you ask? Yes, it is more than just going to the range with the rifles, tearing open a carton or three of ammo, and shooting until I need a cigarette and a nap. Testing without recording the knowledge gained is useless. And testing without a specific and consistent plan to record the data is pointless.

So, the first thing I did with each rifle was run a clean patch down the bore and peer in with a bore scope. The Gradient Lens Hawkeye borescope let me see what was there. Let me tell you, looking down a brand-new mil-spec barrel with a borescope can be a scary experience. If you do this, do not expect to see the perfect, smooth, textbook example of "what a barrel looks like." If you want to see that, spend big money and get yourself a custom barrel. A Shilen, Krieger or other hand-made barrel will look perfect. It should. It has been hand-lapped and you pay for such attention. Production barrels do not look so pretty at 25X magnification, but then I suppose even a Victoria's Secret supermodel wouldn't, either.

Next I measured the throat length, or freebore. The process is simple: use the Stoney Point gauge and a sample bullet to measure just how long the loaded assembly would be before it touched the rifling. The sample bullet used was a Sierra 69-grain Match, the standard "lightweight" Match bullet in use. In the event a rifle had freebore cut to accept long-

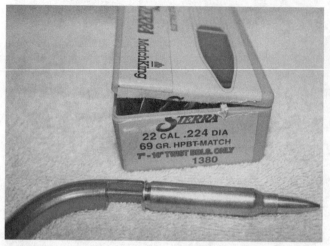

Chamber throat length was measured using a Stoney Point gauge and a Sierra 69-grain match bullet.

loaded 80-grain Match bullets, I would use a Sierra 80-grain Match bullet. The 55-grain bullets are not used, as they are not loaded long to almost touch the rifling. If you are loading those, you either load to match the cannelure to the case mouth, or if there is no cannelure, you load to the OAL that a cannelured bullet would have. The .308 rifles had the freebore checked with Sierra 168-grain Match bullets.

Each rifle had the bolt stripped, the chamber swabbed, and headspace checked. I was not expecting to find any rifle that failed the headspace check, but since I have the tools I might as well find out what I find out. The answer is, unlike the old

Prone is useful to tell how a rifle functions, and for testing the shooter. But it is not the best way to wring out accuracy differences between rifles, and between ammo makers.

Heaven on earth! Testing expensive rifles, using expensive scope, and firing expensive ammo. Short of winning the lottery, can it get any better than this?

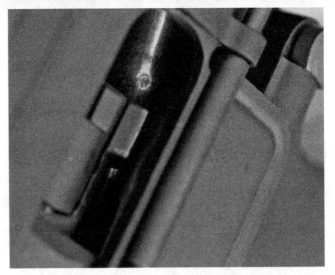

If a rifle malfunctioned, I wanted to know why. The only time it happened was in chronographing, with one rifle, and one load, once.

days where anything but a Colt was suspect, today everyone builds to a higher standard. Back when my customers were home-building ARs, it wasn't uncommon to find a complete parts kit where the bolt and barrel did not properly headspace. Every rifle I checked accepted a "GO" gauge and rejected a "NO-GO" gauge. (some came very close to accepting the NO-GO gauge. The mil-spec measurements have more leeway at the "top" of the dimensions, and a used military rifle might well accept a commercial .223 NO-GO gauge and still be within military specs.) I noted if the extractor had a polymer buffer inside the extractor spring, and what color it was. I recorded the trigger pull of each. I yanked the buffer and spring out, and recorded the buffer weight and the number of coils on the spring as well as its wire diameter.

On the external measurements, I recorded the empty weight, overall length, barrel length, diameter and size of compensator if any. If the barrel was not marked, I check for and recorded the twist of the bore. Flat-top ARs are a subject of intense interest. With a flat-top receiver, you can easily mount optics, a back-up iron sight, or other accessories. But are they all the same? Are the sights the same? To get a handle on things, I measured front sights, flat-top heights, and rear sight heights. The front sights, I measured from the centerline of the bore to the front sight housing deck, the part marked "UP" with an arrow. For the flat-top, I simply "pinched" a dial calipers between the bottom rail of the upper and the top of the flat-top. For the sights, I measured from the inside bottom of the sight housing (the part that rests on the flat-top) to the center of the aperture when the aperture was at its lowest, or short-range zero, setting. Another subject of interest in some quarters is the sidewall thickness. That is, the thickness of the sidewall at the magazine well. As the exterior is not machined, it is the forged surface of the billet, it is subject to some variation. Small differences in the temperature of the billet (within the forging specifications) alter the plasticity of the billet. A slightly hotter billet will be "squished" a bit more, and when machined out, end up with a smaller wall thickness. Likewise, a cooler billet will end up thicker. Does it matter? Probably not, but since I have all

these rifles on hand, I can measure them and see what kind of a spread we end up with.

Why all this? On the flat-top rifle, Colt M-4 carbines are reported to have a front sight .040 inches higher than standard, to accommodate the taller rear sight created by the flat-top receiver. If you have the "wrong" combination of front and rear sights, you could have great difficulty in getting your rifle zeroed. With a base to work from, we can start to get a handle on what combinations might work out. At the very least, if you find that your home-built AR has zero problems, and need a rear sight taller or shorter than the one you have presently, you can consult the chart to see if something else works.

And no one wants a thin, tinny receiver. Thus I measure and record it all. Even the thinnest lower receiver seemed plenty stout enough, so after all the testing I wouldn't worry about wall thickness.

With the measuring tools out of the way, it was off to the range for each in turn, for accuracy testing. Where possible I secured the same Leupold scope to each, and then shot them off the bench for record at 100 yards. I used all of the factory ammunition that was appropriate, from Black Hills, Hornady and selected reloads I've worked up. By "appropriate" I mean I didn't bother to test 80-grain Match ammo in rifles with barrel rifled one turn in 9 inches, as the chances of success were so low as to not be worth the ammo. I did do some small amount of testing with other heavy-bullet loads in accurate 1/9-barreled rifles, but just to see if it would work. (Results in the Barrel chapter.) Those rifles I could not mount a scope on (or couldn't easily) I shot with iron sights at 50 yards using the Lahti rest as a holding fixture.

Each load and its performance, was recorded with each rifle. In testing rifles I have found that while I am a reasonably good shot, I am not a machine rest. And I do not have eyesight as good as eyesight enhanced by optics. So testing for

I chronographed all of the loads. This is not as much fun as the other testing, but someone has to do it, and my volunteers will only volunteer for the fun stuff.

The test crew on a rainy day. Of course they're smiling, their only work was picking up brass.

accuracy is a relative thing. At the top end, we have rifles fired with top-notch optics (and Leupold certainly fits that bill) from the Lahti rest. A step below is me, using sandbags and the same optics. Last is my with iron sights. What I have found is simple: the Lahti, if the rifle is up to it, generally fires a group half the size I can at 100 yards. And I can fire a group that size (me off the sandbags) at 50 yards with iron sights. So, where testing for absolute accuracy, say, comparing one batch or brand of ammunition against another, I used the Lahti. To determine useable accuracy, I fired 100-yard sandbag groups with optics, or 50-yard sandbag groups, with irons. A rifle that I fired average groups at 50 yards of an inch with iron sights, and a rifle with a scope at 100 yards that averaged and inch, would both be described as "One MOA" rifles.

Short of some sort of machine rest that holds the rifle repeatably (FN-USA has one they use to test-fire their sniper rifles with, but are reluctant to loan it out, and I don't blame them) I have to be clear that any descriptor includes me as part of the equation.

Then it was on to the fun part of the schedule. I and my test-fire crew (no lack of volunteers for this project!) would use a rifle or rifles on the steel plates. We were looking for sharp edges the might bite or cut, to see how the rifles handled, if the zero would wander as they heated up, and in the case of rifles with a compensator, how effective the comp was. Once each rifle had a couple of hundred rounds through it, we'd set it aside to let it cool, and let the carbon to harden. Then we'd test it again, to see if the extractor was up to the job. We tested each rifle on three different sessions. In order to avoid being accused of abusing the barrels, I cleaned the bore of each rifle with brushes, solvent and patches. But I avoided as much as possible cleaning the chamber, and I

did not clean the rest of the interior. I wanted to see how well each worked when the carbon had had time to set and harden.

Also part of the testing and analysis was asking the test crew their impressions of the various rifles. How was it in weight? Balance? Were the handguards comfortable? Did you like the trigger? Did it seem accurate shooting offhand? And last, in each batch tested; "If you were spending your own money, which of these would you be most likely to buy?"

In each range session, if there was any doubt as to how well a particular rifle was doing, I'd get it back on the bench and shoot for groups. As an additional step, if a rifle seemed like it wanted to shoot particularly well, I locked it in the Lahti rifle rest and shot it without human influence. As a side test, I tried my hand at shooting several rifles off the sandbags as a check against the Lahti rest. To no great surprise, the Lahti shoots better than I do.

The test session was not thorough, not definitive, and certainly not to destruction. Were I in charge of a testing program to select likely candidates for military approval, or adoption by a police department, I'd do things differently. I'd use a test procedure like this to cull the group to half a dozen candidates or so. I'd purchase more rifles from those makers, and not depend on loaners. I would then test those new rifles until they broke, failed or otherwise proved they weren't up to snuff. The last rifle would be the victor, and get the contract. I can't very well ask politely of Colt to borrow a rifle, and once done with it, return a box full of shattered parts. Well, I could, once. But I'd never get another loaner again. Not from Colt, and not from anyone else, once word got around. There are limits to what I can do. Reasonable wear and tear, up to and including a shot-out barrel, is all fine and good. But I can't go

One of the "heat 'em up" tests we did with the Wolf ammo. All the rifles passed.

Mike Gibson was kind enough to send a pair of his spring-loaded rifle poppers for the testing. They managed to survive the onslaught of my testers without a problem.

Scopes lacking target knobs are best used in a test session with these Stoney Point external adjustment caps.

dropping rifles to see if the sights are as tough as they look. Not unless I want to buy them and then test to destruction.

The general conclusions relevant to a subject (like barrels) will be found in the chapters devoted to that subject. The particulars for each rifle are with the rifles' chapter, in a summary at the end.

And for those of you who are green with envy, wondering how to get either the job of doing this, or on the test fire crew, it isn't as fun as you'd think. After all, I had to schlep all the gear to and from the range many times. My test fire crew and I had to show up rain or shine, hot or cold, and shoot whatever was on the schedule. And since the clubs' range rules are quite strict, and we didn't want to get into trouble, we had to pick up all the brass before we were done in each session. Still not buying it? I don't blame you. We

had a blast. So get over your envy by finishing your read, and then contribute to the economic good health of one of the manufacturers who were so kind as to loan me a rifle, and buy one. Or two.

Sights, Lights And Mounts

In testing, the sighting mechanism used can influence greatly the results and impressions. As a preliminary to Volume 2, I tried a number of sights to see what their strengths and weaknesses were, and get an impression from the crew on each sight. I also handled a few lights to see how they worked, and talked to my crew who had used them in classes, matches, and on duty. The sights fall in three categories: optics, red-dots and irons.

Optics

The optical sights I tested came from two makers, Leupold and Elcan. The Leupold sights I had were their Mark 4 CQ/T, a Mark 4 3.5-10X40 LR/T, and a Mark 4 3-9X36 MR/T. All three have illuminated reticles.

CQ/T

This is the Leupold answer to the need for a close, fast tactical scope. It is a variable, from straight 1-power to 3-power, using a circle with a dot in the middle. The scope uses batteries, to illuminate the reticle, but the reticle is still present even in the absence of battery power. Unlike red-dot scopes, if the battery dies you still have an aiming point.

My first impression of the CQ/T was that it was too big. With all the other things being bolted to rifles today, the last

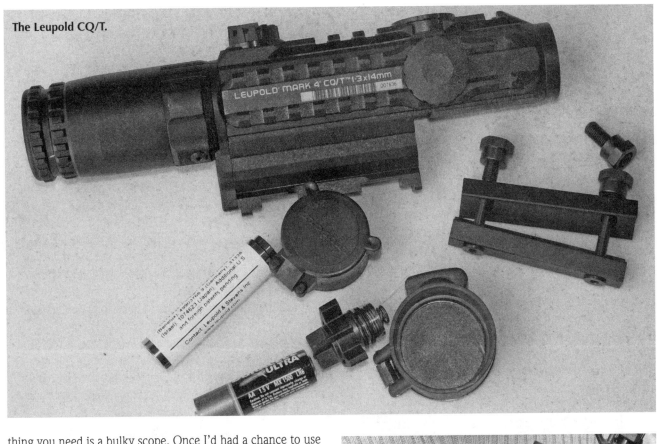

The Leupold CQ/T.

thing you need is a bulky scope. Once I'd had a chance to use it, I found it much better than I had thought. At 1-power the scope is very fast, but I think I'd prefer a slightly larger dot. (I was surprised, on reading the manual, to find that the dot is 9 MOA at 1X, and 3 MOA at 3X. It seemed smaller.) At one power, your front sight post is visible in your field of view. I built an AR Scout Rifle back in the late 1980s, using a Burris Scout Scope. I found that the front sight was visible in that setup, but with a little work I could easily ignore it and soon forgot it was there. But some shooters who borrowed that rifle could not get used to it. So it was with the CQ/T. I didn't even notice the sight, but some of my testers commented on the front sight post being there. Once you had turned the power up to about 2X, the front sight went out of focus and none noticed it after that.

The ring is very fast at close range, and if you have a wide open target to shoot it is hard to beat for speed. If you need to skate a shot past hard cover or a no-shoot target you'd better slow down and use the dot, or your score will suffer. (Or in real life, you or others might suffer.) At 72 MOA in size, the ring is huge.

The scope comes with adapter clamps, so you can attach it directly to a flat-top upper. To mount to a carry handle, don't use the clamps, and instead set the base directly in the handle, and use the included bolt to secure the scope at a proper eye relief location. Personally, I've given up on scopes in the carry handle. They are simply too high, and it is difficult to keep any kind of face contact with the stock while shooting. But if it is all you have, then it is better than irons.

The Leupold LR/T, a big scope, on an M-4. Small rifle, big scope, big results.

The test crew's impressions of the CQ/T mirrored mine. They expected something larger, and found it reasonable in size. And since most are competition shooters, they would have preferred a larger dot and smaller ring. But most of our competition shooting is done 100 yards and closer. If we spent more time at extended ranges, I'm not sure we'd be as well served by a bigger dot.

Mark 4 3.5-10X40 LR/T

The Long Range Tactical scope came in a 30mm tube, with a ¾ mil dot reticle. The use of mil dots is an old and accepted practice in aiming, survey work and range estimation. The idea is simple: if you know the spacing of the dots (and their size) in your scope's reticle, you can use them as a measuring scale against an object of a known size. Knowing the formula, eyeballing the dots a target subtends (extends across) and you know the distance. In the days before laser rangefinders, the mil dot was the essence of cool. However, you have to know the values, and be able to calculate the distances with the formula. For a long-range shot where you have time to calculate, it works great as traditionally done. Another use is to zero the rifle to a known distance, and then know the "holdovers" for additional ranges. With a laser sight, you can do very fast work if need be. For instance, if you zero your 7.62mm rifle for 300 yards, and you test to find that the second dot down is dead-on at 600, then when your spotter calls a target at 580 yards, you can take a shot quickly if you need to by simply holding the second dot down on target and pressing the shot off.

Even a big scope is fun to shoot, and the steel suffered for it.

I bolted the Leupold LR/T in the Armalite scope mount they sent me. It locked in place without a problem, and fit on every rifle without a hitch. I must confess to Armalite that in the process of moving onto and off of some two dozen rifles I kind of chewed up the locking knobs. Despite the damage, the mount worked without fail, and the cosmetic damage can be undone by a simple bolt knob swap.

As you can imagine, the large Leupold on the M-4gery rifles was quite a sight, and not a handy tactical combination. But, as a tool to test for accuracy, it was a very good one. The external knobs of the LR/T allowed me to quickly crank the scope around to get each rifle zeroed. In the proper use, on a single rifle, you'd zero the rifle, then re-set the knobs to "zero" so you would always know where your scope was set compared to its normal zero. For testing, it didn't matter to me where the knobs were, as they'd be someplace different on the next rifle.

The illuminated reticle is a grand thing to have if you are working in semi darkness or the dark. Also, it allows you to see your reticle when aiming into a dark area. If you're shooting through a gap in the trees, at a target in shadow in the forest, a black reticle can get lost. But with a variable brightness reticle you can add just enough light to see your aiming point, without overwhelming your vision.

Mark 4, 3-9X36 MR/T

The medium range tactical is a more compact scope then the LR, but still with a 30mm tube. It has the same external scope knobs, variable-brightness reticle, and matte finish as its big brother. Were I building an SPR, or a police precision rifle on an AR, I'd be tempted to use this one instead of the LR. The slightly smaller size would make for a less-bulky package.

I put the MR on a few rifles but spent most of the time in accuracy testing using the big one. Were I building an SPR (look for that in Volume 2) I would select the MR/T instead of the LR/T. It is just enough more compact that it would be a handier package, and we aren't looking to use an AR as a 1,000-yard rifle, right?

Elcan

The Canadian Defense Forces have been doing some vigorous experimenting on the AR and sighting systems. The Elcan is a sight developed to be used as a durable scope for combat use. While it is not the smallest and lightest scope out there, it is hard to fault it for durability. Where many rifles in use in Iraq sport a Leupold, EOTech or Aimpoint, the Elcan appears on many SAW and M-240 machineguns. I would think for two reasons: the slightly larger bulk of the Elcan is not noticed on an already large and heavy machinegun, and the government bought them for use on machineguns, and that's where they are used. (Hey, a 50 percent rational reason for something in the government is a fantastic rate.)

The Elcan is a sealed scope that uses range and zero adjustments in its built-in base. With no apertures for

The Elcan, a very nice scope even if the eye relief is a bit short.

adjustment rings to leak or admit dust, the Elcan is potentially better-sealed from the environment than its competitors. The built-in base clamps directly to the flat-top of an AR, or the scope base mil-spec 1913 base built on to SAWs and M-240s.

If there is a fault of the Elcan, it is that the eye relief is short and unforgiving. Where you can have your eye positioned within a couple of inches behind a Leupold scope, or anywhere behind a red-dot scope, the Elcan requires that you be close to, and within a narrow range of, the scope. Once you get it mounted and positioned for yourself, it is great. But if someone else mounts it, you may find yourself adopting odd positions to keep your eye in the right place.

The Elcan has a post with rangefinding stadia alongside. The mount has a built-in range adjustment. Once you determine the range, you simply turn the dial on the bottom to adjust for it.

Red-Dots

The idea of a red-dot scope is simple: the scope uses an upright glass or plastic screen. It projects a laser dot onto the screen, which the shooter sees and uses as an aiming point. Everything else about the design is simply a matter of the mechanics of fabrication, housing of the laser and battery, and building for durability and attachments. The simplest are tubes, to be mounted much as an optical scope would be. The more involved designs include a mounting system. The red-dots I tested were the EO Tech Holosight, the Aimpoint ML2, and the C-More rail sight.

Holosight

Hell for tough, the Holosight uses a three-dimensional holographic display. Where all other sights project a dot onto a screen, the Holosight projects its laser on the entire screen. And the screen reflects a three-dimensional representation of the reticle back to you. On many other red-dot sights, damage to the screen can mean the sight is useless. The Holosight, as long as there is enough screen left to see, shows you a reticle. I visited the factory, and there saw a sight that had been used in a DOE force-on-force training session. The operator who had been using it had gone through the training scenario, and upon exiting the other side, one of the others there said something to the effect of "Dude, what's up with your sight?" His Holosight had taken a direct hit on the screen from a Simunitions shot, and was busted and splattered with paint. But it still worked, and he was still able to aim with it.

The EOTech Holosight, here on a Bennie Cooley front mount.

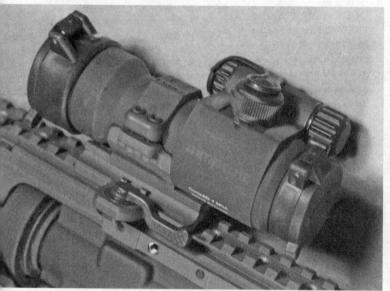

The Aimpoint, here in an ARMS mount on one of their excellent S.I.R. forends.

In testing the prototypes, the development engineers mounted the scopes on a "blue gun" AR carbine, and then dropped it off the roof of the loading dock. Scarred from the multiple impacts, it kept working and didn't change its zero.

Where many red-dot scopes become useless in the rain, due to fuzzing or dispersion of the reflected dot, the Holosight does not. Also, where other scopes can be seen at night when observed by the opposition with NVG, the Holosight cannot. There is no laser light reflected in the target's direction to be observed.

You can see many Holosights in use in Iraq and Afghanistan.

Aimpoint

Aimpoint got the first big contracts for red-dot optics with the U.S. Armed Forces. The Aimpoint scopes are very tough, and almost ubiquitous in Iraq. Combined with a tough base like the GG&G or A.R.M.S., it is easily mounted or removed, and will not shift zero while on the rifle. The military model of the Aimpoint does not turn off. The dot is continually on,

but the first few settings for intensity are meant for use with night vision gear. At the lowest setting the battery is good for 10,000 hours. For those not good with math in their heads, that is almost 13 months of use. If you simply changed the battery in your Aimpoint on your birthday, you'd be good in the rack forever. Cranked up to higher intensity the battery doesn't last as long, but still plenty long enough.

C-More

The C-More sight got started as a competition sight, and it is very good for that. Some might feel it is a bit fragile for combat use, with the exposed ring of the viewscreen, but even IPSC shooters find it durable enough for three-gun use. And you'd be hard-pressed to find a red-dot that has won more matches than the C-More. The one they sent me was

their railway, meant to be bolted directly to the flat-top of an A4 type rifle, complete with back up iron sights.

The differences between optics and red-dots can be summed in one word: speed. At distances inside those where magnification is useful, the red-dot sights, with their lack of parallax, can be shot at speeds that would amaze the uninitiated. Parallax is the optic displacement between the reticle and point of impact, caused by the shooter's eye not being directly on the centerline of the scope. In an optic with parallax, if you move your eye off center, you can still see the reticle, but the point of impact will not be on the reticle. Red-dot scopes either have parallax so small as to be inconsequential, or none at all. If you can see the dot, that is where the bullet will hit.

The problem with red-dot scopes is that they do not magnify. So, unless you have eyesight light a fighter pilot, the longer the distance the more difficult it is to extract all the accuracy a rifle has. While a rifle/ammunition combination may be good for sub-MOA accuracy, at 300 yards you can't see that small. That is, the rifle and ammunition may be able to shoot a group of only 2 inches out there, but your eyesight, and ability to aim, may only be good for 10 inches. Plenty good enough to hit a standing man, but not one peering around a corner. The SPR-armed rifleman, using the 10-power scope it has, can see the peering enemy, and use the accuracy of the rifle. But, the same SPR-armed rifleman is hampered by his variable (we all hope the good guys are armed with variables) scope only going down to 3.5 power, when trying to deal with a bad guy on the other side of a room.

Which you choose depends on what you expect to need.

The C-More rail mount, with built-in back-up iron sight.

Disassembly And Maintenance

The AR-15 is easy to take apart and clean. Ideally, all military small arms are. After all, what good is a rifle, submachinegun or machinegun that needs a vise, hammer, drift pins and special wrenches just to get it apart for cleaning? If there is one thing you can count on in the military context, it is that rifles will get dirty. If it is so easy, why is this one such a large chapter? Because while it is easy, it is also detailed and exacting. If you take care of a few things, your AR will give you years of trouble-free service. If you do not, it won't. And some things have to be explained in detail simply because (in my experience) they otherwise get neglected. Or they simply aren't known. Even if you "know everything" about the AR, or really do know everything because your DI and PMI taught you everything, read on anyway. You might be surprised, and you might pick up a few tips that you (and your DI and PMI) didn't know.

What tools do you need? At a bare minimum you'll need one loaded full-metal-jacket round, and a cleaning rod with patches, brush and lubricating oil. If you want more, you can add a bore solvent, a small screwdriver, a push-pin punch, several brushes for scrubbing various areas of the rifle, and a large, flat, clean surface on which to work. You can get kits that will require a toolbox to cart around, on down to kits that will fit into the buttstock of a fixed-stock AR, the pistol grip, your pocket or your web gear.

If you are cleaning at home you might consider using rubber or latex gloves. Any drug store or medical supply store can provide you with a box of 100 pairs for a few dollars. When you get to the bolt, you'll really appreciate having gloves to wear, as will your wife or significant other.

One thing you should be aware of when cleaning the bore is the need to avoid a jointed rod. For emergency or field use, using a jointed rod is OK. But for the majority of your cleaning (for those not engaged in the field in dusting bad guys) you want to use a single-piece rod like a Dewey rod, or an Uncle Mikes, and a rod guide. More on that later.

The AR-15 runs dirty. Unlike other gas-operated rifles, where the ported gas acts on an operating rod, the AR valves the gas right back into the action. There, the gas tube tip pressurizes the carrier through the key, and blows it back, rotating and then pulling the bolt with it. Every time you fire, you spew hot, carbon-laden gases into the action. As the AR

If you want dust, the Marine Corps can arrange that for you. In this environment, a wet lubricant is not desired. You also want to make sure your rifle works, but a checklist is helpful only if you use it.

(U.S. Marine Corps photo by Lance Cpl. Kenneth E. Madden III)

is a tightly-fitted mechanism, using a high-pressure round, there is a lot of gas and a lot of places it can do mischief. An afternoon of shooting will turn the inside of your rifle into something that looks like it came from London during the Industrial Revolution: soot-laden, oily, disgusting and a mess to clean up. Luckily, it doesn't take 75 years to clean, as the air of London did.

Disassembly And Assembly Note

You should not need a hammer to take the AR-15 apart, except for a brand new, unfired rifle. The pins and springs on a new rifle may be tight enough to need some "encouragement" in coming free. But only a little. If you have to use a hammer to get things apart or back together, then either your rifle is fitted improperly, or you are doing something wrong.

In any class, when we're working on the disassembly or assembly, as soon as I hear tapping hammers I get to that rifle quickly. Almost invariably, the student is hitting something that only needs a push, if it were simply aligned correctly.

Don't use a hammer. Make sure things are lined up.

Disassembly

First make sure it isn't loaded. Long-time readers of mine will in many cases gnash their teeth at being reminded again. (And again, and again.) Others will be encountering this advice for the first time. I long ago lost count of firearms presented to me with the exhortation that "it's unloaded" only to find out otherwise. Even with extreme diligence, over a lifetime of handling firearms you'll at least once in your life pick up an "unloaded" firearm, only to discover in short order that it is indeed loaded.

To check, make sure the safety is on. If it is off, and won't go on, the hammer is forward, making it unlikely it is loaded

but not impossible. Go right to the step of opening the rear pin. If the safety will go on, the hammer is cocked. Now pull the operating handle back partially, and look into the chamber. Look closely, and with a strong light if you have one available. You can't get a finger in there to check, so look again. Empty? Good. Ease the bolt forward.

With the action closed and the safety on, look at the gap between the upper and lower halves. At the front you'll see a pin. At the rear, just in front of the stock, is another. You'll find the front pin in three configurations; Double push pin, Colt large-head screw and Colt small-head screw. The DPP style is simple: a plain pin with a head on the right, and just "proud" (above the surface of the receiver) on the left. The double push pin is the standard, and military configuration.

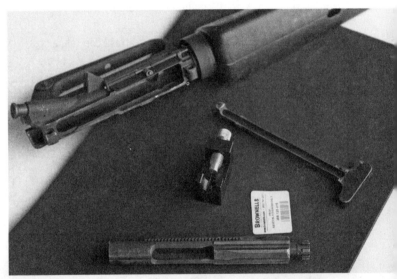

Taking your rifle apart may be done with your bare hands, but you need tools to clean it.

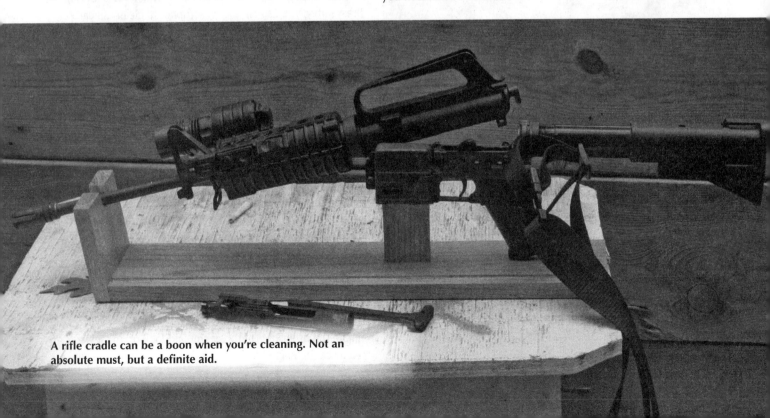

A rifle cradle can be a boon when you're cleaning. Not an absolute must, but a definite aid.

The pins are a nominal .250 inches in diameter, and captured, that is, they stay attached even when they are pushed out for disassembly.

The Colt large-head screw was an attempt many years ago by Colt to placate anti-gun legislators. By using a larger-diameter pin (nominal 5/16, or .312 inches) Colt hoped to avoid the use of military surplus upper receivers on their lowers. The idea was that by taking this measure, Colt could show that their rifles were not military rifles, and could not be converted into machineguns. As a placating measure, it failed, as all such measures Colt has taken in the last 30 years have failed. As a means of foiling the use of surplus parts it also failed. The Colt large-head screw has a large pin that goes through the receivers, with a small screw that threads into it from the left side. To take it apart you'll need a pair of screwdrivers, to disassemble you hold tight one while unscrewing the other.

The Colt small-head screw is, as near as I can tell, a cost-saving measure that attempts to keep the Band-aid of the large-head screw. The small screw is the same diameter as the

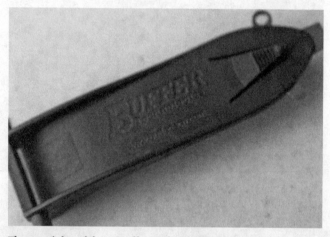

The special tool from Buffer Technologies helps you disassemble the rifle, magazine, and tighten the straps on your MagCinch.

Use a mop to clean after you scrub, just like windows or floors.

double push pin. It is also cut with a shoulder, and retained by the standard upper fence. But it is held in place by a small screw on the left side. You only need one screwdriver, on the left, to take it apart. The standard double push pin uppers will fit a Colt lower with the screw-head small push pin. There is a small complication: not all Colt small-screw lowers have the fence drilled for the spring and plunger. If yours lacks the hole, you'll have to retain the screw/pin to keep things together. Otherwise, vibration from firing will cause a standard pin to work loose and drop out.

Now that you've determined which front pin your rifle has, begin disassembly by pushing the rear one out. Push from left to right. If a rifle is very tight you may need to hold a drift pin against the disassembly pin and tap it. Don't hit too hard. The sidewall on the retaining plunger is thin, and you can break it by striking too hard. Once the pin is completely to the side, the action will hinge open.

With the action hinged open, grasp the operating handle and pull back. Once the carrier comes clear enough, grasp it and pull it and the bolt out. Set the bolt assembly aside for the moment. Pull the operating handle back, while gently pressing down towards the lower receiver. When the operating handle retention tabs reach their clearance slot, it will come down out of the receiver. Set the handle aside. Now turn your attention to the front pin. If your rifle is a double push pin, push the pin over. You may have to wiggle the upper to the lower, to free the pin from binding. Once the pin is completely over, the two halves can be separated. Many times, this is far enough. At Second Chance, where we'd go through a couple of cubic feet of ammunition in a week's time, this was all a rifle would get during the day. Each night it would be detail stripped and cleaned. Ditto a USPSA/IPSC Three-Gun match in a dirty or dusty environment. Once to this level of disassembly, you use an aerosol scrubber to clean the carbon, dirt and dust off, you turn a chamber brush into and out of the chamber, run a patch down the bore, lube, reassemble and get back into the match.

But at night, or after the match, you do more.

Upper Disassembly

The only thing you might need to take off would be the handguards. Most of the time, not even that. Once the parts are out, there is nothing else you need remove from the upper in order to clean it. The handguards are held on by the round, ribbed nut on the back. It is spring-loaded. Pull the ring back towards the receiver, and the rear ends of the handguards will be uncovered. Pivot them away from the barrel. They are hooked inside the front cap. Old triangular handguards are made as rights and lefts. Round handgurads are identical and interchangeable, and go together as upper and lower pieces.

Bolt Disassembly

Take the disgustingly-grubby bolt and look on the left side. You'll see the loop of a cotter pin. Hook it with your small screwdriver. In the field, you can use a bullet tip or the tip of a knife. Pull the pin out and set it someplace where it won't get lost. Turn the bolt upside down, and the firing pin should fall out. If it doesn't, pull it out. (This is a clue your rifle is overdue for cleaning) If it pulls free with a sucking sound, you really have been neglecting it, haven't you? Do not bother looking for the firing pin spring, for the AR-15 does not have one. On the top of the carrier, under the key, is a rectangular knob. Push the bolt back into the carrier. Then rotate the knob so the long side is parallel to the carrier length. Now lift the cam pin (for that is what it is called) up out of the carrier. With the cam pin out, you should be able to pull the bolt forward out of the carrier. Look at the bolt. You'll see a large-ish pin through it. A solid pin. Use your small screwdriver (or in a pinch, the firing pin) to push this pin out. Once it is free the extractor comes out. The only pin left is the small roll pin. It keeps the ejector in place. At this point, let me abandon my usual path of home-made gunsmithing tools, or using ad-hoc tools.

Holding the bolt while you use a 1/16-inch drift punch and a small ball peen hammer to remove the pin is not easy. I did it for years by carefully positioning the bolt in a vise, or in the field getting someone to hold it while I got the pin started. Getting things back together was even more difficult. The first time I used a bolt tool from Sinclair, I mentally forehead-slapped myself for not having gotten one sooner. If you are going to remove the ejector pin and ejector more than once in your life, the money spent on the Sinclair tool is a wise investment. Don't begrudge the dollars, get one.

The ejector is spring-loaded. Put the bolt in the tool, line up a lug in the bottom slot, and turn the screw until it stops. Then back the screw out a quarter turn. (Bottomed out, the screw presses the ejector against the pin. By backing it out, you take pressure off the pin and make it easy to remove.) Take your drift pin and hammer, and tap the pin out. Unscrew the knob, and remove the ejector and spring.

Lower Disassembly

Remove the buffer and spring. Use a thumb to press the buffer back into the tube slightly, then press the retaining plunger down with that same small screwdriver you've used for so many things. Ease the buffer forward past the plunger, and pull the buffer and the spring out. You can swab the tube (A good idea in a sandy environment, wasted effort anywhere else.) but be sure you don't leave a patch or something behind.

The fire control parts are next. Put your thumb over the hammer. Press the safety off with your other hand and press the trigger, releasing the hammer. Ease the hammer forward. If you let it slam into the receiver without the bolt in place, you can damage the receiver or even the hammer.

Take your medium drift punch, the 1/8-inch one, and press the hammer pin. If yours is tightly-fitted you may have to tap it with a hammer, but most will come apart with finger

pressure. Once the pin is out, lift the hammer out. Then push the trigger pin out. Lift the disconnector out. Some rifles will have enough clearance that you can work the trigger out with the safety in place. If not, get your medium screwdriver and look in the pistol grip. The screw in there has to come out. If yours is an allen-head, you'll need a long one to reach. It is common in law enforcement classes to modify the allen head screw by using a hacksaw to create a slot, so you can use either an allen wrench (not common) or a screwdriver (common) to remove it.

As you unscrew the pistol grip, you'll see the safety plunger and spring come into view. Do not lose them. Set them aside, and once the grip is off and the plunger and spring are out you can remove the safety and then the trigger.

You now have a pile of carbon-covered parts on your bench. Let's get to cleaning them.

Basic Cleaning

Wipe everything down. Scrub the bolt, carrier, fire control parts and chamber with brushes and solvent, wipe clean. Run brushes and patches down the bore until "clean enough." Lubricate everything, reassemble and arrange as your needs dictate. In Fallujah, that means load it and put it where you can find it when you wake up. As a police officer, it means load according to departmental policy, rack it and lock it. At home, well, it could be anything from lock it in the safe to stand it up next to your bed.

Many rifles will perform admirably for years with no more than a basic cleaning. Some might want (if we can anthropomorphise a rifle) more bore cleaning for good accuracy. Others might want more action cleaning for reliability. You'll have to determine if a basic cleaning is good enough for you. If it isn't then there is the detail cleaning and the time and effort it takes.

Detail Cleaning

Here you'll scrub every surface of every part that matters. And the surfaces that don't matter get wiped, just to keep the dirt from migrating.

Detail Upper Cleaning

What matters here is the chamber and locking lug area, and the bore. The interior of the upper matters only in that it is a repository of gunk. If you don't at least wipe it clean, your carrier will be "re-grubbified" the moment you reassemble your rifle. The outside matters only if it matters to you, your wife, supervisor or buddies. As for the bore cleaning, it is a specialized matter, and I've put the particulars on cleaning the bore in the Barrel chapter. What you have to keep in mind when cleaning the upper is this: you scrub the bore after you scrub the chamber and locking lugs. Chamber scrubbing can push gunk down into the bore, and you can't leave it there. So scrub chamber first, then bore.

To scrub the chamber you need a chamber brush and a T-

You need a special, big, brush to scrub the interior of the upper.

The chamber brush is meant to scrub the chamber and the locking lugs.

The gas tube blows hot gases into the lubed interior of your rifle.

The BoreSnake is great to keep going in a match or in the field, but it does not replace a thorough bore cleaning.

handle rod. You can swab the chamber and locking lug area with a solvent-soaked patch prior to brushing it, but it isn't required unless your rifle is so caked with carbon you can't brush it all loose. Screw the brush into the rod, and then press the brush into the chamber while slowly turning clockwise. Keep turning once the brush bottoms out, then pull the brush out while rotating. If you simply push the brush in and pull it out you won't scour the carbon off, and you'll break the

bristles off of the brush. With the carbon loosened, press and turn a chamber swab, then pull it out. Finally, clean the locking lug area with a Sinclair rod and swab made specifically for the task. Or, use the Brownells chamber swab. The Sinclair uses replacement swabs that fit on their handle. Swab the lugs clean and toss the grubby swab. The Brownells mop is a chamber-brush-shaped mop that wipes clean, but must be cleaned to be re-used. They both work, you just have to decide which is more convenient.

Once the chamber is clean, wipe the interior of the upper with a solvent-soaked patch. Then brush. You can use the military brush, the one that looks like a toothbrush, or a Sinclair brush, which looks like a bore brush for a small cannon. Use the small end of the military brush to scrub the slot the operating handle rides in. With the carbon loose, wipe it out with a paper towel. You'll be surprised and even horrified at how much comes out.

Finally, scrub the bore. (See the Barrel chapter.)

You can lube the interior of the upper if you like. In many locales it acts to soften the inevitable powder residue. In extremely dry and dusty environments, it simply traps carbon and dust into an abrasive slurry. Here in the Midwest, with hot summers and cold winters, we use a light lubricant, but keep them damp to wet with lube. But compared to the Middle East, our sand and dust is the size of pea gravel. We don't have to worry about as sandstorm caking the rifles into a solid mass. You will have to lube according to your local conditions and time of year.

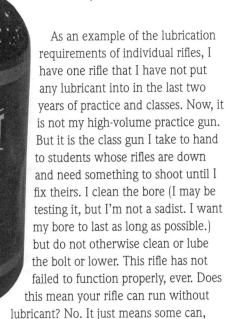

You need a special solvent to get the copper residue out of your bore.

As an example of the lubrication requirements of individual rifles, I have one rifle that I have not put any lubricant into in the last two years of practice and classes. Now, it is not my high-volume practice gun. But it is the class gun I take to hand to students whose rifles are down and need something to shoot until I fix theirs. I clean the bore (I may be testing it, but I'm not a sadist. I want my bore to last as long as possible.) but do not otherwise clean or lube the bolt or lower. This rifle has not failed to function properly, ever. Does this mean your rifle can run without lubricant? No. It just means some can, sometimes. In the wet, cold, gritty dusty Midwest, we keep them wet with lube. In a drier climate, I would use TW-25 from Mil-Com. In testing I've found that it keeps rifles running quite well, and the carbon and dirt clean off easily. What the TW-25 avoids is the gooey, oily mess of the carbon suspended in lubricant. The bolt and carrier of the rifles that get TW-25 wipe off with a lot less mess.

TW-25, a most-excellent dry lube for dusty conditions.

Detail Bolt Cleaning

The bolt is what most often keeps the rifle from working properly. You must get every part of it scrupulously clean, because it gets very dirty very quickly. If it starts off dirty from a casual cleaning, then you've simply shortened the time before it lets you down.

Even for a detail cleaning you need not remove the ejector. Only if your ejector seems weak or sluggish, or the ammo you are using leaves large amounts of brass shavings behind, do you need to remove it every time. With the extractor off, scrub the bolt squeaky clean. Do not scrub the tail, behind the gas rings. There you must scrape the carbon off with a flat brass tool. If you brush the tail, you might snag and sling out a gas ring or two, turning your rifle into a straight-pull bolt-action rifle.

Scrub and degrease the bolt body, lugs and bolt face. Inspect the gas rings. There must be three of them. You can carefully arrange them so the gaps don't line up, but I haven't found a rifle yet that short-stroked when I lined up the gaps. (None of the rifles in this book did, nor do any of my personal ones. Somewhere, out there, is a rifle that does short-stroke when the gaps line up. The solution would be to install new rings.) The carbon on the bolt tail must be scraped off. I use a short section of flat brass bar that I machined a slight chisel edge on. My friend Jeff Chudwin uses a modified .50 BMG empty case to do the same thing. Do not use a brush or wire wheel to ge the carbon off. You can easily snag a ring and sling it off the bolt. Even if you see it go and find it, it will probably be damaged and not useable. If you don't spot it, your rifle could short-stroke as a result.

Scrub the extractor. While you've got it out, look at the edge. It should be sharp and crisp. If the extractor hook is chipped or rounded, you may need a new one soon. You can either keep using it until it fails you (to see how long that takes) or install a new one. Look at the extractor spring. It must have a small plastic cylinder inside the spring. The current ones are the strongest, and are black. Older ones are blue, and work well almost all the time. Anything else (red, white, ivory, etc) is older, weaker, and not to be trusted. If you have regular instances of empty cases left in the chamber, you might need extractor spring help. If your spring lacks a booster, install one. While you're at it, install a new spring, too. (The old ones often get damaged in removal.) If you have a good spring and blue or black booster, you must step up. One way is to use a heavier spring. You can get a heavier spring from Wolff or Specialized Armament Warehouse. To remove the old spring, you must know that it is seated under a lip in the extractor. You'll have to carefully pry it loose. To install the new one, you must start one side of the spring in the hole, under the lip, then use your small screwdriver to press the spring under the lip, as you press the screwdriver around the perimeter. Just like getting a tire on a rim.

Another approach is to use an Armforte D-fender from

The big brush scrubs the interior, but doesn't get into the charging handle slot. There, you'll need a smaller brush.

Make sure you have three gas rings, and that the gaps don't line up.

There is a lot of carbon buildup on the bolt tail. Scrape it off carefully, without marring the bolt, or removing gas rings. Don't use a brush.

Your extractor should have a blue or black internal buffer. Better yet, add a D-Fender.

Mack Gwinn. The D-fender doesn't replace the spring, it supplements it. You place the D-shaped polymer booster (thus its name) with the straight end towards the extractor hook. However, you do not want to "gild the lily." DO NOT use both an extra-power extractor spring AND the D-fender. The extractor must cam over the case rim on closing, and by double-boosting it you make it impossible for the extractor to flex. The bolt won't close on a chambered round.

Once you've got your bolt apart and clean, inspect it. The lugs should be un-marred, and not chipped. Any chips or peening indicates one of a host of bad things: Chips usually mean your rifle was built with a used, military-surplus and high-mileage bolt. If it is chipped it may break. Peening means it is too soft. It is either a sub-standard product, or somewhere along the way it was overheated and lost its hardness. Look at the cam pin hole. One side should be peened to prevent cam pin entry. The peening prevents you from assembling the bolt wrong-side out. If you assemble the bolt with the extractor on the left side, it will try to extract the fired case out through the solid sidewall of the receiver. The empty won't go, the bolt won't let go, and the rifle is tied up. I found this out from a club member who had survived unscathed 13 months in Vietnam, carrying an M-60 when he wasn't packing an M-16 in the bush. The bolt on his AR-15 wasn't peened. He got it together wrong. He was very, very P.O.'d about the non-standard bolt his rifle had. If your rifle lacks the peening, you can't peen it, it is too hard. You can (and should) complain to the maker. If they can't or won't help, you'll just have to be very careful every time you assemble your bolt and carrier, to get it together correctly.

To reassemble, press the extractor into the slot and push firmly. The new spring, or spring and D-fender, will add resistance. Then press the extractor pin through until it is flush.

Lube the bolt, paying particular attention to the extractor and ejector, and the extractor seat.

Carrier Cleaning

There is nothing to take off the carrier for cleaning. First, scrub the exterior. The front tunnel on the carrier, where the bolt rides, will be carboned up quite severely. There are no brushes that work well there. What you'll need is a carbon scraper from Mark Brown, which you can get from Brownells. Insert the scraper, turn, and extract. The carbon will be scraped out, or at least what the scraper can get. Don't worry about what it leaves behind, it is very little and not going to be a problem. With the carrier clean, proceed to your inspection.

First, check the carrier key. It must be tight on the carrier. You'll see two screws holding it on, screws that should be staked in place. Grab the carrier with one hand, and with the other try to move the key. If it moves at all, it must be tightened. If it is loose, proceed to take it off. (You cannot simply tighten the screws and count on their holding. They came loose once, they'll come loose again.) Scrub the key and carrier and degrease them, and the screws and screw holes. Apply Loctite to both key and carrier, and the screws and holes, and tighten the screws back down. Wipe the excess Loctite off the exterior, and use a Q-tip to wipe up any inside the bolt tunnel. Then re-stake the screws. (This is one of the two applications of Loctite I recommend on the entire rifle. Others use it a couple of other places, but I do not.) Sinclair makes a carrier key brush for scrubbing the key. I'd never cleaned a key before I saw this brush. When I used it on my rifles an embarrassing amount of crud came out of each and every one of them. Does it matter? I don't know. On my rifles it obviously didn't, as they all ran fine without getting the key scrubbed. Might it matter on your rifle? Perhaps, only time and testing will tell. All mine will get at least an annual key scrubbing from now on.

When re-securing the key, why not just tighten and re-stake? Once the screws come loose, oil and powder residue works its way into the threads. Once oil and powder residue get there, you cannot tighten the screws as much as they had been, and that obviously wasn't enough anyway. And screws can work loose even under staking, and simply lift the key with them as they turn. Instead, remove it, scrub it, and secure it again.

Inspect the front of the carrier, on the top. Look to see if it is cracked from the front to the cam pin hole. If your rifle had been built with a high-mileage surplus carrier, it may be cracked or become cracked after you've shot it. Cracked is bad, and you'll need a new carrier.

If it passes the inspection, lube the exterior and the bolt tunnel.

The Rest Of The Parts

Wipe the firing pin, cam pin and cotter pin clean. Scrub them if you need to, to remove all carbon. Inspect the firing pin for burrs on the tip, and on the rear collar. AR firing pins and M-16 firing pins differ in collar diameter, and depending on what parts your rifle was built with, the collar may get burred from being banged against the hammer. The cam pin gets a buildup of carbon right at the edge where it bears against the cam slot in the carrier. The cotter pin gets grubby, but doesn't really take a load of any kind. You usually find them knarfed from heavy-handed assembly, and not from shooting.

Reassembly Of Bolt And Carrier

Wipe the tail of the bolt clean and then lubricate it. Make sure the gas rings are staggered. Push the bolt back into the carrier, line the cam pin up with the slot, and push the cam pin into place. Make sure the extractor is on the right side of the carrier, as seen from above. Rotate the cam pin. Push the firing pin in the rear of the carrier. If you have an M-16 or modified M-16 carrier, you'll have to hold the carrier vertically and drop the pin in through the rear. AR-15 carriers have enough clearance that you can work the firing pin in from

underneath. Push the bolt forward, and then press the firing pin as far forward as it will go. Press the cotter key in from the left side. You may have to rotate it to get both legs into the far side hole.

Once assembled, check assembly. Turn the carrier onto its rear and tap it against your hand or a table. If the firing pin comes out, you didn't have it far enough forward, and the cotter pin didn't catch it. Remove the cotter pin, press the firing pin forward, and make sure the firing pin shoulder is forward of the cotter pin on assembly.

Once together, check the gas ring tension. Pull the bolt all the way forward, then stand the bolt and carrier assembly on the face of the bolt. If the weight of the carrier is enough to collapse the assembly, you need new gas rings. If it stands, there is enough friction.

Reassembly Of Upper

Run the operating handle forward into the upper, then hold the front end of it up against the interior of the operating handle slot. Pull the handle back, and you'll feel the locking tabs of the operating handle click into the access slot. Push the handle forward just enough to keep it from falling out. Make sure the bolt is forward, and insert the bolt and carrier assembly into the upper with the carrier key entering the slot on the underside of the operating handle. Once inserted, push the carrier and operating handle all the way forward, until the carrier is flush with the receiver, and the handle locks in place.

Lower Receiver

On the table in front of you are the trigger control parts of the lower, the buffer weight and spring, the pistol grip and

Make sure your key is tight. Wiggle it. If it moves, tighten it or replace the screws and use Loctite.

The lower uses a different brush.
Get the internals out, first.

screw, and the spring and plunger of the safety selector.

Scrub the carbon off of the fire control parts. Leave the disconnector spring attached to the trigger. Scrub the interior of the lower, where the hammer and trigger reside. Swab the gunk out of the buffer tube. For those of you with a tele-stock, there is no need to remove the stock unless you've fallen into water, mud or the peculiar combination of the two they have down in Louisiana. Then, you simply pull down on the whole locking assembly, and slide the stock off of the rear of the tube. Those with solid stocks need not remove the stock. But the buffer tube can collect debris. So, you swab it out. Wipe the buffer and spring clean.

Inspection

Look at the hammer and trigger to make sure the springs are correctly installed. And to memorize the correct orientation. In almost every class, we have at least one range session where a rifle that has been incorrectly assembled fails to work.

Look at the hammer, trigger and disconnector for cracks, peened areas or corrosion. On the hammer, look to make sure the internal spring, the one that acts to keep the hammer on the pivot pin, is there. They have been known to break. A broken spring can result in a hammer pin that walks, and a malfunctioning rifle. On both the hammer and trigger, look at the sear surfaces. Make sure they are not chipped or worn. There will be scuff marks, because they slide against each other in normal operation. Chips or rounded corners are bad. Look at the disconnector. The front tip, on the bottom, is the timing tab. If the disconnector was advanced in timing too

much, excessive amounts of metal may have been removed, weakening it. Look for cracks at the rear of the tab. If the tab is cracked, you'll have to replace it and re-time the new disconnector.

Look at the buffer. If the face is heavily marred, and had not been originally, you may have a rifle that is getting too much gas. While you can replace the buffer, if the problem is a too-large gas port, the new buffer won't last any longer than the old one had. The buffer should have solid weights in it that "clack" back and forth as you shake it. The weights turn the buffer into a dead-blow hammer. Do not use the buffers made of plastic, with lead shot in them. They may weigh the same, but they do not work the same.

Count the number of coils in the buffer spring. A standard spring should have 41 to 43 coils, and a tele-stock rifle should have 37 to 39. And the appropriate buffer. Do not use a short buffer in a standard rifle. To do so allows the carrier to over-cycle, and the key may strike the rear of the receiver. If you're lucky, you'll shear off the key screws. If you're unlucky, you'll crack the receiver. A shorty with a standard buffer will not cycle, as the buffer is too long to allow the bolt to fully travel.

Reassembly

First the buffer and spring. Competition shooters like to heavily grease the spring, to reduce or eliminate the "boing" of the AR when it cycles. However, in a defensive application, you should avoid heavy grease. Use a light oil or TW-25 aerosol. Push the spring into the buffer tube, then the buffer itself. Press it back past the retaining pin.

Insert the trigger into the lower, and press the pivot

pin partway into the trigger. Press just enough to catch the trigger. Then insert the disconnector. Holding the lower on its side, look through the hole on the other side and line up the disconnector hole. Press the pivot pin all the way through. Insert the safety. You may have to press the tail of the trigger down to clear the safety. Take the safety plunger spring and wrap the end of it with a bit of masking tape. Stuff the taped end down into the pistol grip hole. Press the safety plunger into the receiver, and then install the pistol grip. Keep the spring lined up with the plunger as you tighten the screw.

Grab the hammer between thumb and forefinger, and press the legs of its spring down onto the pivot pin of the trigger. Then press the hammer down into the lower, lining it up with its pivot pin holes. Press the pivot pin into the hammer. Turn the lower over, and looking through the receiver hole, line the hammer up with the pivot pin hole on your side. Then use the tabletop (benchtop, etc) to push the hammer pin through until it is flush.

Now look down into the lower receiver. Are the legs of the hammer spring on each side of, and outside of, the trigger spring? If not, use a small screwdriver or knifetip to move the legs over.

AR-15 Checklist

The checklist is not just for buying a used rifle. You could find yourself as a law enforcement officer being handed one for the first time, or handed one in an emergency. Or being handed yet another anonymous rifle out of the rack, as your department doesn't issue particular rifles to individual officers. (A bad idea, by the way, to issue at random. It is far better to individual-issue.) Or you find yourself in a red-hot screaming emergency defensive situation, and you've got one minute to make sure the rifle you've been handed has all its necessary parts before you'll be shooting at people who are shooting at you.

And for those who are looking to buy a used rifle, just what should you look for to see to it that you don't end up with a lemon? In none of the situations described do you have the time or opportunity to function-fire the rifle in your hands. In a law enforcement situation, you're expected to sign the paperwork (after checking serial numbers, something of far more importance to the issuing desk than "does it work?") And when buying used, unless you're at a range, loading it and shooting it is going to get you ejected from the gun show, arrested and probably prosecuted.

(U.S. Army photo by Staff Sgt. Charles B. Johnson)

Now is not the time to be wondering if your carrier key is tight. You can bet these soldiers in the 82nd Airborne knew their rifles worked long before they found themselves in Fallujah.

Short Checklist, What You Can Do In A Minute:

All Present And Tight Check

Give the exterior a quick look-over. Is the stock tight? Are the handguards tight? Is the front sight housing secure to the barrel, and upright? Is there a front sight, and how tall is it? (Is it screwed 'way down or up? It might be mis-zeroed, or it might be zeroed and that's where the sight has to be. Both are bad signs.) Is the rear sight present? Centered? If an A2, is the rear drum three clicks up from bottom, with the sight at 3/6 or 3/8? Is the upper slightly or greatly loose on the lower? Or rigid and unmoving?

Bore Check

Open the action and remove the bolt and carrier. If the pins are very tight and difficult to move, and the rifle is not built as an NRA High Power or Service Rifle competition piece, ask why it is tight. Once the bolt is out, look down the bore to make sure you see daylight. (You'd be surprised.)

Firing Pin Check

Make sure the firing pin is forward of the retaining cotter pin. If it is behind, it will fall out, and even if it doesn't fall out it won't fire. Push the bolt back and then push the rear of the firing pin forward. Does it protrude from the bolt face? If it does, good. If not, something is wrong. That something may simply be storage grease, but it might be a broken or short firing pin. Find out.

Bolt Face

While you're looking at the firing pin, inspect the bolt face. A re-used and refinished bolt that has seen a lot of rounds will have wear on its face around the firing pin hole, where the primer radius is. Some will be burnishing, and abused ones will show pitting from the occasional leaky primer.

Gas Ring Check

Snap the bolt forward, and then stand the bolt and carrier assembly on the bolt. The weight of the bolt should not cause it to collapse. If the friction is so slight that the carrier drops down on the bolt, it needs new gas rings.

Gas Key Check

Is the carrier key on to of the carrier tight? If not, the rifle will short stroke. To quote the movie "Casablanca:" "Maybe not now, but soon, and for the rest of your life." Or at least until you get it secured.

Fire Control Check

Does the safety flip from Safe to Fire easily? Too easily may mean it is a worn, used, replacement part. Or that it has been abused, neglected or mis-assembled. If it is difficult to move, it may just be storage grease, or it may be incorrect assembly.

Once you've checked movement, then check by dry-firing and checking timing. If the owner won't let you, or the gun show regulations require that the action be cable-tied shut, then you can only go by the owner's assurance that it works. Get it in writing!

Five-Minute Checklist: Bore Check

In addition to looking down the bore, inspect the crown for dents, dings or uncleaned powder residue. Some people like to sell used guns as new, but neglect to clean the flash hider. New rifles are test-fired at the factory, but not very much. If you have one, a chamber mirror (Brownells has them) gives you a chance to see if the chamber is crusty, pitted, neglected or needs a cleaning. A chamber brush is useful to scrub the chamber clean, as is a cleaning rod. If you can, run a patch down the bore to see how clean it is, and to get a feel for any roughness.

Firing Pin Check

Pull the firing pin out and look it over. Check to make sure it is straight. Is the tip clean, smooth and rounded? A rifle that has seen blown primers may have a chipped or eroded firing pin tip.

Gas Key Check

Make sure the gas key is tight, staked, and straight. Inspect the front for wear, banging or chips. A banged-up gas key may work just fine, but if it is on a rifle that is offered as a "low mileage creampuff" then there is something wrong.

Gas Ring Check

After you do the headstand check, disassemble the bolt and carrier and look at the gas rings. There should be three of them, the gaps should not line up, and they should not be worn. Gas rings are cheap and easy to replace, but worn gas rings on a supposedly new or low-mileage rifle should be a warning.

Fire Control Check

Does the lever move smoothly? If so, then check the trigger timing and trigger pull weight. Check that the safety does indeed prevent the hammer from falling: Put the safety on, then pull the trigger. It must not fall. If it does, there is something seriously wrong, and it must be fixed. Then, release the trigger, push the selector to Fire, and dry fire. Is the trigger pull markedly different than before? (When you hadn't pre-loaded the trigger.) If it is, then the safety is not completely blocking the trigger, and the trigger is moving slightly when the safety is on. Again it must be fixed.

Magazine Inspection

Do magazine insert smoothly, and without binding? Do they fall free of their own weight when the bolt is locked back.

Magazines For The AR-15

The AR-15 is saddled with the worst magazines of any rifle I've ever encountered. They are flimsy, delicate, poorly designed and in many cases shoddily made. They can be maddeningly variable in their reliability, prone to damage simply from being dropped, and even when working properly always a cause for suspicion. The basic 20-round USGI magazine weighs a mere 3 ounces, while the 30-round magazine weighs in at an ounce more. The ammunition they hold weighs two and a half to three times as much as the magazine itself does. One's first impression of an AR magazine is that if it were any less substantial it would be disposable. And there were some early efforts at making disposable magazines for the M-16. My friend Duane Thomas, a fellow gun writer, was a jump-qualified Clerk-Typist in the 82nd Airborne in the 1980s. (And proud of it. Someone had to do the paperwork, and despite what some might tell you, not everyone with jump wings has led a life of danger.) His comment to me on the subject of magazines was: "In 10 years on active duty, I only ever made it through one 40-round qualification without at least one malfunction. However, my own personal belief, I think this had a lot more to do with the state of the magazines than any flaws in the gun." The magazine of the AR's direct competitors, and contemporary rifles, are all durable and reliable to a fault. The AK magazine is so tough that when loaded with steel-cased ammunition it can actually be considered low-grade body armor. The magazines of the M-14 and the FN-FAL are so sturdy you can literally run them over with a truck or car and justifiably expect them to work. So how is it that the AR-15 is stuck with such a wretched excuse of a magazine? Remember, when we were talking about the fits and starts of the M-16 adoption and production? The magazine was part of that dysfunctional process.

That said, I've always had extraordinarily good luck with AR magazines. All my magazines were picked up at gun shows, or bought along with used rifles, or police department rejects that I rebuilt or simply cleaned up and used. And once I tossed the absolutely wretched magazines, the ones that wouldn't work in any rifle, I had no problems with the remaining ones. I suspect that part of my good luck with magazines stems from their being owned and used by a gunsmith. All my ARs through the years have been tuned to work 100 percent. If you want to improve the odds of your magazines working all the time you should tend to the particulars of your rifle and its feed system. And if you pay attention to magazine maintenance and selection, you will have a rifle that is an exemplar of reliability.

Just as the rifle was adopted without serious input from Ordnance, and as a result had teething problems, so was the magazine treated. Had the M-16 gone through a rational adoption process, the weaknesses of the magazine would have been identified and addressed. What probably would have happened was that the flimsy construction of the magazine

These Sig magazines are made of a tough polycarbonate, they clip together, and they are nearly indestructible. Too bad we can't make them work in our ARs.

The magazines of the rifles the AR replaced, the M-14 and the FAL, can survive being run over by a car or truck.

would have been addressed in one of two ways: by using a heavier thickness of aluminum sheet as the starting point, or making them from steel to begin with. The former would have required adjusting the magazine well dimensions to accommodate the magazine (a small problem early enough) or altering the fabricating dies to accommodate steel instead of aluminum. Again, a simple process early-on.

Instead, the magazine was adopted as-is. Just as the rifle itself was not to be altered (the McNamara Whiz Kids said it was perfect, so leave it alone) so were the magazines. So, we began with 20-round magazines of aluminum, which actually aren't too bad.

Tour Of The Magazine

The AR-15/M-16 magazine, like all other detachable rifle magazines, is a rectangular tube containing a spring, follower and baseplate. On all magazines I can think of, the baseplate is removable for cleaning. Unlike the old design of 1911 magazines, weaseling the follower out of the top of the magazine between the feed lips is not feasible. The spring is too strong, the follower too tight a fit, and the feed lips too close together to allow such a system. The follower in all magazines is meant to fit and function only when

The AR, like other rifles, is a double-feed, that is, rounds feed alternately from one side then the other.

installed correctly. Ditto the spring. Baseplates can be put on incorrectly, but it is obvious (unlike the spring) and won't stay without the use of duct tape.

On the top you'll see the feed lips. The AR feeds from a double-stack/double-track magazine. (Also known as double-stack/alternate-feed.) A 1911 is a single/single, and the Browning Hi-Power or Sten gun is a double/single. The ideal feeding method for any magazine-fed firearm is single/single, simply from the viewpoint of cartridge control and uniformity of feed. However, the double/double is plenty reliable enough. (Some have their doubts about the double/single, but in a properly engineered and fabricated magazine it works just fine. When badly done, however, it can be a sorry mess.) The feed lips are critical, for if they are not properly shaped they will not reliably present the cartridge to the chamber each time. Cracked, bent, altered or "adjusted" feed lips are not to be trusted. If someone hands you a magazine with the advice "I think I've got the feed lips working properly now" you should decline the opportunity to shoot any more of their ammunition, or use their magazines. Even when expensive, magazines are cheap enough that trying to get a recalcitrant magazine working by bending the feed lips is an utter waste of time. With one exception. I have seen magazines altered to be single-stack/single-feed, with the intent to use them to feed reloads using 80-grain low-drag Match bullets. The result is a 20-round tube that holds about eight shots, and allows the use of the extra-long bullets.

The feed path of the cartridge is not the smooth, even experience you'd expect. I've watched high-speed video (1,000 frames a second) of AR-15s and M-16s firing. The cartridge practically rattles around on its way to the chamber. I've seen rounds get the rim up to the top of the bolt, before camming back down into line with the chamber as it went forward. In the end, the only measure you can use is this: does it work? If it does, it is a good magazine. If it doesn't, it isn't a good magazine for you and your rifle.

Materials Of The Magazine

Original magazines were made both of steel and aluminum. (Not in the same magazine, mind you.) But when volume production got started, they were all aluminum. As all aluminum magazines are either actual surplus, or contract over-runs from manufacturers making them for the government, there isn't a supply of cheap, soft, aluminum magazines. Which is good. If you have a magazine in good shape, i.e., no hammer marks or tire tracks, and the finish is mostly there, you're most of the way to having a reliable magazine. If the follower moves smoothly up and down when you check it, and the baseplate doesn't have egregious marks from abuse or heavy-handed disassembly, go ahead and bargain a good price on it. (Well, after you check the reports on particular brands you can find on many web pages.)

I do not want to quote prices, as the market can change quickly. If the law changes, or the government insists on

The H-K high-reliability magazines are just that. They could also be called the H-K high-cost magazines, too.

purchasing all magazines made (like there was a war on, or something) the market value of existing magazines could skyrocket. If the law relaxes, there could easily be a glut of brand-new magazines, bringing prices down. And those of you who live in such places as California, Hawaii or New Jersey, with state laws covering magazines, are not helped by improvements at the federal level.

But a magazine in good shape, from a recognized manufacturer, is always worth bargaining over, in case you can get it at a price you can feel good about. They don't go bad on the shelf.

There are bad magazines out there. Some are steel, some are plastic, and some are abused.

Steel Magazines

The bad ones are (almost without exception) USA brand magazines. There will be others lacking a name, but they look the same as the USA. You can recognize them by their relatively bight blue finish, their near-gloss surface, and their soft metal. In the course of teaching rifle classes for over a decade now, I have seen a literal bushel basket full of magazines from USA that were not reliable. (And I cannot recall a single one that was immediately and obviously reliable.) I have seen a few that seemed to be, but no one, not even the officer they were issued to, was willing to try them long enough to establish a track record. The problem is, the steel is not tempered, and the lips will bend. If they are dropped the magazine can stop working immediately. Any impact can reduce their reliability. And being soft, the temptation is to bend them back to shape, which invariably makes things worse. Until USA tempers the feed lips to make them strong enough to resist impact, I will not use them and cannot recommend that you use them. If USA does decide to heat-treat the feeds lips (at least the feed lips, the whole tube would be better) I'd be happy to test and report on them. Until then, pass on them.

There are good steel magazines. When Great Britain decided they were going to adopt a 5.56 rifle for their Armed Forces, they decided to design and manufacture their own.

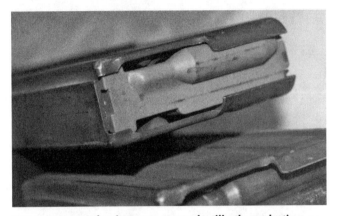

Some mags are aluminum, some steel, still others plastic. What works, works, but you'll have best luck with GI aluminum magazines.

Steel magazines from Singapore are very reliable and durable. Of course, steel rusts, but you can't have everything.

The Enfield 80 turned out to be a hopeless mess, an unreliable rifle, and an embarrassment to all involved. (Even after H-K was called in to fix it, they couldn't.) The one bright spot was that it was intended to be able to use standard M-16 magazines. The British, not fond of aluminum, had theirs made of steel. The "Made in England" steel magazines you see have all been reliable and durable magazines. Ditto the near-identical ones made in Singapore. I have both, and have found them to be as reliable as my tested aluminum magazines. If you must have steel, get one (or a bunch) of these. As with all things mechanical, there are no guarantees. In the course of testing all these rifles, I found a couple that didn't like the British or Singapore steel mags. One rifle would drop the magazine when firing. Use aluminum magazines and it was fine. Again, your rifle is your guide. If it won't work in your rifle, it is a bad magazine. ("Bad magazine, bad magazine! Go to your room!")

And if anyone tries to convince you that USA are as good as the British or Singapore magazines, take anything else they say with a grain of salt, too.

When H-K attempted to improve the SA80/Enfield 85, one of the engineering projects they undertook was to improve the magazine. As you would expect from the people who

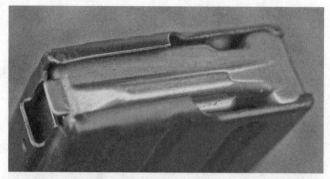

The stainless steel follower. It will rust, just not very quickly.

designed the G-3 rifle, the H-K magazine is tough, reliable and gorgeous. The government procurement office refers to it as the "High Reliability Magazine" and it is just that. It is also expensive, rare, and did I mention expensive? As I said, the H-K magazine came about as a result of their attempt to improve the British SA/80 Enfield 85 to something more than "dreadful." The result is a thing of beauty. The tube is steel, seam-welded and sturdy. The tube is a bit longer and ends in a sharper angle than USGI magazines. Whether that is to accommodate a stronger spring, or the follower, I don't know. The follower is stainless steel, and moves like there are ball bearings between it and the tube. Are they great magazines? Without a doubt. Are they worth the cost? You'll have to decide that for yourself.

One source of steel magazines that can be good or bad, is Sterling. Back before the British government banned guns in a futile attempt at controlling crime, Sterling made AR-180 rifles and magazines, and exported them to the United States. Among the magazines they made (which worked in both AR-180 and AR-15 rifles) were 20-, 30- and 40-round magazines in steel and aluminum. You might never see the 20-or 30-round magazines, but the 40s show up at gun ranges on a regular basis. In an attempt at gaining an advantage, some shooters will cross their fingers and use a 40-round magazine in a practical rifle course. Not all work. However, I've had good luck making them work with a complete

The 40-round magazines can be reliable, but you should replace the springs, and you must test to be sure.

Thermolds are plastic magazines of pretty good quality.

internal transplant, as covered in the Maintenance section. The aspect of the Sterling magazines that kept them in play is that they were designed to work in both the AR-15 and the AR-18 or AR-180. Anyone with an AR-18 or 180 is always on the lookout for magazines that will work in their rifle.

One drawback to steel magazines is rust. Unless you keep them lightly oiled, they may rust in some climates. If you know a plater or refinisher, you can get yours heavily parkerized or plated with something protective. Otherwise, you'll have to stay alert and perform maintenance.

Plastic Magazines

The fashion, as we have all had drilled into us by Glock, is to call them "polymer" magazines. I guess I just got started too soon, as they are all plastic to me. I have a pair of plastic magazines marked "Eaton" that were an early attempt at "one-size-fits-all." They are intended to work in AR-15, AR-18 and Ruger Mini-14 rifles. They do not seem terribly sturdy, but I have now gotten well over 15 years of service out of them without any failures in my AR-15s. Which only goes to show that there is always an exception to any blanket statement. They never worked all that well in my Ruger Mini-14, and were worse in my AR-18.

The best plastic magazines are the Orlite. Made in Israel, they are tough but have some peculiarities you need to watch out for. The earliest production apparently lacked metal reinforcements at the lips. (I've never seen one, only been told of them, in 20 years of AR use. They must be rare.) Look for the mesh pattern of the metal stiffening insert to be sure. Original production magazines have side fences that prevent over-insertion of the magazine into the rifle. The fences were proportioned to work with Colt lowers. Other makers' magazine wells were not tapered so sharply, and Orlites can fail to lock in place in other rifles. Later production magazines had the fences altered (or rather, the mould to make them was altered) to allow their use in non-Colt rifles.) And they can be good bargains. The problem with Orlite magazines is that they were surplus from the Israeli Defense Forces. The highest level of maintenance you're likely to see in an IDF unit is "Benign Neglect." Below that are; "Utter Neglect," "Equipment Prop" and "So, that's what a cleaning brush looks like?" Any Orlite you get will have led a hard life before it ever saw this side of the Atlantic Ocean.

Less durable are the Canadian Thermold magazines. Original American Thermolds are OK magazines. The Canadians went with a less durable formula of plastic, and their magazines have been dubbed "Thermelts" by the CDF. Apparently, when you're pressing your M-4 (or in the case of Canadians, C-8) into service as a SAW, you can get the rifle hot enough via full-auto fire to melt the feed lips of the magazine. You can recognize the Canadian Thermolds by the maple leaf moulded into them. The others come with two mouldmarkings, "21" and "22." Apparently, the 21s had the fence moulded a fraction of an inch too high to fit

The patent number is on the baseplate, if you want to look it up.

There is a Thermold mold number 21, and 22. If your AR is picky about it, you'd better check before you buy.

into all lowers. So the mould was adjusted, re-marked, and production resumed. If you have Thermolds that won't lock in place, look at the mould number.

Lowest on the list of plastic magazines are all the others. I have the Eatons I mentioned (which bear a remarkable resemblance to Ramline magazines of the time), and a clutch of Orlites, and they have worked. I've seen Thermolds used. All other plastic magazines for the AR-15/M-16 that I've seen have failed.

It is interesting to note that after experimenting with synthetic magazines, both the CDF and IDF ditched them all and went with aluminum USGI magazines. Many shooters I know use Orlites and Thermolds only as range mags. They practice with their plastic, but their duty or defense magazines are aluminum. I do not know any shooter who does it the other way, practicing with aluminum and packing plastic when potentially going in harm's way.

Aluminum

Stick with aluminum magazines, from recognizable manufacturers, either magazine makers or rifle makers. I've had some shooters bad-mouth magazines made with rifle manufacturers' names on the baseplates, but those I've seen have worked. They were obviously a sub-contract from the original, no-doubt USGI, magazine maker. If you buy enough of anything, the maker will put your name on it. Offer to buy 1,000, or 10,000 magazines, and the maker is likely to be pleased as punch to put anything on the baseplate you want. (Provided it isn't libelous, treasonous, or offends the sensibilities of the manufacturing staff.)

Aluminum magazines will have a hardcoat anodized finish in silver, with a black anodized aluminum baseplate. The followers may be bright or dull alloy, black plastic, or the new bright green anti-tip. Some aluminum magazines will have a black Teflon coating. The Teflon is not a USGI-approved treatment, although it wouldn't surprise me to see some of them over in Iraq. When there's a war on, you use what the makers are making.

The Twenty

The original magazines were basically scaled-down 20-shot magazines derived from the M-14 magazine. As that rifle had had a decade of engineering done to it, it was a sturdy and reliable piece of gear. While the aluminum AR-15 magazines aren't as tough as the steel M-14 magazines, they are still quite good. The 20-shot M-16 magazines are so good that many shooters prefer them over all others. The compactness of the tube creates a stiff construct, and the feed lips hanging loose in the air is actually a good thing. As they are not attached at the rear, they can flex slightly against impact and survive. I've dropped 20-round mags on their feed lips and had them survive. The 30-shot magazines, with welded feed lips, have been known to crack if they fall on the lips.

Original 20-round magazines have bright or dull aluminum followers. Later ones have black plastic followers. The latest followers are the bright green anti-tip followers. However, as the 20-shot magazines are not prone to follower bind in the tube, you needn't swap out your existing followers for the green ones as a matter of course. If you do, be aware that the 20- and 30-round followers are not interchangeable. If you want new green followers in your 20-round magazines, be sure to order twenties and not thirties. The 20-round AR magazine fell off the charts for military orders in the early 1970s, being replaced by the 30-round magazine. If you do find some, good old NSN 1005-056-2237 will last you a long time.

Types Of The Twenty

You won't find a whole lot of variety in 20-shot magazines. Collectors and some shooters desire them, but many shooters want only 20-round magazines. Basically, you'll find lots of Colt-marked aluminum magazines, and some Simmond-marked ones. Some of the Colt magazines will be blocked to hold only five rounds. Colt made them to offer their customers who had hunting regulations prohibiting the use of magazines greater than five rounds while in the field. You can recognize them by the rivet on the baseplate. The rivet holds the baseplate to the retaining tab on the inside of the magazine. Inside the magazine you'll find a sheet metal "U" that restricts the travel of the follower. If you drill out the rivet, disassemble the magazine, and pull out the U, you have a 20-round magazine. Doing so may not be permitted in some states, so be sure you aren't committing a felony (I'm not kidding!) if you do it. Other short magazines you'll find are a result of the late and unlamented Assault Weapons Ban of 1994. In the AWB/94, no new magazine could be made that held more than 10 rounds. The "Post-Ban" magazines were all made with a plastic lower half, or a pinched and crimped middle section. It you tried to alter the magazine to make it hold more rounds, it will come apart on you. With the sunset of the AWB, makers are no longer fabricating the 10-shot versions. I'm sure those unfortunate shooters stuck in states with laws against hi-cap mags would be happy to take the AWB 10-shot mags off our hands.

One curious 20-round magazine you may see are what appear to be short 30-round tubes. These 20-round magazines have a short, curved section at the bottom. Why? I don't know, as those who make magazines are remarkably closed-mouthed about what they do and why. All I can surmise is that the idea of 20-round magazines being more reliable than 30-round magazines has gained such currency that the magazine manufacturers are slipping the short plates into 30-round forming dies. (So to speak. It isn't just that easy.) You need not worry about seeing too many of them, as the design did not come about until after the AWB/94 was enacted, so all the ones as of this writing (August 2004) have been made for law enforcement use only. The markings mean nothing now, except as curiosities.

There are some interesting 20-round magazines: they look like shortened thirties. Here is a pair in a Redi-mag carrier.

The Thirty

As you'd expect, the grunts of Vietnam felt a bit put out by all the changes. It was bad enough giving up a "real" rifle for a plastic toy. But the little toy, despite its light weight, didn't have any more rounds than the big ones did. And the bad guys had 30-shot magazines! Everyone immediately recognized that a larger magazine was desirable and possible. Except for one thing. Colt. You see, the previous AR rifles had not been made on a continuous production line. Rifles then were not like automobiles, where once the line was set up product poured off the other end. Rifles were made in batches. Each order or contract caused the tooling to be hauled out, set up, tested and rifles made. Colt wasn't sure the government was going to actually buy a bunch of AR-15s, and if they didn't, then target shooters and hunters probably wouldn't, either. Colt had better uses for their shop floor than leaving the AR-15 tooling standing in place. And as long as the existing rifles, of whatever production batch, reliably used 20-round magazines, everything was fine. When the word got out that the troops desired 30-round magazines, the Colt designers went to work. The correct geometry for a 30-round magazine using the 5.56 cartridge calls for a gentle arc. The tube should be curved along its entire length. The only problem was, the rifles had been made for straight-tube 20-round magazines. The magazine wells in the rifles would not all accept curved magazines. And the only way to tell was to try those curved magazines in each and every rifle in the government inventories.

As the procurement of M-16 rifles was already a snarling pit of accusations, recriminations and attempts at scoring political points, Colt didn't want to admit that their previous rifles might not all work with a properly designed magazine. So they got to work stalling the government, while trying to come up with a design that would work in all rifles. What they came up with was, in effect, the bottom of a proper magazine attached to a straight magazine. Yes, that is why your AR magazines are all "straight and curved." Because Colt couldn't afford to 'fess up. (If they had, the AR-15 probably would have died there and then, as there were still competitive designs the Ordnance Department favored.)

The problem, then and now, is that the stack of cartridges, and the follower lifting them, gets down past the curve below the straight section. (If it didn't, you wouldn't need longer magazines to fit 30 rounds, just the straight section would do.) So the rounds, and the follower, have to make the turn from the straight to the curved section. Why not make the magazine all straight? You could, but it would probably feed worse than the current ones. The curve accounts for the natural curve of the stack of tapered cartridges. If you leave the tube straight, by the time you stuff 30 rounds in, the bottom rounds are going to be at a very sharp angle, in relation to the tube walls front and back.

Up at the top, the feed lips of the 30-round magazines are

The 30-round magazine has its feed lips secured at the rear, to take the spring tension when loaded.

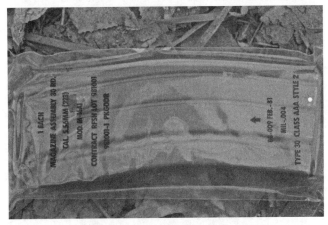

These curious magazines can't be found in any contract listing. They look mil-spec, but aren't even though they are professionally packaged. Just one of the curiosities of the AR.

If anyone knows the history of these magazines, let me know for Volume 2, would you?

folded continuations of the spine of the magazine. Again, why the change from the 20-round magazines? The spring of the 30-round magazine has to lift half again as much weight as the spring of the 20-round magazine. The feed lips have to resist the force of that spring. So, they're designed to be attached to the spine for more stiffness.

The early 30-round magazines, as with the twenties, had bright or dull aluminum followers. Later production magazines had black plastic followers. The 30-round magazines, with their straight and curved shape, were more

The REAL Hi-Caps

The old Rock 'n roll adage "too much is never enough" has been applied to everything. Including magazines. If a 30- or 40-round magazine isn't enough, then what? Well, there are drums. One was the M.W.G. magazine, a 90-round magazine built as a spiral. Made out of plastic, the MWG is one of those "God its goofy, where can I get one?" kind of things. The weight is all on the left side, the friction of the rounds, follower and spring going down that spiral makes it hard to load, and not always reliable in feeding. It definitely falls in the "mall ninja" category of gear.

Other mall ninja magazines are the Chinese drum magazines brought in before the AWB/94. Made from the body of an AK drum, with an AR vertical adapter, they looked solid, being all-steel. But all steel is not the same, and precision parts made by slave labor in a third-world "people's republic" are not all that precise. If you can get one at a good cost, make sure it works reliably before shelling out any money at all for it.

The really cool magazine, one that falls into the "CDI" and not mall ninja, is the Beta C-mag. While it seems it is like the MWG and made of plastic, the Beta is made of a filled thermoplastic, using fibers for added strength, and a heat-curing resin for strength. It uses two spiral feeds that come into a vertical feed tube. It holds 100 rounds and does not project lower from the rifle than a 30-round magazine does. It is very reliable, and it should be for the price. After the AWB/94 was passed, the seemingly "high" price of $250 shot up to "whatever the marker

would bear." As in, $600 to $700 dollars on the open market. Curiously, those who had Class 3 licenses found the price not going so high. After all, if you're licensed for a machinegun, getting a hi-cap feeding device was no problem. The rest of us had to pay big bucks to get one. And Law Enforcement sales were at the original price.

Now that the ban is gone, the price is down to normal levels. I'm still not sure what use a Beta mag has, but they can be a whole lot of fun. Especially if you have access to someone else's select-fire rifle. A hundred rounds can be hard on a barrel if fired in less than a mnute.

The Beta top is just like a standard AR mag, and locks in place normally.

The Beta even comes in a special mag pouch to mount on your web gear.

The Beta mags are reliable 100-round dual drums, guaranteed to be the fastest way to wear out a barrel or wallet.

prone to feeding problems than the 20-round tubes. In an attempt to solve the problems, we have just recently been treated to the new, anti-tip followers. They have longer "legs" front and back, to keep them from tipping and binding in the tube. The new anti-tip followers can be recognized by their bright green color. (Except for the followers from MagPul, which are coyote brown) Combined with a new spring, the combination can resurrect some otherwise unreliable magazines.

Through it all, the 30-round magazine has been known by its national stock number; 1005-00-921-5004. You can actually go on line and do a search using that number, and come up with all sorts of interesting information. Like, how many get made in a contract, and how much they cost. Usually, 300,000 to 400,000 at a time in a big order, and 50,000 to 100,000 in a "small" order. And the latest price

I recall seeing was $7.40 per. Delivered, in sealed plastic wrappers. So, if someone is offering you new in the wrapper magazines at $11 or $12, you're getting a good deal.

Markings

The whole subject of who makes magazines, how many they make, and what goes into it (and comes out of it) is so shrouded in secrecy that you'd think it was something of a national security subject. (Geez, they're just magazines!) I've had magazine manufacturers hang up on me once they found out who I was and what I was doing. Another gave me the phone number of a DoD office I could call and ask about magazines. Except they gave it so hurriedly I had to call back and get the rest of the number. You'd think I was calling to find a good price and location of the nearest black market for plutonium. The DoD office still hasn't gotten back

The date codes don't mean anything now that the AWB/94 has sunset. Thank goodness.

to me, by the way, some nine months after my request. One manufacturer said they'd answer any questions I submitted in writing. (I'm still waiting for answers there, also.) One offered a few bits of info, but swore me to secrecy. And I thought radio broadcasting was a competitive, secretive, cut-throat business.

One firearms wholesaler who worked with a magazine manufacturer said it was frustrating in the extreme. Samples were out of spec, and wouldn't work in test rifles. GI followers would bind in the new tubes. Spring wire was under dimension, short of coils, or quickly took a set. They almost gave up on the whole thing. "Pat, we weren't going to carry something that we couldn't get to work in our own rifles." After that, I understood better why the whole subject is secret. In that kind of an environment, if I found a supplier who delivered quality stuff, I'd keep them a secret, too.

Add to that the "non-compete" and "non-disclosure" clauses in government contracts, with the associated thought of a slavering pack of Department of Justice lawyers being loosed on you, and you'd be closed-mouthed about what your company did, too.

Magazines are almost anonymous. You'll find markings on the baseplates of who made the magazine. But, unless you pull the new magazine from a sealed wrapper (which tells you who made it) there is no guarantee the baseplate and the magazine are the pair that left the factory. But, as few people swap baseplates (and the government doesn't let anything out as surplus any more) the chances are good that the baseplate maker is the tube maker. Some few magazines will be marked with a CAGE code. The CAGE code is simply a manufacturers code assigned by the government. Unless you are an accepted defense manufacturer, with a CAGE code, there are things you can't get. You can't get the full Mil-spec specifications. You can't bid on contracts. For all I know, you can't get phone calls returned.

Magazine tubes were typically not marked before 1994. During the AWB/94 they had "LEO Only" and sometimes a production date stamped on them. But few makers stamped

the tube with their name; one I saw recently was from Center Industries. Clearly stamped on the side with name and production date, you had no doubt who made and when. I understand that revisions have been made to government contracts, and now the tubes will be marked with the manufacturers CAGE code and also the date of manufacture. I know the "black helicopter" crowd is going to see some sinister plot in all this. I don't. After the tales of woe my friend Duane Thomas told me of aged and trashed magazines in inventory, I can understand the desire to get some kind of a handle on magazine quality and age in a military environment.

It is fashionable to rank, or sort, magazines, by the "good" manufacturers and the "bad" ones. I've looked over all the lists, and found that I own magazines made by all the names on any list. (I've got a few drawers full of them lying about.) And all of mine work. It may well be that I've got some of the few reliable ones from the unreliable manufacturers. More likely, the large variables in both rifle and magazines allows for some to work, others to not work, and some to have a larger percentage of rifles in which they don't work.

Identifying magazines is not always easy. The baseplates and followers can easily be changed. The exterior is not a guarantee, as there are several companies that make an aerosol coating to duplicate or replace the original finish. Standing there at a gun show, holding what appears to be a pristine Colt magazine, you could actually have in your hands one of the dreaded "bad" maker magazines, with a Colt baseplate, new finish, and current USGI anti-tip follower. Approach any magazine I.D. with caution.

That said, here is the list of makers of the 20-round magazines, and the 30-rounders, also known as NSN # 1005-00-921-5004, general comments, and my experience.

Adventureline

An early maker that ended up being bought by Center Industries. Mine have all worked 100 percent from the day I acquired them. When I began shooting AR-15s, Adventureline was the whipping boy of choice. I guess their reputation went up when other makers made magazine with less-savory reputations.

AdventureLine

Center Industries

Having acquired Adventureline, Center also bought up Parsons. They produce many magazines on contract for DoD, and make LEO magazines as well. Center Industries has continued to make magazines. I just looked over a Center Industries magazine at a recent class (August 2004) marked for LEO-only. The production date on it was August 2003. Mine, and the ones I saw in that class, are 100 percent reliable.

Center Industries

Armalite

Original Armalite magazines, from the beginning, are rare and collectors' pieces. New magazines are made for the new Armalite company, by one of the big USGI makers. Who? It differs from batch to batch, and no one will say. All I have tried have been reliable and durable. As makers of the rifles for the magazines, you'd be correct to think Armalite would have a good handle on proper magazines.

Colt

While many magazines are marked "Colt," Colt does not make them, and as far as I know, never mass-produced magazines. They were all made on contract for Colt, primarily by Okay Industries. I have never encountered a bad magazine marked as coming from Colt, either 20- or 30-round capacity.

Colt baseplates have been made a lot of ways through the years. Collectors are happy, the rest of us don't care.

Cooper Industries

To date, this is the only magazine contractor to lose their contract due to sub-standard magazines. They apparently did not provide enough welds, and Cooper also apparently mixed rejects back in with passed inventory. Some won't even fit into rifles. I searched my gear bins, and managed to come up with a single Cooper Industries magazine. It has only three large spot-welds on the spine, vice six by other makers. However, it has a spray-painted my-magazine stock number on the side (I number all my mags) so I must have tested it and found that it worked some time in the past. Even the bad brands have good examples. If you can afford to risk five bucks on a Cooper that you might be able to salvage, go for it. Mine works fine, yours could too.

D&H Industries

A new to me manufacturer, based on Oconomowoc, WI. Which is curious, because LaBelle is in Oconomowoc, and the CAGE code for D&H (04TQ4) is different than that of LaBelle (90435). Can Oconomowoc be such a hotbed of metal stamping that it has two USGI magazine manufacturers? As I received no reply to e-mails and letters, I can only surmise that some change in corporate ownership or structure lead to a new CAGE code being issued. The D&H magazines I inspected were LEO-only, made during the AWB/94 period, 30-round capacity and completely standard USGI magazines bought by a police department in Illinois. They worked flawlessly during a week-long class.

D&H Industries, which used to be called LaBelle.

DPMS

Magazines with the DPMS logo on the baseplates are generally thought to come from LaBelle, now D&H Industries. They are black Teflon coated, curved 20- and 30-round magazines, and many with LEO-only or production date markings on them. All I've seen worked 100 percent, no surprised since they all came from various law enforcement sources.

DPMS

Eagle Arms

Eagle was the company name before they bought the rights to use Armalite. I have a clutch of Eagle mags (and the Eagle rifle they came with) and they all work fine. They are Teflon-coated, indicating that they probably came from LaBelle, but there is no way of knowing. I used them exclusively at Second Chance, where ammunition consumption in competing in the Light Rifle Pop and Flop was measured not in boxes or even cartons, but in cubic feet. They never failed. Nor did the Eagle Arms rifle I was using.

Eagle Arms

General Stamping

Buying LaBelle in 1995, General Stamping magazines are all post-ban, and thus government or LEO-only marked magazines so far. Those I've seen have worked just fine. I don't expect any change now that the ban has ended, just changes in tube or baseplate markings.

H-K

The Mercedes/Beemer/Porsche of magazines, the H-K magazines, since they were made only after the AWB/94 passed, are all marked LEO-only. The only one I have seen (and played with for a short time) had been left behind on a police range by some Federal agency that had used the range. The Officer who was holding it was waiting for a phone call so he could get in some gentle ribbing, and I had the opportunity to try the mag for an afternoon. It worked fine, loaded easily,

and might be worth the money. With the sunset of the ban, do not expect to see many H-K magazines on the market. H-K is well-known for both going for the police market, and restricting the sales of items they deem to be law-enforcement only.

LaBelle

LaBelle differed from regular magazines in offering a Teflon coating on some production batches, but all their USGI magazines were hard-coat anodized. They were bought by General Stamping in 1995. For a while at gun shows, LaBelle mags were all anyone had. Mine work, and I've not heard bad things from other shooters.

LaBelle

Okay Industries

The sole maker of magazines for Colt. If you dig into the warranty specs of Colt rifles, you'll find that they will guarantee the reliable function of their rifles with Okay, and only Okay magazines. I've seen some negative comments about Okay magazines, but I've never seen one that failed to work. As the sole-source magazine for Colt, the exemplar of AR-15 manufacture, we can expect them to set the standard for magazine function.

Parsons

Bought up by Center Industries, Parsons made magazines until the 1980s under their own name.

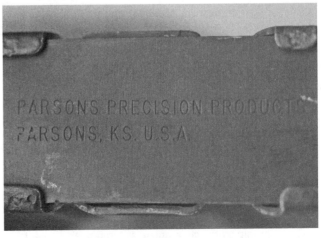

Parsons

Sanchez Enterprises

Another of the "marginal" manufacturers. Apparently the Army found that some were unreliable in full-auto fire, but could never figure out what the cause was. They were in spec, and the mystery was "solved" by using them as the test-bed for the new green followers. Problem solved. Mine has a black follower and works fine. (Although I haven't had a chance to test it in full-auto fire, worse the luck.)

Simmonds

Another early maker. Boringly reliable and utterly indistinguishable from other magazines except for the baseplate. All my Simmonds are 20-round magazines, and I used them for years along with Colt-marked mags while under the impression that 30-round magazines were unreliable. Once I got over that, I loaded them and stashed them in a bandolier. I lost track of the bandolier, and came across it three years later. The magazines worked fine.

UI, Or Universal Industries

A division of Okay Industries, the interlinked UI logo is found only on 20-round magazines. Apparently they were made by UI, as a part of Okay, for Colt. However, I have some 20-round Simmond-marked magazines. I acquired them some 20 years ago, before anyone cared about assembling bogus collector's magazines. And the chance that they are mis-assembled is almost nil. (Back then, I only bought new, untampered, magazines. I didn't want to risk buying someone's rejects.)

Brownells

For those out of the loop, Brownells is the biggest supplier of gunsmithing tools and supplies in the country. As the U.S. is the biggest place to do it yourself, that means the World. Always looking for products, the crew at Brownells decided that what with the hi-cap magazine ban sunsetting, the market might be ready for a top-quality 30-round magazine. So they contracted with a G.I. producer for magazines. They were not happy with what they got at first. (Brownells won't tell me who the supplier is, just a known magazine maker.) So, the magazine got bumped up from "mil-spec" to "Brownells-spec." They kept sending back design change and dimensional change until they had a magazine that worked in every rifle they could lay hands on. Then they tested them in even more rifles. Once the pre-production magazines worked, Brownells ordered a bunch of them. They feature chrome-silicon springs, so they won't take a set. They have the new green anti-tip followers, They are hard-anodized and given a dry lube coating. They're first-class.

Government "Surplus"

There are surplus items, but mostly what people buy from the government is "scrap." The "surplus" ammo cans you buy are actually sold by the government as scrap steel. The fact that they all have lids is simply a recognition by all involved that cans without lids will receive far lower bids than cans with lids. Back at the shop we used to buy ammo cans by the pallet. (So does every other gun shop out there with reloaders and shooters who aren't skeet and trap shooters) We'd find all sorts of things in the cans besides sand from Georgia and clay from Texas. But don't count on finding anything valuable.

As for the "surplus" magazines, there aren't any. Not any more. There used to be, for I distinctly recall buying a big pile of magazines that were all used. Some even had burn marks and tread marks on them. But not any more. The whole idea of valuable and sensitive products getting out of government hands is so touchy that there none are allowed to get out. (Imagine an anti-gun Senator or Congressman finding out we can buy surplus items! The horror!) I've known of people even being investigated and prosecuted for attempting to trade in "scrapped" government parts fished out of scrap bins, dumpsters and salvage yards.

Apparently President Clinton signed an Executive Directive to the effect that all equipment owned by the government was to be controlled "cradle to grave." The effect, 10 years later, is that even fired brass is now to be considered metal, and destroyed as brass before being sold as "surplus."

No, if what you're seeing are "surplus" magazines what you're seeing are production over-runs. Especially if they are presented as "new in the wrapper" surplus. Let's say a magazine manufacturer gets a contract for "X" thousand magazines. Since they're set up and running, they might as well finish the contract by running for an extra day or two, or week or so. Since you're (the manufacturer) are already buying aluminum by the ton, you might as well add a few thousand pounds extra at the volume price you're getting, and run the machines for a while longer. The extra magazines, once the contract has been fulfilled, can then be sold as "surplus." Is the government "cool" with this? I don't know, for no one will tell me. If the government looks the other way, or if the contract specifically forbids it, I have no idea.

Magazine Maintenance And Upgrades

Magazine failures come in three ways: failure to feed early; (commonly the "bullet-shaker magazine") failure late; sometimes the "bolt-over-base" failure, often a trapped empty or failure to strip the top round off (sometimes failure to lock open when empty) and failure randomly and frequently. While the failure early (with a near-full magazine) is sometimes the spring, it is usually the follower that is causing the problem. In early-failure, the follower binds in the tube, shoved by the spring and the stack of rounds, and thus stops lifting. The bolt closing on an empty chamber is your first clue, and when you pull the magazine out it rattles from the loose ammo. Failures near the end (almost empty) are more often the spring, weak or tired and not able to lift the rounds fast enough to get the top one in front of the bolt. The bolt-over-base failure happens when the spring is weak, or the follower binds a bit, and the top round is not lifted parallel to the bore. The base lifts late, and the bolt crashes into the side of the round. Closing on an empty chamber or failure to lock open when empty comes from the weak spring not having enough force to get the next round in the bolt path, or lift the follower forcefully enough to get the bolt hold-open up in time. Random and frequent failures are tube-related, from the tube being bent or badly made, or the feed lips being bent or cracked. To fix the solvable problems, you have to take the magazine apart.

Taking a magazine apart is relatively easy, if seemingly hazardous. On 20-round magazines you press a bullet tip or rod through the access hole and flex the internal spring tab out of the slot it locks to in the baseplate. Then slide the baseplate out. On the 30s, you just flex back the tab at the

Magazine Testing, The Hard Way

My standard procedure, up until now, has been to put several boxes of ammo through each new magazine, first by loading only five rounds and seeing if it has bolt-over-base problems, and ensure it locks open. Then I do another couple of boxes, loaded full, firing five rounds then topping it off to make sure it can lift a full stack. For a new test, I volunteered two magazines to science. First up is the dry and dusty environment: I took a pair of tested and reliable Okay Industries magazines, stripped and cleaned them. I then sprayed the magazine spring of one of them with water-displacing oil and dried it with a blow dryer. I then treated the other spring with TW-25 aerosol and also dried it.

I then reassembled the magazines and dropped them empty into a five-gallon pail with an inch of fine, dry sand in the bottom. I put the lid on and treated the pail like a maraca for a minute. (Harder work than you'd think. You shake a pail for a full 60 seconds.) I then loaded and fired the magazines. My plan was to repeat until they failed. Well, dried, they did not fail. After the fourth time through, I was getting tired and the rifle was getting hot. And I'd gone through 240 rounds with nothing but practice and empty brass to show for it.

So I took them apart and re-sprayed the springs. I let them dry only as long as they could until I could get them back into the bucket. Success! As in failure to function. The third time through, the oil-treated magazine closed on an empty chamber. The TW-25 continued on.

With even a limited baseline to work with, I then took them both apart and cleaned them. I then sprayed the interior of one (spring and tube)

with TW-25 and let it dry. The other I left bone dry. For the next test I loaded the magazines before subjecting them to the sand test. Once I was done shaking, I cleaned them up as much as I could with my bare hands and by blowing on them.

The first time through, they both worked. By the third time they would not function reliably, but the mag treated with TW-25 worked a bit better than the dry one did. But they both were very cranky.

The next test duplicated the first, with magazines sprayed with oil and TW-25, left wet and then dropped in a bucket of loamy soil and water. Our range is mostly sand, but there is enough clay and black dirt that grass does grow in places. On a rainy day, a magazine dropped is a magazine made muddy. I dropped the magazines in the mud and swirled the bucket around to get them good and grubby. I then swished them around in another bucket with clear water, loaded and fired them. After the fourth treatment the magazines began to act up, closing on an empty chamber. A quick unload/swish/re-lube and they worked fine.

The lesson to be learned is simple: you cannot lube your way through a dusty environment. At least not where magazines are concerned. You must brush the powder residue, grit, dust, lint and other stuff out of them. In a wet environment you can "clean" them a bit by using a bucket of clean water or a relatively clean puddle. But that only works for the muddy magazines, and you'll eventually have to give them a proper cleaning.

And when conducting tests like this, you want to be wearing a full face shield, or at least a good pair of goggles.

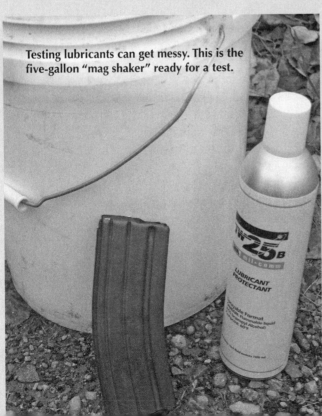

Testing lubricants can get messy. This is the five-gallon "mag shaker" ready for a test.

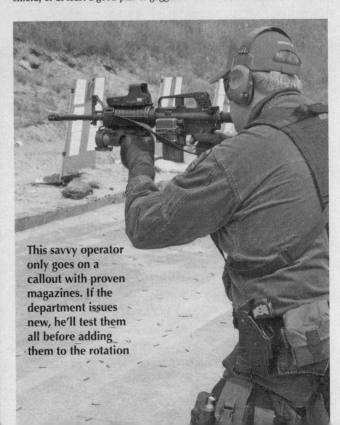

This savvy operator only goes on a callout with proven magazines. If the department issues new, he'll test them all before adding them to the rotation

To disassemble the 20-round magazines, you press in on the tab inside the magazine. For the 30s you pry the baseplate up. Then slide either off the tube.

Of course things are proportioned that a bullet is useful. What else can you guarantee that a soldier will always have?

back of the baseplate, using a rod or round stuck in the hole provided in the baseplate. The seemingly hazardous part is that the plate on the 30 doesn't flex without protesting, and the tabs on both the 20- and 30-round tubes grab and resist extraction of the baseplate. The whole while the spring inside is rubbing on the plate, making the process more difficult. Resist the temptation to "make it easier" by bending the tube tabs out a little bit, reducing friction on the baseplate. The tabs keep it together when loaded.

With the baseplate out, the spring will catch on the tabs. Work the spring side to side and get it past the tabs, and pull if down. The follower will get to the bottom, and you'll have to wiggle it past the tabs. That's it, you're done taking the magazine apart. Unless you need to swap springs, you need only clean and reassemble.

For many uses, I spray the springs with a water-displacing oil. In triggers I hate water-displacing oils, as they often form a lacquer as the more-volatile components evaporate. Since a magazine spring does not have to work in tight dimensions, and the lacquer can act to protect it, they work fine for me. A spray with WD-40, and an hour in the sun, and they're dry enough to assemble. However, those in a dusty environment might not find an oil of any kind to be very useful. For dusty applications, I favor one of the dry lubricants like Hoppes Dri-

slide or TW-25 aerosol. I spray it on the spring, try to keep it off the follower, and after I swab the magazine out, assemble the magazine. I don't lubricate magazine interiors.

For the gunk inside of a magazine, use a brush. Or a brush with a cleaning patch wrapped around it. Just as the rifle interior has powder gases blown into it each time it is fired, so is the magazine treated. Granted, the magazine doesn't receive the full blast of the shot, but the receiver still has swirling gases in it when the bolt cycles, and some gets down into the magazine.

Wipe the follower clean.

Reassemble by the famous "reverse the order" method. Make sure the front of the follower is forward. The little cartridge-shaped lump on its top will help. Wiggle it past the tabs, then push it all the way up with the spring. Compress the spring and slide the baseplate on. Check follower function by pushing it down and letting the spring push it back up. If it binds, find out why.

New Spring

The spring should not come off the follower for regular maintenance. However, if you're changing springs (or installing new spring on new followers for old tubes) you'll need to get it right. The follower has a stump underneath, near the front. You'll notice the spring passes through the stump. That is the correct assembly of the spring and follower. Remove the old one by turning and pulling it to thread the tip out of the stump. Install the new one by reversing the order. And you need only pass one loop of the spring through the follower stem. If you loop more (I once found a magazine assembled that way "for more spring tension" or so the owner said) the follower will not be properly lifted by the spring. If you assemble them any other way the magazine will not work. (The hassle of just getting it back together with the spring and follower wrong should be a clue.) Why would you need a new spring? Springs do not wear out from being compressed. They wear out from being cycled. A loaded magazine, if the spring was good to start with, will be good for years to come. The magazine you use all the time could wear out from being cycled as you load and fire, load and fire. If you regularly unload your magazines to "rest" the springs, you are actually causing them more wear than if you just left them loaded.

Do you need new springs every "X" time period? No. Changing springs every few years is a waste of time, springs and money. Get good ones if you don't trust the ones you have, test them, and leave them alone.

For springs, I go to one of three sources. ISMI, Wolff, and Specialized Arms Warehouse. The ISMI springs will replace the existing ones and not change capacity. The SAW springs (in the 30-round magazines) will reduce capacity by two rounds.

How is it that a weak spring can cause failures when it has few rounds on it, and not so often (or at all) when it is lifting a full stack? Compression. At the end of its cycle, the magazine spring (or any spring) has its least amount of force to bear on the problem. The compressed spring may be weak, but it has all of its lessened power to use. At the end of its length, the spring is weaker both from lack of compression, and being a weak, tired or abused spring. A new spring will solve the weak spring problem, but not other problems.

Once back together, go test.

I have seen advice that you should "restore" a tired spring by stretching it. Anyone who does that does not understand just how a spring works. In an attempt to explain, I will summarize a Bachelor's degree in Mechanical Engineering in a few paragraphs. Springs work via the non-plastic deformation of a metal or plastic. ("Plastic" deformation in Engineering-speak means it stays bent.) The object (let's call it a "spring," just to keep from confusing things) bends away from the force bearing on it. As long as the force does not exceed the tensile strength of the material, it will flex back to its original configuration when the force is removed. However, a smaller than tensile strength force, but a significant percentage of the tensile strength, applied to the material work-hardens it. (Given enough repetitions.) Making a spring harder does not make it stronger. What happens is, the work-hardened portion flexes less, shifting the stress to the nearest non-work hardened section. If enough of the spring is work-hardened, the stress becomes concentrated on a small enough area that failure occurs. Or, if the whole spring becomes sufficiently work-hardened, it takes a set and fails to return to original dimensions. Springs wear out from either being bent past their limits, or being flexed too many times. The accumulated load can be millions of flexions at a minor percentage of strength, or a few hundred happening just under the load limit the material can take.

So, what happens when you stretch a tired spring to "restore" it? That's right, you work-harden it. You've bent it past its limit in the direction opposite to the load it experiences when working. The stretched spring works marginally better for a few more flexions, then takes a worse set than it had before.

My brother Mike, who has several degrees in the Engineering Arts, commented on the spring problem: "Since you already have the spring out to look at it, why not replace it with a new one and get on with your life?" Makes sense to me. The only way to restore a tired spring is to replace it. To judge when, place the new spring next to the old spring. If the old spring is more than three coils shorter than the new one, install the new one.

New Follower

Should you swap out the follower? Older magazines may have perfectly good followers. Don't swap yours if the one you have has proven to be 100 percent reliable. I know a lot of shooters who have been using USGI 30-round magazines with black plastic followers, who have not had a lick of trouble.

The new followers are bright green, and improve the feeding reliability of many magazines.

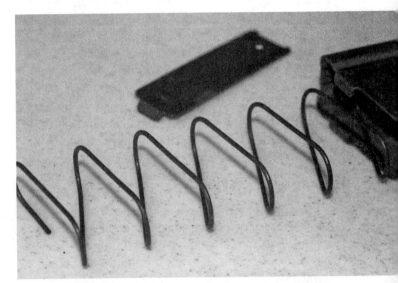

To install the Sinclair followers, disassemble your mags and remove the old follower.

The Sinclair follower allows single-loading for long-range target shooting.

I also know guys who shoot with 20-round mags with alloy or black plastic followers that have never failed. For them, swapping followers is a waste of money. (Even if it is only a buck each, it can add up.) However, if you have a recalcitrant magazine, spending a buck or two can sometimes salvage it. Considering that in some states the magazines you've got are all the magazines you'll ever have (at least hi-cap ones) salvaging an unreliable magazine for a buck or two is a boon. Even for those of us who live in more reasonable jurisdictions, getting a magazine up from the category of "lightweight doorstop" to "reliable practice magazine" for a buck is a good thing.

The new anti-tip followers are easy to identify: they are bright green and have a long leg on the front. The idea is that the longer leg prevents the follower from tipping inside the tube, and a follower that "tracks" straight up and down the tube is going to be more reliable. Why did it take more than 20 years to develop the new follower? Remember our discussion of the development of the M-16? As long as something worked reasonably well, it was left alone. The politics of the whole sorry mess were such that any investigation was bound to cause problems. Not until Sanchez made a batch of magazines that checked out in all the specs, but still posed mysterious feeding problems in full auto, did the powers that be investigate. The solution was to use the new followers. They proved so successful that soon after (the early 1990s) all government magazines were required to come with the new follower. Why is it such a hot aftermarket product? Because with the AWB/94, all new government magazines were verboten for civilian use. So, we all kept using our black-follower magazines.

As they needed rebuilding from use, shooters would investigate the new followers, and spread the word. Now, it is pretty common to see even old magazines with new followers.

The swap is easy. Disassemble the magazine. If you're replacing springs, too, install the new spring on the new follower, reassemble and go test. If you're just replacing the follower, work the old spring off the old follower, install it on the new, and reassemble.

High Power shooters sometimes need a new follower for a different reason: slow fire. At 600 yards you aren't going to be loading up a magazine and blasting away. As a matter of fact, the ammo you'd be using there may not even feed in a follower. If you've got 80-grain bullets loaded long for more case volume, they won't fit in the magazines. You need to load your rounds one at a time. Doing so with a standard magazine can be clumsy. Sinclair makes followers that replace the standard followers. They hold the bullet up out of the feed lips, so you can simply place a round in the new follower (which acts as a tray) and then press the bolt hold-open to close the bolt. The Sinclair follower is bright yellow so you won't confuse it with a magazine set up to feed. Simply strip your magazine, replace the old follower with the Sinclair, and

reassemble. The neat thing about the Sinclair follower is that since it doesn't use the feed lips of the magazine, you can use any busted old magazine as your slow-fire mag. You can have a 20 (you'll want a 20 to get low in prone) with cracked lips, busted tabs, anything so long as the magazine stays in the rifle and the feed lips aren't so busted up they interfere with the Sinclair follower. Me, I ditched all non-working magazines a long time ago, but the next time I'm at a gun show and see a scrapped 20 lying on a table for a buck, I'll get it.

Rebuild Kits

You can buy a whole new set of internals, to rebuild an existing magazine. Do you need such a kit? I haven't yet, but you might. The questions are, how often will you need all three parts (follower, spring and baseplate) and is it more cost-effective to buy all three than buy just what you need?

Tube Maintenance

Basically, scrub it clean every now and then, and wipe grime, dirt, mud and the other gunk off the exterior. If the feed lips get bent, or the tube gets tweaked or kinked from being dropped or stepped on, consider it an experimental/range-use magazine. You can learn a lot by trying to bend the lips back, or using a rubber mallet and a hard backing surface to try to flex the tube back to spec. But even if it works well after that, consider it a training/practice magazine only. Don't depend on a tweaked magazine for a match, or worse, as a defensive magazine. It just isn't worth the hassle.

Too-often taking it apart, or heavy-handed disassembly, can bend or break the bottom tabs that keep the baseplate on. Be gentle. If you must brush the interior, use a proper brush. Using a wad of cloth on the end of a cleaning rod is a sure way to hook a tab and bend or break it.

One question that comes up now and then is how to refinish it. Basically, you don't. You can use a durable aerosol paint if you want, but you need not refinish your mags. The best line I've heard concerning AR magazines is "They have plenty of self-esteem. As long as they work reliably they don't care what they look like."

If you want to re-paint them, go ahead. Refinished will require the services of an anodizer, a shop that can remove the old hard-coat and replace it with a new anodized finish. Save your money.

Testing

It takes good ammo, and a bunch of it, to really test a magazine. You also have to have a rifle in good working order, to test magazines. It doesn't do any good to test magazines in a rifle that isn't running 100 percent, as you will be driven crazy trying to sort the magazine malfunctions from the rifle malfunctions. I've known shooters who would spend $150 on a high-cap handgun magazine, have it tuned by an expert, fuss over the spring and follower, and test it thoroughly, putting hundreds of rounds of ammo through it before depending on it in a match. The same shooter will put 30 rounds through a 30-round magazine of their AR, and declare it "good to go." Excuse me, but are you crazy?

The primary malfunctions of a magazine happen in either the first five rounds or the last five rounds. So, you can catch a break in testing your AR magazines by not shooting a full capacity amount each time. The first test is to see if it fits. Does the test magazine insert easily, and drop free of its own weight? If it is such a tight fit that it has to be pushed, or won't drop out on its own, pass on it. Or trade it to someone whose rifle has a more accepting magazine well. The tolerances of both rifles and magazines are such that it is entirely possible to find rifles and mags that are not compatible and others that are.

Then, does it lock the bolt back when empty? Insert the magazine and pull the charging handle back. Lock open? Great. No? Not so great. You can replace the spring and try again, or look at the rear of the follower to see if is damaged, worn or has been altered. At a good enough price, a tube that fits your rifle can be rebuilt with new internals, and if it works 100%, it's a good deal.

Now, test for function. (Obviously, at the range.) Load five rounds and fire a group or a drill. Repeat several times. Does the bolt lock back when empty? The last five rounds is the place for bolt-over-base failure, and if your magazine is prone to it you'll find out here. In classes we spend a lot of time doing five-round drills with magazines with five rounds in them. We do it for two reasons: One, we quickly discover if a magazine is prone to failure. And Two, the students get more practice at handling magazines and learning the skills of magazine handling, rifle controls and loading. Once you're satisfied that your magazines won't give you a bolt-over-base malfunction, load them up. Now, shoot a five-shot drill, put the rifle on safe, pull out the magazine, and reload five more rounds. Reload, and repeat. You want to see if the follower will tip and bind with a full load. Repeat until you're satisfied. It can take 50 or 60 rounds to do a basic test of a new magazine, and several hundred before you can be completely sure it will work fine in your rifle. With that much invested in it, its little wonder anyone with any sense wants their own magazines back in a match or training session.

Which leads us to a subject many shooters "know about."

How Many Rounds Do I Load?

The advice we all know, that comes from Vietnam, is to load a 20-round magazine with 18 rounds, and a 30-rounder with 28. Why? Supposedly, the top rounds can cause malfunctions. Me, I've never seen it. I've always loaded mine full-up, 20 in a 20 and 30 in a 30. My friend Jeff Chudwin has a different experience in this. He's seen magazines that sometimes malfunctioned when fully-loaded. He saw repeated episodes of properly-loaded magazines where the top round stubbed against the feed ramp. Or the top round wouldn't feed, and the buffer spring hadn't enough force to

strip it out of the magazine. He also saw officers who could not press a fully-loaded magazine home when the bolt was forward. When he wrote his departments patrol rifle policy, he felt strongly enough about it that he mandated 20-round magazines loaded with 18 rounds. No 30's, and nothing fully-loaded.

Colt encountered this problem when they were working on the M-4. They found rounds stubbing on the receiver due to the very slightly different feeding cycle of the M-855 round as opposed to the M-193. They solved the problem with the M-4 feed ramps.

All I can tell you is what I know, and that is I have never used a magazine that caused malfunctions when fully loaded until this book. In the course of testing the rifles, we encountered one rifle that stubbed feeding the top round from a 20-round magazine. So, it can happen. The ammo was factory ammo, the rifle new and factory-built, and the magazine was one of my tried-and-true 20-round Colt-marked magazines. But there can be other sources of problems. You see, many magazines will actually accept an extra round. You can stuff a round number 21 into a 20-round magazine, and a number 31-into a 30. And there you will have problems. If you have a 21/20 or a 31/30, and you go to insert it in your rifle when the bolt is forward, you won't be able to get it to lock in place. You can beat on the magazine with a mallet, and it won't seat. The "stack", the column of rounds, follower, and spring, has to have some flex. That flex allows the top round to ride under the carrier, but have spring tension to lift it into the bolt's path when the bolt cycles. By forcing the extra round into the magazine, you've used up the flex. The stack can't compress under the carrier. The magazine won't lock in place. If you are reloading under fire, you are well and truly in a bind. And even experienced shooters can make such a mistake. One of my test crew loaded 21 into a 20-round magazine in the course of testing, and of course the round would not feed. So if an experienced competition shooter, on

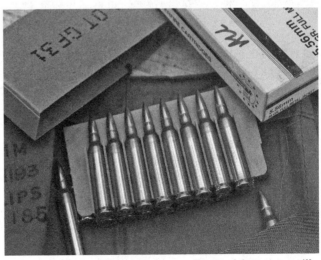

Even loading from boxes, you have to be careful. You can still get more in than should fit.

Stripper clips avoid the need to count. Just strip in two in a 20, and three in a 30.

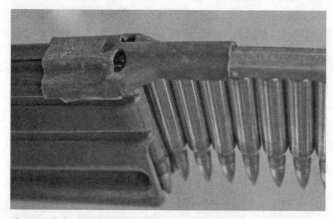

The guide makes loading a lot easier and faster.

a fun afternoon of shooting, using ammo from 20-round boxes can overload a 20-round magazine, what were the odds that an exhausted GI in the rain, mud or darkness, would do it in the field in Vietnam?

And it won't help to lock the bolt back. The extra round is under great spring tension. The tension adds friction to the feed cycle. The bolt may not have enough force to strip the top round (21st or 31st) out of the magazine, and still be able chamber and close. You might have the rifle close up, but if the bolt is out of battery, pulling the trigger gets you a "click" instead of a bang.

My observation and speculation on the origins of the 18/20 method is that early in Vietnam GIs would have been loading magazines from boxes of ammo, not stripper clips. If you're loading from loose ammo, or a box dumped into your lap, helmet, or on a tarp on the ground, it is easy to load an extra round. To prevent that, it would have been common sense to simply "load it full and strip two rounds out." Thus, the 18 in a 20-round magazine. When 30s became available, the same process would deliver 28 rounds. With the supply of stripper clips, with ten rounds each, the possibility of getting an extra round in the magazine becomes very unlikely. But the old routine would carry on.

As I've said before, I load my magazine up full. I then test, by pressing the top round down, to make sure I have flex in the stack. If the stack won't compress, I unload and check to see what is wrong.

One additional advantage to using ammo on stripper clips is the bandolier. Old bandoliers came in pockets of 20 rounds. Each of the seven pockets held two stripper clips, with the end pocket also containing the stripper clip guide. Loading 20-round magazines was a snap. And best of all, the loaded magazines fit snugly into the bandolier itself, giving you 140 rounds loaded and ready to go in one carrier. As a field-expedient, or poor-man's web gear, a bandolier loaded with loaded magazines is quite handy. Not necessarily fast in use, but handy. And each magazine has exactly 20 rounds, with no chance of an extra causing problems. Later, the bandoliers were changed to five pockets of three stripper clips. The bandolier was made deeper, and has a quick-remove line of stitching along the middle. Use the strippers to load your 30-round magazines, yank the middle stitch out, and the bandolier now has pockets long enough to hold your 30-round magazines.

While it may be a bit slow if used as a primary carrier, the best use of the bandolier as carry pouch is as backup. If you have enough magazines available, you can load magazines, stuff them in the bandolier, and then fold the bandolier and put it in your gear. An extra 140 or 150 rounds, in magazines, in a rucksack, are comforting to have. Or, folded and put in a buttpack, to augment your load-bearing vest supply in a dire emergency, can be literally lifesaving.

How Long Can I Leave My Mags Loaded?

No one really knows. I once grabbed a bandolier of loaded magazines off the shelf to go to a match (they were my backup supply) and later that day forgot about them. I got back to the shop, dumped the bandolier into a drawer, and left it. Almost three years later, I came across the bandolier. (Yes, there were drawers in the shop I didn't look into for years at a time. I was a horrible pack rat back then.) I took them to the range on the next range trip, and tested them. They worked fine. They were a mixture of brands of USGI 20-round magazines loaded to 20 rounds capacity. My friend Reid Coffield served in Vietnam. He arrived at a fire base to discover there was a shelf of loaded magazines in his office. No one on the base knew when they had been loaded, just that "they were loaded when I got here." During one firefight to repel an assault on the base, he used all those magazines and more. And they all worked. So, we know from these and other incidents that good magazines, with good ammo, in good rifles, given even a modicum of care, will work for years after they are loaded. Now that's not to say that magazines left loaded on the floorboards of your truck will still work after even a few months. The storage conditions matter more than anything else. Keep those magazines dry, clean, out of the sun, away from vibration, and in a moderate temperature range, and they will probably work just fine any time in the future you need them. Do anything to abuse them, and they won't.

That said, you must take care of magazines and ammo that get exposed to bad storage. If you depend on a rifle in your car, or the trunk, swap out the ammo every six months at the longest. Magazines that get dunked should be unloaded, stripped and cleaned. And mostly this care is for the ammo. Take care of the ammo, and the magazine will take care of you.

Magazines that get bounced around should have the ammo inspected and swapped out on a regular basis. My friend Jeff Chudwin experienced this first-hand. He had a bunch of magazines loaded and in his gear bag. He hauled the gear bag into and out of his squad car every day. Some of the magazines were loaded with soft-point ammo, and he found that the repeated impacts had jolted the bullet noses against the inside of the magazine tube. The soft-points were riveted back. In testing, he found they had an absolutely horrible feeding reliability. Check your magazines regularly, even if you don't unload them.

Marking

Since you've gone to the trouble of buying good magazines, and testing them to make sure they work properly, why risk losing them, or getting them mixed up with someone else's junk? At the classes, it isn't unusual to have 15 or 20 officers on the line at once. In a 15-shot drill, that means 45 to 60 magazines on the ground. Do you really want someone else's magazines? (Well, if yours suck, yes. But will the guy next to you be happy once he discovers he's got your discards?)

I run into unreliable rifles in every class. The first step (if the problem isn't obvious) is to hand the officer some of my magazines to use. I have rock-solid, ultra-reliable magazines I bring to classes just for that. I take two steps to make sure I get them back: I hang on to the officers magazines, and I mark mine. Marking can be done in a number of ways. You can use paint, felt-tip pens, tape, marking labels or engraving. You can even use those adhesive-backed metal labels "Property of.." business, municipalities and departments are so fond of marking furniture with.

I use tape to mark new magazines, ones I haven't fully tested yet. That way, if it proves unreliable I can take the tape off and hand the mag back. I tape with a couple of circuits at the base, and then initial and number them. That way, if one of a batch is bad, I know which one from paying attention to the number.

Felt-tip pens work as temporary markers, too. The Sharpie brand, which comes in black and silver, will stand up to a days worth to testing and training. The markings will come off if you use solvents, so if you want something temporary until you can use paint, they work fine.

You can spray-paint or use paint markers. The paint markers

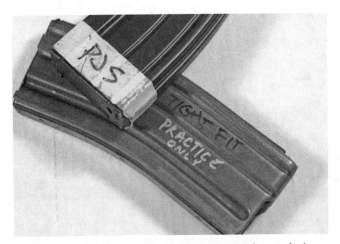

Mark your mags, or you risk getting them mixed up or losing them.

are often found in art supply stores, or the pockets of gang members who want to "tag" objects. Simply shake, and then write what you want on a clean, dry, degreased surface. For spray paint, use a cutout to spray the design, initials or numeral of your choice. Use subdued colors, unless you're a competition shooter and you want your magazines to match your eye-searing spectrum of colors your gear and clothing is painted, anodized or dyed. I put my initials and a magazine number on each one. That way, if "number seven" has had a bolt-over-base failure for the third time, I know to pull it out of rotation and see about getting it rebuilt.

Engraving is a classy way to mark your magazines, but can cost more than the magazine itself cost you. And, you should ask before showing up at the engraving store at the mall. They may not do aluminum, they may not do "gun stuff" and they may call security to ask you a few questions when you come back to pick the magazines up.

The adhesive-backed labels can be very good, but you have to be careful. The printed label tapes can work well, but they are not always going to stay when they get hit with cleaning solvents. I've seen smart-looking labels get stripped off at the first exposure to bore solvent. The institutional labels use a better grade of adhesive, and will often stand up to solvents. But beware: Marking your personal magazines with labels that say "Property of Riverdale PD" may not be the smartest thing to do. At the very least you might find yourself making a "donation" of magazines to the PD (they are marked, after all) and may find people asking in their official capacity "Why do you have city property?"

The labels are not that expensive, so if you want to order a batch with a special "Property of…" marking on them, you can.

Remember, all markings should be on the magazine tube, and not the baseplate. The tube determines what magazine is reliable, not the baseplate.

Modifications

Once you've got them tested and marked, you need

The Magpul Ranger bases give you a means of fishing the next mag out of a tight web pouch.

(sometimes) a means of getting them quickly. Many mag pouches hold the magazine or magazines so tightly you need to wrestle them out. One method is to use tape, or tape and 550 cord. Or, you can use the old Magpuls or their new Ranger Plates.

The best method of putting old-style magazine pulls on your magazines is to take 4 inches of 550 cord. Burn the ends to build up a knob of nylon. Lay the cord in the bullet guide channels on the side of the magazine, and then tape-wrap the bottom of the tube to trap the cord in the channel. The adhesive secures the cord, and the knobs add to the security, wedging in the tape if the cord is pulled hard. The ugly way is to stuff the knobbed ends into the tube, and force the baseplate closed. To do so flexes the tube. And, you're putting the stress of yanking a loaded magazine out directly on the bottom tabs of the tube. (A bad thing to do.)

Magpul solved the problem by making moulded synthetic pulls that were a tight fit on the bottom of the magazine tube. The old style Magpuls come in a variety of sizes and colors. The newest approach is to use their Ranger Plates. The Ranger Plates replace the baseplates, and the moulded grasping loop is your pull. If the 550 cord inserted in the tube and wedged by the baseplate is bad, how can the Ranger Plates be good? Because you aren't flexing the tube to start with.

Do you have to have every magazine with some kind of magazine pull on it? Not really. Only when a magazine pouch is full, and you can't get a good grasp, is getting one out a problem. So, if you have one per mag pouch, as soon as that one is out the others are a lot easier to grasp.

Another accessory for the complete AR-15 magazine are mag covers. I know, I know, half of you think they are mall ninja, and the other half think they're old-fart High Power stuff. Guess again. The last three-gun match I was at, a nationally-known Grand Master pulled his AR mags out of his shooting bag, stripped off the dust covers, and got ready for the stage. He'd loaded them in the hotel room, then covered them and put them in his shooting bag. Why the covers? "You ever try to finish a stage using a magazine that has a dime rattling around in it?" It seems he had dumped his pocket change into his shooting back at a match, and missed the pocket. His change went into the pocket with the AR mags. You guessed it, a dime worked its way into one of his magazines. Would it have shown up in practice? Get real, there's a reason it's called Murphy's Law and not Murphy's Suggestion.

Issued Magazines

Back to Duane, and his time in the 82nd Airborne: "Rifles and magazines were issued from the arms room when we needed them. As soon as we got back to the unit and cleaned the guns, they and the magazines were turned back in to the arms room." And magazines weren't sorted, maintained or otherwise looked after by the supply sergeant, either. "Every time I came back to the unit and told the arms room guy something like "I had two double feeds with THIS magazine," he just shrugged and threw it back in the pile. I think the main problem, reliability-wise, with the M-16 in military service is 30-plus-year-old, beat-to-hell aluminum magazines." As the critical part of the rifle, and something that can get you in a world of hurt if it fails to work properly, magazines are important.

What do you do if you're issued magazines, and can't go sorting, trading, rebuilding and otherwise marking them? That depends. If you are in a police department, you use masking tape and a felt tip pen to mark them until you've tested them. Go back to the clerk/officer/sergeant in charge of issue, and if one is a problem, say so. If the reply is "That's what we've got, that's what you get." Then you'll have to decide how much your safety is worth. If it is worth a lot, buy your own. Label them. Safely store the department's magazines in your locker, properly labeled. When you have to turn the rifle and/or magazines back in, turn in the department's magazines. If the department is very fussy about using personal equipment instead of issued, then you have a real problem. I cannot advise you to break departmental regulations, but again, how much is your safety worth? Perhaps you should just buy replacements, and let the departmental magazines disappear from the light, never to be seen again. (A big problem, if the department marks them in a permanent fashion.)

In military unit, you will be faced with the problem Duane had: magazines are near-disposable, and your problem is your problem. One "solution" is for the irretrievably shabby magazines to become accidentally damaged. A heavy vehicle makes a mess of magazines, but not so much they can't be recognized when turned in for replacements. What with an actual shooting war going on, the supply personnel are a lot more understanding of the need and desire for good magazines. And Duane's peacetime magazine experience is less likely to be the norm. If you do buy your own, to replace, supplement or add to the issued magazines, be sure to clearly mark them before you go where you're going. And that your Senior NCO knows and approves. While spending money for your own gear, only to have to turn it in to the government when you're done isn't a big cost, it may well be an avoidable one.

Take care, stay safe, come back.

Myths Of The AR-15

The myths are legion, but most of them are concerned with a few details. In the course of debunking the ones I can stand to discuss (some are too ignorant to even dignify with a response) I'm sure I'm going to step on some toes. If you've been repeating one of the myths I list, don't take it personally. If you think I'm wrong, test it for yourself.

The AR-15 Is Unreliable

Well, 40 years ago, in the jungles of Vietnam, you would have had some takers. But that was then, and we've learned a lot (and the makers have changed a lot) since. The primary causes then of malfunctions were the unchromed chambers and bores, using the wrong powder, and lack of maintenance. If you use a rifle that is properly set up (that is, factory-built or assembled by someone with knowledge and not just a few minutes of instruction) if you feed it good ammo, and you keep it reasonably clean, the AR-15 is as dependable as most. I won't say it is perfect, for nothing is. But even the best mechanisms need some TLC.

A later cause for malfunctions are poor magazines. My friend Duane Thomas served 10 years in the Army, as a jump-qualified enlisted man. In that time, he only had one annual 40-round qualification that did not have a magazine-related malfunction. The bad magazines were tossed back into inventory along with the good ones when he turned them in, despite mentioning the problems to the supply sergeant.

The Israeli Defense Forces use the M-16, preferring it to the AK, or even their own Galil. (some might say that free M-16s from Uncle Sam was a big factor, too.) The Israelis use a lot of firearms, because everyone serves and everyone protects. If they had problems with the M-16, they'd figure a way to "solve" the problem. That they issue box-stock M-16s should tell us something.

The AR-15 Is Fragile

It is made of aluminum, and can't take the knocks that a "real" rifle can take. Well, not all "real" rifles are made the same. Compared to an AK, which you can't hurt with a ball-peen hammer, or an H-K G3, which you can run over with a truck, yes the AR is fragile. But, take a match-conditioned M-14 or M1-A, and drop it off a shooting bench. It isn't match-conditioned any more. Afford an AR-15 the same treatment and all you'll need to do is wipe off the scuff marks and perhaps bend back an inconsequential bit of aluminum, and you're good to go.

I've talked to Marines fresh back from boot camp about their issue M-16s. Used so much, and cleaned repeatedly and excessively, they were worn white. And yet they would shoot clean to 500 yards if the boot holding it knew what he was doing.

I saw a photograph (not a hi-res file, sorry) of a tank commander in Iraq: he had an M4 lying on top of the turret, within easy reach, while the tank was in service. If he needed it, he could pick up the M4 and deal with a threat a lot faster than he could slew the turret around. And if he had to deal with a sniper, or someone trying to launch an RPG from an alley, that M4 was going to save his skin. Would it be there if it couldn't take the dust, vibration and heat?

The 5.56 Bullet Tumbles

Not until it hits the target, it doesn't. Any rifle, in order to be accurate, has to keep its bullet properly spun and stabilized. Some are more stable than others, which is where the 5.56/.223 round derives its wounding potential. The bullet is less than stable in flesh where it overturns, breaks apart, and works out of proportion to its size or energy. (Or, that is how it is supposed to work.) Using the wrong bullet or bullet/twist combination can radically diminish that effect.

The AR can be an unreliable rifle, but it doesn't have to be. With proper maintenance, it is as reliable as any.

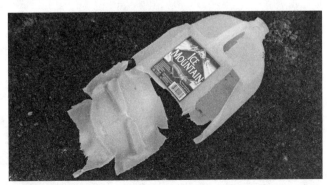

Ideas of how powerful the .223 is, and how the bullet works, come for many people via the very unscientific method of shooting a plastic jug of water.

The AR-15 Is An Assault Weapon

Perhaps, under inane state law, written by legislators with no practical knowledge of firearms. The standard definition of an assault weapon is that it is a lightweight shoulder weapon, fires a round of medium power, and is select fire. That is, you can choose to fire semi, burst or automatically. By that definition, the M-16 and M-4 are assault weapons, but the AR-15 is not. If we use the typical legislative approaches, we find that a whole lot of other rifles, not usually associated with assault weapons, fit the definition. Such as the Remington Model 8, so named from its year of introduction, 1908. Semi-automatic, capable of accepting a detachable magazine of high capacity, medium power, and there were even a batch made for military trials in the 1920s that accepted bayonets! Try to convince a deer hunter using granddad's rifle he's using an "assault weapon." Or, the first real assault weapon, the M-1 Carbine. Well, when they rolled out the M-2, the select-fire one, it was an assault weapon. What is really a scream, is that by the logic of the gun banners, the M-1 Carbine should be first on the list. It was, after all, the first, and the Army found it absurdly easy to make it into a full-auto carbine. But almost no list ever published of "assault weapons to be banned" includes it. I guess it just shows how little such people really know.

The typical approach is to use cosmetics to define a firearm. So, if it has a bayonet lug, takes a magazine, has a pistol grip, it is an assault weapon? I guess then, if I take the neighbors Ford Escort, paint a big number on the side, affix a lot of advertisers tickers on it and install a roll bar, I have a NASCAR Stock car?

The AR-15 isn't an assault weapon. It's a rifle, like many others. Get over it.

The AR-15 Is Easy To Convert To Full Auto

I guess that depends on what your definition of "easy" is. Give me an afternoon, a machine shop, and a rifle, and I can make it full auto, too. Any rifle except perhaps a single-shot. Don't believe me? When John Browning had an idea for a machinegun, he converted the first extra rifle lying around his shop as a test project. (Don't panic, it was the 1890s and no one was up in arms about it. There wasn't even a law against it!) That rifle was a lever-action rifle. When the Australians had the little problem of the Japanese intending to invade, they found they had few machineguns but lots of bolt-action rifles. So they designed and converted a bunch of bolt-action rifles to be light machineguns, complete with 20-round box magazines.

You can be pretty sure that when you're talking to someone, when they say "the AR-15 is easy to convert" that they've never done it. And probably have no idea how to do it, nor even seen one that had been so converted. And you can include a lot of police chiefs in that group.

If it isn't easy, why is the ATFE so strict on trying? Because there are a large number of people out there who are not as clever as they think, and who don't know the danger they are running. I've read of some of the methods, and let me tell you, I'd rather learn to juggle chain saws than try some of them.

The M-1 Carbine is often overlooked as an "assault weapon" but was, in its M-2 form, actually the first.

If the AR was easy to convert to full-auto this police officer would be more than happy to arrest you for doing so. The "easy conversion" is a convenient fantasy many cling to.

This 9mm subgun actually penetrates interior walls more than a .223/5.56 bullet would.

Penetration testing of the .223/5.56 shows that the high velocity causes bullets to break up on interior walls very quickly.

The 5.56 Round Shoots Through Walls

Not really. This is partly from extrapolation, and partly from never testing. The high velocity of the 5.56 causes the bullet to be destroyed on any object with more resistance than tissue. Watching a .30-30 bullet go through a tree in the woods (greater distance, stouter bullet, better-stabilized) and then extrapolating that to a .223/5.56 on an interior wall 5 feet away is not correct.

Just because it is a rifle, and has a scope, doesn't mean it is a sniper rifle. All rifles carry farther than handguns or shotguns do, but it is just one bullet.

If you want potential liability headaches, consider that this shotgun shell could launch nine to 20 pellets downrange for each shot fired. That's eight to 19 more chances for an innocent bystander to be struck in the event of a miss on the suspect.

Testing has shown that a .223/5.56 bullet inside a house blows drywall into the next room along with fragments, and they do not penetrate the wall after that. On the other hand, the 9mm, which is often selected "because the AR is too powerful" will travel through wall after wall, and unless the building is of masonry construction, will exit the structure.

The AR Shoots Too Far

I've heard police chiefs rail against the AR, because "the bullet will travel for miles, and still kill someone." Well, all bullets will go more than a mile. And all will fall with enough force to cause harm. However, the 5.56, along with all other rifles, will launch but a single bullet at a time. The often-selected shotgun (won't travel so far, don't you know?) will launch nine to 12 pellets each time it is fired. Since all things that go up must come down, do you want to risk one or nine?

The big advantage of the AR is that same velocity we just spoke of. If you (as a police officer or citizen firing in defense) miss, the bullet will likely shatter against the first object it hits. A street, curb, brick wall, etc will cause the bullet to become a splatter of fragments that will then travel a few more yards and be done. That shotgun? The pellets, because they are malleable lead, and the velocity is low, will ricochet. When resting from shooting the BCBC at Second Chance (shotgun slugs on steel plates) we would always notice the misses. Those that went low threw up sprays of wood from the log glacis. Those that went high, left or right would skid off the ground, usually traveling in a low arc to the treeline. Occasionally, one would hit a buried rock, and the bright lead slug could be seen popping up into the air. They ricocheted so frequently off the earth that it was not a remarkable sight to see them hitting the trees 50 yards behind the targets. It was remarkable watching them rocket into the air.

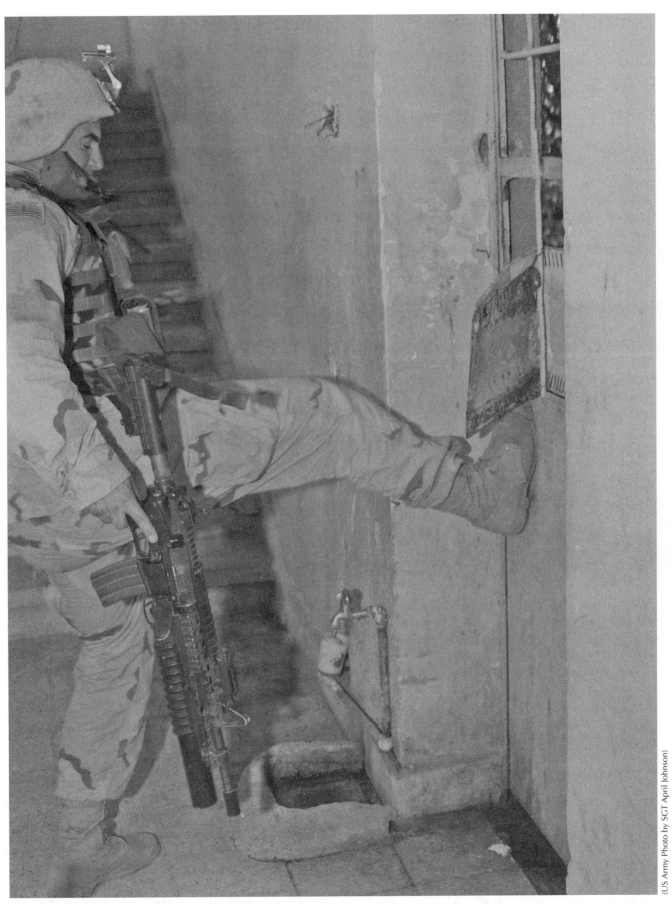

Not every rifle ever made is mil-spec. The government goes to a lot of trouble to ensure that this trooper has a properly-made rifle while "on the job." Not everyone who makes AR parts or rifles wants to incur the cost of testing, and then have to pass it on to the customer.

The AR Looks Aggressive

This was a much more common complaint before 9/11. Now, the aggressive looks of the AR are seen as an advantage, as it plays into the "perception of attention" some seek. (That is, really solving the problem is not as important to some as the perception that the problem is solved or being solved. Don't find homes for the homeless, just move them someplace I can't see them, would be an example.)

Aggressive is as aggressive does, in my book. (Say, it is my book, isn't it?) If you are handling an AR safely, you aren't aggressive to me. If you are waving around a single-shot trap shotgun in an unsafe or unfriendly manner, you are aggressive.

Still some felt that way and I'm sure some still do. Thus, the Ruger Mini-14 is accepted some places, while the AR is not.

Every AR Is Mil-spec

Not really. Technically, none are truly mil-spec unless they are M-16 and once or currently owned by the government. Which means that only unmodified, legally owned, M-16s that somehow got into the Class 3 community are really mil-spec. What makers of ARs probably mean is that their parts would pass the mil-spec testing and inspection if they got that far. Or, that they are mil-spec production that came off the same lines as real military guns, but were production over-runs. What most makers really mean by "mil-spec" is this: "It looks like the real thing, you have no way of knowing if it isn't, and I don't have the tools to tell. So buy it because the price is right."

Real mil-spec stuff costs more money than non mil-spec stuff does. Why? Because military specifications (what we call "mil-spec") requires a lot of inspecting, measuring and testing. Colt, when they make military rifles fires every single one of them for function and proper zero. Colt takes several from each production batch and tests them for 6,000 rounds. Does "Bobs House of ARs" do that? Even if you went and assembled an AR from parts that were all themselves meeting mil-spec you would not necessarily have built a mil-spec rifle.

If you want the good stuff, don't expect to pay the lowest price. And take any claim of mil-spec with a grain of salt. Perhaps what we need is a new standard, a "close to mil-spec" or "80 percent of mil-spec" that manufacturers can use. Because if something really is mil-spec, it is either unlawful to own, being a select-fire rifle, or hazardous legally, being full-auto parts or stolen from the military or the original manufacturer.

Now, a manufacturer could rightfully claim their parts or even rifles were "made to mil-spec" but not that they "were mil-spec." A further example: you can make a car to NASCAR specs, but unless it has actually been on a NASCAR track, in a race, it isn't a real NASCAR vehicle. The same holds true with mil-spec rifles.

There Are Lots Of Surplus Parts And Rifles

No, no way, nada, zip, zero, zilch. If a dealer at a gun show tells you he "has a box full of FN uppers" you should be suspicious. If he tells you he has a "carton full of take-off M-16 uppers" he bought from the government when they scrapped them, be suspicious. There are two current M-16 manufacturers, Colt and FN. Bushmaster has supplied rifles to the government in the past, and there are a number of makers of accessories who are on the DoD short list. But only those two make rifles right now. Colt makes military and commercial rifles, and sometimes you can find parts, uppers or lowers for sale "surplus." I'd bet they are production over-runs, and sold to generate some quick cash for Colt. FN, by contractual agreement with the government, to make M-16s, does not offer their production or parts for sale on the commercial market. They make their own barrels and uppers and lowers, so you aren't buying "over-runs from the subcontractor."

That said, I have seen new in the wrapper FN barrels for sale. I have seen one FN-marked upper for sale. How did these get out? Who knows? They might have been shipped as replacement parts to some unit, and then as excess were sold. (Probably against regulations.) Or, they were spirited out of an NG armory by a G.I. (Definitely against regulations.) You may see one or two, now and then. But nobody has boxes of them for sale. If someone says they do, then one of two things has happened: Someone in the production and distribution stream has unlawfully diverted said parts. This is a federal felony, worth big fines and serious prison time. Or, someone along the way has lied about the provenance of the parts, and the dealer is passing on the lie.

The AR Has To Be Kept Scrupulously Clean to Work

Well, I don't want to be telling my readers that they can slough off in cleaning, but some parts are more important than others. And some rifles are more picky than others. I have a rifle I haul to classes to hand out as a loaner. Part of my job when teaching some classes is keeping rifles running. When an officer has a rifle go down, I fix it. I hand him my rifle (usually with the admonition "don't touch the sights") and work on his. He keeps getting instruction while I solve his problem. The rifle hasn't been cleaned in three years. I'm not a complete sadist, I turn a chamber brush in the chamber now and then, and swab the bore out occasionally. But otherwise it doesn't get cleaned. And unless the officer using it squirts some lube into it, it hasn't been lubed, either. And in three years of classes, it has not failed yet. At least not with good magazines. There was one incident with USA brand magazines, but once we were done throwing them over the berm, there were no more problems.

(DoD photo)

Not every military barrel gets scrapped from too many bullets going down the bore. Banging on walls, doors, windows and people cause barrels to get bent. Dust in the bore when fired prematurely wears them. Treat yours right and you'll get years of use, even decades.

How well will your rifle work without cleaning? I don't know. If you're really curious, test it. A good rifle will work for a very long time.

You Have To Change AR Barrels Every 3,000 Rounds

I think this one came from the same dynamics that caused people to think 1911 barrels only lasted 5,000 rounds: Marine Corps shooting teams. I know the Marines used to start each target season with new barrels in their 1911s. (Back before the Beretta became the mandated Service pistol.) I know because many of those 1911s ended up at Bar-Sto for new Bar-Sto barrels each off-season. A season was about 5,000 rounds, so of course, the assumption was they were worn out. They weren't, but who wanted to use an old barrel when the Corps would install a new one?

Likewise with rifle barrels. When a long-range target shooter replaces barrels on a regular basis, he isn't doing it because the old one is worn. He's doing it to prevent the potential loss of a match by finding out the lost accuracy limit the hard way. The question is not; "How long does a barrel last," but "How much accuracy can you give up before it matters?" To someone shooting 600 yards, a barrel that goes from a 0.5 MOA performance level to a 1.0 MOA level represents lost match points. To a USPSA Three-gun competitor, that is a sign it probably only has a season or two left in it. To a police officer, that is as much of a change as he sees switching from one lot of ammo to another.

I have one rifle that I acquired the hard way: the customer who left it for work ended up going to prison and could not own it again. Via a mechanic's lien, it ended up staying with me. As I had nothing in it but labor, I used it hard in practice.

I even used it in a winter rifle match we used to do called "Mad Minute." The layout and rules were simple: two targets, one at 50 yards, one at 100. You fire one shot on each, alternating between the targets. Every shot that hits is scored, within the 60 seconds available to shoot. When we started the match, getting 20 or 30 hits was a good score. But then we got warmed up and practiced. I finally maxed the course with 60 shots and 59 hits in one minute. And the barrel was smoking. A few years of regular practice, and annual Mad Minute matches, and I quickly had 15,000 rounds through that barrel. And it still shot 1.5 MOA. That may not seem like much, but it is still within military specs for an issue rifle.

As a 600-yard rifle, that barrel was hopeless. For 100-yard practical competition, defensive and police use, it had plenty of life left in it. And even at long range it wasn't useless. I used it on the National Guard 300-meter pop-up course, and easily got my hits at 300 meters. (1.5 MOA at 300 meters is still a 5-inch group, on a target 16 inches wide. A piece of cake.) I ended up trading it off to someone who wanted to build a beater rifle for his Father-in-Law, and knew his Father-in-Law was never going to put more than a couple of hundred rounds through it, ever. And those would all be plinking.

Use your barrel until it demonstrates a loss of accuracy. Thoroughly scrub the bore and test it again. (It might just be heavily-fouled.) If it is still poor in the accuracy department, get a new barrel. They aren't expensive, as shooting costs go.

There Are Two Sets Of Magazine Tooling

This is variously reported as only two sets, or two sets of mil-spec tooling, or two sets that are owned by the government, shipped to different manufacturers, and usually with the breathless announcement that the winners won due to minority set-asides or some such thing. I have a hard time believing this one, for a number of reasons. To be clear, we're talking about the actual metal-bending parts that you fit to hydraulic presses to cut, stamp, bend and weld sheet metal. Not the presses that do the work. The idea is silly for several reasons:

1) Tooling doesn't last forever. If there were, indeed, only two sets in 1974, there are a lot more now. Or, that tooling is so shabby as to be useless. Tooling has to be maintained, rebuilt, replaced and updated. If you're making one, it is easy to make more.

2) Tooling doesn't fit all machines. The tooling that fits an ABC 2-ton press does not necessarily fit an XYZ 10-ton press.

3) Tooling is cheap, presses are expensive. A production-level hydraulic press purchased, moved, installed and fitted, takes bales of money. As in, $100,000 per step up in capability, or more. You could install a new top-grade high-speed machine, and not have enough left from a million dollar loan to buy your production crew lattes from the local coffee shop. The tooling itself, the part that bends metal to make

the magazines costs less than a luxury SUV. A company that has millions invested in presses would not blink at spending $50,000 to make their own tooling. They are going to be maintaining it anyway, and the cost of making it is tax-deductible, so who would want worn, 30-year-old government tooling, anyway?

A typical government contract calls for 50,000 to 400,000 magazines, at approximately $7.50 each. The small contract is $375,000, the big one is $3 Million. For a $3 million contract, I'll build my own tooling, thank you very much. And in a few years, (or less, with a War on) I'll gladly pull my own tooling out of storage, and make more.

4) There are more than two companies making magazines at any given time.

5) They look different. I have shooting friends who are tool and die makers, production-level mechanical engineers, and machinists. More than one has remarked that they see different stress patterns in the sheet metal of the aluminum of the magazines. If they were all being made on the same tooling, (and thus on the same model presses) the stress marks would be remarkably similar. They aren't.

6) The idea that something critical to military operations would depend on two sets of tooling, is so absurd I can't imagine even a parsimonious accountant going along with it. Forget other sabotage, all you'd have to do is arrange two fires in one weekend, and there wouldn't be new magazines for a while.

Where did such an idea get started? I don't know, all I can do is speculate. All I can figure is that early in the adoption of 30-round magazines, there may have been only two sets of tooling. After all, two plants would have been making enough for Vietnam, and once the handwriting was on the wall and production would diminish, who kept track?

Israel Adopted The AR Because It Was Free

Yes, we gave them warehouses full of M-16s in the past. And they also captured many AKs, and built their own version, the Galil. And with all that, they've selected the M-16 for almost universal use. Units don't pay for rifles and reservists don't make a check out to the IDF when they are issued something. (Not unless they lose it, and can't account for it, but that is a different matter.) The cost of the rifle does not matter to the end user. And the Israelis are nothing if not pragmatic. If there wasn't any difference, or the AK was markedly superior, then the citizens of Israel, who make up the Defense Force and the Reserve units, would insist that the AK be issued.

That should tell us something. Like, we've been paying too much attention to the Vietnam-era teething problems of the M-16A1, and not enough attention to the track record of the current designs and production?

AR-15 vs. AK-47

As the two rifles made in the largest volume, they are the ones you'd most likely run into at a range, in a match, or in a shooting encounter. Lest you think I'm swerving off into tinfoil-hat territory, or contemplating some TEOTWAWKI (the end of the world as we know it) paranoid fantasy, I'll recount an experience some fellow shooters had. We had traveled for over a day in one or another 747 to the Philippines, to compete in the World Shoot. In the scramble to nail down hotel rooms, some of the shooters had used web pages (this was in 1999) as their sole source of info and made reservations. One group joined us at our hotel on the second day, having spent the night at their previous hotel, their web choice hotel.

While "picturesque" described the neighborhood in the day, at night it turned into a setting from a cow town of the 19th century, when the cattle crews were in for some fun. The competitors locked and barred the doors, and loaded their competition guns, they were so alarmed by the goings-on outside. In many parts of the world, if things turn noisy what you'll see and have to use (if it gets that bad) won't be five-shot Mossberg pump shotguns. The hardware will be AKs of various iterations.

Their experience aside, I found my trip to the Philippines to be fun, safe, hot and humid, and a great time.

Over in the sandbox, when our Armed Forces were early into the fracas, we found that there were a whole lot more soldiers and Marines who needed rifles than there were rifles to be issued. It wasn't unusual for a tank crew to have two rifles and two pistols issued for the four of them. Pickup AKs were quite common. And since the AK is ubiquitous, it would be useful to know how to use one, and what the strengths and weaknesses are. Besides, there are a whole bunch of shooters who are interested in getting into Three-Gun competition, who aren't ready to break the bank for a hi-zoot AR competition setup. Getting started with a much less expensive AK is a viable option, as long as you know the strengths and weaknesses.

There is someone still, five paragraphs into this chapter, who thinks I'm some sort of a survivalist loonie for suggesting that they should know how to use an AK in case they are

(DoD photo by Staff Sgt. Charles B. Johnson, U.S. Army)

Early in the Iraq war, while all infantry units had all the small arms they needed, not every tanker had one. As in earlier wars, tankers simply used picked-up enemy weapons. This soldier on patrol is carrying an M-4 with all the toys. That gold thing behind him? A satellite antenna.

Ready to go, a shorty AR and an AK are just about the same size, have the same sight radius, and work very well.

The new flat-top ARs offer a quick means of attaching optics. Advantage: AR.

someplace where AKs are common. Do you know how to swim? Do you know how to use a fire extinguisher? At the very least, if you happen to encounter one at the range, or while helping a friend clean out the home of a deceased and elderly relative, do you know how to check if an AK is loaded? (You'd be surprised what you'll find when the day comes.) There are a whole lot of skills and knowledge that are useful and helpful to know beforehand, and where to find the best latte shop in town is not on the top of my list.

With that in mind, I hauled my AK off to the range (hey, someone has to do the work of testing and evaluating, right?) and spent an onerous afternoon comparing it to an AR. OK, I'll admit it, it wasn't onerous at all. My AK is a Bulgarian, a relatively rare import. Apparently there were just a few thousand of them brought into the country back in the late 1980s. I came to acquire it while working at the gun shop. We were visited by an ATF agent, with a federal offender and family in tow. It seems the current owner of the rifle (and a couple of footlockers full of other gear, too) had previously been a Pharmacist, gun collector and FFL holder. However, he had been caught selling prescription drugs without the benefit of the proper prescriptions. So the last official function of his federal firearms license, before it would be revoked and he was to go to prison, was to liquidate his firearms collection. Once we heard the story, took in the scene of the unrepentant felon, his nagging, shrewish wife and crying child, we found out we were the last gun shop on the list. The rest had either decided to pass on the offer, or offered so little money the ex-pharmacist was insulted. After us it was the smelter for the guns. So we put our heads together, estimated the wholesale cost of the guns (two footlockers and assorted cardboard boxes full of AKs, Beretta 92s, 1911s, Mossberg shotguns, ammo, magazines, assorted other gear) cut that in half, and Tim, the owner, went to make the offer. And when he spoke, he mentioned a figure half of what we'd just calculated. The felon almost broke down in tears, said yes, and that was it. Apparently we had offered a lot more than anyone else.

As was the custom on big collection buys, the staff (John

and I) got our pick of one from the bunch, at cost plus transfer fee. I think I ended up paying about a hundred dollars for the AK, a couple of cans of ammo, another ammo can full of magazines, and a bayonet, web pouch, cleaning rod, all the assorted "stuff" that comes with a rifle. (To mis-quote the fashion model, "don't hate me because I'm lucky.") John also bought an AK, and the rest went out for sale. At the prices we could offer, they didn't last long.

To be fair in the comparison, I used a like model of AR. Since the Bulgarian AK is an iron-sights version with folding stock, I used an iron-sight tele-stock AR, and not one with a tuned trigger. In comparing two different rifles, we need to understand how they stack up in a number of categories: Accuracy and terminal ballistics, manipulation of controls, comfort to shoot, reliability, durability, and availability and cost. And all must be considered as well in the potential for improvement in each category. I ran the two rifles through a set of standard drills that you would be almost certain to encounter in either a competitive environment or a defensive encounter.

Accuracy And Terminal Ballistics

I tested them by shooting groups off a sandbagged rest at 100 yards. I also used the Lahti rest as a backup, to make sure I was getting repeatable results. I was.

Accuracy depends a lot on the ammo you are using. If you feed your AK primo ammo, like Winchester, Remington or Federal, or imported Lapua, you'll find it shooting a lot better. If you buy the cheapest Chinese import ammo at the guns shows, then you'll have less accuracy. Considering that per 1,000 rounds, the Win/Rem/Fed would run you over $500, and the Chinese under $100, most shooters shoot the import stuff. Expect 3 inches at 100 yards at best. Some combinations will do worse, and at the outside you can expect to just barely be able to keep all your shots in the USPSA "A" zone, 6 inches wide, at 100 yards. With an AR, 3 inches is the worst you'll see, and many can do a lot better.

The rear sight of the AK is meant to be durable, not target-grade accurate.

Even with long hands, I have no hope of contacting a standard AK safety with my index finger.

The sight radius of the two is not so different: the AR has a sight radius of 14.5 inches on a shorty, while the AK is 15. (The numbers surprised me, too.)The sights of the AK work against marksmanship. The open notch and blade setup is less precise than an aperture sight, so precision work is less likely. For speed, they work fine, but a fast miss isn't much use.

Terminally, the argument between 5.56 and 7.62X39 will never end. Either will get the job done. As a base gun/ammo combo, we have to call this a tie. Were the AK switched to the 5.45 Soviet round, the results would be much the same. The longer 5.45 does more work when it overturns, but being a steel jacket (usually) it isn't going to fragment.

For improvements, we have to give the nod to the AR. You can easily find replacement barrels to swap out a shot-out or poor quality AR. The tools are easy to come by, the work not difficult. AKs, on the other hand, aren't nearly so easy. Most do not use barrels screwed into the receiver trunnion. The barrels are pressed into place and use a large-diameter cross pin to lock them in. Without a press to remove and replace the barrel, you're out of luck. AR barrels are everywhere, and AKs are not. While you can replace an AR barrel yourself, you'll need to find a gunsmith familiar with the job to re-barrel and AK. And .223/5.56 ammo of better accuracy potential is also much more common than AK ammo.

Finally, if you want to get better sights, you can find a veritable host of optics, red-dot sights and improved iron sights to install on your AR. None of which is the case for the AK. You can fit optics, but none are durable or inexpensive. Improved iron sights? Fuggedaboudit.

Advantage, AR-15.

Manipulation Of Controls

Part of the manipulation of controls involves magazine changes. In a competitive environment, the sole act of replacing a magazine is measured against the clock. In the real world, the difference in time between them is overshadowed by the nature of the problem itself. In real life, you do not do a standing reload in the open against stationary opponents. However, to get a handle on the time difference, I did a standard IPSC drill: Vice Presidente. Three targets, ten yards away, a yard apart. Two hits on each, reload, and two hits again. In El Presidente, you start with your back to the target. In Vice, you face the targets.

Since the timer records all shots, I can write down the three relevant times: the time to first shot, which requires I push the safety to fire, the split times between shots, and the time to reload.

First, the safety. The safety on the AK is also the ejection port cover. Unless you have hands like an orangutan, you cannot reach the cover and push it off, while maintaining a firing grip on the AK. You have to use some sort of off the grip motion. The AR is great, in that the safety is right under yoru thumb. Advantage, AR.

The split times are a function of trigger, stock, and caliber.

I have to reach up to swipe it to "fire."

Once swept, you then have to get your hand from the safety to the trigger.

The trigger on some AKs can be wretched. Mine is OK. The stock on an AK is usually too short, so I adjusted the AR slider until it was as close as I could get it to being the same as the AK. At the short distance involved, the recoil difference between 5.56 and 7.62X39 is negligible. Here we have a draw.

The reload is complicated in the AK. Unlike the AR, with a magazine button, the AK uses a paddle right behind the magazine. Where the AR magazine goes into place straight up the well, the AK locks by rocking. You hook the front tab of the magazine in the receiver, then pivot the rear up until it locks into place. Fast, secure, durable, and requiring two hands. The AR is much faster. Advantage, AR.

One situation that is particular to the Israeli Defense Force and Israeli civilians is in carry: it is required by law that a weapon being carried in some circumstances be carried with the chamber empty. Many reservists use public transportation, as do many civilians. It is too easy for a safety to get pushed off in the crush of a bus for anyone to be comfortable with a chambered round. The AR is easy to carry that way. You can leave the hammer cocked and the safety on. Or, you can leave the hammer forward and keep the safety on Fire or Auto. And the dust cover is closed. When you rack the action, the cover opens and you are ready in whatever condition you desired. The AK, on the other hand, uses the safety as the dust cover. To enclose the action and keep sand and dust out, the cover must be closed, which puts on the safety. And blocks the operating rod. In order to chamber a round, you must first push the safety/dust cover down, then work the operating handle. Two motions, to the ARs one. In this particular situation, advantage AR.

Comfort To Shoot

The AK stock was designed for short-statured Soviet troops. With little space in an armored vehicle, a long weapon would have been clumsy indeed. Add cold-weather clothing, short-statured Asian troops, and you understand why the stocks are so short. The final touch is that it is easier to use a stock that is too short than it is to use a stock that is too long. As a result, it is not unusual for taller-than-average American shooters and soldiers to use an AK with their nose pressed against the receiver dust cover.

You can increase the length of pull on a wooden-stocked AK, and if it happens to be less than elegant, who is going to complain? Your fellow shooters might not even notice. The folding stocks of various designs for the AK are simply wretched. While it can be a bit uncomfortable at times to shoot a tele-stocked AR, the various folders on AKs are simply awful. With some you can't even get a good sight picture, a proper check weld is out of the question, and they are all uncomfortable.

Advantage, AR.

No way will it reach.

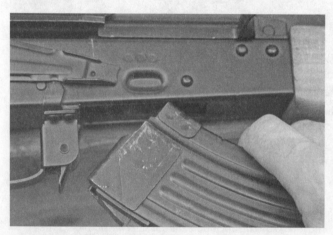

To seat a magazine, hook the front,

Rock it back,

Until it locks.

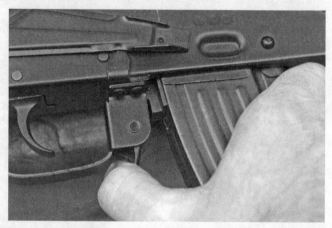

To start a reload, hook the paddle with your thumb before rocking forward.

Reliability

Here we have to categorically cede the field to the AK. It is possible, literally, to deal with a mud-caked AK by taking off the dust cover and swishing the rifle around in a reasonably clean puddle, creek, lake or whatever. It will clean up well enough to work. You can shoot an AK without ever cleaning it, and except for the absolute worst conditions, expect it to function. I've seen videotapes of AK testing that included firing one in a dust chamber, where the power-driven dust was so thick and at such velocity that the test-shooter had to wear a full protective suit. Otherwise, the dust would have stopped him before it stopped the AK. (The AK worked just fine, by the way.)

Advantage AK

Durability

There are two kinds of durability to consider: How well would a rifle stand up to utter neglect, and how well would a rifle stand up to a reasonable amount of care with regular, if occasionally hard, use? For the former, the AK is the standout. Short of running over it with a truck, it is hard to get a well-built AK to stop working. But with a bit of care, the AR can last years, the same as an AK. A tie.

Where they differ is in magazines. AK magazines are hell

The AK stock works for short shooters, but tall shooters might have a problem.

for tough. You can run them over and they'll still work. If you are hard on magazines, then the AK gets the nod.

Availability And Cost

Here we have a problem. Do we consider simply the financial cost of acquiring one or the other, the cost of the initial purchase and maintenance, or the purchase, maintenance and upgrade costs? For simple purchase, the AK wins. There are AKs of various manufacture in all the wholesale catalogs in the $300-$350 range. Yes, they're basic guns, but we're considering the threshold cost. At the same "get a gun and consider accessories later" level of the AR, a good one will run twice what the AK does. I'm considering wholesale cost not because I'm trying to reveal any "inside" secrets. Retail costs vary depending local taxes, local laws and the dealers desire to make a profit. Wholesale costs are the same across the country.

But then you have to add stuff. A rifle without magazines

is a clumsy single-shot. AR and AK mags cost pretty much the same, with choices ranging from $12 to $20 each. The magazines last a long time, but the AK magazines are definitely more durable.

Ammo costs are all in favor of the AK. Depending on the current state of imported ammo from the various previously or still communist countries now in business with us, ammo can run from $75 to $125 per 1,000 rounds. Less, if you buy in volume when a new boatload arrives and the wholesalers are flush with it. It doesn't matter much as to cost, between 7.62X39 and 5.45X39, but your rifle can only use one or the other. Good .223/5.56 ammo starts in the $150/K range and goes up. Nod to the AK.

For maintenance costs, a simple cleaning rod, some patches and lubricant are all you need for the AK. The AR will require a lot more, as well as special tools to take some of the mechanism apart for annual cleanings. The cost difference isn't much, but it is there, so the AK wins here.

The AK round penetrates a lot of material.

As for rebuilding, upgrading, replacing worn parts, the AR is the winner. You can buy all the parts you need to replace every single component on the lower receiver (the actual rifle, by law) and the upper of your AR. And do the work yourself, once you know a few tricks. Except for replacing the stock and handguards, there isn't much you can do to the AK. If you're a machinist, and insist on making changes, you can do more, but not anything like the extensive list of things you can do to an AR.

Conclusion

One situation pointed out by advocates on both sides is the Israeli Defense Force. With many, many AKs captured through the years, and even their own design produced in-country (the Galil) the IDF, reserve forces and many civilians are seen with the M-16 in various iterations. If the AK was so good, wouldn't they be using the readily-available AK? Those favoring the AK point out that the IDF has more than once received large shipments of M-16s free of charge. And that using U.S. loans Israel can buy rifles at the U.S. military unit

The 7.62X39 round makes holes in many things, mild steel plate among them.

This is a steel-core AK round, after going through sheet steel, drywall, plywood, glass, and lodging in ballistic gelatin.

cost, a significant cost savings. Except, that once the rifles are in the warehouses, the units that draw them don't see or care about cost. It isn't as if the IDF Special Forces has to fork over $650 for a Galil, $450 for an M-16/M4, or $250 for an AK. It is simply a matter of filling out the requisition paperwork and signing for the shipment. And the Israeli experience has been that with care the AR works as well in the desert as the AK.

For most work, there isn't a lot of difference between them. If you need fast handling and manipulation, or precise work for target shooting, the AR is the one you want. In a defensive predicament, the shortcomings of the AK can be overcome. For someone who wants to get shooting, on a budget, the AK has a definite appeal. The "answer" own both, shoot both, learn both, and have all the bases covered.

Patrol Rifle Conversion

Not all surplus is suitable for patrol work. My Father carried an M-3 through France and Germany, and loved it. But it isn't what you want in patrol cars.

Did you know your police department can get an M-16 for $39? No, that's not surprising, because a lot of police departments don't know it either. What they get is a government-surplus M-16A1 from storage, for the cost of shipping. It comes out of the wrappers as a silver-gray anodized, fixed stock, triangular handguard, 1/12 twist 20-inch barrel A1 with the assurance that it has passed inspection well enough to be put in storage instead of having been destroyed by the government as used-up scrap metal.

Yee-ha! Except, as it comes out of the box, it is usually smeared in grease, and set up so that it isn't very useful for issue on duty. It isn't compact enough to easily fit in a patrol car. It isn't set up for tactical slings, for a SWAT or Entry team. The thin barrel does make it light to carry, and the 1/12 twist isn't a problem for ammo, as all the "good stuff" is available in 52-, 53-, 55-grain weights.

It can be made better. My friend Jeff Chudwin, President of the Illinois Tactical Officers Association, came up with the basic idea. Fellow gunsmith (and artist in metal) Ned Christiansen and I added a few refinements, and I then found myself making them for departments around Chicago that had bought rifles but needed them upgraded.

What is wrong, that needs changing? The barrel is too long. The stock, fixed, is too long for short-statured officers and those wearing body armor. The handguards are fragile, and don't lock into the car racks made for AR-15/M-16. And, the triangular handguards don't work well with tactical slings. Finally, they come Safe-Semi-Full on the selectors, and no one needs an Auto setting for patrol work. Maybe for some SWAT or Entry work, but even there I have my doubts. So, we changed the rifles.

First, change them to Safe-Semi.

Law Enforcement Use Of
The AR-15/M-16, Full Auto

One of the attractions of law enforcement is the opportunity to get hands on neat gear. Yes, that's right, some people join because they get to use the lights and siren, wear the uniform, and play with the automatic weapons. It isn't noble or pretty, but it's the truth.

That said, just how useful is the selector switch on an M-16? In a military context, it can be useful, but not always. As a short-term option, using an M-16 or M-4 as a squad automatic weapon is a sure way to use up a weapon in short order. The military use of an automatic weapon falls into several firing rates; "sustained," "denial," and "final protective fire" or "cyclic rate." In Sustained, a machinegunner will fire short, controlled bursts into a small or well-defined area. "Three- to five-shot bursts every five seconds down this street until I tell you otherwise, or if a viable target presents itself" would be a typical order for sustained fire. Sustained, because at that rate the machinegunner can continue to fire until he has exhausted his ammunition, two or three hours later. He has plenty of time to let the barrel cool, and if need be, can change barrels between bursts. In Denial, the rate is

upped. He'll fire five- to seven-shot bursts, he'll direct it at specific areas, and he can just manage to keep the gun cool by furiously swapping barrels as needed. Final protective fire is hard on weapons, but harder on units that haven't planned for it. In FPF, the machinegun position will have special limit stakes driven into the ground. (You do not do FPF off the bipod if you have a choice, and do it on a tripod only when it can be locked.) typically, FPF lines are parallel to a unit's front line. When an FPF is called for, the machinegunner shifts his weapon to the limit stakes and fires at the cyclic rate of the weapon. Typical application? To deal with human-wave assaults on positions on a Korean ridgeline at night.

One other use, but not in the training or field manuals, comes from my friend Bruce Britt, an M-60 gunner in Vietnam: "In an ambush, I would fire a full belt in one burst, sweeping the ambush kill zone. When it ran dry, I'd kick out the barrel, install a new one, and see if anyone needed any extra attention. They never did." And his gas tube was often a dull red by then, too. Full auto fire is very hard even on the weapons designed for it, and the barrel Bruce "kicked out" was unusable, worn to scrap.

Even at the slowest rate, Sustained, using an M-16 or M-4 as a squad automatic weapon is a good way to burn out

The MP-5 has been the SWAT long gun of choice for many years, but it is after all just a heavy 9mm pistol.

If you work in a place where a belt-fed machinegun is useful, it isn't anyplace in the United States the rest of us want to live. This FN M-249 is a great tool, but not a suitable one for law enforcement.

Putting accurate fire onto an offender, full-auto fire is not much use. At least not outside the military environment. Here, Ned hammers the steel in an LEO class.

the barrel in short order. I'd be surprised if an M-4 lasted 15 minutes used as an emergency SAW. One Ordnance test designed to see what would happen called for firing an M-4 at an emergency rate until it failed. What they found was that in the space of a couple of minutes, you could fire on the order of 400 rounds through an M-4. The barrel would heat to the point the rifle began to cook off immediately, until the barrel softened to the point where it drooped (in the range of 1,200 degrees Fahrenheit) and a bullet then exited through the side. Now, if you need the firepower, don't have an M-249, and have spare M-4s, then by all means, go for it. (Keep your

non-firing hand off the handguards, for when that errant bullet exits the side of the barrel!) But there is no police equivalent of any of these firing rates or needs. No police department or SWAT team is going to deny an area to an offender by filling it with bullets.

There is one situation where some think the select-fire option is useful: assault fire. In a military context, assault fire calls for short, controlled bursts on the assault objective or enemy positions by the assault team as they walk, run, crawl or scramble those last few yards before they can throw explosive gifts. Again, the idea is to fill the air with

Full auto fire is hard to control without a lot of practice. And that means lots of ammo. Here, a patrol rifle conversion gets tested before being shipped to a police department.

so many bullets that the enemy can't poke their heads up to shoot back, as you close in on with them and blow them up. Imagine the outrage if a police department were to do just such a thing. What does that leave? It leaves full-auto or burst fire as a means of getting multiple fast hits on a target (offender) in the shortest possible time, so as to deny him the opportunity to shoot police officers.

OK, perhaps we're on to something. Even the fastest shooter can't keep up with a moderate-rate full auto weapon. An IPSC Grandmaster can shoot "splits," the time between shots, aimed on a target, of .12 seconds. The low end of the cyclic rate of an M-16 is 750 rpm, and mil-spec allows up to 900 rpm. At the low figure, that produces split times of .080 seconds, and the 900 rpm figure gives us .066 seconds. But not all firearms are equal. You see, we have to manipulate them, and for that we need thumbs. The common law enforcement full-auto firearms are the MP-5 and the AR-15/M-16. Both have problems as far as the safety and full-auto are concerned. The MP-5 simply has a safety apparently designed to be operated by orangutans. The lever is so far forward of the pistol grip that only shooters with huge hands can manipulate them. This has lead to strange "Ready" postures with the MP-5 held at odd angles and positions, to allow the operator to reach the safety. Or decisions like that of L.A., where the SWAT teams stack and enter with the safety of their MP-5s in the "Fire" position.

You and your team may elect to enter on a high-risk warrant service, drug raid or other operation with the safety off, but not on my team. And don't call me as an expert witness when things go awry, for I don't think it is a prudent thing to be doing. So, we'll have to consider entry using rifles in the "Safe" position. At some time you'll need to challenge or fire on an offender. Let's construct the experiment thusly:

We'll be facing a target 5 yards away, with the need to react to the start signal (or in real life, the offenders drawing a firearm with intent to fire), move the selector to the desired position, aim well enough to get hits, and fire three rounds. All rounds must hit. Misses in a match are penalized, but in real life the penalties can be much higher than simply lowered score and diminished match standings. In real life misses can be fatal to others. So we'll insist on hits.

The process requires four steps:

React to start, moving rifle up from low ready,
Push selector to desired position,
Confirm that aim is "good enough" for proper hits,
Fire appropriate rounds.

Steps one and three require the same amount of time, regardless of your decision to fire in semi-automatic or burst or full-auto mode. What differs is firing time and selector selection time. Lets take the last step first. In full-auto mode or burst, an M-16 or M-4 will cycle at a minimum of 750 rounds per minute. That gives us a between shot time (known as a "split" in competitive shooting) of .080 seconds. A super-fast competition shooter can fire splits of .12 seconds. Even an average shooter can manage splits under a quarter of a second, or .25 seconds. The full-auto selection thus gains from

Full auto is fun, but not often used or needed even in the law enforcement world. Here, a patrol rifle conversion that has been left select-fire is being tested.

.080 seconds to as much as .34 seconds over semi-auto fire. There are only two splits in three shots, as the first shot is the same, coming from the initial firing stroke.

This leaves us with the manipulation time to get the selector from "Safe" to "Fire" or "Auto." The total time for a fast competition shooter to react, lift, confirm aim and press the trigger for the first shot is under a second. If we simply make it a full second for convenience, and then add in the split times, we come in at 1.25 to 1.5 seconds for three shots, all A hits at 5 yards. Now, the question is, how long does it take to push the selector from Safe to Auto? And the answer is, a long time, relatively speaking. You see, the selector works great going down to Fire. The safety moves in a direction that conforms to your thumb. Your thumb goes down, the safety pivots, you're at "Fire" and ready to go. To get from Fire to Auto, you must then push your thumb in a different direction, to continue the pivot of the safety lever.

It can take an additional full second. Or more. The shooter firing semi can have all three hits on target before the shooter selecting full auto or burst has his first shot off.

Counter-intuitively, full-auto fire is actually slower than semi in the close confines of a drug raid. When I suggested this to a group of police officers the reaction ranged from "You're wrong" to "You're full of *bleep*" So I set it up as a test. We each faced the target with rifles in low ready, safety on. On the buzzer, the rules were, all three shots had to be A hits, get them done as fast as possible. The results were consistent: all shot three hits faster in semi than in full auto or burst.

So, if your department won't authorize full-auto M-16s, don't sweat it. You haven't given up anything useful.

After I wrote the section above, I went to a tactical officers annual conference, and sat through a briefing on an incident that opened my eyes: A tactical team went to serve an arrest warrant, on one offender. They had to hit two adjacent houses, not knowing which one he was in. Well, the one he was in was barricaded, and when the entry team tried to break down the door, he opened fire. In the ensuing half-hour firefight, he killed two officers and wounded several others. The SWAT team members, pinned down and unable to locate the offender in the barricaded house, receiving accurate and intense rifle fire from the offender, tried to gain control with burst-fire suppressive fire. They did not succeed, and ended up using up their ammunition so quickly they had to reload dropped magazines with boxes of ammunition thrown to them by fellow officers.

Wow. I guess there are instances where burst or full-auto fire might be called for. Still for a Patrol officer, semi is a much better choice.

The simplest conversion of an M-16 to semi-auto only means removing the auto sear. But not all chiefs are comfortable with that. And it is still a machinegun as far as the paperwork is concerned.

Fire Control Mechanism Conversion

The simplest means of converting (mechanically, at least) an M-16 to semi-only is to remove the auto sear. The selector will still turn all the way around, and that might cause problems in some marginally-timed rifles. The next step would be to remove the auto sear and swap the M-16 selector for an AR-15 selector. But, all administrators I've talked to were less than comfortable with that. "What if one of my guys buys an auto sear and selector at a gun show? He can convert a departmental rifle to full auto if he wants." I don't see that as a problem, but I must confess that they would know their officers better than I would.

So, I yank out all the M-16 parts, place them in a sealed bag with the rifle's serial number, and replace them. That way, the department can keep them on hand as proof of conversion, and proof of retention of the nasty, evil, full-auto parts. I've found that the DPMS fire control parts kits available from Brownells work great. I install the parts and do the timing and function tests to make sure it works as it is supposed to.

The lack of the auto sear is obvious by the empty hole above the selector lever, and the selector only turns from Safe to Semi.

Stock Conversion

To make the stock better-suited for short people, I remove the fixed stock and buffer tube, and replace them (along with the buffer and spring) with a tele-stock kit. When required I use the current mil-spec Colt or mil-spec provider tele-stock. But I much prefer the old style. The new stocks lack the upper

This SIG 552 has the folding stock engineered as part of the rifle. ARs have to be re-built for something close.

A patrol rifle conversion in-process. Once re-zeroed and function tested, it gets shipped back.

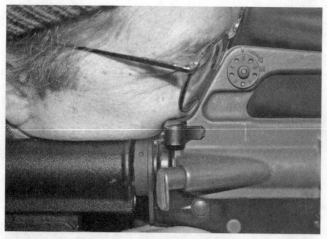

The sliding stock should be locked or taped out one spot. Otherwise you risk banging yourself in the eye if you haven't extended the stock before firing.

enough to capture the buffer. (Trust me on this one, I've opened more than one AR that had a no-longer-captured buffer. It comes out of the tube with gusto.)

The one drawback to the tele-stock is that it can be made too short. In fact, when telescoped to the minimum length, it can be so short that a shooter under stress can raise the rifle to shoot, and slam the rear sight into his eye. Starting a gunfight by injuring your sighting eye is not a prescription for success. To solve that problem, we bring electrical tape to the fore. A wrapping of electrical tape just past the second to shortest stock setting keeps it from being collapsed to the minimum. At that length you can shoot it in a pinch without injuring yourself. And it can always be extended. (One of these days I'm going to design something to short-stop the slider. But until then, tape will do the job.)

sling swivel loop, and many tactical slings slide off when the loop is missing.

The trick with this change is in fitting the new tube and nuts. The standard buffer tube has an external shoulder, and stops at the correct spot to trap the buffer retainer plunger. The tele-stock tube does not have an external shoulder. You must screw it in far enough to trap the buffer retainer, but not so far it keeps the retainer from raising far

Barrel

At 20 inches, even with a tele-stock on it, the rifle is too long. A squad car is not a roomy place, even if it is a full-sized SUV. (As with so many other instances, inventory increases to fill available space. If the chief issues you a full-size SUV, he also issues you enough gear to fill it.) But barrels are expensive. The solution is simple: shorten the existing barrel. I have done a bunch, and haven't had to mess with the gas port yet.

(US Air Force Photo By Staff Sgt. Stacy L. Pearsall)

The Steyr AUG has quick-change barrels. You can make any rifle shorter or longer by simply installing a new barrel. (It takes about five seconds.) But ARs aren't AUGs, so we must follow another path.

The best way to shorten a barrel and cut new threads is with a lathe. Lacking that, you risk making a mess of the job.

A shortened barrel. I have yet to test a rifle thus shortened that didn't work 100 percent.

Not everyone wants a Vortex flash hider. (I don't know why not, it is the best.) So some rifles just have the old flash hider re-installed.

Installing a tele-stock on a full-sized rifle is not new. Nor is it rare. There are a number of M-16 rifles in Iraq that have been so altered. For a unit that spends its time in vehicles, a shorter rifle is a great thing. A unit can order the needed stocks through the system, and with luck, get them. Then it is a simple matter for a trained armorer (or someone who knows what they are doing) to swap stocks, test and re-

issue. Why not just get M-4 uppers? Or rebuild the M-16s to M4 configuration? Because M-4 uppers can't be ordered through the system (it is a long, detailed and messy story) and you can't turn M-16s into M-4s. It just isn't done. Why not shorten them? You'd then face charges of defacing or damaging government property. Swapping parts is one thing, but taking cutting tools to government barrels is something else entirely. The new SPR is being built with a tele-stock, even though it is a medium- to long-range sniper rifle. Luckily, in the law enforcement environment, we only have two constraints: What the chief wants, and state law.

You cannot simply shorten a barrel with a hacksaw and some lapping tools to clean up the muzzle. To do it right takes power tools. I use my lathe, and shorten the barrel to 16.5", re-thread it for a flash hider, and re-cut the crown. If you have a lathe and some experience, it is an easy job. If you do not, you risk knarfing it beyond repair. I lathe-cut the threads to make sure they are concentric to the bore. If you try to cut the threads with a die and die handle, you'll almost certainly get the threads cut at an angle, and your flash hider will screw on at an angle (and with great difficulty, too).

Many question if the result will be starved for gas, and short-stroke. I wondered too, 15 years ago when I did it for the first time. I conducted a test. I fired the modified rifle at a range session to get it good and dirty. (I practiced on the club's simulated plates for the Light Rifle Pop and Flop. It was easy to put a couple of hundred rounds downrange in an afternoon.) I then left the rifle and ammo in the back of my truck (in the winter) until the next range session. The morning I was there to test it and other rifles, the overnight low had been 17 degrees Fahrenheit. The rifle, dirty and frozen, with frozen ammunition and magazines, worked just fine. Since then I've done the same test to a number of other rifles, for the same result: the rifles work. (For some reason, every time I go to do this test, the overnight temperature ends up in the upper teens. I've done it a bunch of times from 16 to 19 degrees.)

Once shortened, I run a patch down the bore to clean out any stray machining chips, clean out the cutting lube, and then take it to the range for zeroing. It is a rare rifle that requires more than a couple of clicks to re-zero it. And the accuracy of military-production 1/12 "pencil" barrels can be surprising. The last batch of rifles I did all produced 25-yard-zero targets that were tight clusters. Two rifles each fired final groups of five shots into a single hole. Each group could have been covered with a single paster.

Since I ship them back to the department with the final test-fire target, those two got extra attention. What I heard from the training officer was that there was some argument over who would get one of the two tack-driving re-built M-16s, and who would have to "settle" for one of the brand new commercial AR-15s the department had also bought. Apparently, given a choice, the officers wanted the two most accurate M-16s, then preferred the other M-16s, then took

PATROL RIFLE POLICY
Anytown Police Department

Special Order #223, 2004
   AUTHORIZED PATROL Rifle / CARBINE

   A. The authorized patrol rifle / carbine may be provided by the Police Department or individually officer owned.

   B. All authorized patrol rifle / carbines whether personal or issued, must meet the following specifications:

1. Unless otherwise authorized by the Chief of police, authorized patrol rifle / carbines must be AR-15/CAR-15 type. (1) Butt stock may be either fixed or collapsible.

2. Authorized patrol rifle / carbines must be chambered for 5.56 x 45mm rifle ammunition. (2) Primary magazines are to be 20-round capacity / loaded with 18 rounds. Back up magazines may be 30-round type loaded with 28 rounds. Ammunition shall be of a type approved by the chief of police.

3. Authorized patrol rifle / carbines must be semi-automatic only unless otherwise authorized by the chief of police. (3)

4. Authorized patrol rifle / carbine barrel length must be at least 16 inches unless otherwise authorized by the chief of police. (4)

5. Authorized patrol rifle / carbines must be equipped with a sling system suitable for tactical deployment where the weapon may be retained hands free yet ready for immediate use. (5)

6. Only the iron sight system will be employed unless otherwise authorized by the chief of police. Any supplemental sight system authorized for deployment must be suitable for tactical close-quarters engagement and either allow for immediate access to the iron sights, or be quickly removable to allow for access to the iron sight system if the supplemental sight system fails for any reason. (6)

7. Other than the below listed modifications, no modification of the patrol rifle / carbine from manufacturer issue is permitted without prior approval of the chief of police. Requests for modification must be submitted to the chief of police through the range officer and training commander. Recommendations regarding the request will accompany the request through the chain of command.

8. Generally approved options:

   1. Front Post Night Sight

   2. Surefire Flashlight attachments

   3. Redi-Mag magazine carrier

   4. Vortex Flash Hider

   5. DPMS Ambidextrous Safety

9. Authorized Patrol Rifle / Carbine Deployment Policy

   a. Authorized patrol rifle / carbines will be deployed consistent with Department Rules and Regulations. The officer on scene, given the known totality of the circumstances, shall make the decision as to deployment of the patrol rifle / carbine in the same manner as with the duty handgun or any other defensive tool. (7)

   b. Authorized patrol rifle / carbines are recommended for field deployment when any of the following conditions are identified:

      i. Any potentially dangerous / deadly force situation where the officer has reason to believe that deployment of the patrol rifle will contribute to the safe resolution of the incident or diminish risk to officers or the public.

      ii.The officer is assigned as a Rapid Deployment Contact or Search & Rescue Team officer.

      iii. The officer is assigned as a cover officer on a perimeter containment team.

      iv. The officer has cause to believe that the suspect is wearing ballistic body armor or is shielded by an intervening barrier.

      v. The officer has cause to believe that the suspect may be engaged at extended distance.

10. Officers employing the patrol rifle / carbine will maintain control of the firearm at all times or insure that the weapon is controlled / secured by another police officer. (8)

11. Officers must complete department approved patrol rifle / carbine training prior to field deployment. Officers must successfully complete departmental re-qualification and training to remain eligible for field deployment of the patrol rifle / carbine. (9)

12. Prior to duty deployment; the rifle / carbine must be inspected by the department range officer or other qualified armorer for proper mechanical function and overall condition and be serial numbered for department record.
   The patrol rifle /carbine must be properly sighted in according to department range protocol. No patrol rifle / carbine may deployed on the street that has not met the above requirements.

   By order of:

   Chief of Police

My comments on my version of the model policy, not what the chief would send (were he or she to copy this);

(1) To make sure all officers are using the same type of rifle, in case an officer needs to use one grabbed from a patrol car. Yes, the AK type is certainly reliable and rugged enough, but a department has enough to do getting everyone up to speed on the AR. Adding more rifles to the mix just makes the job harder.

(2) No special varmint chambers, no tight, accuracy-improving .223 chambers, just mil-spec chambers that will work with all ammunition the department issues or approves, and will work under all conditions.

(3) No select-fire or burst rifles, without departmental approval.

(4) Shorter barrels may be a violation of state law, and shorter barrels have less terminal effectiveness.

(5) Any sling except the military sling is approved.

(6) If a scope is installed, it must be readily removable. The cold here in the Great Lakes region kills batteries. The rain and snow fogs optics. Only irons are always ready, so if the scope croaks you have to be able to remove it quickly.

(7) Some departments have special restrictions on the use of a rifle. Ideally, the rifle is just another firearm, one with better sights and more capacity than a handgun. It should be just another tool in the toolbox, not some special gizmo that requires a decoder ring and personal phone call from the chief to use.

(8) The only way to ensure control when handcuffing a suspect, or transporting a prisoner, is with a sling. Or another officer, whose hands are free.

(9) Yes, the Marine Corps taught you a lot about how to use a rifle. And a lot of what they taught you is irrelevant to police work. Regardless of how much you know, you go through the departmental course so we know you know everything we'll hold you accountable for. Nothing personal, just making sure.

---

the commercial ARs. Not a fair test, as the M-16s had been test-fired and zeroed, making their jobs easier.

Sling

The last thing we need to do to convert a box-stock M-16A1 into a Patrol Rifle is to install a sling. Yes, we can just install a tactical sling of some kind, but making a SWAT rifle was not our original intent. I'm not knocking patrol officers when I say a tactical sling can be too complicated. A tactical sling does a lot more than just keep a rifle off the ground, but it does so with extra webbing, or clips, or hardware. Our patrol rifle has to fit into a vehicle rack, and come out cleanly. If the rifle has so much extra webbing it risks getting hung up on the car when you exit, it isn't much help. I've known officers with loose slings who had the rifle snatched out of their grasp when running (doorknob, fencepost) or couldn't exit a vehicle (rifle sling tangled with radio cable) or couldn't get it out of the rack (excess sling caught in rack). We need a sling that is compact, can be extended when needed, keeps the rifle off the ground, and is easy to extend.

Let's back up for a moment: Why a sling? Because an officer can't just lay a rifle down on the ground when it comes time to put the cuffs on a suspect. You risk damage to the rifle, you are leaving an unsecured, loaded rifle out of your reach, and out of your reach it may be grabbed by someone else.

The Chudwin sling uses a plain Uncle Mike's strap. Loop the bow end through the upper sling loop of the tele-stock. Run the secured end through the slider, and then tie, stitch or otherwise secure it to the front sight housing. To store it in a rack, run the slider forward until the slack is gone. When you need it, pull the slider back (you can do it one-handed) and put the sling over your head. You can get more length, or a bit more freedom of movement, by using 550 cord on the rear. Make a multi-layer loop of 550 cord through the sling loop on the stock. Then run the Uncle Mikes sling through the looped

550 cord. If you find you have a little too much sling, bunch or fold it and secure it to the stock with a large rubberband or a wrapping of masking tape. When you pull the sling free, the tape will tear or the rubber band will snap free.

But the basic sling can be improved. Two changes make it more versatile. One is to use a "Ned loop" on the front. The second is to incorporate a Fastex buckle for quick-release. Ned Christiansen devised a front loop. He uses a short section of coated cable, a stiff plastic spacer, and clamps the loop with an aluminum crushable cable clamp. Take the Ned loop and loop it through itself, either on the rear upright of the front sight housing, or on the gas tube channel. If you use the rear upright, the sling works both right and left-handed, but you risk blocking the front sight. If you use the gas tube channel, it works right or left depending on what you set it up for. And there, it doesn't block the front sight. The Fastex buckle is for those who want a quick release, usually when working on or around bodies of water. Once you've gotten the gear and done the work, you probably have as much invested in our sling as if you'd just bought the "cool gear" sling the SWAT cops have. But yours will serve a different purpose, and much better than, the "CDI" sling.

Patrol Rifle Policy

A department that issues a rifle has to have a policy for its selection, issue and use. No department (or administrator) with any sense is just going to send out a memo "Use what you want, and be careful out there." In the modern world of incident review, criminal and civil liability, and concern for safety, officers have to be trained and supervised, and equipment and ammunition issued or approved.

As I am not an attorney, nor a police administrator, rather than coming up with a policy on my own, I gathered the best policies and distilled them into a model policy. I've added my comments as to why a particular positon is mandated.

Competition With The AR-15

When it comes to any form of shooting competition, there are the old divisions, and the new ones. I'd like to suggest different ones. As far as competitions with the AR are concerned, there are four: Benchrest, short-range run and gun, long-range run and gun, and NRA High Power. A fifth type of competition is also a type of hunting: varmint shooting.

The rules of these competitions are varied, and just because a particular rifle is allowed in one, does not mean it is allowed in others. Some competitions don't care. If you want to show up to a High Power match with a 16-inch tele-stocked shorty, no one will tell you "No." Your scores won't be very impressive, but you might learn a few things. Like, shooting a shorty offhand at a bull's-eye 200 yards away is even harder than it looks. And that the shorter sight radius of the shorty

If you use iron sights, you need a means of adjusting them. To adjust the front, you need this tool. Get it. If you loan it, don't let the borrower walk away with it.

Practical shooting course designers love windows. They force you to move, think and be aware of your sights.

is not helpful when trying to shoot 600 yards. Likewise, if you show up at a USPSA Three-Gun match with an 18-pound DCM Service Rifle gun, your scores are likely to suffer. As in, trying to sprint to the next box while carrying the heavyweight you brought, and reload your magazines while holding up the rifle one-handed, is no fun.

Benchrest

Most gun clubs have some sort of benchrest competition, even if they don't have a full-house benchrest setup. The full, formal benchrest competition you may be aware of calls for a level of precision that seems to require zen-like abilities. Serious competitors will shoot groups at 100 yards where the distance center to center of the two holes farthest apart is less than two-tenths of an inch. The aggregate, or compiled score of groups fired at 100 and 200 yards, can be under half an inch. The rifles used are single-shot, machined to incredible tolerances, and use specially prepared brass used in that rifle, and that rifle only. The groups are fired off of the bench (hence "benchrest" shooting) using supports on stock and forearm. All serious competitors use various gadgets to estimate the wind direction and velocity, and account for it when firing. (Some "Account for it" by waiting for the conditions to settle down, and then firing their five-shot group in less than a minute.)

Enter the AR shooters. The groups are not quite as small, but are single-hole groups. At the club level, you may not be shooting for smallest group size, you may be shooting for score on a bull's-eye target. But in all cases you'll be shooting as accurately as possible.

Short-range Run And Gun

Mostly, you'll find USPSA Three-Gun competition, and a group of single-match organized tactical rifle competitions. The USPSA is a National organizing body, and if you go to an approved or sanctioned USPSA event you will find the rules are the same. Unless there are local rules for safety, or you happen to have crossed into a state with some onerous restrictions, like 10-shot magazines. By short-range, I do not mean that you are only shooting short distances, but in many cases that is what you'll be doing. There are a great many ranges where the longest distance you can shoot is only 100 or 200 yards. Now, for a handgun shooter, 200 yards seems like a long way. In rifle shooting it is no big deal. No, the "short" in short range run and gun refers to the distance you will travel. A long field course in the short-range run stages will have you traveling 50 yards. You'll go from one box or port to another, shooting at targets as you go, but you not run very far.

USPSA

Three-Gun grew out of USPSA/IPSC handgun competition. The targets are the same buff cardboard, and where the club has steel that can take the impact, steel plates. Some clubs or matches will have separate handgun, rifle and shotgun stages. Others will have "multi-gun" stages where you may be required to fire two or even all three in the conduct of a single stage. A match is a collection of stages. Each stage is fired separately, and the scores for each stage are ranked only in that stage. Then the stage percentages are totaled, (the actual scoring, stage weighing, calculations and ranking system

Practical competition means obstacles, to maneuver around and shoot past.

Sometimes you'll start with your AR on a table, or on a rack.

Fresh air, bright sunshine, a reliable AR, and a ticking clock. The only other thing you need is good competition and camaraderie. You'll get those at a USPSA match.

is worthy of the term "Byzantine") and a match winner declared.

The simple explanation of scoring is this: the points you earn while shooting the stage are divided by the time it took you from start to finish. Each shooter fires the stage in turn, with scores and times recorded. The higher your points total, the better you do. The faster you shoot, the better you do. Any problems you encounter during the stage are problems you have to solve while the clock is ticking. And misses or shooting the wrong targets call for penalties, deductions from your points total.

In the rifle portion of the competition, and the match overall, there are three categories of equipment; Open, Tactical, and Limited or Standard.

An Open rifle has pretty much no restrictions on it. Any caliber, any size, any capacity magazine, any sights. You can have a compensator, bipod, GPS unit, laser designator, etc. Anything. The "typical" Open gun is one with a compensator, bipod, and two optics: a magnifying optic for longer shots, and irons or a red-dot for the close targets. You may engage targets in a stage, or in a match, from 5 yards out to the longest distance the club can manage. Most clubs have a 100-yard

Some sights have four positions, some five. Be sure which your rifle has before you get a tool. Ah heck, get both, they're not that expensive.

An excellent sight such as this EOTech Holosight moves you out of Limited Division. You can shoot Tactical or Open.

As exotic as this sight is, it is still an iron sight, and allowed in Limited USPSA. It won't fly as a Service Rifle in NRA High Power, though.

range. Some have much more, but you will be hard-pressed to find many shots out past 300 yards. Partly because not many clubs have that much room, and partly because it is so hard to run a match quickly with targets that far out. (If they are scored, someone has to go out there and call the score and patch the holes. Steel stargets speed things up.) A 300-yard target can be difficult with iron sights, but a telescopic sight makes the shooting much easier and faster.

A Limited or Standard rifle cannot have optics. It cannot have a bipod. It is allowed a compensator, but only one no larger than 1 inch in diameter and no longer than 3 inches. Why a comp, but no optics? The AWB/94. Rifles could not be made with flash hiders. But they could be made with compensators. Many rifles thus left the factory with compensators silver-soldered on the muzzle. Rather than require competitors remove them, the USPSA simply allowed their use. And in the old days, the division was simple: optics made it open, and irons were the default, or Standard configuration. You can have a very tricked-out rifle that is still a "Limited" or "Standard" rifle. It just can't have optics or a bipod.

A Tactical rifle is one that otherwise meets Limited rules, but has a single optical or red-dot sight on it. Tactical came about due to two things: the recognition that in real life (see any photograph from Iraq) IPSC has made its mark: optics are viewed as real-life relevant. And two, other Three-gun competitions had been allowing their use in otherwise tactically relevant rifles. So, rather than restrict participation, USPSA decided to make it more open.

In USPSA Three-Gun competition, the highest level of any three guns is the level you compete in. That is, if you shoot an Open rifle, but have a shotgun and handgun that are in "Limited" your overall score will be in Open. Your shotgun and handgun scores will be compared or listed in the partial results in their respective equipment divisions, but your overall score will be Open. By the same token, if you shoot an Open handgun, and a Limited rifle, you're in Open for the overall.

There are other Three-gun matches like the Mystery Mountain, the DPMS Tri-Gun, or the North Carolina Tactical. A quick web search will give you the dates, locations, and current rules of those matches. While the USPSA is a national organization, and the rules will be similar if not identical in all clubs shooting USPSA matches, the individual matches can vary from year to year. You really should peruse their current rules (and even find new matches) on the web.

Long-range

In long-range events, we have matches that have some farther distance shooting, but primarily have long distances to cover. The big match as the exemplar is the team tactical put on by D&L Sports each year. You and a partner will leave the start line carrying all your gear. You'll have handguns, water, lunch, one of you will have a carbine (such as an AR built to SPR specs) and the other will have a sniper rifle. You have a maximum time to hike to the firing position (which could be a mile away). Once there, you locate and engage all targets on the clock. You then saddle up and hike to the next firing position. Each leg is timed and scored, and each shooting problem is timed and scored.

Such a match is not for the faint of heart or weak of back or knees. You'll do a lot of walking, a bunch of shooting, and learn a whole lot about your shooting skills, stamina and your gear.

Unique Mike Gibson

And then there is the extravaganza: the Mike Gibson Ironman Marathon. Again, the rules change over time, and the requirements with them. But the basics are the same: the maximum amount of shooting possible. In a USPSA club match, you might shoot three or four stages, with a combined total of handgun, shotgun and rifle ammunition between 100 and 200 rounds. At the MGM, you can approach that in one stage. It is like the American Handgunner Shoot-off in that regard: you can go to the MGM Ironman and shoot a couple of thousand rounds. It is possible to risk burning out the barrel in your AR. Check Mike's web page for the latest info and dates.

NRA High Power

These are the traditional, cast-in-stone, long-range bull's-eye shooting match with rifles. The real course calls for scored shots fired offhand slowfire at 200 yards, sitting rapid-fire at 200 yards, prone rapid-fire at 300 yards, and prone slow-fire at 600 yards. How slow is slow? At 200 yards, it is 10 minutes for 10 shots. Plenty slow. But then, the bull's-eye is not very big. The sitting rapid-fire is also not easy. First, you start standing, and can't go sitting until the targets appear.

Then, you have 60 seconds to fire 10 shots. Oh yes, you have to reload, too. Those shooting the Service Rifle category start with two rounds in the rifle, and then reload with eight more. All others load five and five. At 300 yards, you get a generous 10 extra seconds. But, you have to start standing, and still have to reload. At 600 yards, the shooting is slow-fire again, 20 shots in 20 minutes. All the slow-fire shooting is done by single-loading the rifle.

Wow. Anyone who can do all that, and produce a decent score, certainly knows how to shoot a rifle. But it is far more specialized than other competitions. There is no movement, there is no way to make up a bad shot, and for some there just isn't enough shooting. It is possible to shoot in a match where the volume of shooting is increased, and instead of a 50–shot course you fire 80 or 100 rounds. But compared to a USPSA match, where there could well be over 100 rounds of rifle, and then shotgun and handgun as well, it is a lot of work for (in the view of some shooters) not a lot of shooting.

In NRA High Power, there are two equipment divisions: Service and Match. A Service rifle is an M-16A2 clone. You must have the rifle built so it has "no external changes" from an issue M-16A2. But the "no external" part allows for a whole lot of differences. And potential expense. First, the

Ted Puente, with a high-zoot USPSA Limited Division gun: iron sights, Redi-mag, comp, tactical forend with vertical grip. He shoots as good as the rifle looks, too.

A rack of guns, one squad at a club match. If you want to see what is hot, what is happening, and what to get, get yourself to a USPSA 3-gun match and start asking questions.

Carts to haul gear are the newest rage at Three-gun matches. With three guns, ammo, magazines and the rest to haul, why not?

barrel. Instead of a 1/7 chrome-lined, serious Service rifle competitors will have a very expensive, match 1/8, stainless barrel with a match and not 5.56 chamber. A hand-lapped, precision-chambered barrel, installed in your Service rifle, can quickly eat up a handful of hundred-dollar bills. (Start with a barrel blank from Krieger or Shilen, (nearly $300) then turn it over to a gunsmith who finishes lathe-turning it, reams a chamber, installs a barrel extension, installs a front sight housing, then headspaces, fits a bolt, and installs the whole thing in an upper, and you'll eat up just as much again. A Service rifle, while it must have a trigger pull heavy enough to satisfy the rules, will have a two-stage trigger for the cleanest possible pull while holding a 4.5-pound weight. (Add another couple hundred dollars.) The barrel is free-floated, so the handguards cover a steel free-float tube. The sights are often hand-fitted, and have been re-machined to offer quarter-minute click adjustments instead of the standard, coarser adjustments on a rack-grade M-16A2. Then, many competitors will add lead weights fore and aft to balance the rifle while making it as heavy as possible. A top-grade Service rifle can tip the scales at 18 pounds, and have cost the owner two grand or more. The DoubleStar DCM rifle tested is a perfect example of just what a competitor in the Service category uses.

The Match rifle differs in a few regards. The main one is that you need not hide anything. So the barrel is free-floated in a tube handguard. Optics aren't allowed in some sub-divisions, so the iron sights are parked out on the end of a hollow tube installed on the barrel itself. The extension, called a "bloop tube" from the sound it often generates, exists simply to get the front sight out as far as possible. The stock is adjustable for length of pull, cheekpiece height, buttplate angle and drop, and the trigger weight is allowed to be lighter than that of a Service rifle. To avoid getting the charging handle banged against (or stopped by) the cheekpiece, the bolt is machined, and the upper as well, to allow for an operating handle bolted directly on the carrier itself. The bolt hold open is extended, so the shooter can manipulate it when prone without having to take his left hand out of the sling.

If you thought the Service rifle, or a USPSA Open rifle was expensive, then you haven't priced an over-the-course Match rifle. For a look at a Match rifle, check out the Fulton Armory match rifle tested.

Varmint Shooting

There is no organizing body, no book of rules, and no national scoring method. There are simply the hunting regulations, and the score you and your buddies keep that day, weekend or season. The plan is simple: You get a license, if needed. You find a farmer or rancher who has a problem with burrowing rodents of some kind. You approach him about solving or at lease easing his problem. Once you have permission, you go to the site and settle on a safe firing direction. You and your buddies then drag your gear out of your trucks and set up on a convenient hill or ridgeline. There you proceed to shoot all members of the family Rodentia who are unwise enough to appear.

Scoring is whatever you and your buddies agree to: ratio of hits to misses, total hits, longest hit, whatever.

In the interests of greatest accuracy and painless and instantaneous demise, you load your ammo (or buy factory) that uses hollow-point bullets. In the interests of building a good relationship with the farmer or rancher, and making sure you can count on getting a "Yes" answer to future requests, you clean up all your brass, leave no trash, and refrain from indulging in victory donuts in the pasture with your truck when you produce the highest score.

Competition shooting not only tests the shooters and their rifles, but their gear as well. Short of a shooting war, you can't do more testing, nor find the faults with rifles and gear, like you can in a rigorous competition. Competition is what brought us rock-solid 1911 pistols, and it brought us optics, rails, handguards and other improvements in ARs. And it produces spectacular shooting skills. If you want to be a better shooter, don't spend all your time at the range plinking with your buddies. Swallow some of your pride, spend a bit of time and money, and shoot some competition.

Varminting requires long-range precision. There are no time limits, just hits or misses.

Carry Options For The AR-15

The "correct" way to carry an AR-15 depends on a lot of things. If you live in Arizona, you can simply carry your AR out to your car or truck, stick it in the rack, and drive off. In a lot of places, that would get you so arrested. If you are carrying it around, you might have a different idea of correct if you are out working over a prairie dog town, riding in a squad car in the suburbs of Chicago, or have the job of adjusting the sights of an M118 Light Gun, 105mm,

outside of Najaf. Are you carrying it ready? Or are you simply transporting it to where you'll be ready? Does the chief, sheriff, special agent in charge or other boss have a policy as to where and how you'll carry?

No, saying there is one "correct" way to carry an AR is like saying there is only one "correct" size for shoes, and we'll all get a pair. Carrying an AR comes in three modes; slung, racked and cased.

AR Slings

Slings come in a dizzying variety of styles and intended uses. We have the military sling. There are tactical slings, which come in top-mount, side-mount and single-point. Slings also come in one-piece or multi-piece, and all are designed to be carried on the shoulder, neck, or "tactical" which is neck and shoulder.

The first was the simplest: The military carry sling. A simple webbing (later nylon, later still various synthetics) strap between the front and rear sling swivels, the military sling is fine for military carry. Also known as "hunter's carry" muzzle-up, and "African carry" muzzle-down, the rifle is more or less vertical while hanging on your shoulder. As a means of carrying the AR like any other piece of gear or luggage, it is fine. And you can get your hands on it and point it at the target pretty quickly. But it is in the way. (Truth be told, all means of carrying a rifle are clumsy, and the rifle gets in the way regardless of the sling. If you want an unobtrusive firearm, get a holster and put a sidearm in it.) Target shooters

Sometimes, carrying a rifle means resting it on the web gear that you are festooned with. That gets the weight on your shoulders, if the web gear/vest fits right.

(U.S. Army photo by Staff Sgt. Vernell Hall)

The newest accessories have multiple locations for your sling to attach. That was not always the case.

use the military sling or some variant of it that attaches to the standard sling swivels on the bottom of the rifle. But there are faster, more convenient ways of carrying a rifle so that it is ready when you need it.

The first of these is called the "Israeli sling." The sling involves 5 feet of webbing, and a steel clip that fits into the front sight housing. The clip goes through the housing, the strap goes over the top of the rifle, and is secured to the buttstock on the top. That is, it is tied, taped, wired or otherwise lashed so the sling leaves the rifle from the top of the stock. Typically, you'd see an IDF trooper with the rifle somewhere down around his or her waist. The Israeli sling hangs from your neck, with your shoulder left out of the action. Convenient to the hands, if they're hanging down, but not fast to use. You can pick them up at many guns shows, as they were all the rage a few years ago.

The problems with the Israeli sling come from the steel clip. First, it quickly rubs the finish from the edges of your front sight housing. And if you leave it long, the rifle flops around. Last, the steel clip lets the sling flop around, and sometimes it flops in between the sights. Then you can't see, due to your own sling. The Israeli sling was improved on by my friend Jeff Chudwin, and then improved again by Ned Christiansen. First, Jeff hit on the idea of using a utility sling from Uncle Mike's. He used loops of 550 cord to attach the rear, and looped and secured the front on the front sight housing. With no metal involved, the rifle finish didn't get worn. And the slider in the sling allowed you to pull the sling tight for storage. Ned then refined it by using cable ties to secure the 550 cord, to keep the knots from coming untied. And, he designed a coated cable loop that you could put on the front sight, to attach the sling. By putting the loop on the rear of the housing, you made it universal, right- or left-handed. But it can get in the way of the sights. If, however, you put the cable on the connector bar, it kept the sling out of the sights, but made it a right- or left-handed sling. The last refinement came from me. I added a Blackhawk 1-inch side-release buckle and tri-glide to the front, for a quick-release capacity.

In use, you leave the rifle racked or stored with the sling tight. To sling it, you grab the slider and yank the sling back until there is enough loop to get it over your neck. And if you need to ditch the rifle, the side release lets you "cut-away" in less than a second, rather than try to get the sling over your head. Why the cut-away? Here in the Great Lakes' region, many Sheriff's Departments have a Power Squadron. If your

THE GUN DIGEST BOOK OF THE AR-15

A military sling offers two options; muzzle up or muzzle down. It works, but there are more convenient methods.

(DoD photo by Chief Journalist Dave Fliesen, U.S. Navy)

You don't have to get very far from shore before the water gets too deep to wade back if you fall in. It is a good idea to have quick-disconnect buckles on your gear if you go over water.

County has a large lake, or shoreline on one of the Great Lakes, you've got boats to deal with. If you are one of the 30 million or so people who live in the Great Lakes region, you only have to drive five minutes to find a body of water deep enough to drown in. I can tell you from personal experience that if you go over the side in full tactical gear you'll sink like a rock. With a rifle, sidearm, and tactical vest with ammo and gear, there is no buoyancy vest that will keep you floating. The Marine Corps has known this for some time, and all current gear must be quickly removable. I can see someone in the back, waving a hand. "Isn't this gear expensive? Aren't you responsible for any firearms you abandon?" Yes. However, if you cut away from your gear, and the water isn't too deep, we can send in a diver later that day or the next. If the water is too deep for recovery, you can buy new gear. However, standing on the bottom, wearing gear you refused to abandon, you cannot buy more air. And we'll have to call in the divers to recover your body, not your gear. You tell me which is preferable.

The good thing about the Chudwin/Christiansen/Sweeney tac sling (we've got to get a snappier name for it) is that you can fabricate it yourself for less than 20 bucks. And you may have some of the parts on hand already.

One option for a top-mount sling without making yours is the Uncle Mike's tactical sling. It fits over the top, but does not use a metal ring to attach, and won't wear the finish.

Not every one wants to make their own sling, and yet they wanted an improvement over the Israeli sling. The first improvement came from Giles Stock. Giles was a Sergeant with a big PD in Arizona, and when I met him, an instructor at Gunsite. The Giles sling combined the Israeli and the H-K MP-5 sling, but eliminated the bad parts of both. Available from The Wilderness, it comes in Standard and Tele version. (The webbing can't fit both, so you have to pick one or the other, depending on what you have.)

The Giles Sling is a multi-strap sling, and it fits over your neck and shoulder. The main strap goes in front, and the second loop goes over your neck and shoulder, to rest against you. The question always is, "which shoulder?" If you put your head and left arm (for a right-handed shooter) through, the rifle ends up hanging almost vertically at rest. If you put your head and right shoulder, it rests more in a horizontal

Even when armed, there are lots of people who cannot have a rifle on their person. These artillerymen have their rifles close at hand while they solve someone else's problems.

(U.S. Army photo by Sgt. Christopher Kaufmann)

The GG&G Sling 'n Light Combo offers a way to have a sling and mount a light, too. (And even leave room for an M-203 underneath.)

axis. Me, I prefer head and left, as I want it pointing straight down when I'm at rest or doing a transition to sidearm.

A side sling that can be a neck or tactical depending on what straps you use comes from GG&G. Their hardware consists of the Sling Thing or the Sling 'n Light Combo (SliC). The rear bolts onto a tele-stock, using the lower strap slot. The front clamps to the front sight housing. The Sling Thing is just a sling swivel, while the SliC incorporates a light rail on the offside of the front assembly, where you can mount a light or laser. You can attach a simple neck sling to it, or use a multi-strap tactical sling. While it may seem pricey to get the hardware and then still have to get a sling, it has advantages; it comes off easily. By using the GG&G, you can attach a side sling and light to a departmental rifle without making

permanent modifications. If you have to turn in the rifle to get issued another one, you unbolt your gear and install it on the new rifle. Two minutes with a set of allen wrenches, and you can move your sling and light from one rifle to another.

Single-point rigs attach without using the standard sling at all. The Chalker sling uses a strap around the buffer tube, a strap with a ring on it. The Chalker slig comes in two parts, the strap with ring, and the harness/suspenders you wear. The harness has a clip that secures to the ring on the strap. Despite its complexity, the Chalker sling has two advantages: the harness distributes the weight of the rifle evenly on both shoulders, making it less of a burden. And the center attachment makes it easy to swing the rifle over to shoot from either shoulder.

Another single-point sling comes from The Wilderness, using a GG&G sling adapter. The GG&G adapter replaces the buffer tube plate on a tele-stock, and has a loop on one or both sides. The sling attaches through the loop, and the quick-disconnect buckle let you bail at a moment's notice. The wide strap is easy to carry, but makes swinging to shoot from the offside cumbersome for some people. Possible, but not as fast as the Chalker.

A variant of the single-point is the bungee sling. Here, the sling has a section of bungee cord incorporated in the sling. The springiness of the bungee adds comfort, and makes it easy to swing from one to the other shoulder for firing. The bungee sling seems to be a "love it or hate it" proposition. Me, I hate it. I spent entirely too much time in martial arts training, learning how to use my opponents clothes or gear against them, to be comfortable with the idea of a "spring-loaded' rifle someone can grab, yank, and let go of. But there are those who love them.

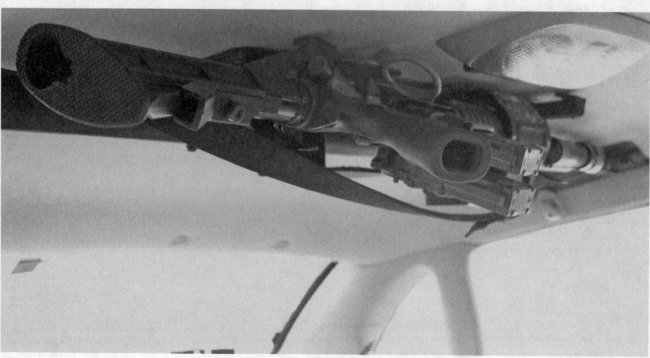

A rifle rack is the only way to have a rifle in a car. It must lock or it is simply a license to steal.

Racks

Racks can be simple: my friend John Simon simply had a bar and mesh steel shelf welded up for his collection of rifles. The rack was bolted to the concrete wall of his basement, and had welded-on rings at each end. He simply ran a coated cable between the loops, through the triggerguards of his rifles. With a padlock on the end, all the rifles were stuck in the rack, which was bolted to the wall. To get to them, you'd have had to get through two locked doors (past a very large dog) and then figure out how to cut the cable, lock or rack.

Racks can also be more complicated, in which case they are called safes. You store a rifle or rifles in a safe for long-term storage, not for tactical readiness. If that means you keep the combination written down on a file card you keep behind your Great Uncle's portrait, fine. The important thing to keep in mind about safes is that you cannot make them heavy enough by themselves to prevent loss. If you want your safe to stay where it is, bolt it down.

Tactical racks. Police cars, to no one's surprise, often have firearms in them. The trick is to have them locked but accessible. Thus, locking racks made by Big Sky are the thing to have. If the vehicle is large enough, you can rack the rifle between the seats. If not, then on the ceiling it goes. One thing to keep in mind: if you have a Redi-Mag on your rifle, you'll have to tell Big Sky when you order a rack or racks, and tell them you want the "Olympia Fields" model.

At home, if you plan to keep a rifle handy for defense, you'll have to balance security with access at a point where you are comfortable. I've been places where the comfort zone was; loaded, in the room with you, and carried from one room to the next with you. Many other places, a locked or latched rack, with ammo on your person, is plenty accessible enough.

Cases

A case is a luggage-like container for your AR. While you may, in some places, be able to just walk out to the car and put your rifle in, no case needed, it isn't smart. Rattling around in the trunk without protection is simply asking for your rifle to be damaged. You need a case of some kind. A trip to the range can simply call for a fabric case of some kind to keep the gear together, while an airline flight calls for a hard case that can be locked.

And when you have your rifle in a case, you have to consider how to protect it from whatever else is in the case, too. I've seen more than one AR pulled out of a double-gun case with the front sight damaged by the other gun in there. In police work it is always damaged by a shotgun, and the department is too cheap (or the trunk too heavily loaded) to get two cases, one for each gun. So, sometime in all the hauling, lifting, riding and storage, the shotgun shifted and banged against the rifle sight. Guess which was damaged? Of course, the one that depends on good sights for proper function.

Uncle Mike's cases are traditional, rugged, and obvious gun cases. I still use them, and mine have lasted for years with no wear to speak of.

Soft Cases

The ballistic nylon or cordura case is the standard. You can get something obvious like the Uncle Mike's cases, which are vaguely rifle-shaped, and have magazine pockets on the outside. If you have a short rifle, the short or long cases will do. But the standard full-size AR only fits in the big case. I've got cases that have worked for me for years. Back when I was doing full-time commercial gunsmithing, I'd be doing regular range trips to test-fire customer guns. In the months leading up to opening day of the deer season I'd be buried under a deluge of rifles and shotguns. Some weeks I'd make two or three range trips with the back of my truck absolutely stuffed with cased rifles and shotguns. I can tell you from personal experience that even when a rifle is on the bottom of the pile, with 3 feet of cased rifles on it, they are well-protected by the standard case.

For a number of years I lived right in the middle of what I called "studentville" the area of town mostly populated by university students. I did not want everyone to know I was hauling guns to the truck each Sunday morning I was headed off for a match. First, I didn't need the lectures from students with their first semester of Philosophy or Political Science under their belts, telling me of the evils I was committing. And second, any place students gather off-campus to live, there will be break-ins. How I wish back then I had the Blackhawk Discreet carry case. I could have ditched the various guitar cases I used to haul guns. Now, to someone who knows what they're looking at, it is a rifle case. But to those who don't, and those who aren't really paying much attention to anything while they're walking around, it could pass for an art portfolio, or a guitar case, or any number of other things.

The Blackhawk cases are slick. The case is flat, rectangular, with stitched-in sides to hold its shape, and uses Velcro straps

You also have room and pouches for ammo and magazines in the Blackhawk case.

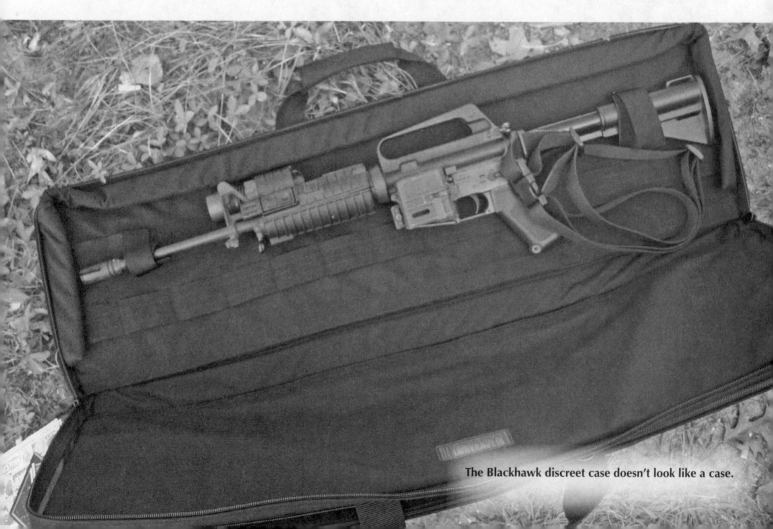

The Blackhawk discreet case doesn't look like a case.

inside to keep the rifle in place. As an un-obvious means of hauling a rifle around, it is great. And as a bonus, it comes with magazine pouches inside, that are Velcro-attached to the case interior. With the rifle with a magazine, and magazines in the inside pouch (which comes out and can be slung or belt-mounted) you can have a low-profile means of carry combined with a reasonably fast deployment. And even if you don't have occasion to rapidly deploy your rifle, it does a very good job of protecting your rifle.

For less discreet carry, and more specialized use, Blackhawk also makes a case that is a carry case/drag bag/shooting mat. Folded like a suitcase it is a gear bag and shooting mat. If you unfold it and flip out the lengthening panels and uncover the shoulder straps, it is a backpack carry case. With the nose loop, you can use it as a drag bag, to haul a tactical precision rifle (we used to call them "sniper rifles" in the old days) behind you while you crawl through the brush. And once there, you can unfold it and use it as a shooting mat.

Another product from Blackhawk is a dedicated shooting mat. You can't carry a firearm in it, but it rolls up to such a compact size that you can pack it and not have it get in the way. (And in a pinch you could even use it as a sleeping pad.)

If you are packing a spare rifle long distance, but can't take (or don't need) the extra protection or weight of a carry case, then at least you can protect the optics. With your patrol rifle slung and handy, you pack your tactical marksman rifle on your back. To protect the optics, you use something like the Balckhawk scope protector. The one they make for Acog is large enough to cover a compact optical or red-dot sight. If you need to cover a larger one, they make a scope cover with muzzle protector. The two covers are connected with a webbing sling, but if you don't feel the need for muzzle protection you can take it off and just use the scope protector.

Hard Cases

The case company that seems to have the hard case market for the manufacturers locked down is Doskocil. Of the rifles shipped, five did not come in a Doskocil case: three Armalite rifles, in cardboard boxes, Colt in a cardboard box and sleeve, and Wilson, in a Wilson soft case. The Doskocil case is the right size, but it does suffer one failing, one I saw time and again: the foam inside is thin and not secured to the case exterior. More than once I pulled a rifle out of the case to find it had slid to the bottom. (I kept the rifles stacked against one wall, stood on their ends, where I could read the label.)

Along with the rifle, you need a supply of ammunition. And, sometimes you'll need extra tools, too. At the range, if you find you have a problem and need to tighten a screw or swab the bore, you can ask around. Or hike up to the clubhouse, open your locker, and get out what you need. If you're stationed in Dirt, Afghanistan, which is halfway between "Nowhere" and "The Road doesn't go there" the only cleaning supplies may be what you brought with you.

You have to make sure you have what you need with you, whether the trip is to the range, to a prairie dog site for some varminting, or an all-expenses paid trip to Dirt. Hence:

Web Gear

A rifle by itself isn't much use. Outsiders look on all firearms as "guns" and things to shoot people or critters with. However, handguns and rifles fall into two distinctly different camps: Offensive and defensive. Those who carry a firearm with the idea that "this thing might save my life someday" invariably carry a handgun. A rifle is too bulky, too heavy, always in the way, and not at all concealable. However, if your job is to go looking for troublemakers (not necessarily looking for trouble, although the two are linked) you will always take the biggest firearm you can. You will also take friends, also armed with the biggest firearms they can manage. Many friends, and much ammo. And a radio to call for more help.

You cannot take a meaningful amount of ammo into a fight, just by putting ammo or magazines into your pockets. Even modern style, baggy pants with multiple pockets won't carry enough.

Competition shooters have a different problem: sometimes the rules prohibit pocket carry. And even if they allow it, pockets are notoriously bad magazine carriers.

And in the case of a magazine malfunction, if the only one you have is the one giving you fits, your rifle is useless or nearly so. When the second gunman of the North Hollywood shootout was stopped, he bailed out of his getaway vehicle and opened fired on the L.A. police officers who had stopped him. As the officers exited their own vehicle, one officer lost all the spare magazines in his pockets. The only magazine he had, that was in the rifle, proved to be faulty. The feed lips were bent, and the rifle fed in slow motion. (He could watch the bolt going forward, it was so slow.) Luckily, the offender took cover behind the car and fired ineffectually at the police. They shot and hit what they were aiming at. However, that damaged magazine could have proved fatal.

I repeat: You need extra magazines for more reasons than just running out of ammo.

And unless the next magazine is on your person, or on the rifle, it might as well be on the moon. Incident after incident has proven that spare ammo in the car, the next room or the next person is essentially non-existent as far as its usefulness to you in the fight is concerned.

The matter of spare magazines, and places to carry them, falls into three categories: On the rifle, on your belt, and in a high-volume load bearing vest or web gear.

On The Rifle

One magazine isn't enough, but for a whole lot of uses two magazines is more than you'll need. That is, a study of shooting incidents uncovers the fact that many are finished before the capacity of a magazine is exhausted. But you need a spare in case the main one fails. In many cases, the rifle with two loaded magazines will be all you'll need. And by putting the spare on the rifle, you save valuable belt space and comfort. Even police officers don't always need a lot. Unless your job is standing in front of the "high value target" in full SWAT gear, getting your picture taken, you aren't going to be wearing a vest full of loaded magazines. More likely, you'll have a rifle clamped in an overhead or between-the-seats rack. Even around the home, a rifle with two magazines in the ready rack will probably be plenty. So, if you've decided that two is enough, where should the second one be? Your choices are: Stock pouch, as in Blackhawk, the stock itself, from Rase, the Redi-Mag carrier, and the second magazine attached to the first, using the Mag Cinch.

Blackhawk Stock Pouch

I've been seeing a lot of these in photos in Iraq. While the ones I've seen have been on the stocks of rifles soldiers and Marines are carrying on patrol, they have even more use to someone not on the street in full combat gear. If you feel the need for a ready rifle, it is a lot more convenient to have your spare ammo on it, than have a loaded vest next to the rifle. The stock pouch secures with straps around the stock. The typical version (and the version by Blackhawk I have) goes on a tele-stock. The rear strap goes through the sling slots, keeping it more or less in place. What I've found works is to re-route the strap so the buckle acts to keep the pouch from rotating around the stock tube. Fixed-stock versions use an additional strap, and secure to the rear sling swivel. The big advantage the stock pouch has (that all on-the-rifle methods have) is that the spare is right there. If you have the rifle, you have more ammo. The big disadvantage is that with the ammo on the right side of the stock, you can't shoot from the left shoulder very well. It is possible, but not fast, fun or easy. The disadvantage must not be that great, as I've seen photos from Iraq where every other trooper in the photo has a stock pouch on his rifle.

Rase

The Rase stock replaces the standard fixed stock. Instead of the solid stock filled with foam, the Rase is hollow and cut on the bottom to receive a magazine. At the front of the opening is a spring-loaded latch. In use, you stuff a loaded magazine into the stock, feed lips towards your shoulder, bullet tips pointing up. Swing the latch out of the way, and stuff the bottom of the magazine in. then let the latch swing back and hook on the mag. The magazine is in very securely, and I have not yet found an impact that will dislodge it. At least no impact I'm willing to withstand along with the rifle. From testing, I suspect it would take a fall of over 50 feet to dislodge the magazine. At that height, I'm not sure either I or the rifle will be in any shape to continue, so whether or not the magazine stays with us hardly matters.

In use, you reach back with your left hand and grasp the spine of the magazine, thumb on the left side. Use the back of your hand to press the latch open, and pull the magazine down and forward. It will pivot in your grasp as you pull, and come forward of your right hand (on the pistol grip) with the feed lips up. Press the mag release, drop the old, and insert the new. Yes, that fast.

Redi-Mag

The Redi-Mag, from The Wilderness, is a sheet steel housing that clamps on to your rifle and provides an additional magazine well. The Redi-Mag is arranged such that when you press the magazine button to release the magazine in the rifle, you also release the magazine in the Redi-Mag. To start, you put a loaded magazine in each, and then load or don't load, depending on the ready state you want or are required be in. Once you begin shooting, the spare magazine is right there next to the one feeding. When you need more ammo, reach back with your left hand and grasp the spare magazine. Press the magazine release button and let the old magazine drop free. If your hands are big enough, or if you practice enough, you can grab both, with a finger in between them. Then, pull the new mag straight down, move over, and insert it in the magazine well. If you've done a "reload with retention" and have the old mag still in your hand, put it in a pocket, empty mag dump bag, or someplace else.

Practice is easy, if a bit hard on the magazine falling to the ground. Once you've had a little practice, you can reload quite quickly. You can also transition to a different kind of ammo, if you want. Entry teams might go in with frangible ammo in the rifle, with barrier-defeating rounds in the spare magazine. A team leader in an infantry unit might have the spare as all-tracers. That way, if he spots something his machinegun team needs to be dealing with and isn't, he can transition to the all-tracers mag, and mark the offenders for appropriate treatment. Once done, he can switch back to ball ammo.

The Redi-mag adds more weight than the others, but the second magazine is handy, protected, and close to the reloading hand.

Mag Cinch

Mag Cinch is the modern update of the old "jungle clip" of taping two magazines together. Instead of wrestling with sheet metal clamps, or duct tape, or "hundred mile an hour" tape, Larry Bullock got with the future. Plastics. He makes a simple plastic bracket and nylon strapping arrangement that holds magazines securely. It is one of those forehead-slapping "Why didn't I think of it" ideas. How secure? Well, I had one of those Israeli sheet-metal jobbies, that held two magazines, that I was using a lot in our club's Three-gun matches long ago. I lost the extra mag during a field course a long time ago. I turned a corner, it didn't and I had to go back for it, adding a great deal of time to my run. So, I used duct tape on it to keep the assembly together. A couple of years later, I'm shooting another Three-gun match at the club, in the dead of winter. The tape dies in the extreme cold, dropping the spare mag.

Luckily that match, it didn't cost me anything, as I was too far ahead for anyone to catch me.

The Mag Cinch won't die in the cold, nor if properly assembled will the spare magazine drop off. You do have to take care with two things when using the Mag Cinch: offset and cartridge shift. You must clamp the two magazines together so the one on the right is lower than the one on the left. Otherwise, when the left magazine is in place, the right magazine will block either the brass during ejection, the dust cover door as it opens, or in some cases wedge against the open door, damaging the door and/or magazine. When you fire a full magazine, the top round on the spare magazine will sometimes shift forward due to accumulated recoil. If you try to just jam the magazine straight up, the top round will be too long, and cause a problem. I found that a slight rocking action, to get the nose of the round in first, then lift the rear, pushing the round back, solves that little problem. Not all magazines will have cartridge shift, but those that do are easily dealt with. (Or swapped out.)

On Your Belt

You can make your own. Back in the old days, we all did. Some took Vietnam-era nylon magazine pouches and cut them down. Others sewed together leather bits to make mag pouches. Today, you can forget all that. I've seen the future, and it is Kydex. If you are going to shoot in a match that may call for a reload, use a Blade-Tech Kydex magazine pouch. It will hold the magazine, the assembly will stay on your belt, and it won't slap you silly when you run. And it won't suffer if you should drop it and then step on it. Some Three-gun or tactical matches do not allow pocket carry, while others are not keen on web gear. The Kydex carrier from Blade-Tech passes muster with both sides, holds the mag securely, and is so tough I'm not sure you can wear it out.

Shooting Mats

The best shooting mat is a bed. However, hauling one to where you need to be shooting from is very difficult. Either of the aforementioned Blackhawk cases/mats work well. If you are planning to use a shooting mat, you should look for a few things: how wide is it and does it have non-slip panels, how long is it, how padded is it, and does it have pockets? A mat that is not wide enough to keep your elbows in the pad, or lacking a non-slip surface, isn't much use. If you can't get on it, or stay on it, what's the point? Also a pad that is too short isn't much use, either. If it stops at your waist, then it isn't protecting much of you from the dirt, water or rocks. Yes, yes, we're all tough guys (and gals) who don't mind a little dirt or dew now and then. But what's the point in hauling gear that only offers a little protection, when for a little more weight you could have had it all?

A non-padded "pad" only acts to keep the dirt off. It doesn't do anything about the rocks. I've shot on more than my fair share of ranges with rocks, gravel and God knows what else

A shooting mat keeps you off the ground, out of the mud and water.

A versatile bag, like this Blackhawk, can be gun bag, drag bag, shooting mat and seat cushion.

underfoot. Throwing a blue plastic tarp down is a nice thought, but all it does is keep the dirt off your uniform. (If that's all you've got, then don't turn it down. But go for the real pad if given a chance.) Padding is more than just comfort. You can injure your knees or elbows going prone on gravel. If a sharp rock, or empty brass is in the right spot, it can even put you on medical leave. One of my two accidental discharges came at Gunsite, with Jeff Cooper watching. I knelt down to shoot, caught a rock under my kneecap, and the pain was so intense I prematurely fired my 1911. My knee became so swollen that in the hotel room that night I actually contemplated cutting my jeans off. I walked around like the Deputy in Gunsmoke for days afterwards.

Pockets are a personal thing. Some love them and some hate them. They add bulk and weight to a carry case/shooting pad. But they can be very handy places to stash things that you might need once you're right there in shooting position.

Match Transport

In many three-gun matches, you only need to carry the firearms you're using on the individual stages where you'll fire them. When not on the stage, you rack the guns, and help with the scoring, pasting and re-setting of steel. A small club three-gun match would be three or four stages. You might even be able to leave gear in your car, and haul out what you need for each stage. A bigger club, or a state or area match, will have eight to 12 stages, and the parking lot will be too far away. A Nationals will be fifteen to twenty stages, and you won't see your car all day long.

At my home club, a three-gun match is often seven or eight stages. In the course of walking to each one in turn (you shoot on each stage, and haul your gear from one to the next) you'll haul your gear over half a mile. For some, the match is simply a series of trips to and from the parking lot to haul what they need. But the smart ones have all they need in one package. A gear bag with magazines, ammo, holster, handgun, lunch, etc,

The Blackhawk mat rolls up into a compact package. You can even use it as a sleeping bag mat.

A scope cover can protect your scope while you haul your rifle around a match.

a gun case for the rifle, and a gun case for the shotgun. Even pared-down that is a lot of gear, but it isn't too bad. But some shooters make carts, or buy them. With a gun cart, you simply pull your gear around, rather than carry it. You definitely want something to protect optics, and covers over the ejection ports to keep dust out. But for those who believed in the wheel, they are great.

Not all three-gun matches allow carts. Some tactical matches will require that you haul everything you need over the whole course. (Many are team events, with no shotgun shooting, just two guys, two handguns, a carbine and a sniper rifle.) You'd better have comfortable slings, a source of water, good boots and sunscreen. Luckily, you probably won't need elbow and knee pads (but they are still a good idea) nor a

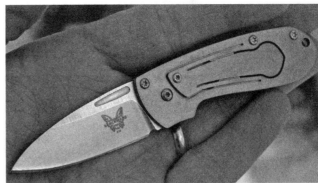

When it is a razor-sharp Benchmade, even this little BenchMite is a useful tool.

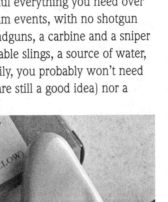

Sinclair makes iron sight covers. NRA high Power shooters use them.

The Benchmade Mini-Griptilian is a tough little non-tactical-looking knife. Do yourself a favor, get one.

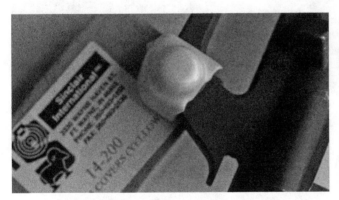

A cover can keep idle fingers from making adjustments to your sights, and keep dust, dirt and pigeon droppings off them, too.

Non-serrated, the Griptilian is not a "threatening" knife.

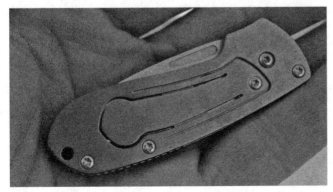

A handy little knife can be used for many things.

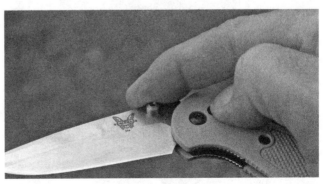

The advantage of the axis lock on the Griptilian is that your fingers need not be in the blade's path to unlock it for folding.

The Eikhorn-soligen Rescue tool.

The side button is the lock.

The button is a glass-breaker, and the shielded blade is a seatbelt and strap cutter.

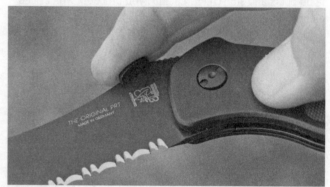

You need not get your fingers in the blade's path to unlock and fold.

It looks like this trooper is using an Israeli sling, but he has the new Colt side sling adapter on his M16A2.

(U.S. Army photo by Staff Sgt. Joseph Roberts)

shooting pad. Generally, you hike against the clock to the shooting area/box, and once there identify the targets. You then shoot for score, and pack up and hike off.

Extras

If you are going to be geared-up on duty, or shooting a full-dress tactical match, you'll need a couple of extras: a knife and a helmet. A knife, not because you plan to get in a knife fight, but because you might have to open lunch, modify gear or cut rope, or cut your gear off and follow the bubbles back up to the surface. I received a few new ones for this book, and the small and large knives were covered with one item each, while the medium had two: A Benchmade BenchMite, a Benchmade Mini-Griptilian, an Eichorn-Solingen Rescue Tool, and a Benchmade Nimravus Cub.

The helmet is a vanilla-plain PASGT, but the modification that made it comfortable to wear is the Oregon Aero suspension kit.

You need a knife for a lot of things. Sometimes you only need a small one. Rather than pulling out the huge, serrated, teflon-coated folder or fixed-blade, and "scarin the wimmen 'n children" a gentleman's folder is called for. The BenchMite doesn't have a pocket clip. The body is anodized aluminum, with the lock built as part of the body. It locks both open and closed, so you'll need both hands to get it open. (There's probably some place where a knife that can be opened with one hand is illegal. Then this knife is for you.) The 2-inch blade, at least in the 154Cm steel, is scary sharp. You know the flimsy, thermal-print paper they print store receipts on nowadays? The BenchMite will cut that unsupported. As something to have in your pocket to open whatever needs opening, it is a great little tool.

A step up in size is the Mini Griptilian. The one they sent me came in a bight green synthetic body, and a reversible clip. The Griptilian series uses the axis lock, which is the lock Benchamde uses for their automatic knives. This one isn't automatic, but the lock is slick. The blade thumbs out easily, and the lock, which is a post that rides front-to-back in the body, locks it open. The slick thing about an axis lock is that you don't have to get your thumb out in the blade's path to unlock the blade, as you do with a liner lock. This knife is so perfect in size that when I made the mistake of showing it to my wife, I lost it. With a non-serrated 3-inch blade (this one made of 440C steel) it is the perfect size for daily carry and use. And, clipped to your web gear, perfect for regular, non-tactical use, when you don't need to be using a knife as a prybar.

The Eichorn-Solingen Rescue Tool is a tactical folder with a Solingen steel blade. (By definition, good steel.) It has as carbide window breaker, and a safety web cutter built into the handle. By hooking the safety cutter on a seatbelt, web gear, rope or the like, you can cut the belt without risking cutting the person trapped by the belt. The glass breaker will shatter a side window, allowing access. The Eichorn-Solingen Rescue Tool is not just something to have strapped to your web gear, it is something you could benefit from having in your car. (Just be sure local law allows it.)

As a bigger knife, on your web gear, the Benchmade Nimravus is a good knife. The Cub is "only" a 3.5-inch blade, but tough, with a full-width tang and made of either 154CM or M4 high-speed steel. For those who are content with a tool for the job, and not a "status blade" Rambo knife lashed to their gear or person, the Cub is plenty. My friend Ed Mohn pointed out that the members of his team often start out with big knives, but get tired of the weight and go to smaller ones or tactical folders. They need them to cut rope and webbing, and are not looking for a prybar to open doors.

A few years ago, before 9/11, the federal government offered excess PASGT helmets to the states, who then turned around and sold them to police departments. The price? $15 each. Every police department I know of bought a store-room full of them. (At the time, the wholesale price, new, not in volume, was over $200 each.) The PASGT is the German-looking Kevlar helmet that will stop most anything. While it isn't rated for 7.62X39, it has on more than one occasion saved the life of the soldier or Marine who was wearing it. The problems it has are that it is heavy, and it does not balance well. Add a pair of covered protective goggles and a mounting kit for night vision gear and the balance improves but the weight goes up. They arrived at the PDs lacking suspension gear, so each department or officer had to build them up themselves. And found out that while the state-of-the-art on the outside had improved, the inside hadn't moved much since my father ditched his helmet in northern France in the Fall of 1944. The webbing, leather and strap suspension system sucks. (Pardon my French.) Adding the crown pad and the airborne pad only makes it suck less. When every Junior High School football team is wearing state-of-the-art suspension helmets, why are we going on callouts with stuff from WWII? We needn't, with a call to Oregon Aero. The pads come with complete instructions, and once you are done it actually makes the helmet wearable. You start by pulling all the old mounting and attachment points out. As the Oregon Aero pads are held in place by adhesive, you should get a bottle of rubbing alcohol and a roll of paper towels. Then, follow the instructions to fit and attach. You will not be disappointed.

Why did the government ditch the old helmets? Back then there wasn't a war on, so they were surplus. And, there was a new helmet being introduced, the MICH, which gave almost as much protection, was better balanced, and allowed the wearer to actually use a radio handset while wearing the helmet.

Many, many PDs have SWAT teams using the old PASGT, and all who do not have the Oregon Aero pad kit installed probably hate the helmets.

Training With The AR-15/M-16

Many who purchase a firearm would be better off buying a magic talisman. Those who think that simply having invested in some safety devise, that they will be safer as a result, are at best mistaken, and at worst deluded.

If you invest in anything more involved than a smoke detector, carbon monoxide alarm or radioactive radon recorder, you must learn how to use it. You cannot simply plug a battery and ammunition into your AR, and expect it to alert you and shoot the "bad guys." No, you must learn the law, you must learn your rifle, and you must learn you. One

way to learn firearms manipulation, safety and marksmanship is in a competitive event. Another is to go to class. The advantage of competition is that you can regularly reinforce your skills. And you can do so at a reasonable cost. It may cost you $2,000 to go to a class and learn how to use an AR. For that same money, you can drive to and enter into a rifle match every month of the year for a couple of years, cover the cost of the ammo, and even go to a bigger match or two. However, the drawback to using competitions as your sole teaching method is that you cannot learn more than you already know, or can easily extrapolate.

These Royal Marine Commandos don't assume that just because the Queen has issued them a (wretched) Enfield they are ready to get the job done. They train. You should to, even if you aren't going to be boarding ships.

Training also means learning from other students. You can learn much from watching others learn.

It is bad tactics to stand and shoot at a 300 meter target. But it can be a great learning experience, if you have a good instructor.

Only by going to a school can you learn to work with a partner (there are few two-man competitive events) enter a building safely (and not just for the highest score) and what works in the real world and not just the competitive range. The two are not competitive, but complementary.

But, which one or ones? I can only comment on the people and places I have been, or know well. So you will not have a comprehensive list of who teaches (I'm not sure anyone could do that, short of a web search) and a review or overview of each one. (Not even Bill Gates has that kind of time and money.)

Gunsite

Based in Paulden, Arizona, (which is just a wide spot in the highway, with a store and post office) Gunsite is on a path upwards. Founded by Jeff Cooper, and starting out as a handgun school, the new owner is investing large amounts of time, money and effort to make Gunsite once again the state-of-the-art school. What you will learn is not how to win competitions. Gunsite is staffed with instructors who are law enforcement and military veterans who have been on the tip of the spear. They teach a solid, real-world approach that is geared to making you a shooter who can perform in tough circumstances. You can go on to win, but they will not be looking to push you to the limits of competition speed: rather, they will drill you so your performance will be rock-solid regardless of circumstances.

Live-fire, tactical, moving training is the pinnacle of any skillset. You must be trained to this, you can't just pick it up on your own.

The basic AR class is a week, in which you will consume a case of ammo or more, tear at least one pair of trousers, heavily scuff your elbow and knee pads, and work on drills, simulators, and more drills. You'll probably also start the class with too much gear bolted on your rifle, and spend part of your downtime removing the heavier or more superfluous items. Gunsite teaches the basic moral aspects of defensive force, but cannot go into great detail. They have students coming to them from all of the states, and foreign countries. No lecture could cover all the bases, so you will have to supplement your Gunsite education with a consultation with your attorney as to just what is legal in your home base.

For many, Gunsite is THE place from which to have a diploma. Once you've gone and graduated, you'll find Gunsite Grads in every range you ever go to. In that regard it is sort of like being a former Marine.

John Farnam

Unlike other instructors, John ("Uncle John" to many students) does not have a home range. He travels the country holding classes at ranges that are the home base for his network of senior students and long-time friends. What it means is that you will not get the kind of simulators and environmental immersions you'll get trying to clear out the Funhouse at Gunsite. What it does get you is John Farnam, who is interested in teaching his students how to stay alive in a dangerous environment. You'll also get the benefit of having

John's wife, Vickie is an excellent instructor as well, and you can't slack, and won't get sloppy with her watching.

John Farnam gets you off of shooting groups, and into shooting tactically, just as fast as possible.

The best give one-on-one instruction, and you'll get that from John.

you will be corrected by those around you, for no one wants to learn first-hand from your mistake.

As a very fast, thorough learning experience it is amazing. And un-nerving for those who have spent their entire lives loading rifles or handguns to get ready for a match, hunting, or qualifications.

Clint Smith

Clint used to run Thunder Ranch, which many felt (and I thought unkindly) to be "Gunsite in Texas." Clint is a veritable idea factory, with many innovative ideas and approaches to firearms instruction. He is in the middle of moving Thunder Ranch from Texas to Oregon, and scaling back the class sizes. Where he was running classes up to 24 students in Texas, in Oregon, he will (by choice) be running classes from one to eight students.

Clint is not a competition-oriented guy. He doesn't care about competitions except those that bring you home safe. As at Gunsite, you'll probably show up with a rifle that is too heavy, or has too much gear on it, and end up unbolting stuff as the class progresses.

The Site

I met Herschel Davis at Gunsite, He was an instructor there, soon after retiring from the Navy, where he had been the highest-ranking NCO in the Navy. He had joined UDT before there were SEALS, and then spent time "with the Teams." Herschel is a no-nonsense guy, who like so many other SWAT/spec ops operators has no interest in competitive shooting. The Site is in Illinois, and while (as I write this) Herschel is once again in the employ of the government in a sandy place which no one can bring themselves to mention, the school is being ably run while he is gone. (How tough an old bird must the be, if the government is willing to hire him to go riding a chopper around Afghanistan. Ooops, I mentioned it.)

The Site is a law enforcement and military-oriented, defensive school, but not all their instructors are solely ex-ops people. One I know is Peter Milionis, a Chicago cop and top-ranked USPSA/IPSC competitor.

You can go to The Site and learn a great many things, primarily how to use the AR as a tool in an emergency, and thus stay alive.

Competition

Competition is different. There, you are not looking for an experienced SWAT cop, or a special ops operator. Those fellows can teach you many things, but winning shooting competitions is not what they are good at. To find out how to win matches, go to those who win matches. One place to go and person to see is Jerry Miculek. Jerry is perhaps best-known as the best revolver shooter of our time, or even the best revolver shooter ever. But Jerry is also very good with other firearms, including the AR. He made many trips to

an assistant to John who knows the local laws. If you take a class in your home state, the person who is arranging the class is likely to be an experienced firearms instructor or police officer, and they can tell you of the intricacies of the use of defensive force in your state.

John is not interested in what wins competitions, except the competitions where your own life, limb or safety are concerned.

One thing in particular you must know about a John Farnam class, is that he believes in immersion in the environment you wish to learn about. No, he isn't going to be some sort of a D.I. out of the past, harsh and violent. What he will do is give the class the opening classroom work, take you out to the range to check rifle zeros, and then he will switch the class to a 24/7 armed environment. You will load your rifle, sling it and you will stay loaded for the rest of the class. When you leave the range to go home, you'll unload (unless local law permits loaded carry) and each morning when you arrive, you are expected to safely load and sling. A firearm used for defense is of no use if it is not loaded. You will learn to exist in that environment. If your safety habits start to slip,

Pop-up computerized targets can be good instruction, with proper coaching. As a controlled competition, it can be really, really, fun.

Jerry Miculek is best-known as a revolver shooter, but legions of bowling pin shooters know he is also know he is first-rate with an AR, too.

the prize tables at Second Chance, and it was a rare year he wasn't "on the table" in the Light Rifle Pop and Flop, the event set up for rifles.

Jerry teaches in Louisiana, so you must travel to a hot and wet place to learn, but learn you can. His "Bang" academy is a place to learn many things about shooting fast and accurately.

Matt Burkett

I first met Matt at a group dinner in town, at one of the Second Chance shoots. He was this brash, fast-talking and big-talking kid up from the dusty ranges of Arizona, there to show us all how pin shooting was really done. As I recall, he didn't do as well shooting that first year as he did talking. But he picked up pin shooting very quickly, and earned more than his fair share of loot in later years.

Matt teaches, and you can go to Arizona to learn. Or you can absorb how the AR is used from his DVD instruction. While not the first to offer instructions on tape, Matt jumped in with both feet, and then went to DVDs as soon as they became common enough to form a market.

If you start with a solid, reliable AR, and follow the course of instruction, you will be 'way ahead of the competition at your gun club. If you augment the DVD with occasional trips to bigger matches, and take notes of what you did, how well it worked, and then go back to the disks to work on your skills, you can be shooting to your potential in a lot less time than it took us in the old days.

Legalities Of The AR-15

First things first: I'm not a lawyer, and I don't even play one on TV. So, I cannot give you legal advice. Nor would I, unless you were present and paying me for said advice. What I can tell you is what I have learned from being a dealer and gunsmith for over 20 years, and from my conversations with various ATFE agents and state, county and local law-enforcement officers during those years.

Second, it is fashionable among many gun owners to vilify the ATFE and try to make them out to be thugs, miscreants with badges, and the worst kind of politically-driven, subject to the whims of the powerful, bureaucrats. Those I've talked to and worked with were all fine people. However, they cannot know every regulation by heart. (Although during the last compliance inspection I had, the agent didn't have to crack open the book a single time to answer, by regulation number, my answers.)

And, many agents didn't know anything about firearms before they signed on with the bureau. Before you snort in disgust over that, ask yourself this: How many Secret Service agents knew anything about counterfeiting before they went to the academy? How many FBI agents had a clue about embezzlement, bank fraud or wiretaps before they raised their right hand to take the oath? No, the Bureau of Alcohol, Tobacco, Firearms and Explosives enforces the laws as they are handed to them. And tries to interpret (as in, make sense of) the laws passed by Congress in the face of the incredible creativity of gun owners, experimenters, inventors and competition shooters. Since the ATFE is vastly outnumbered just by licensed Federal Firearms dealers alone, they have to work hard. Do not be put off by not getting a clear and quick answer from your local office. If they dash off a quick, and wrong, answer, they'll be years cleaning up the mess.

I can't cover the details of each and every state in the union vis-a-vis the AR-15. For that you'll have to inquire of your local gun shop, or ask the State Police about the laws where you live. Just be aware that some states are a lot harder on what is allowed than the Feds are. And, that not every police officer you meet knows the law. If you can't find it in the compiled statutes of your state, or the law is not clear, get it in writing from the state Attorney General. You can find out what is or isn't allowed in your state from a surprising source: your State or Area Director of the United States Practical Shooting Association. As the USPSA is involved in Three-gun competition, and the AR is viewed as the tool to have for those competitions, the members will know more about what is and what is not allowed in your state.

Basically, you have two things to be aware of: that the AR-15 was a machinegun to start with, and as a result a lot of the parts floating around out there are machinegun parts. And second, accessories meant for said machineguns (Yes, they can be legally possessed in some places; most states, as a matter of fact.) can turn an otherwise legal and semi-auto only rifle into a rifle covered by the National Firearms Act of 1934.

First, we need to set some definitions. We need to set out just what it is we're talking about. Barrel length is a big one. Barrel length is measured from the face of the bolt when closed, to the forwardmost part of the barrel that is permanent. Overall length (OAL) is another. OAL is measured parallel to the bore, from the front of the assembled rifle to the rear of the stock. If the stock folds, then measure when folded. "The firearm" is the part that has the serial number on it.

And all declarations I make can be changed for you, depending on the state in which you reside.

A welded-on extension is good enough for the ATFE. As long as it is long enough, that is.

This rifle is too short on both ends. The barrel is too short, and the stock folds. Good thing the owner is properly licensed, or he'd be in trouble. (Jeff A. shooting a DS Arms FAL shorty, brought to the range by DSA.)

Barrel Length

The minimum length allowed in any standard rifle is 16 inches. How much more do you need? There is no "safety margin." You must be over 16, is all. Measure from the face of the closed bolt to the forwardmost part of the barrel that is permanent. A screwed-on flash hider is not permanent, and doesn't add length. However, the ATFE allows barrel extensions that are permanently attached. By permanent, they mean something welded on, silver-soldered (hi-temp, not low-temp solder) or that uses a blind pin or welded pin. There is no chemical bond strong enough to satisfy the ATFE. You cannot use any grade of Loctite, or J-B Weld, to secure an extension onto your barrel. You can have a short barrel with a long flash hider, and if the total is permanent and over 16, you're in. It is possible to obtain a 14.5 inch M-4 barrel, and then permanently attach a flash hider that bumps it up past 16, and be kosher.

Be aware that some places make it tougher. The ATFE doesn't care if there are threads under the weld, but the state of California apparently does. And some States might not allow flash hiders.

Overall Length

As far as the federal government is concerned, 26 inches is long enough. However, a lot of states insist on 30. Which brings some rifles into a very curious situation: they are handguns under state law, but rifles under federal? My home state of Michigan is one such state. If your rifle is 29.5 inches long, it is too short to be a rifle under state law. So, we have

to get it "Safety Inspected" as a handgun. (Too weird, but what can you do?) On the other hand, the attorney general of Michigan has declared that folded length only counts if the firearm can be operated when folded. Now this obviously includes the AR-15 and all its clones. But something like the Kel-Tec, which can't work when folded, would be OK if it were over 30 when unfolded and ready to shoot. The thing is, the state of Michigan doesn't allow stocked handguns of the "normal" type. That is, if you were to show up with a Luger or a Browning Hi-Power with a stock attached, to register it, you'd be told to get that NFA weapon out of sight before you were arrested. (If you weren't just arrested.) But, we can "register" a rifle on a handgun safety inspection form. No one said the law had to be rational, just consistent. Sort of. I guess we should just be glad that they've given us an avenue to own said hardware, instead of simply saying "It isn't 30 inches, you can't have it."

If your State follows federal law, then you can make yours shorter, but not on the muzzle end if it is already at the 16-inch limit.

Short-barreled Rifle

It is possible in some states to have a short-barreled rifle. Where allowed by state law, you fill out the appropriate paperwork with the ATFE. Once you have gotten approval (and not one minute sooner!) you can legally trim your barrel down from 16 inches to whatever you want. However, it is not all a bed of roses. You must be very careful in what you do. For instance, in applying for the conversion, you must be

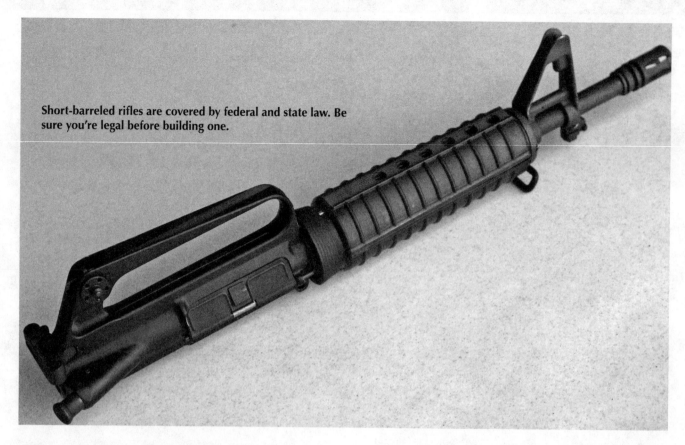

Short-barreled rifles are covered by federal and state law. Be sure you're legal before building one.

careful in how you fill out the paperwork. If you fill it out to convert the rifle to an SBR with a 14.5-inch barrel from 16.5 inches (say you want an M-4 clone) you are stuck with 14.5 inches until you amend the application. If, however, you fill it out as "less than 16 inches" you can make the barrel whatever you want in the future. Ditto overall length. Put down "less than 26 inches" and be content. Once you get approval, do not, I repeat DO NOT ever put that shortened upper on a lower other than the one you listed as the serial-number lower for conversion. Despite having approval for a short-barreled rifle, you do not have approval for THAT, second, rifle to be short-barreled. You will have created an unlawful weapon. I'm not kidding, you could be in big trouble by assembling the wrong combination.

You must be very careful then, if you own an AR that has been turned into an SBR, and another rifle that has not. Inadvertent parts swapping can lead to a legal mess.

M-16 Parts

There are differences between the internals of the AR-15 and the M-16. In the manufacturing process, some AR-15 parts were first M-16 parts. They then had additional machining cuts made to them, to remove the offending characteristics. For example, the hammer of the M-16 has the full-auto sear lump on the top of it. If you look closely at many a hammer in an AR-15, you'll see the pad left behind when the lump was cut or ground off. The disconnector was often an M-16, with the tail cut off to make it an AR part. The trigger is the opposite: you can make an M-16 from an AR, but not the other way

around. The AR trigger is boxed in at the rear, to prevent the longer M-16 disconnector from fitting. The M-16 safety could be made from an AR safety, but the additional cuts make it likely they are done on separate machines. The auto sear is the one M-16 part that has no AR-15 compadre. There is no equivalent, as the auto sear is the key.

The big one is the carrier. The M-16 carrier has the bottom rear enclosed. The lower shoulder of the enclosure is the engagement surface that trips the auto sear in an M-16, and on an M-16 the lower lip is the same distance forward from the buffer end as the upper lip.

What are you allowed to have in your AR-15? After all, very many rifles out there have been assembled from surplus parts (back when surplus was actually available) and may have some M-16 parts in them. I have seen collector AR-15 early production rifles (new in the box) that have full-auto M-16 carriers in them. They just weren't drilled for the auto sear, and obviously had no auto sear nor any other M-16 parts. Kosher? Back in 1963/4, who cared? Now, no one would make them that way. What can you do?

To make sure we're all on the same page (literally) for the following discussion, I have quoted the ATFE on the relevant section from their web page www.atf.gov:

The National Firearms Act, 26 U.S.C. section 5845(b), defines "machinegun" to include any combination of parts designed and intended for use in converting a weapon to shoot automatically more than one shot without manual reloading by a single function of the trigger and any combination of parts from which a machinegun can be assembled if such parts are in the possession or under the control of a person. Such combinations of parts are subject to all provisions of the Act.

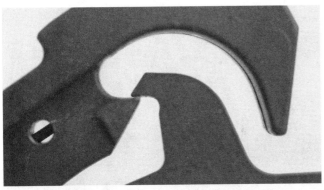

The hammer for an AR must be "slick" on top. That is, the knob on top used to engage the autosear must be ground off, or it is an M-16 part.

Don't worry about the burst-fire sear on the side of the hammer. No one cares about it, as long as the hammer is clean on top.

The safety must be solid in the middle and not slotted. The slots allow other M-16 parts to be installed.

The rear of the AR trigger is closed to preclude installation of an M-16 disconnector.

The critical parts you need to keep in mind are: combination of parts designed and intended for use in converting a weapon to shoot automatically. And: any combination of parts from which a machinegun can be assembled. If you cruise the gun shows and collect a complete set of M-16 parts, and you own an AR-15, you are in technical violation of the law. Now, you can own all the parts if you don't own an AR-15. You just can't have them all including the rifle. You can't have the AR in your den, and the auto parts in your garage. You can't have them. Shooters being shooters (i.e., some of them incredibly cheap) someone will ask "Can I own just some of them?" The only answer is "Yes, but...." There is no advantage to using auto parts in a semi rifle, except for one part. And all the parts can be easily converted to semi configuration, at least those that matter. The one part in question is the carrier. An M-16 carrier is heavier than an AR carrier. Some shooters like to use the auto carrier for the greater mass it has over the cut-back AR ones. A carrier by itself cannot turn a rifle into a machinegun. But if you have an M-16 carrier in your rifle, and a bunch of parts here and there, well, you can see where that leads to.

Engineering Warning!!!!!

Let us suppose you assemble a rifle with all auto parts that will fit an AR: carrier, hammer, trigger, disconnector, safety. (Leave out the auto sear.) Correctly done, the rifle will not fire except in semi-automatic mode. However, if your work is not perfect, you could end up with a rifle that doubles now and then. Bingo! You just made a machinegun, and earned a trip to Ft. Leavenworth. The fact that you didn't correctly adjust the timing of the disconnector is no defense. You have the requisite machinegun parts, the rifle fires more than one round. Slam dunk, it meets the definition of a machinegun exactly as written.

As you remove parts one at a time, and replace them with semi parts, the likelihood of full-auto (defective) fire diminishes. But, one full auto part and a bad trigger job that doubles is suspicious.

Engineering does not trump Law. And intent does matter. Intent, or evidence of intent, can be a really big problem. Let's go at it from the other direction: You have a rifle with all semi parts, but the lower receiver has been drilled to accept the auto sear. I think we can all agree that despite the fact that the rifle will only fire semi (The parts are all semi) we have clear intent on the part of someone (the work may have been done before you bought the rifle) to create parts designed and intended for use in converting a weapon to shoot automatically. That someone else did the work, and you were unaware, is no defense. At best, it will get you a warning, and a confiscated rifle. At worst, you're in the slammer.

The ATFE is not composed of gunsmiths with years of experience. They can't handle an AR and in a few seconds determine if it is correctly timed, badly timed, or has been subjected to experimentation to make it into a machinegun. In order to make that determination, they'll confiscate it, give you a receipt, turn it over to the experts back in the lab, and await the report.

Leave the full-auto fire control parts out! Use an M-16 carrier if you want, but be aware it is an M-16 part and could lead to trouble if someone wants to make trouble for you. The chances of that trouble are very slim, but they are larger than if you did not have that M-16 carrier in your semi-auto only AR.

LEO-Only Marked Rifles

Unlike the full-auto parts conundrum, the LEO-marked rifles are easy: they don't mean squat, federally. The ATFE has posted a letter on their Web site explaining it all:

Check out the Web site: www.atf.gov/firearms/saw-factsheet.htm

As of September 13, 2004, the provisions of Public Law 103-322, the Violent Crime Control and Law Enforcement Act of 1994, covering semiautomatic assault weapons and large capacity ammunition feeding devices are no longer in effect. The regulations implementing these provisions also are no longer in effect.

Law enforcement officers and police departments who obtained semiautomatic assault weapons are no longer required to use such firearms only for official use.

Law enforcement officers and police departments may now sell or transfer semiautomatic assault weapons to persons who are not prohibited from receiving firearms.

Law enforcement officers and police departments may now sell or transfer large capacity ammunition feeding devices to anybody.

SAWs and LCAFDs are no longer prohibited. Therefore firearms with the restrictive markings are legal to transfer to civilians in the United States and it will be legal for non-prohibited civilians to possess them. All civilians may possess LCAFDs.

A "SAW" was a semi-automatic assault weapon. An "LCAFD" was a large-capacity ammunition feeding device.

You can now own magazines and rifles marked "Law Enforcement Only" if you wish. There are some who wring

The "police only" markings on magazines are also a thing of the past. Let us work to keep it that way.

You can build your new receiver into anything legal; the law no longer restricts you at the Federal level. (We'll be building in Volume 2.) Just be aware, other Federal and State laws have not sunset. Build carefully.

their hands at the thought of being stopped by some nosy backwoods deputy who hasn't gotten the word. If you really are worried, go the web site, print out the letter, and put it in a plastic sleeve. If someone starts to give you a hassle, show them the letter. There may be some states where the ban was enacted at the state level. If you live in one of those states, the markings may mean a great deal. Find out, before you invest in a rifle or receiver that could bring you grief.

What Can I Build?

As long as it conforms to the current laws, anything. Assuming you don't live in a "Peoples Democratic Republic" like California, you can build from parts a rifle any way you want. Make sure it is longer than 26 or 30 inches overall, has a 16-inch or longer barrel, and doesn't have full-auto parts in it, and you're good to go.

You can re-build your post-ban rifle into whatever you what. Go ahead, thread that barrel, swap out the stock for a tele-stock, add a bayonet lug if you like. But what about the "stealth" rifle you built a few years back? The one that had the forbidden, banned parts on it? As long as we're not talking about a too-short barrel, or full-auto parts, no problem. (We'll

The markings put on rifles mean nothing now. Well, at least those required by the AWB/94. If a rifle is marked "Property of CPD" and not being sold by the city, you might inquire before buying it.

You can own magazines made during the ban, provided your state allows it. The Feds care not, now.

overlook for the moment that you did commit a felony when you assembled that rifle in the spring of 2001.) You cannot be prosecuted at this after-ban time, at least not federally. The law no longer exists. It would be like trying to prosecute your grandfather (or great-grandfather) from his nursing home, for having brewed some bathtub gin in 1929. The Volstead Act no longer exists, and there is no mechanism by which the government could prosecute him. Likewise your semi-automatic assault weapon you built between 1994 and 2004.

However, prosecutions undertaken during that time still have the force of law. If you were arrested for possession of that rifle on September 12th, 2004, or had it confiscated and given a warning, there is no going back. The former will not have their record expunged, and the latter isn't getting the rifle back.

You are not allowed to assemble an AK into a configuration that is prohibited for import, unless you use enough U.S.-made parts.

What About Magazines?

Again, the markings mean nothing. You can own an "LEO-Only" marked magazine if you want. You can assemble them from parts, salvage or new, make what you want, and experiment to your heart's content. The old restrictions mean nothing.

The Ban Is Dead Can I Build My AK?

Not necessarily. The AWB/94 was a different law than that covering the assembly of AK-47 rifles and other imports. And the AK law is still in effect. The law began with an Executive Order in 1989 by President G. H. W. Bush, disallowing the import of certain firearms deemed "unsuitable for sporting use." Expanded in a later Executive order by President Clinton,

The 20 parts are: frames/receivers, barrel, barrel extension, mounting block (trunion), muzzle attachments, bolt, bolt carrier, operating rod, gas piston, trigger housing, trigger, hammer, sear, disconnector, buttstock, pistol grip, forearm/handguard, magazine body, follower, floorplate.

So, to build an AK up from its thumbhole stock style, you must replace enough parts with USA-made ones such that there are no more than 10 imported parts left in the rifle. And, you still have to stay within length restrictions, don't use any full-auto parts, and make sure your work is safe.

Building an AK is not only outside the purview of this book, but something that could be a book in itself. I just wanted to mention it so some reader doesn't go off modifying their AK unwisely, in the euphoria of the sunset of the AWB/94.

What About The Future?

Some worry about a future ban. Will the old markings come back and bite the owners? How can you ensure your rifles are grandfathered then? The answers are; No, and there is no way to be sure. If there is a new ban, the ATFE will have to approve new markings that don't cause confusion with the old markings and the new law. (If such a law ever happens. The best solution is to make sure new laws don't happen.) And there is no way to guarantee old rifles are grandfathered under a new law, as the new law (if such a thing happens again) will have all new language.

The AWB/94, once sunset, cannot be resurrected by Congress simply voting "bring the old law back." Any new law, even if it was an attempt to resurrect the old law, would have to be proposed, and then be subject to being amended, language re-written, changes made, etc. There is no way to guarantee anything, except by making sure a new law doesn't get passed.

A folding stock on an import? Maybe, if it was imported before 1989, police-owned, or papered as a Class 3 firearm.

it became a federal regulation in 1993, as 27 CFR Section 178.39, later shifted to 27 CFR Section 478.39: "No person shall assemble a semiautomatic rifle or shotgun using more than 10 of the imported parts listed in paragraph C of this section if the assembled firearm is prohibited from importation under section 925(d)(3) as not being particularly suitable for or readily adaptable to sporting purposes."

Some things are completely controlled under some state laws. This suppressor is forbidden even to police in Illinois.

Armalite

The Armalite company used to be known as Eagle Arms a few years ago, and was in Coal Valley, Illinois. I ended up owning one of their rifles (a parts kit, really) back in the waning years of the 1980s, and it was a durable, reliable, tackdriver. Still have it.

When the rights to the Armalite name became available in the mid 1990s, Mark Westrom bought them in a heartbeat and started marking the rifles. Armalite is now located in Geneseo, Illinois, right around the corner from Springfield Armory. (You've got to wonder just how much shooting the city fathers liked to do, to lure two such companies there!) Armalite, unlike a number of AR makers, machines their own uppers and lowers from forgings, machines many of the smaller parts like sights, buffer tubes and barrel extensions, and turns barrel blanks to their own specs on CNC lathes.

They send out for the specialized things like the forgings of upper, lowers and front sight housings, chrome-plating the bores of barrels, and mil-spec anodizing. For the book, Mark and the folks at Armalite not only sent me three rifles (a bonanza of gear) but let me wander the plant, taking hundreds of photos of the rifles, production, assembly and testing. As near as I can tell, the only place off limits was Mark's personal gun safe. Everything else was open to inquiry, photographs and discussion.

What I learned was that the Armalite staff spends a lot of time making sure the parts are made right, and the parts are assembled right. They must be on to something, as when I was there they were loading three rental trucks with the nearly 800 rifles just purchased by a state police department. And the buy did not sweep the shelves clean, as there were

When you make rifles, and lots of them, you need someone to install and check every part. Assemblers don't build whole rifles, all the time.

plenty more on hand. The three they sent me were an M-4gery with Mil-Std 1913 railed handguard, known in the Armalite catalog and inventory as the "M15A2 w/1913 rails" their tactical marksman/varmint model, an M15A4(T), and a .308 carbine, the new AR-10.

M-4gery, 1913 style

The M-4A2 w/1913 rails sent was a post-ban, but since the sunset you can have it in correct trim. The comp on the end of the correct M-4 profile barrel is quite effective, and it would be good if Armalite offered it threaded for those who want one for competition. The barrel was slightly smaller in diameter than the M-4 we use as a benchmark (.718" vs. .741") but unless you put dial calipers on it you'd never notice. The barrel is not marked, is chrome-lined and has a twist of 1/9. The front sight height was correct for a non flat-top rifle, which this one is. The upper is an A2, with the rear sight housing lightly marked. The dial is marked "8/3" which is correct for an A2 rifle and not a carbine, but I'd bet you'll find a bunch of M-4s in Iraq with dials marked "8/3". They work on both, and since no one is shooting a rifle past 300 without optics, no one cares. The front sight housing is an Armalite, and uses two large, high-grade allen screws to

clamp it to the barrel. The screws do not contact the barrel. While it is much easier to machine and assemble (you don't need a fixture to hold the barrel while you drill it for cross pins, for example) it is slightly less durable than a pinned unit. For anything less than jumping out of perfectly good aircraft, I wouldn't worry. I'm sure my friend Jeff Chudwin, who has seen far more ARs abused than I have, would worry over it. But I wouldn't until someone demonstrated otherwise. What the design does is allow Armalite to make sure their front sights are top dead center over the barrel, and that you aren't faced with the problem of cranking some windage into the rear sight to get the rifle zeroed, a problem I've seen on other rifles.

The handguards appear to be a one-piece tube, but are not. They are made of identical top and bottom units, held together with six allen-head screws. The base tube "diameter" (it is actually machined to look as if it is a square or octagon) measures 1.630 inches and is comfortable. The tube, while edgy, is not uncomfortable, and small enough in diameter to be graspable.

The buttstock is the old synthetic with a sling loop on top, the one I prefer. As I received a neutered rifle (before the sunset) this stock wouldn't slide, but Armalite is now making

One assembly room of one part of the Armalite plant.

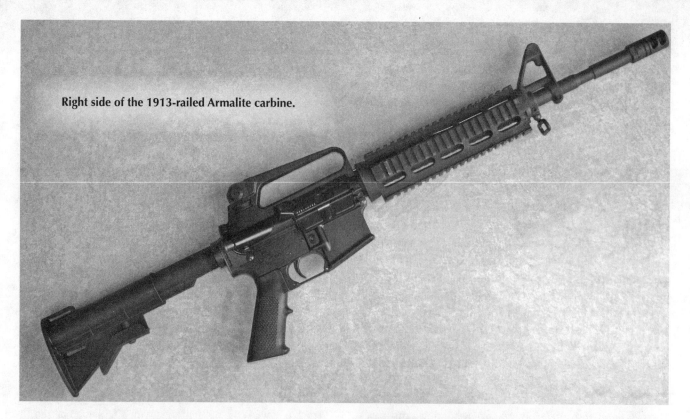

Right side of the 1913-railed Armalite carbine.

Armalite makes their own, so the receivers are dimensionally and feature-correct.

The sight clamp screws are large, and torqued down tight. Don't mess with them.

The slider on the telestock has the top sling loop, a feature I like.

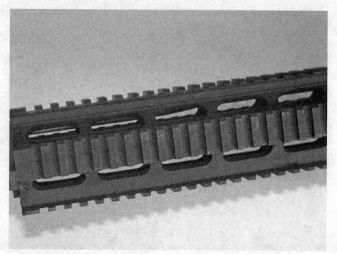

The handguard is not one-piece, but two halves tightly fastened together.

Plenty of cooling air can flow through, which is good if you have testers like mine.

them as sliding units. The buffer tube is the larger, non mil-spec diameter that most stocks are. No problem, unless you want to go swapping the existing slider for something else.

Internally, the fired control parts are all AR. The hammer, trigger, disconnector, safety and carrier are the correct Colt-style AR parts. The carrier, while black-coat treated, has the interior chrome plated. The carrier is not marked with a manufacturer's letter code, but does have a pair of patent numbers on it. They are patents of Mark Westrom's, concerning the design and modification of bolts to increase durability. The bolt is marked "AR 9D", obviously an Armalite bolt, and production lot 9D. (Or perhaps inspector 9D, there are some things Armalite won't say.) The extractor is unmarked, and the spring has instead of an internal bumper, an external donut to increase extractor force.

The upper and lower are machined by Armalite from forgings provided by their contracted forge company. The company uses Armalites own forge dies, so the upper is marked with the Armalite forge marks, a cross in a circle and

No failures with the Armalite rifles.

For varminting, a good scope (Leupold) a laser rangefinder (Nikon) and a way to carry lunch and ammo (rucksack from London Bridge Trading Company)

The flat-top A4(T), right side.

Left side of the A4, with the selector offering only Safe and Fire.

The front sight clamping screws.

For the test sessions, we put the Elcan on the A4, and the testers had a blast.

Armalite puts their proof mark on all rifles assembled.

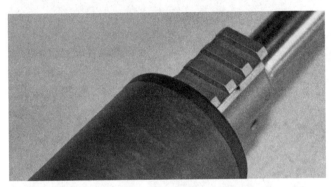

The reinforced synthetic handguard free-floats the barrel for best accuracy.

"AR." The lower is marked with the Armalite logo, city of manufacture, fire control markings, and serial number. The finish is a deep black, fine-grain matte of uniform texture and color, matching well the Colt control rifle. The trigger pull has a 4- to 5-pound take-up step, then holds solidly until you get to the 7.5-pound pull that drops the hammer. The disconnector is timed very late (correctly) and releases sharply and solidly. The safety moves positively, but does not require undue force.

The Armalite 1913 carbine is well-balanced, and was well-liked by the test-fire crew. The accuracy was suitable for all uses except varmint or ultra-precise shooting. For duty, defense or competition it had more than enough accuracy. Clamped in the Lahti test-fire rig it was quite content to deliver MOA to 1.5 MOA groups with the best ammo. As it is a carry-handle model, mounting a scope was not feasible, so I had to use 50-yard iron-sight groups as my test groups fired off sandbags. Using match ammo that it likes, (this particular rifle is very partial to Hornady TAP Urban 55-grain ammo) the Armalite 1913 carbine is a one-MOA rifle.

The test crew firing produced some expected results, and some unexpected ones. First, is when you have an aluminum tube handguard, even one extensively vented to allow for cooling, a lot of shooting will heat the handguard. Not anything new, we knew about it 20 years ago when experimenting with tube handguards for Second Chance and

IPSC shooting. If you are going to heat the barrel up, it would be prudent to have rail covers to protect your hands. The surprising thing we discovered was that the carbine had no problems with Wolf steel-cased ammo. This was one of the first rifles we tested, and magazine after magazine, we were waiting for the inevitable hiccup. We're still waiting. This rifle just didn't want to quit. When we ran out of the Wolf ammo, we went back to Black Hills, Hornady and reloads. All-told, the Armalite 1913 digested some 2,000 rounds and never failed once.

If you're looking for an M-4gery, or some variant of one, you can do a lot worse than Armalite. Based on anyone's cost/value calculation, this one ranks near the top.

M15A4(T)

The target, or varmint, rifle, the A4(T) is a shooting wonder. The upper and lower are standard Armalite, with this upper a flat-top. The color, texture and look are all correct. The upper has the Armalite forge mark, and the top rail measures 1.842 inches from the upper's lower edge. The slots are not numbered, but numbering the slots is a military "belt and suspenders" approach, anyway. The stock is an A2, longer, stronger and with buttplate trap door for storage. The handguard is a synthetic, reinforced tube, 2.25 inches in diameter. Both buttstock and handguard, and the A2 pistol grip, on this rifle are OD green. The barrel is a bull barrel match stainless 1/9 twist barrel. The gas block is a clamped block, using two large allen screws to hold it on, and has a picatinny rail on top for a removable front sight. The barrel measures .875 inches under the gas block, and .800 inches forward of that to the muzzle.

The M15A4(T) is noticeably heavier than other ARs, but it isn't meant to be a lightweight patrol rifle. It is meant for target shooting, precision marksman work (we used to call them snipers) and varmints. To that end, it has a heavy barrel and a very nice trigger.

The trigger is a two-stage trigger. For those who don't know the minutia of firearms design, a one-stage trigger is what the standard AR trigger is. It uses a disconnector to recapture the hammer, but there is nothing to stop, time or alter the trigger pull other than its spring and its friction on the hammer sear. A two-stage trigger uses some other part (usually the disconnector itself) as a spring-loaded part to adjust the trigger pull without adding spring tension or sear engagement friction to the parts.

A single-stage trigger simply pulls the trigger nose out of the hammer sear. On a two-stage trigger, the hammer sear engagement can be much greater, and the surfaces smoother and at a gentler angle. When you pull the trigger back, you take the slack out until the trigger contacts its spring-loaded stop. Then, you continue the trigger pull working against that spring to finish the pull. With the much larger sear engagement surfaces of a two-stage trigger, you can make the initial pull very easy. The second spring then controls final pull. What does all this mean? On the A4(T), the two-stage trigger can have an initial take-up of a couple of pounds, and a final pull under 4 pounds. With a standard AR trigger, getting the trigger pull down under 4 pounds is asking for trouble. In the A4(T) you get a completely safe and reliable trigger, with a pull under 4 pounds. Heavy enough to be allowed in NRA High Power, and light enough to be useful hosing down a prairie dog town.

When it comes to precision shooting, a lighter trigger pull is almost always a benefit. (A lighter trigger pull will not in and of itself make you a better shot. But if you are already a good shot, a lighter trigger lets you shoot better than a heavy one.)

And this rifle shoots. With the Leupold Mark 4 on board, it was absurdly easy to shoot sub-MOA groups. I used this rifle to test the ammo, and rank them in relative accuracy. While shooting it offhand, or in a field course in a USPSA 3-gun match would be work, shooting it from the bench was pleasure. The heavy weight dampened the already soft recoil of .223/5.56 ammo, and the tack-driving accuracy made me look good.

AR-10

The original AR-10 was the design that the Armalite company in the 1950s tried to market against the M-14, FAL and other competitors for the new (then) military rifle trials. Coming in just a bit late, it failed to make any headway against the M-14 and FAL. Redesigned, it became the AR-

If you're close enough to read it, you're close enough to realize that the proportions are a bit "off."

From a distance the AR-10 looks like just another AR in .223. It isn't.

AR-10 magazines started as M-14 magazines, but got changed along the way.

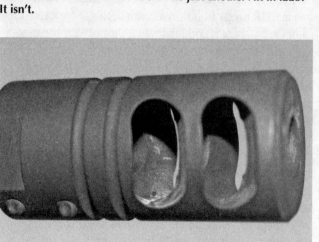

The comp on the AR-10 is great. It makes the light AR-10 soft in recoil.

One of the changes was re-machining the feed lips. Another was installing a new follower, with a spring-loaded plunger for the bolt hold-open.

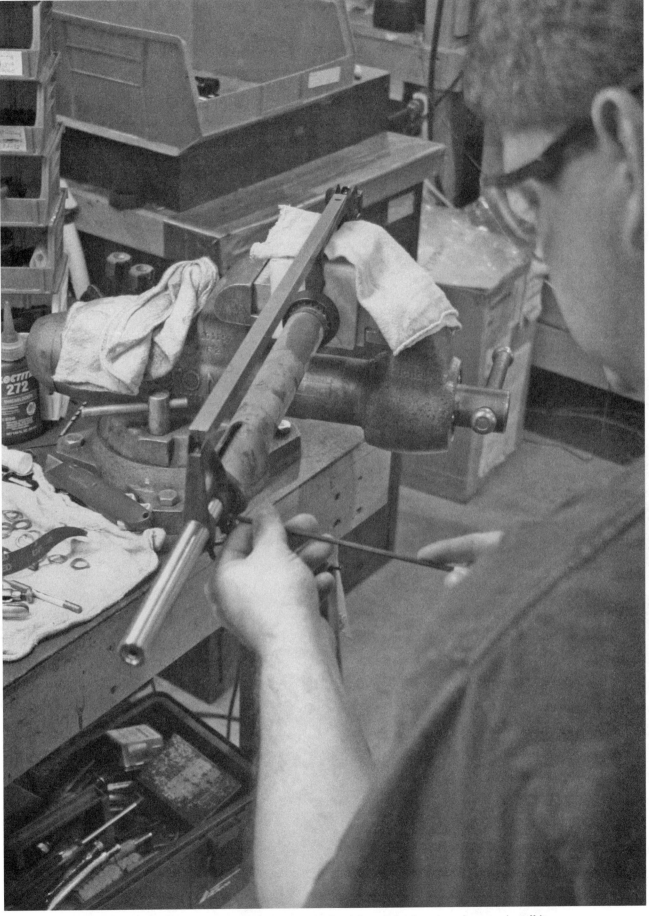

The advantage of a clamp front sight housing is that you can get the sight top dead center when you install it.

Here you can see the transitional magazines, with the locking block that allows use in M-14 type rifles, too. Note the bolt hold-open plunger in the back of the follower. It is there on all the Armalite magazines.

15. When computer aided design became common, Mark Westrom was able to use those methods to solve the niggling little engineering problems that had been in the original design. Then, teamed with computer-aided machining, he could offer a debugged AR-10. This rifle is the culmination of that work.

As you can tell looking at it in the "flesh" it is larger than an AR. It has to be, the cartridge is bigger. But the increased size isn't much, and only where needed. In handling, the rifle is quite handy. The obvious changes are in the size of the magazine well, and the reinforcements of the rear takedown pin area. The one shown here is a carbine, and now that I've handled it I'd prefer a carbine to a full-sized .30 rifle. As a post-ban, the barrel is not threaded, and the comp on the end is pinned. The comp is a little less than an inch in diameter (.937 inches) and a bit more than an inch in length (1.140 inches from muzzle to front baffle) and as a result is compact enough to fly as a Limited or Tactical comp in USPSA Three-

Lots of forged receivers on their way to becoming Armalite rifles.

Gun Divisional rules. The front sight/gas block is flat-top, to match the receiver, with picatinny rails for a place to clamp a front sight. The upper and lower receivers are stretched to accommodate the larger magazines, which are derived from the U.S. government M-14 magazines. The stock on this rifle is an A2. Given that the AWB/94 has sunset, you might be thinking of getting one with a telestock. More on that in a little bit.

The upper and lower receivers are forged, machined in-house, and anodized a matte, dead black. The lower is marked "Armalite Rifle 7.62MM" and "AR-10A4" along with the serial number. The Safe/Fire markings are on both sides. The upper does not have any forge marks on it, but as I saw platters, forged uppers and lowers, and partially-machined uppers and lowers in the plant when I visited Armalite, I have no doubt about who machines them: Armalite.

On the AR-10A4 the rear sight is a detachable one in a carry handle, just like the A4 versions of the M-16 and AR-15. due to the larger size, the unit is much larger than that of its 5.56 little brother.

The trigger is an entirely serviceable and clean trigger, and the accuracy this rifle demonstrated was almost as good as the best of the .223/5.5 rifles. I say almost, as the extra recoil of the .308 made it a bit more of a handful on the bench than rifles in the smaller cartridge. The trigger internals are standard AR-15, on small-diameter pins. The bolt and carrier are purpose-built for the .308 cartridge. So if you wanted to change the already decent AR-10 trigger for something smoother, lighter or more adjustable, you can simply drop in and fit something meant for the AR-15.

What really made the AR-10 stand out was the comp. If you're going to get a light, handy big-bore rifle, and you want to get the telestock, go for it. But if you're thinking of ditching the comp to get a flash hider, think again. We happened to have the Armalite AR-10 carbine and the Bushmaster .308 full-sized rifle along in the same test one day. All the shooters remarked that the Armalite was softer in recoil than the heavier Bushmaster. I had noticed the same thing while chronographing 7.62mm ammunition, that the Armalite was soft in recoil compared to heavier rifles. Lighter rifle, less recoil, that is the comp at work. Yes, it was not fun to be next to, but then no comped rifle is. However, unless you're going to be using it in a team environment, the comp of the Armalite is very effective and worth having.

The magazines sent were 10-shot, modified M-14 magazines. The mag catch is machined as a slot on the left side of the magazine, like the AR-15. The rear and the lips are modified, and the spine of the body is stamped with the Armalite patent number concerning the modifications. Now that the ban is done, Armalite is getting new, purpose-made 20-shot magazines made up. One addition to the older magazines (and probably the new ones) is the hold-open device. On the original M-14 magazines, the follower contacted a lever that pivoted up and stopped the bolt. There

isn't room for that in the AR-10, so Armalite made a new follower with a spring-loaded plunger in the rear. When you load magazines, you can get the first round in, no problem. Then, for the second, you have to also push the plunger in. Once the second round is in, you can continue to load. The magazines sent were the latest, lacking the locking block the original M-14 magazines had. Transitional magazines could be used in both AR-10 and M-14/M1-A rifles, but the newest design is AR-10 only. I have no use for "one size fits all" magazines, and that the new AR-10 magazines are AR-10 only doesn't bother me. The rifle still works with the transitional magazines, so if you have some you aren't left out in the cold.

The AR-10 fed everything, and shot some loads spectacularly well. The Black Hills load using Barnes bullets was extremely accurate, as were the Federal Gold Medal Match, with Sierra 168-grain MatchKing bullets. On the other end, I had some Radway Green 1969 British surplus ammo on hand, so I tried it. While the Armalite chugged through it reliably, it didn't like it, shooting groups that could best be described as "casually accurate." Which only goes to show, you get what you pay for. (I paid $50 per 1,000 rounds for a bunch of it a few years back, and it all works reliably, if not to match accuracy.)

Why would someone want a big rifle like this? First, it isn't so big. And second, some people just aren't happy with the power of the .223/5.56. A sheriff's deputy out in wide-open spaces may find that he needs to reach farther, or hit harder, than his urban compadres. Special bullets work well to increase the performance of the .223/5.56 on automobiles, but you don't need special bullets to reach inside of cars with a .30 rifle. State police departments have to spend a lot of time in rural areas and on highways, and they are a group interested in a big-bore rifle.

For a department looking for a big-bore precision marksman rifle, with fast follow-up shot capabilities, the AR-10A4 could be just the thing. It is plenty accurate, and if you need more you can get more simply by swapping the standard handguards for a fiberglass or carbon fiber free-float tube handguard. Leave the irons in your rucksack, and mount a scope on it. Zero the rifle, and you're good to go. And if you need to switch ammo types, say from a match hollow-point to a barrier-defeating round, you can do so by simply swapping magazines and re-chambering a round. A few seconds of work, and you're ready.

So, which Armalite would I want? Actually, I'd want all of them. I think I'd want them changed a little bit, but all three could find a happy home here. Specifically, on the shorty, I'd swap the handguards for standards and take the faux telestock off for the real thing. The Varmint/marksman rifle only needs a non-blasty comp to make it a smashing precision marksman rifle for light-caliber law enforcement use. And the AR-10, the only change I'd make would be to swap the solid stock for a telestock as a patrol rifle, or leave the stock as-is and rebuild it slightly for a law enforcement precision marksman rifle.

DPMS

No doubt who made this one.

on the rear sight wing. The upper is a flat-top, correct height for an M-4 and marked with an "M" on the front face of the receiver. The slots in the upper are numbered. The rear sight is a clamp-on with adjustable A2 rear sight, correctly heavily-marked for up and down, and with a 3/6 wheel for elevation. It has the ejector lump and forward assist. You could slap this upper on any lower and not be caught out as not being military-issue.

The handguards are the full-diameter current-issue size, but instead of being the double heat-shield military design, they are DPMS' own "Glacierguards." Instead of a metal heatshield, they have thick ribs of the synthetic the

Only the lighting makes the steel on the DPMS look lighter. It matches closely the black anodizing of the upper and lower.

DPMS, also known as Defense Procurement Management Systems to old hands in the AR-15 world, is located in St. Cloud, Minnesota. (No jokes about "Minnesota" meaning "How cold does it get?" in various Indian languages, please.) Less than an hour's drive outside of Minneapolis, St. Cloud is listed as having a population of 48,000 residents. DPMS, incorporated in 1986, is a maker of quality ARs that many of you may not have heard of. That should change. One shooter who did know of them, Bruce Piatt, is that rarest of all people: a police officer who is a superb shot. He does not skimp on gear, and he uses DPMS ARs in Three-gun competition. I've had the privilege of being trounced by Bruce (I think I have beaten him once or twice, when he had the flu) and he is not one to cut corners on quality nor in technical approaches to solving a problem.

For the book DPMS sent me two rifles, at the opposite ends of the spectrum: an M-4gery, and their long-range .308 marksman rifle. Both are excellent examples of the type.

DPMS Mod A-15

The DPMS M-4gery is a near-perfect example of the civilian version of the current military-issue carbine. The receivers are beautifully made and finished, in a beautiful matte finish without any machine marks, mars, knarfs or mistakes left in the metal. The color is dead black, a product of the mil-spec anodizing and the additional Teflon coating that DPMS gives their receivers. The upper does not have any forge marks, but the rear sight assembly does have a Cardinal Forge marking

The current, no-loop-on-top telestock slider.

Fat, double heat shield handguards.

The DPMS is an exemplary version of what is being issued.

You can clearly see the chromed carrier installed on the DPMS M-4gery. Easy to clean, even though it has fallen out of favor in the military.

handguards are made of. How well do they work? In the Wolf testing (more on that later) we heated the guns up and chambered a round and left it in the rack. In handling it, I hadn't noticed any heat from the handguards. But my

hand brushed the barrel in getting it into the rack, and I almost immediately had a blister. The barrel was smoking hot (literally, when it hit the painted rifle rack) and I hadn't noticed it.

The DPMS proved reliable even when being torture-tested with steel-cased ammo.

The barrel is a correct M-4 barrel, with M-203 mounting cut and profile, made of 4140 chrome-moly steel and button rifled 1/9. It is chrome-lined and chambered for 5.56mm. The front sight is a forged housing, and is the correct height for a flat-top carbine. The barrel is threaded, and out on the end was a comp. For all the world it looks like a Miculek comp, complete with the rear slot shading cuts on the top. If DPMS is buying comps from Clark Custom and Jerry Miculek, great.

The Long-range .308 is one big rifle, made to take a scope and only a scope.

If not, then they flatter him greatly. That said, many of the comps mounted on the rifles looked very much alike. The testers all commented on how flat the comp was. That is, the sights did not lift off the target on recoil, and the light M-4gery did not hit as hard as its lack of weight might suggest. As a competition comp, it is great. I'd hate to be in a hallway with a team, armed with carbines with this comp mounted on them. After the first few shots we'd be shooting through a haze of blasted-off paint and wallpaper.

The pistol grip is A2, and the stock is the current synthetic military-issue lacking the upper sling loop. Curiously, it appears to be a sliding telestock that has been pinned open (for the expired AWB/94) with a couple of blind roll pins. The slot is there, and a locking hole is visible. I'd say you could turn this into a real telestock by removing the pins. As this is a loaner from DPMS, and not mine (though I'd really like to keep it) I won't go trying to machine or remove the pins. And

Mount a scope like the Leupold LR/T on it, and the DPMS Long Range .308 delivers tight groups way out there.

The rear takedown pin has its own reinforcing boss, and doesn't come out as far as the front on disassembly.

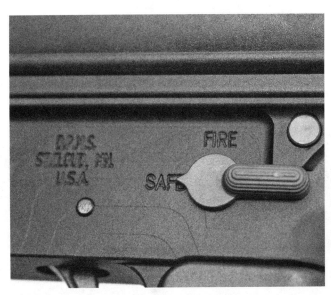

The controls work the same as any other AR.

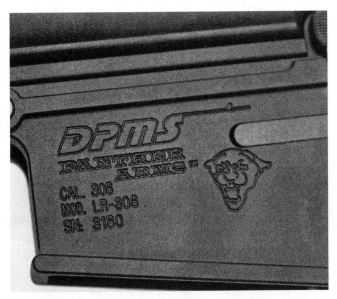

Clearly marked, you won't mistake the DPMS for any other rifle.

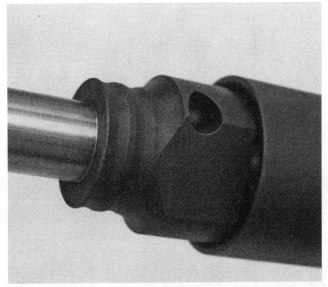

The gas block has no provision for mounting a front sight. Scopes only on this rifle.

since the ban is no more, a real telestock is an option now.

The internals are a modified M-16 hammer and all other AR-15 parts. The carrier is an AR, chromed (not something you see a lot of today) and marked with a large "D" on the left side. The bolt is marked with a similar "D", the extractor is unmarked, and uses a blue buffer inside the extractor spring.

The trigger pull is one of the nicest bone-stock, military-issue triggers of the test. For most shots, and most dry-firing, there was no creep at all. You simply pressed on the trigger until you reached the 7.25 pounds it took to make the hammer fall, and the rifle fired. Every now and then a pull would present itself with a tiny step in the takeup, not enough to notice except when dry-firing. Once you took up the step, the trigger again stood still until the hammer fell.

The soft comp, and the clean trigger, made the DPMS one

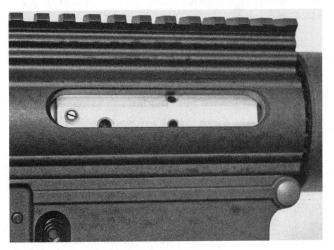

The .308 has no dust cover door.

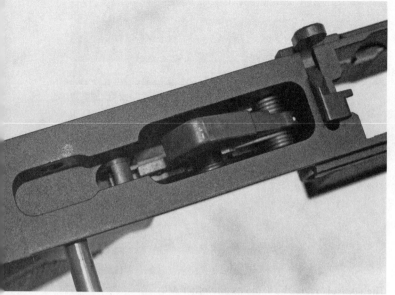

Inside, it is all AR. The walls are not that thick, you're seeing the web to blend the lower to the upper.

The weak spot right now, the plastic magazines don't stand up to much shooting.

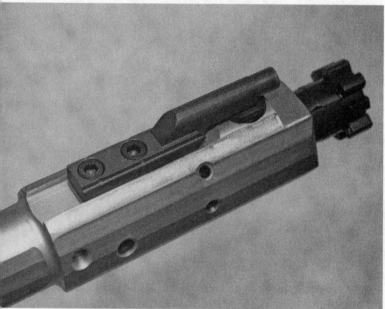

The carrier is over-sized to take the .308 bolt, but the rear is standard AR size.

of the testers' favorites. We spent some time working over the plates and the Mike Gibson poppers, and it was selected for further testing in the steel-case sessions. I have to confess here that I had forgotten that DPMS is not keen on steel-cased ammo in their rifles. They would prefer you not use it in the .223/5.56 rifles, because the cases cause accelerated wear. You may find your chamber chewed up by the steel. The .308, they are clearer about: don't use steel-cased ammo. Well, I forgot that when we went to test the .223/5.56 rifles, and as the DPMS was a solid, accurate, rifle we included it in the second test. We shot 120 rounds through the DPMS and other carbines, in five minutes or so. Then chambered a

round and left them to cool in the rack. To no one's surprise, the DPMS carbine worked just fine. It was hot enough that when we put it in the rack the paint smoked, and the barrel got some white heated-on scuff marks on it. But he chamber didn't get lacquered, it looks fine when viewed with the bore scope, and it worked flawlessly after this test.

As for accuracy, I can see why Bruce favors DPMS rifles. This one produced MOA iron-sight groups with Hornady 55-grain TAP Urban, and shot like a house afire with Federal Gold Match 69-grain ammo.

If you are looking for a tactical carbine, or a carbine for tactical matches, the DPMS M-4gery would be a fine one. For duty or defense, I'd get a flash hider instead of the comp, and make sure the telestock does slide. For competition in USPSA Three-gun matches, in Tactical Division, I would leave the comp on, not worry about the stock, and be sure and get some Brian Enos Slide Glide or Brownells trigger goop on the sear and lower the trigger pull a pound or so.

The DPMS, as so many of the rifles also demonstrated, had no problems with any magazine I had to feed it. Do yourself a favor, be like Bruce Piatt, and get a DPMS.

Long-range .308

The DPMS is not a rifle I'd want to pack for long distances. At 11.25 pounds, empty, stripped, it ends up a bit over 13 pounds once you add a scope and bases, sling, magazine and ammo. But, if I wanted to be shooting an AR long distances, the DPMS .308 would be near the top of the list. Unlike Armalite and Bushmaster, DPMS is not trying to make their .308 look like a scaled-up AR-15, or an AR-10 knockoff. First, the lower receiver is milled from a billet of 6061-T6 aluminum. It takes a standard AR-15 pistol grip, and the internals are all AR-15 (so you can swap parts if you need to or want to improve the trigger pull). The milling marks are not obvious, but they are there. The other thing you have to know when taking it apart is that the rear pin does not come out as far as the front ones does. As the front and rear are different widths (at least where the pins go through) the pins don't have to be the same length. When we were at the range, one of my testers was taking it apart to add some more lubricant (we did a bit of shooting) and he said "The rear pin's stuck. It won't come out any farther." That's how we discovered the difference.

The upper is a flat-top, with raised rib, so you can mount a long-range optic on top. Machined from a 6066-T6 extrusion, it is thick-walled for stiffness. So thick, in fact, that the magazine hold-open button has to fit in a recess machined into the upper. And for this rifle you want good optics, for you'll be able to do some real shooting. The barrel is a bull barrel of 416 stainless, button rifled and with 1/10 twist. The forend is an aluminum freefloat tube, 2.25 inches in diameter, that gives you a place to hold, mount a bipod, and covers the gas tube. The threads for the tube, and the receiver, are not the same as other .308 rifles so you cannot substitute other handguards for the tube.

That is no provision made for iron sights.

The trigger would disappoint an NRA High Power match shooter, but for anyone used to a military-issue trigger or what's known as a "rack-grade" issue rifle will find it very nice indeed. Clean and crisp, it is around 5 pounds in pull and entirely manageable even for long-range shooters. As for accuracy, the rifle has it in spades. Fed the ammo this one likes, Federal Gold Match 168-grain hollow-point, it shoots sub-MOA for as long as you can stand to take the .308 recoil.

It also was very fond of my dwindling supply of Hornady Match 175-grain Moly-coated ammo. I didn't try it for long with that, as I didn't want to use it all up, but every group with that ammo was also sub-MOA.

The DPMS Long-range takes original, waffle-pattern AR-10 magazines (pricey collector's magazines) and Knight's Armament SR-25 magazines. While the Knight's aren't as pricey as the collectibles, they are still expensive, and DPMS is arranging for magazines of their own. What you won't like are the 10-shot magazines that came with this rifle. During the AWB/94, everyone had to come up with a supply of 10-round magazines. The plastic ones that came with the rilfe are not very good. In fact, it is entirely likely that the crew at DPMS saddled up, rode off to the suppliers, and burned the place to the ground when they found out just how bad these magazines are. I started the test with two plastics, and in less than 100 rounds they were shattered bits of magazine parts. One magazine lasted most of that, but finally the feed lips cracked and broke off. The second one split down the rear seam in less than 20 rounds. If you get plastic 10-shot magazines, consider them disposable. I managed to locate, and borrow, an original AR-10 magazine for use in testing, and the moment I was done the owner wanted it back. (I can't say that I blame him: in 30 years in the gun business, it was only the second one I'd ever seen.)

If you are capable of packing the weight, then the DPMS would be a great regular-duty rifle. But for the rest of us, it is a long-range shooting, and not a long-range walking rifle. What you'll get is a rifle fully capable of delivering head shots on IPSC targets out to 400 yards, once you dial in the drop.

CHAPTER 17

Bushmaster

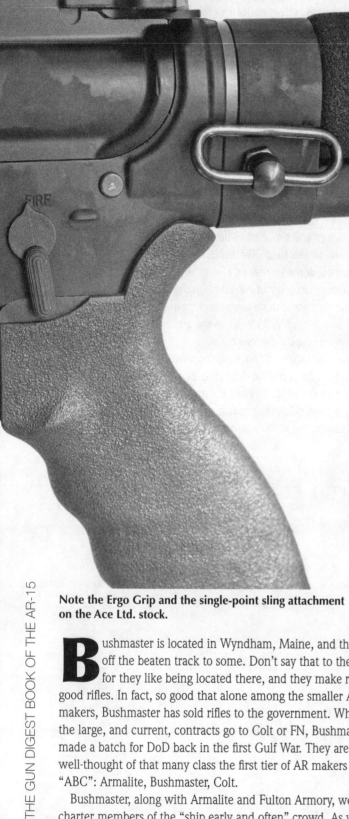

for testing. Jon Clark at Bushmaster wrapped up and shipped a Modular tactical carbine, a Carbon 15, and one of their .308 full-size rifles. And all three were a blast to test, and tempting to one or another of my test-fire crew.

Modular Bushmaster

The "M Gun" as one tester put it (after tripping over "modular for the third time) is a different approach to the AR-15. The barrel is a fluted, chrome-lined and with a twist of 1/9. Between the flutes you can still see the roll marking of the barrel, a Bushmaster, chromed, magnetic particle

The Bushmaster Modular is built on one of their excellent lowers.

Note the Ergo Grip and the single-point sling attachment on the Ace Ltd. stock.

Bushmaster is located in Wyndham, Maine, and thus off the beaten track to some. Don't say that to them, for they like being located there, and they make really good rifles. In fact, so good that alone among the smaller AR makers, Bushmaster has sold rifles to the government. While the large, and current, contracts go to Colt or FN, Bushmaster made a batch for DoD back in the first Gulf War. They are so well-thought of that many class the first tier of AR makers as "ABC": Armalite, Bushmaster, Colt.

Bushmaster, along with Armalite and Fulton Armory, were charter members of the "ship early and often" crowd. As with those two other makers, Bushmaster shipped me three rifles

Press the button to unlock and stand up the sight.

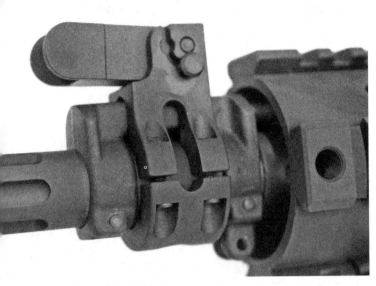

The front sight, folded.

Upright, it locks in place.

The Yankee Hill Machine rear sight.

inspected, 5.56 mm-chambered, 1/9 twist H Bar to start with. No muzzle threads, but that ended in September of 2004. The front sight is a folding unit from Yankee Hill Machine, clamped over a shaved front sight forging/gas block. The sight has a locking plunger, so it won't fold up on you if you bump it against something. How hard a hit can it stand? I don't know, and as I was unwilling to break a rifle loaned to me, I guess we'll just have to guess. As the locking shaft is a good 1/8 of an inch in diameter, I'd guess "a lot" of impact.

The Yankee Hill handguard is a single-piece aluminum tube with picatinny rails on the outside. The base tube size is just under two inches (1.990) and the rails and rail covers end up making it rather large in diameter, but still comfortable. The stock is an Ace, Ltd. skeleton stock, a design I'm getting to like more and more. The buffer tube is covered with a foam tube, and is comfortable to the face. The buffer tube is a standard AR tube, not a telestock buffer, and thus uses a rifle buffer and spring, not a carbine set. The stock is quite durable, and has multiple locations for attaching sling swivels. You can do a stock-to-front-sight-side-sling, a bottom, military sling, a single-point at the front of the stock attachment, or some combination of them. The pistol grip is an Ergo Grip, which was designed to be similar to, but better than, the MP-5 grip.

The Modular Carbine is a flat-top, and the upper bears a Cerro Forge forge mark. The upper rail height is 1.846 inches up, close to the Colt standard. The lower bears the Bushmaster logo, city of origin, fire control marks and serial number. The Bushmaster upper and lower are done in a very dark shade of gray. I'm not sure if the gray is actually the color, or that the texture of the anodizing/surface prep is enough coarser than the others to make it appear slightly gray instead of dead black. In any case, you aren't going to have to worry about color match if you build a Bushmaster upper for your existing lower. The match is plenty good.

The rear sight is another Yankee Hill Machine part, and well made. It is held on the upper by a pair of allen-head screws. Were I going to be using this on duty, I'd make sure they were good and tight, then I'd paint them in to make sure the couldn't move without my knowing about it. One design element I'm curious about, and not entirely happy with, is that the base of the sight does not rest on the upper. When the screws are tightened, the sight clamps on the corners of the

Upright, the rear locks in place, too.

Upright, there is room on the flat top for optics.

The forge marks on the upper.

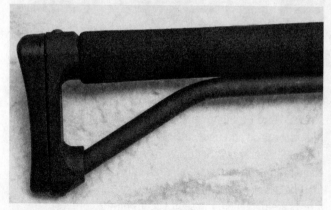

The Ace Ltd. Stock, a design I am getting to like very much.

rail, and does not contact the top deck of the rail. It is more than a place for dust and debris to collect, it also makes the mount slightly weak. As I've seen all sorts of abuse done to ARs, anything that might weaken parts gives me pause. Again, I can't test it to destruction, so I don't know. I just would like it more if they made it differently.

Internally, the Modular has standard AR-15 fire control parts. The carrier is a modified M-16, with the auto sear shoulder machined/ground back. But the firing pin is still shrouded. The carrier is not marked, nor are the bolt or extractor. The extractor has a blue synthetic buffer inside of its spring. The trigger pull is a very nice duty trigger. The only way I can describe it is as a "spring-loaded" slack to break. As you put pressure on the trigger, it kind of feels like the trigger is moving. (If you watch the trigger, you can clearly see it move, but the impression your trigger finger gets is that it may or may not be moving.) the feel is more like you are compressing a spring, than sliding the trigger nose out of the hammer sear. The break is clean, the timing of the reset late, and everything works with authority. If I could get this trigger feel on all my AR-type rifles, I'd be content.

For accuracy, the Modular was quite the showy gun. With irons, I could shoot about 1.5 MOA. If I took the rear off and folded the front, and installed one of the Leupold Mark4s, it delivered sub-MOA groups.

Carbon 15

Using synthetics in a firearms is not new. Gaston Glock didn't invent it back in the 1980s. The earliest production firearm using synthetics was the Nylon 66 by Remington. As a .22 LR it didn't have to be strong to contain the cartridge it fired. And as a plinker/hunting rifle it didn't have to be robust. But it was reliable. The few Nylon 66s I saw at the

The Bushmaster Carbon 15 with its markings.

The Carbon 15, right side view.

S and F on the right side. Note the mag button fence, protecting the mag button.

The Carbon 15 has no dust cover door, nor a forward assist. But it does have an ejector lump.

The rear sight is adjustable for windage only.

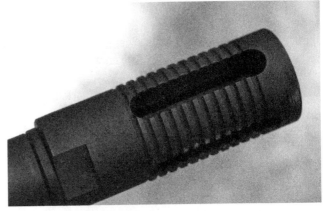

The Carbon 15 flash hider/comp.

gunshop in need of repairs fell into two categories: those that had been taken apart (and the owner either couldn't get it back together, or had lost a part or two) or were so horribly neglected that there was rust involved.

The trick in using polymers in a firearm is matching the mixture and stiffening additives of the polymer to the task the parts are expected to withstand. Too soft, and the parts flex, mis-aligning moving parts or allowing malfunctions. Too hard, and they risk being brittle against impact and the cold.

Bushmaster bought the rights and tooling for the Carbon 15 from the company that developed it but (by all accounts) couldn't quite make it work. I never tested one of the original ones, so I don't know from personal experience, but the reputation was not good. Well, Bushmaster must have taken care of the problems, because we didn't have any malfunctions when testing this one. But first, the rifle.

The Carbon 15 sent is an M-4gery, with carbine barrel and telestock. Built during the AWB, it curiously came with a muzzle brake not permanently attached. It was screwed down against a split washer. The M-4-profile barrel has standard handguards, a fixed front sight, lacked a bayonet lug, and had the front sling swivel riveted in place. The barrel is marked "B MP 5.56 NATO 1/9" indicating that it was made by or for Bushmaster, has been magnetic particle inspected, is chambered for 5.56mm, and has a twist of one turn in 9 inches. All good. The front sight housing is held on with two taper pins, as per proper design specs. The buttstock is a new-style slider, on a non-spec diameter tube. Mil-spec tubes are a nominal 1.14 inches, while most other tubes are 1.16 inches. It can make a difference, and you often cannot get a mil-spec slider onto a non-standard tube. (Only a problem if you plan on changing sliders.) The slider has the Bushmaster logo molded into the stock, an easy change for whoever does the moulding.

In between, we have the upper and lower receivers, made of a glass-filled synthetic. The lower is clearly not a forged aluminum part. The fence around the magazine release is free-standing, and does not have connecting ribs to the rest of the lower. The front disassembly pin fence only extends back far enough to contain the plunger and spring. The trigger guard does not hinge. The Bushmaster logo, and "Carbon 15" are part of the mold on the right side. A slot on the safety, and the "F" and "S" are paint-filled, so you can see where the selector is. On the left side the lower has "F" "S" and the serial number, etched into a metal plate encapsulated by the synthetic as it was molded.

The upper looks even less like a forged part, lacking a forward assist (not a bad thing to lack) and the ejector lump is oddly shaped. The front face of the ejector lump is tipped back from the ejection port, and if you look closely you can see that it is held on with an allen screw. Why? My thought is, that including a large chunk of synthetic on an otherwise cylindrical, thin-walled part, could lead to warpage as the mixture cures. Either that, or getting the part to release from

Inside, the Carbon 15 is all AR. No funky modified parts here.

The Carbon 15 is light, compact, reliable and was a big hit in the test sessions.

The carrier is cut back to preclude any full-auto funny business.

the mold is made a lot more difficult with the lump as an integral part. It works, it didn't fall off, and short of testing to destruction (something I'm sure Bushmaster has already done) it wasn't a problem for us. The upper has a flat rail on top, and the rear sight is part of an attached rail with picatinny slots machined in. At first glance the sight rail appeared to be aluminum, but on closer examination it turned out to be another synthetic. The sight housing and rail are black, where the upper and lower receivers are a gray/green. The sight is an A2 aperture and knob, but it is only adjustable for windage. All elevation adjustments have to be made off the front sight, as is done on the A1. The charging handle was nicely anodized, with curious marks on it. On the right side, just forward of the grasping parts, were some pyramidal indentations. I have seen those dents on other rifles for this book, and can only conclude that they are marks left by a holding fixture. That I've seen them on charging handles on different brand rifles only reminds us that while many makers make their own parts, there are a bunch of subcontractors at work, too. And it wouldn't surprise me in the slightest to find that some big makers sell their production over-runs to other makers. Hey, if it turns out the guy running the CNC mill produced 1,100 more charging handles than you need, why not get some cash for them?

The fire control parts are AR, while the carrier is a modified M-16, with the auto sear shoulder milled back. The firing pin is shrouded by the carrier. The bolt lacks any markings, as does the extractor, and the extractor has a blue buffer inside its spring.

As set up, the Carbon 15 is meant to be a compact and lightweight carbine, which it is. It is also meant to be reliable,

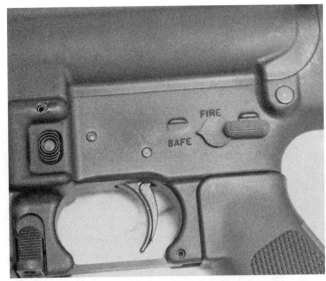

Note the .308 magazine button on the left side, and the bolt hold open below it.

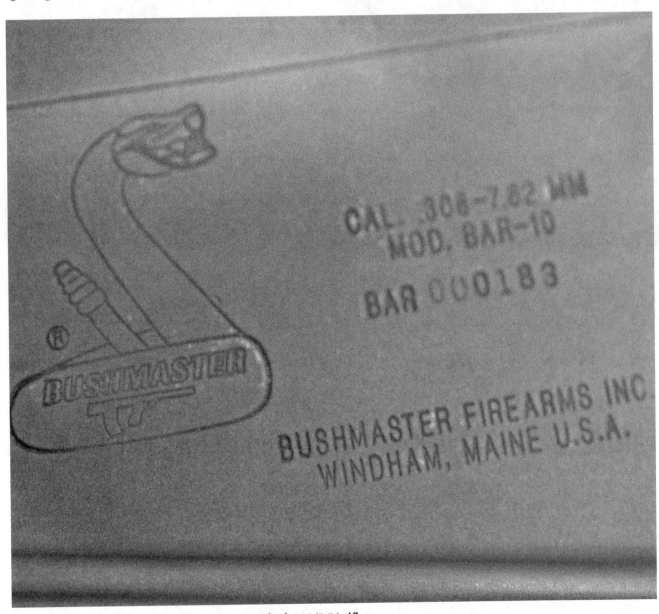

The Bushmaster BAR-10 is obviously not your standard .223/5.56 rifle.

Brass in the air, little recoil, free ammo, a sunny day, and paid to be on the range. Can it get any better?

which it is. In testing, the crew found nothing wrong with it. There were no malfunctions, magazines slid in and out without binding, and it even gobbled its fair share of Wolf ammunition without a complaint. Several shooters did mention that they heard a lot of spring "boing" for reasons we couldn't track down. The buffer and its spring, riding in the buffer tube under your ear (and against your check) can

sometimes create spring noise. Some shooters hear it more than others, and some rifles produce it more than others. This particular rifle seems to produce more than usual. I'd bet that the Carbon 15s that came off the line before and after this rifle probably don't.

The trigger pull was within military specs, heavy by handguns standards, but clean. Very clean. There was no

The ambi bolt catch. Push it down on either side, and the bolt goes home.

Scaled up, but still an AR. The Bushmaster 308 looks good and runs great.

perceptible creep, and only a little bit of the "spring-load" impression as you pressed the trigger.

For accuracy, the Bushmaster barrel delivered just what you'd expect from an iron-sighted lightweight carbine: just under 1.5 MOA. With ammo it really liked (the Carbon 15 was particularly fond of the Black Hills Blue 52-grain match hollow-point, which it shot sub-MOA) it shot a lot better. With everything else it shot well, better than average, and

The comp is not as effective as other comps. But it must work, for the felt recoil is not bad for a .308.

The charging handle retaining button, spring-loaded and catches on the inside of the upper.

nothing was really wretched in it. Which is perfect for what the Carbon 15 is meant to be: a car or truck gun. Something that would be impervious to heat and cold, not rust, be ready to go at a moment's notice, and eat anything you feed it. Not being particular about ammo is a bonus for a defensive firearm, and the Carbon 15 has that virtue. On the negative column, the muzzle brake that it came with wasn't a particularly good one. The brake seemed to have little or no effect on felt recoil. And, as a brake it wasn't very good as a flash hider. However, this rifle, and now current production riles, are threaded, so you could swap it for a good comp or a real flash hider. Were I to use this rifle for defense that would be the first, and perhaps only, thing I'd change. For current-production rifles, the thing to do would be to get a standard flash hider instead of the comp, a tele-stock instead of the faux tele-stock mandated by the late and unlamented AWB, and zero it. Then "paint in" all the sight settings, the sight rail locking screws, and attach a sling. If you really feel the need for a scope of some kind, you can easily attach it to the rail on the rear sight assembly.

Then stash it wherever, and be assured it will be ready for you when you need it.

Bushmaster .308

When it comes to making a big-bore AR, you can scale up the parts, you can re-invent the wheel, or you can mix and match. Bushmaster mixed and matched, and went a different route than others. First, they kept as much of the rifle the same as possible. The handguards, pistol grip, stock, buffer tube, sights, internal fire control parts are all AR-15. The upper and lower are scaled-up M-16A2 configuration, with a windage and elevation adjustable rear sight. Made of 7075-T6 forgings, if you were a few steps away you might not notice the slight difference in scale between the Bushmaster and an A2 AR-15. The barrel is a button-rifled 1/10 alloy steel barrel.

The handguards are standard A2, and fit into the normal-appearing (although bigger) delta ring and front cap. The

barrel is not marked, nor does it have a bayonet lug.

But the differences Bushmaster added, they are almost all brilliant and well-executed. First, the magazines. For a .308 rifle, Armalite modified M-14 magazines. Knight's went with the original AR-10, and then made their own derivative. Bushmaster went with the most prolific, and battle-tested design extant: the FAL. The BAR-10 uses metric FAL magazines, which are so common you could probably go to any big gun show on a weekend, and fill the back of a full-size pickup truck with metric FAL mags for not much more than $5 each. The FAL magazine was made all over the world, from the mid 1950s until the early 1990s. Now, Bushmaster can't guarantee that the BAR-10 will work with every single one of them. Come on, who would guarantee a magazine made by the East Lower Slobbovia State Arsenal? But if you have one made by the big players, you can be sure it will work.

A brief aside here: there are "metric" and "inch" magazines. In the rifles, the designations mean what measuring system was used to determine thread pitch, pin diameter, and so on. In magazines, metric mags have a small, diamond-shaped notch punched into the sheet metal. Inch-pattern magazines have a large, rectangular block welded to the sheet steel body. Metric mags will often work in an inch-pattern rifle, but never will an inch magazine work in a metric rifle. If you buy magazines, inspect each one to make sure you haven't gotten any inch-pattern mags mixed in with the metric.

Then, Bushmaster went a step further. They designed the magazine catch to be on the bottom of the magazine well, not the side of the lower receiver. The BAR-10 has an ambidextrous bolt catch. Push it straight down, and the bolt drops closed. Well, if the bolt drop is ambidextrous, then why not the rest? The hard part was the magazine catch. Bushmaster made buttons on both sides, and pushing them cams the magazine catch out of the way, and the magazine drops free. After that, an ambi safety was easy, but they didn't put one on. Hey, there has to be something you can do for yourself.

In function, the BAR-10 was flawless. The weight helped dampen the recoil of the .308 cartridges, and the accuracy was quite good. With the fixed carry handle it would have been tough to mount a scope, so I had to go with iron-sight accuracy testing. It quite often would put three or four rounds of a group sub-MOA, but the work of the .308 recoil would toss one out of the group. Of course I blame the recoil, and not me. I'm a gun writer, and we can all shoot sub-MOA groups on demand. Or at least for the camera. No, really, the rifle wanted to shoot. It is very accurate, and the trigger is clean and crisp enough to do good work with. It just seemed that every time I was testing the Bushmaster, I was pressed for time, or had just finished another test session and I was tender from recoil.

What the Bushmaster .308 did not have was an effective

Even the shorter testers found the BAR-10 recoil easy to deal with.

comp. Called a comp to comply with the old AWB/94, it didn't do much to tame recoil. If you need recoil reduction, you should get either the AK-74 comp Bushmaster offers, or get a threaded barrel and install your own comp. I've also heard complaints from other users about the charging handle. Instead of the external latch, it uses a spring-loaded plunger inside the handle, and that clicks into a recess in the upper receiver. Some have complained that with enough use the

catch wears and the handle pops free under recoil. I haven't fired this one enough to tell if that is the case, but it doesn't seem any easier to open now that when I first received it.

With a carbine barrel and a comp, the BAR-10 would be a great competition gun for action shooting. With a flash hider, it would make an excellent big-bore duty rifle. And in full size, with a flat-top upper, it would make an excellent police marksman rifle.

Colt:
The Gold Standard

The rifle Colt sent me represents the coup of the book. When I started this project, I was warned that I'd never get a loaner rifle from Colt. The reasons mentioned varied, and I think represent more the experience or frustrations of the speaker. One told me "You won't get anything from Colt, they have so many requests." Apparently Colt gets hundreds of requests from gun writers, police departments, foreign governments, and training establishments, so much so that the cost of these rifles represents a noticeable percentage of their production, and production cost. Or another, who remarked "Colt has spent so much time dealing with the U.S. and other governments, they have more lawyers on staff than engineers." In my discussions with Colt, I did talk to more attorneys than engineers. But I did talk to engineers.

And I did receive a rifle. Colt sent me, assembled before but shipped after the sunset of the AWB/94, one of their Match Target M-4 models, a de-milled civilian-legal M-4 in every respect save the ones legally barred at the time. While we can call other rifles copies, clones or excellent replicas, the Colt is the AR-15, the M-4, and thus is the exemplar, the rifle against which all others much be measured.

The Colt rifle came wrapped like a set of Russian dolls. Working out from the rifle, it was wrapped in a sealed vapor-phase inhibiting pouch. Then an interlocking cardboard sleeve to hold it in place, then the cardboard outer box, with its own locking lid.

The vapor-phase inhibiting sleeve was dated 04/04, for those into collecting minutia. Thus wrapped, it could sit

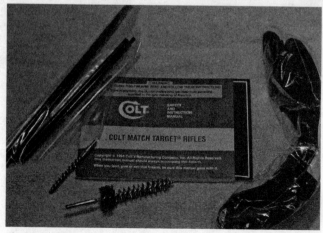

The Colt rifle came with accessories, in a cardboard box.

The coup of the book: an ultra-rare loaner rifle from Colt.

A colt-marked but not Colt-made magazine, made during the ban but legal now.

The forge marks show who did the actual hammering of hot metal.

The markings on a Colt Match Target M-4 Carbine.

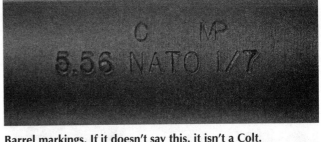

Barrel markings. If it doesn't say this, it isn't a Colt.

Colt Manufacturing, the commercial division.

Only two rifles sent had the retaining castle nut staked, and Colt was one of them.

on a self for years, even decades, and still be ready to go. Curiously, despite being sealed in the sleeve, it was dripping in preservative oil. In the box with it was a sling, cleaning kit, owner's manual, and a magazine. Shipped just after the sunset, the rifle came with a 20-round NHMTG-marked magazine with a production date of September 2003 on it.

The barrel is a 16.5-inch M-4-profile tube, complete with the M-203 retaining slot. The comp on the muzzle is pinned in place. The barrel is marked "C MP" over "5.56 NATO 1/7" Other than being 16.5 inches instead of 14.5 inches,

(and lacking threads) it is an M-4 barrel. Underneath the handguards, right behind the front handguard cap, the barrel was stamped 09/04, the production month and year. The front sight housing lacks a bayonet lug (no great surprise) and has a faint "F" stamped on the left side, indicating it is for a flat-top receiver. The only casting mark on the right is the numeral "1." The front sight top deck is machined high, for the flat-top receiver. The front sight housing is held on the barrel by a pair of taper pins. The pins are machined (or ground, depending on the tooling of the manufacturer) on a taper, and they only go in, and come out, from one side. The front sling is the relatively new side sling, and the lower sling on front is missing. The handguards are the M-4 double-lined, and larger in diameter than older "shorty" handguards.

The upper receiver is a flat-top, with "M-4" stamped on the front face, above the delta ring. (The delta ring is angled.) The rear sight is the A2 design, with the elevation ring marked "6/3" as is proper for an M-4. The upper has no forge marks, but the handle/sight has a keyhole, and the numeral 7, showing it was forged by Cerro Forge, in die number seven.

The M-4 mark on the front of the receiver, again, if it doesn't have this it isn't a Colt M-4 upper.

All Colt bolts are tested and marked.

Colt is now machining the lower with a web, to preclude unlawful conversions.

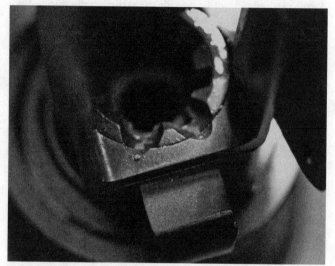

The M-4 ramps are carried down into the receiver wall. Only short-barreled rifles by Colt get this ramp.

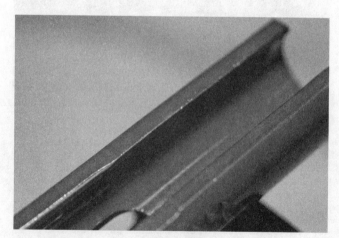

Colt carriers are machined straight back, without any shoulder at all.

Colt bolts comes with a paint "C"

The lower is a double push-pin lower (Colt is moving away from the double-screw-front-pin pattern, as they finalize their lower changes to preclude the use of full-auto parts.) and uses large-diameter hammer and trigger pivot pins. The lower markings are "Colts Manufacturing" a clear sign it is a commercial lower. Military and Law Enforcement rifles are made by "Colts Defense."

The stock is a fixed, telescoping-appearing stock, which were common during the AWB. While full-length externally, it has a carbine-depth interior, a carbine spring, and an "H" marked (heavy) carbine buffer. Internally, the lower lacks the hardened steel block of earlier Colts, but the rear space where you might install a DIAS has a web left across the gap. There's room for an Accu-wedge if you want one, but nothing unlawful. The hammer, trigger, disconnector and safety are all standard Colt AR-15. The carrier has the bottom lip machined off. The carrier key is tight, and whoever staked it on apparently used a maul and a cold chisel, instead of the more commonly-seen drift punch and ball peen hammer. The marks are deep, and the screws are not coming loose anytime soon.

The carrier is "C" marked, Colt-made, and the bolt is marked with a "C" in white paint, and stamped/etched "MPC" as well. Colt, magnetic particle inspected, the real deal. The extractor is marked with a "C" and the extractor spring has a black internal buffer.

The trigger pull is interesting: there is a step of about 5 pounds, where the trigger takes the slack out of the hammer engagement, and then there is no perceptible movement in the trigger until the hammer falls at about the 7.5-pound weight. For someone accustomed to a match handgun trigger, the description and numbers must seem atrocious. They aren't. As AR triggers go (for out of the box, or issue rifles) this is very clean, of moderate weight, and eminently useable. I had no problems shooting tight groups, or clean scores, with this trigger.

In all, this rifle stands as an example of Colt production as of September of 2004.

In function, it was perfect. It never failed with any ammunition, even the steel-cased Wolf. It never failed to lock open when empty, nor to drop an empty magazine when the mag button was pushed. The test crew remarked on how soft the compensator was. For a bolted-on comp to diminish felt recoil, and complete the "look" of a post-ban rifle, it works remarkably well. At least as long as you are shooting it. It is quite "blasty." While not the most egregious when it comes to side-blast, the Colt comp is one you do not want to stand next to. When we were doing the Wolf heatup and lacquer test, the Colt was in the middle of the three rifles. The test-shooters on either side moved away from the Colt. The Colt shooter did not notice the other rifles. Now this is not bad or good, just something to be aware of. The rifle will be soft in recoil, but others will pay for your diminished recoil.

Can you replace the comp? Sure, now that the ban is sunset, and if your state law allows it. But as the barrel is not threaded, you have two choices; thread the barrel, or fit a flash hider to the smooth barrel, and use the pinning method on the barrel. With the ban sunset, there are lots of gunsmiths willing to thread your barrel for you. But you might not want to. Compensators are allowed in many competitions. (Not in NRA high Power, but this isn't that kind of a rifle, anyway.) Comps offer advantages, including higher scores. The USPSA standard for comps allowed in Tactical or Limited, is 1 inch in diameter by 3 inches long, maximum. After careful measuring, I have determined that the comp on this rifle is .9996 inches in diameter; and thus allowed. As it is a mere 1.5 inches past the muzzle, it is well within the rules. If you wanted to shoot this rifle as-is, it would not only be allowed, but be quite useful.

Look And Feel

As the standard against which we will be measuring all other rifles, the Colt bears detailed analysis. First, the finish. The mil-spec anodizing (once I'd wiped off the gallon or so of preservative oil) is a dark black. No gray is to be seen in the aluminum, and the small steel parts match it closely in their finish. The barrel is a dark gray, but still a closer match than a lot of other Parkerizing finishes I've seen. The parts have no sharp edges anywhere. You can rub your hands over the rifle from one end to the other, and except for the sharp corners of

The off side of the Colt side sling adapter.

The sling side of the adapter.

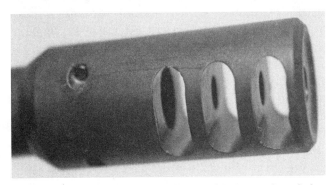

The Colt comp is effective, and if they made it as a threaded part it would be worth getting.

Yes, a big scope on a carbine is a bit odd. But if you want to find the limits of a rifle's accuracy, you get good glass.

the front sight post (entirely proper) you won't get cut or abraded. I've handled "mil-spec" rifles where the handguards had so much flashing left from the molds that it felt like you were running your hand over a rasp.

The front sling assembly is very interesting: it is a two-piece affair held on the barrel with a pair of roll pins. The sling is riveted to the main part, and the whole thing designed to be used on either right or left side. Why? On an issue M-4, if you mount an M-203 grenade launcher under the barrel you cannot use the bottom sling swivel. By mounting the sling on the side the rifle can still be carried slung. And with roll pins and a reversible design, it can be switched with a minute or two of work and a few tools. Too bad the rear sling swivel was

not as well designed. To properly use a side sling, you'd either have to have a tactical sling (and put up with it slipping off the new-design buttstock) or install a GG&G side sling adapter. Were this mine I'd remove the superfluous rear sling swivel, bolt in a GG&G adapter, and put a modified Chudwin sling on the side. (See the Patrol Rifle conversion chapter for the Chudwin sling.)

In function the Colt was utterly reliable. In accuracy, it was more than acceptable. The only rifles to consistently out-shoot the Colt were those set up as match or varmint rifles, like the Clark Gator or the Armalite M-15 with synthetic free-float handguard. When fed what it liked the best, Hornady 75-grain match .223, the Colt, with the Leupold Mark 4 mounted would shoot sub-MOA groups. And that, with no free-floated barrel, and a trigger many would deem too heavy, but is within issue specs.

If you're only going to own one rifle, and you want to make sure that what you have is absolutely correct as an AR-15 and a superb competition/duty/defense rifle, make it a Colt. This particular model would be great for defense if you can live with the comp, and would work very well in a tactical competition. For NRA High Power you'd want a full-size Match Target, and if you were using a Colt as a base rifle for USPSA Open competition, you'd probably want the full-size rifle for the longer barrel. But with a scope mounted this one is going to shoot as well as many longer rifles, just not balance the same.

As I wrapped up this chapter, a couple of items came to my attention. One was that Colt was apparently acting against dealers who were selling LEO-Only marked rifles now that the ban had sunset. Well, a little digging and I turned up a number of dealers who had stock, were selling it, and Colt was not doing what the internet rumors said it was doing. Why the fuss? There are some who worry about having a rifle marked "Law Enforcement Only" marked on it. But we've gone over that in the Legalities chapter. There is nothing wrong with owning such a rifle, and in due time the whole "deal" about some rifles being so-marked will be a curiosity you see sometimes at a gun show. The other rumor is that Colt will not be offering non-ban configurations on their rifles. That is, no threaded muzzles, no bayonet lugs, and no sliding telestocks. And it is true, at least for now. Colt has been much more sensitive to the breezes blowing through various state and Congressional buildings. They feel they should concentrate on their main customers, military and law enforcement, and not get mixed up in any future assault weapons debates. Me, personally, I think it is more ostrich thinking, head in the sand stuff. But I'm not the President of Colt (although I've had long talks with more than one of them) and don't decide for them.

If you really, really have to have those items, you can buy other brands. Or you can buy a Colt and rebuild it. Whatever you do, don't let it make you crazy, or give you an ulcer. Get over it, and get on with your life.

Doublestar

Doublestar is a builder located in Winchester, Kentucky, which is if I recall correctly, the home of Ken Tapp, one of the best bowling pin shooters of all time. I have to admit I had never heard of Doublestar before starting this book. I don't know why, but not many of their rifles made it up to the Great Lakes region, and I'd never heard of, let alone seen, one before I opened the shipping carton. Nor had any of my test crew, and between the bunch of us we've been around and shot a bunch of rifles.

Doublestar sent me a pair of rifles, an M-4gery and a DCM Service rifle. To say we were impressed was an understatement.

The carbine conforms to what you'd expect for an Iraq-bound shorty. Up front it has a comp that looks like a flash hider (as with most makers, you can now get yours post-post-ban) It took a bit of looking to find the blind, welded pin that held it on. The barrel has the obligatory M-203 mounting groove, and is finished in a dark gray/black phosphate finish. It is unmarked, with a twist of 1/9. The front sight forging

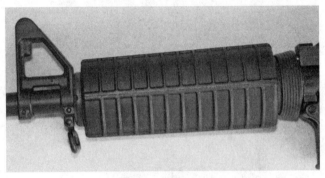

Full-size military handguards, with double heat shields.

The Doublestar logo and markings.

Military-correct current tele-stock slider.

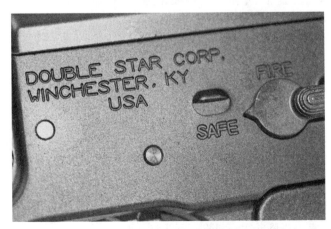

Small pins, double push-pin, the Doublestar is correctly and well-made.

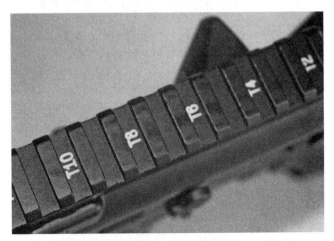

The top rail on the flat-top is numbered, per current specs.

The Leupold CQ/T fitted perfectly, worked superbly, and almost went home with a tester.

is held on with a pair of taper pins, and the front sight is the correct height (within tolerances) for a flat-top carbine. The handguards are the fat, double heat shield and slightly oval design of current military issue. The tele-stock was fixed (post-ban, you can get sliders now) on a non-mil-spec diameter tube. The stock is the current, synthetic without the top sling loop design. The pistol grip is A2. The upper and lower are nicely matted, and black. The markings are machined into the side of the lower, using two or three different end mills. The serial number is punched, with a pantographic or CNC guide to produce digits and numerals. The lower is marked "Safe" and "Fire" on both sides. The upper does not have a forge mark, but the rail slots are numbered as per military usage.

Inside, the carrier is an AR without markings, the bolt and extractor lack markings, and the extractor spring has a blue buffer in it. The fire control parts are all AR. In looks, hanlding, detail and appearance, the Doublestar M-4gery is as good as any of the others. Except for a few minor details (like not staking the tele-stock securing nut) which only Colt and Stag Arms did, I can find nothing wrong with it. For some reason which I can't remember, I did not ask for a back-up

iron sight to come with the Doublestar, so we had to do all of our test-firing with borrowed sights and various optics.

To fire the shorty, I tried it with several different sights, and for the test crew session we mounted the Leupold CQ/T on it. I'm not sure which did a better job of selling the other to my testers, the Leupold on the Doublestar, or the Doublestar for the Leupold. The trigger on the M-4gery is eminently suitable. Once you take up the slack and pre-load on the trigger, it breaks cleanly. The disconnector is timed quite late, as it should be, and my testers and I found there was no problem in transitioning to the Doublestar from any other rifle with a good trigger. The Leupold made hitting easy. Once we had it zeroed, whacking the steel was simple. Even the tiny Mike Gibson spring-loaded poppers took more than their share of hits, especially if the Leupold was zoomed up to 3x. One interesting aspect of the Doublestar was the comp: it was too effective. Regardless of the load used, the comp drove the gun down off the target. Once recoil was over, your sights were below what you were aiming at! Some loads did it more than others. If you're looking for a comped rifle, then this will do, and it isn't as "blasty" as others. With a little patience, you

The right side is marked Safe and Fire, with all correct features

The Doublestar comp, which worked so well it needs de-tuning.

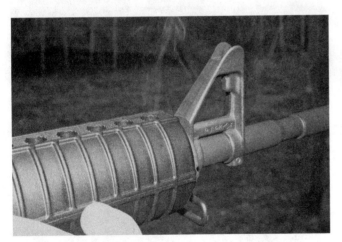

Even when hot enough that oil was visibly evaporating, the Doublestar worked flawlessly.

could ream out the front baffle from its current clearance hole diameter of .290 inches to make it stay on target. Once you'd tuned the comp, your sights would never leave the target.

We found the Doublestar to be 100 percent reliable. So much so that it got volunteered for the second Wolf test: we shot 120 rounds of Wolf through it (and two other M-4geries) in the space of about five minutes. Then I chambered a round of Wolf, and racked it until it was cool. (Don't worry, no one could walk in front of it, and we had the range to ourselves. However, in the spirit of the automobile commercials on television I have to offer this disclaimer: "Professional shooter. Closed course. Do not attempt.") Once it was cool, I extracted the round to see if any lacquer had come off. No. I also looked at the chamber to see if there was any there. Well, there was something there, but I couldn't tell if it was lacquer or powder residue. And since it had gotten close to 300 rounds through it that day, you'd expect the chamber to be grubby. I tried the Doubelstar again later, and it again worked without fail.

Accuracy-wise, the Doublestar M-4gery was a solid performer. It had elevated tastes, shooting the Winchester silvertip varmint load the best, just under one MOA. Everything else it shot between one and 1.5 MOA. With the nice trigger, and the very respectable accuracy, it was a lead-pipe cinch to shoot a clean score on the NEMRT qual course, and I did. As a rifle for Tactical Division in USPSA Three-gun, or a duty, defensive or tactical-use AR, this Doublestar has a lot going for it. Once you've tuned the comp (or simply used a regular flash hider) the rifle would be ready to go.

Were I to hang on to it, I'd swap the non-slider for a proper tele-stock, ream the front face of the comp by steps until it shot flat, and put some Brian Enos Slide Glide on the sear. I'd install a back-up iron sight, and either the Leupold or the EOTech Holosight. And then go about winning Tactical Division in USPSA Three-Gun matches.

DCM Service Rifle

In the long-range NRA rifle game known as High Power, .30-caliber rifles ruled almost as long as the dinosaurs roamed the earth. From 1903, until the mid 1990s, if you showed up with anything except a rifle in .308 or .30-06, you found shooters snickering behind your back. Despite the fact that the M-16 had been The service rifle since the 1960s, shooters who expected to win showed up at Camp Perry with tuned M-14s and M1-A's. That changed when the U.S. Army team showed up, having quickly learned the lessons civilian shooters had been puzzling out for years before. They beat the Marine Corps Team, something that had happened so rarely before it is probably on the list by Nostradamus about signs of the coming apocalypse.

Basically, a Service Rifle for High Power competition has to have the external appearance of a standard-issue M-16A2. (You could use an A1, but the lack of click-adjustable sights would be a severe handicap.) Inside, you can make all kinds of changes. You can install a match barrel, you can tune the trigger as long as the safety works and the trigger pull does not fall under a certain stated weight. You must use iron sights. What kept many shooters from using the AR system was that the sling is attached directly to the barrel. When trying to shoot tiny groups at 600 yards with iron sights, competitors would use a heavy leather sling, and pull it so tight their fingertips would turn blue. At that level of tension, the barrel on an M-16A1, A2 or similar AR-15 would be flexed. A flexed barrel is not always a handicap, but you can't count on a

The Doublestar DCM rifle is a full-sized M-16A2 clone, for target competition.

The Doublestar DCM came ready for storage, and we had to clean it and break it in for shooting. Once shooting, it didn't quit.

The Doublestar DCM does not get any special logo or markings.

flexed barrel that is flexed by a sling always having the same amount of tension. Tension would change with every shift of the shooter's position. As the barrel heated up, it would change. Long-range target shooters hate change. At least change they can't predict and adjust for.

The big deal that altered the equation was the tube handguard. Hidden under the plastic handguards, and with the sling attached to the tube and not the barrel, the barrel is free-floated even though it appears to be a normal barrel.

Once that final piece was in the puzzle, the AR took over, and the .30 rifle was doomed to second-class status.

The Doublestar DCM showed up with a bare muzzle. When the AWB was passed, the powers that be in High Power immediately allowed rifles lacking a flash hider, even though the rules for Service Rifle clearly state "no external modifications." Competition rules must bow to the law of the land, no matter how stupid the law. No big deal to target shooters, the whole flash hider thing was a pain anyway,

Inside is a very nice trigger.

The steel free-float tube keeps the sling and handguards off the barrel

The rear sight betrays its target use: your aperture options are small and small.

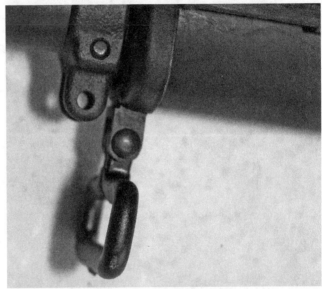

You can see how the sling attaches to the free-float tube, and not the front handguard cap.

sometimes calling for special work to keep it from degrading accuracy. You see, long-range target shooters are very particular about accuracy. The barrel is standard dimension forward of the front sight housing, which is a forging and secured with two tapered pins. Underneath the round, A2 handguards is a steel free-float tube, and the front sling swivel is attached to the tube. At first glance the sling swivel appears to be where it is supposed to be, but take a closer look and you will see it is attached to the front handguard retaining lip. The steel tube adds weight, an appreciable amount of it. The stock is a standard A2, and the pistol grip also an A2. After all, it has to at least appear to be mil-spec. The upper and lower are nicely matted, although the lower seems just a small bit shinier than the upper. The markings on the DCM lower, unlike the M-4gery, are machined-in using the same end mill for all the cuts. The serial number is punched, and the "Safe" and "Fire" markings are on both sides. The upper is an A2, with ejector lump and forward assist, and the windage- and elevation-adjustable rear sight. The elevation wheel is not marked in yardage, starting with "8/3" but instead is numbered. There are 25 clicks per revolution, and the wheel is marked 0, 5, 10, 15 & 20. The aperture is marked "0-2"

but it does not have a large and small, only a small and small. After all, it is a target rifle.

The carrier is unmarked, an M-16 with the autosear shoulder milled back. The bolt and extractor are unmarked, and the extractor spring has a blue buffer in it. The fire control parts are a two-stage hammer and trigger, with an AR safety.

The trigger is spectacular. Once you take up the slack (and the slack is relatively light) the trigger does not feel like it moves until the hammer falls. And then it moves so little, that if you weren't waiting for it, you would not notice the over-travel. It feels appreciably lighter than it actually is, falling at a weighed 4.25 pounds. If you were to pass it around for dry-firing, the estimates would be more like 3 to 3.25 pounds. If you are trying to shoot small groups at long range with iron sights (or a scope, for that matter) this is the trigger you would want.

In accuracy, there was nothing this rifle did not shoot spectacularly. Without mounting a scope on it, I had to "settle" for using the iron sights. Shooting MOA groups with it was a piece of cake. As I am not the best shooter around with iron sights I can't be declarative about it, but of the ammo tested it seemed to really like the Honrady 55-grain

DOUBLESTAR

With the superb trigger and weight, the Doublestar had great hitting potential and no recoil. As long as the sun was out, the testers loved it.

Urban TAP, and the Cor-bon 55-grain Blitz. Which is strange, considering it has a 1/8 twist, which would seem to indicate a heavier bullet preference. But then, I'm judging from groups fractionally different in size, fired with iron sights. That I could not get smaller groups with ammo the rifle almost certainly could do better with simply proves that I'm not a precision, long-range shooter, with a resting pulse of 37 bpm. I tried the Lahti, to see if I could get the rifle to shoot better than I could, and alone of all the rifles, it did not shoot any better in the Lahti than I could shoot it. Curious.

In the first test session, the DCM rifle did not get off to a good start. It was shipped heavily oiled, and all I did to get it ready was to push a patch down the bore to make sure there was nothing there. It short-stroked and failed to fire for the

first magazine, until I pulled the bolt and wiped the firing pin, then squirted some lighter lubricant into the action. Then it began working just fine. (Hey, it is a tightly-fitted target rifle. If it wants to "wake up" before being shot the first time, that's fine with me.) Once we got it broken-in, it worked perfectly. The light trigger and the heavy weight meant recoil was minimal and aiming easy. Of the rifles, it was by far the easiest with which to work over the steel plates with iron sights. As long as the sun was out. On a cloudy day, the tiny apertures of the rear sight made it hard to see the targets.

If you're looking for a DCM rifle, this could be the only Service Rifle you need.

If you've never heard of Doublestar before, you have now. And you now have no reason to pass them up.

Olympic Arms

I've known of, and used, Olympic rifles and barrels for many years. What I didn't know was that I had seen a couple of rifles built on their receivers before I ever gunsmithed an AR, in the form of a couple of rifles built on Palmetto Arms lowers. Those were machined from billets of aluminum, long before the business became known as Olympic, and began making rifles from forged and machined uppers and lowers.

Olympic is the rare AR maker: they make every major component themselves. Olympic machines their own bolts, carriers, upper and lower receivers, they make barrels, and they make the various smaller parts that go into the rifle. They buy molded parts from a supplier, but they own the molds that the supplier uses to make Olympic parts. They buy forgings from those who forge, but as I've pointed out before, who wants the multi-million dollar investment that the ovens, forges and the like represent? About all they don't do is forge the billets, anodize the receivers, and make lattes to go. I've re-barreled many tired rifles with Olympic stainless steel barrels in the past, and even tried to wear them out myself, hosing pins and plates. They make accurate, tough barrels, and they also make them in calibers other than 5.56. If your state hunting regulations don't allow .22 rifles on deer, you can build an AR upper using an Olympic barrel in something bigger, and have a deer hunting rifle without the expense of a complete .308 rifle, or other caliber.

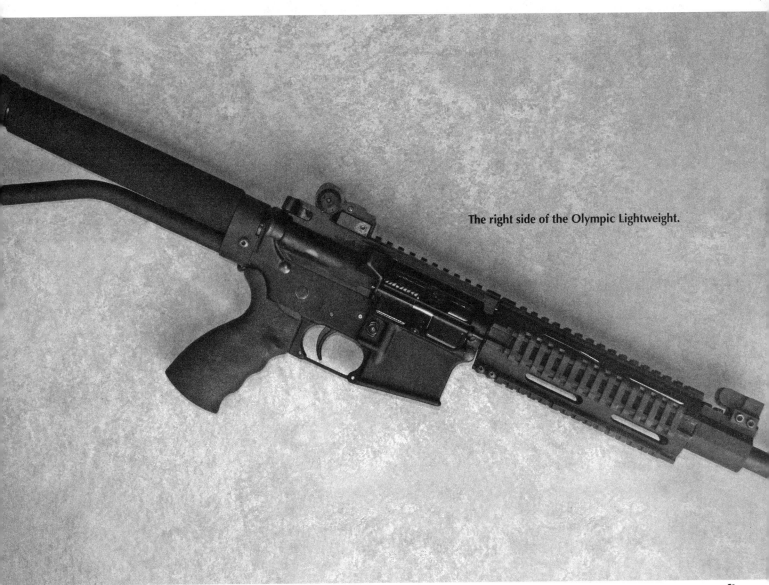

The right side of the Olympic Lightweight.

Olympic has been at the AR business for a long time. I've had this SGW marked lower for nearly 20 years now, and it has always worked perfectly.

Olympic lowers now feature their rampant lion logo.

For the book, Olympic sent me two rifles: a Lightweight Carbine, and an Airsoft M-4gery.

Lightweight Carbine

The LT came with a flush muzzle, railed handguard, and one of the slickest stocks you've ever seen. The barrel is an Olympic, marked "SS 556" (stainless, with a 5.56 chamber and leade) and a 1/9 twist. All Olympic barrels are made of 416 stainless, but only the Ultra Match barrels, marked with "SUM" are broached. All the rest are button-rifled. As I mentioned, Olympic makes their own barrels. Not by simply machining barrel blanks they buy, but in taking a bar of steel and turning it into a barrel. Olympic got into the barrel business by way of a government contract more than two decades ago to produce replacement barrels for M-14s. The hard part of barrel making is the deep-hole drilling, reaming and broaching or button-rifling. Once you've got that down, it is relatively easy to make barrels in other bore sizes, exterior configurations and materials. So, Olympic makes their own AR barrels. The currently fashionable M-203 clamping groove is behind the groove for clamping a post-ban muzzle brake onto the muzzle. (You can now get threaded barrels, too.) The front sight is a fold-down assembly clamped onto a custom gas block with a rail on top for said sight. The sight clamps on using two allen screws. The sight is solidly made, and has two detents to keep it up and down so it doesn't flop around. However, it lacks a locking catch to keep it upright once flipped up. It doesn't take much impact to knock it down. I would much prefer a sight that locks up, and resists inadvertent (and deliberate, too) impacts. The buttstock is an Ace Ltd. Stock. The buttplate and fixing block are connected by a tube. The stock clamps on using the standard buffer tube buttstock screw. The buffer tube is left exposed, unless you use (and you should) the included foam sleeve. The foam sleeve makes the stock much more comfortable, it deadens buffer boing, and on cold days it provides you with a place to put your face on an otherwise frozen rifle. The stock has four locations for sling attachments, and as it is made of aluminum you could drill and tap it for more it you felt the need.

The railed handguard is a single-piece aluminum tube, fitted to a steel barrel nut. The base tube diameter is just under 2 inches, but the rails are as flush as Olympic can make them and still give accessories a place to grab, making it a slender tube even with rail covers. The Olympic skeleton covers take up less volume than regular ones, keeping the tube small compared to others. The testers liked the smaller diameter of the Olympic tube, over others of more portly dimensions.

The LT comes with the excellent Ergo Grip. The upper and lower are matted a little coarser than a Colt, but the color is deep black, without purpling or color changes from end to end. The lower is rollmarked with the Olympic Arms rampant lion logo, serial number, address, designation and fire control markings. "Safe" and "Fire" are marked only on the left side. The upper is a flat-top, with the "broken A" of Anchor Harvey forge. It has the ejector lump and forward assist, and matches exactly the lower in texture and color.

Inside, the carrier is unmarked, and is a shrouded M-16 with the autosear shoulder milled back. The bolt and extractor are unmarked, and the extractor has Olympics "EX-Ring" a rubber ring designed to increase extractor strength, nestled around the coil spring.

The front sight is the proper height for a flat-top shorty, and the rear locks up. It has a small button on the side, and once up you have to press the button to hinge it down. The aperture is an A2, but the sight is adjustable for windage only. It also has the trait shared by so many, of only being able to be folded down when the large aperture is selected. If you click it to small aperture, the sight won't go down enough to be completely folded. A small quibble, I know, but for those of us who prefer to use the small aperture as much as possible, an irritant.

The upper and the railed handguard do not quite match in

The folding front sight.

The Olympic folding rear, which does lock upright.

If only it locked in place, it would be a great sight.

The Olympic rear is windage but not elevation adjustable.

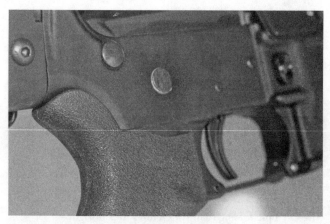

As expected, the lower is normal, with mag button fences, but not marked Safe and Fire on this side.

The Ace Ltd. stock, and its single-point sling attachment.

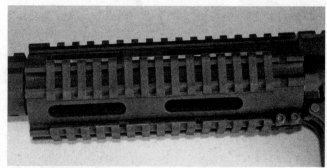

The railed handguard on the lightweight.

The Ergo Grip fills the rear of the lower for those with big hands.

height. They are off by ten thousandths or so. It wouldn't be a problem if you mounted an optic on one or the other, but you can't clamp something on them that bridges the gap.

The trigger is very nice. It has almost no creep or slack, and once you get enough pressure on it to drop the hammer, it releases cleanly. It is heavy enough to keep you out of trouble on duty or in defense, but light enough that you aren't going to be handicapped unless you're using it in NRA High Power or some kind of benchrest match. In testing, we found nothing that would cause the lightweight any problems. It gobbled all the ammo, including the Wolf we had to test. Olympic is not too keen on Wolf ammo. Not that it will turn your AR into a tactical nuke, vaporizing you and the shooting bench if something goes wrong. It is simply that in their experience the steel cases are very hard on the chamber (in the words of Tom Spithaler, my contact at Olympic, "Brutal") and if something goes wrong you have no redress. As Tom put it; "If you have a problem with other ammo, Remington, Winchester, other U.S. makers, we can get your rifle repaired, and get a check for the repairs due to bad ammo from them. If anything goes wrong with Wolf, we're never going to see a check out of Russia." So I crossed my fingers, and resolved that if things exploded I'd own another Olympic a rifle, and tested it with Wolf. The rifle and I survived, and the rifle is fine. It worked 100 percent with Wolf, and looking at the chamber with a Gradient Lens borescope, I can't see where anything is different. Granted, 200 rounds or so isn't a big test, but if it is so bad you'd think we'd see something right away. The test crew remarked favorably on the forearm size, and liked the trigger and handling. It was no problem at all to hammer the steel, and give the Mike Gibson Manufacturing spring-loaded poppers a real workout. All the magazines I had worked just fine, without binding. They dropped free when empty, fed all we had to run through the rifle, and none stubbed, double fed or gave us any other problems. Even my chintzy Eaton magazines, plastic and nearly 20 years old, worked fine, which speaks well for the rifle.

As for accuracy, the Olympic once again proved that a free-floated barrel shoots well. Of the ammo tested, the Olympic had to be contrary: it shot the Black Hills blue, 55-grain full-metal-jacket, and some Federal XM-193 the best. With a scope on board, I was able to easily punch MOA groups for the camera and the notebook. How can you not love a rifle like this, that doesn't need expensive match ammo to shoot well, and gets along well with any magazine I could dredge out of the safe? I'd be a lot more tempted by it if the

front sight locked in place. As it is, this is a rifle I'd not let escape, if I didn't already have a rack full of ARs. The accuracy it demonstrated is also not unexpected. As I said at the beginning, I've had very good luck with Olympic barrels, and used a brace of Olympic-barreled rifles at Second Chance to win more than my fair share of loot in the rifle events.

Airsoft

There are places where a real gun is forbidden. Or at least, so controlled as to be out of the reach of normal people who are not plutocrats or politically connected. (There are also places where an Airsoft is considered a "real" gun, but one need not live in one of those "People's Democratic Republic" paradises.) And, there are those who like to shoot in paintball-type gatherings, but who want their gear to be less "surfer neon" and more camo and tan. One place where real firearms are essentially forbidden is Japan. And that is where Airsoft hails from. Basically, it is a BB gun that fires a plastic sphere instead of a steel pellet. Where the BB is a nominal

The Olympic Lightweight worked with all magazines, including this 100-round Beta drum.

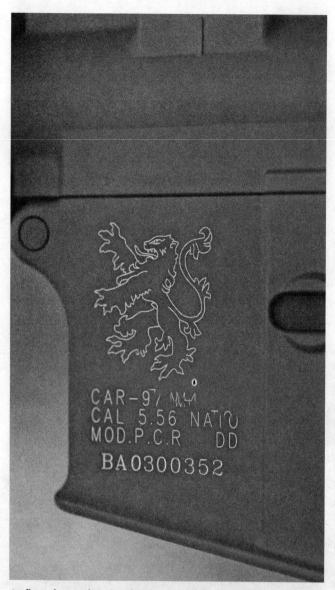

At first glance the Airsoft Olympic looks like another AR.

The rear sight looks real, and adjusts. Although I think 600 yards is a bit optimistic.

Yes, the selector goes all the way around.

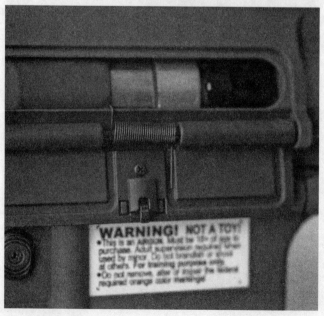

The ejection port gives it away: Not a real firearm.

.177 inches, the Airsoft is a 6mm plastic pellet, around .236 inches in size. The operation is simple: you can use gas, or you can use geared mechanical propulsion.

The Airsoft Olympic sent is a select-fire M-4gery with a fixed stock. In size and weight it is very close, but not exact. The muzzle is sent painted orange, as per Federal regulation, to keep it from being confused with a real firearm. Because unless you're holding it, you aren't going to tell it from the real thing.

In operation, it is simple: you charge the battery. You pour pellets in the magazine, and crank the knurled wheel on the bottom to prime the magazine and provide feeding tension. Insert the magazine, move the selector, and press the trigger. Safe, Semi, Full, it is all there. What you get is a total lack of recoil, reasonable accuracy, and something you must respect. The pellets leave the muzzle at an average of 250 feet per second. Yes, I chrono'd it, and the pellets register on the chrono sensors. They also have enough velocity that at 10 yards they can still merrily sail right through a cardboard target. In the words of all our mothers: "You can put someone's eye out with that thing!"

The interior of Airsoft firearms of the mechanical type use a gearbox to produce propulsion. The cheap, not-likely-to-last-very-long models use plastic gears, while the better ones use metal gears. The Olympic Airsoft M-4geryuses metal gears, and you will likely get a lot of use out of this rifle before you even have to think about an overhaul or rebuild. (What would that be, a dumpster full of plastic Airsoft pellets?)

Accuracy-wise, you can put all the pellets through the same hole at ten yards. A large-ish, ragged, hole, but a single hole none the less. Bursts will chew a larger hole than semi. It is consistent enough that you could use it for primary marksmanship. You could easily set up a range indoors, and with a carpet backstop to stop and drop the pellets, use them repeatedly. With a paper target for score, you could even have indoor matches. (I'm trying to think of a format we could use at our gun club, indoors, for the monthly meeting days.) The only drawback I've found is that the rifle is not noisy enough to trip a shot-sensitive timer. So you can't use it competitively in a speed-type match, except for practice. At least not until I figure out some kind of hit-sensitive falling plate to stop the clock.

Which brings me back to Japan. At the Steel Challenge, there is always a squad or two of shooters from Japan. They either "own" or borrow guns here in the United States to shoot the match. At home, they practice with Airsoft guns. As the pellets can be re-used, and the "cost" of shooting is battery power (rechargeable with an adapter) they can practice all year for only the time and effort. And the practice is good enough to place well, and even at the 2004 Steel Challenge, win the combined overall.

If you really wanted to get better, you could set up a practice range in your basement, and emulate the Japanese Squad. I can also see the Airsoft as a remedial training tool. If a police department has problem shooters, officers who just haven't gotten the basics down,10 minutes before each shift with an Airsoft and a target set up in a closet would pay big dividends.

How much fun is this rifle? The included bottle of Airsoft pellets went downrange in less than 15 minutes. Which is how I came to find out that you can get pellets in a range of eye-searing colors, even glow in the dark pellets that look like tracers when fired at night or in a darkened room. As money-sucking, extremely fun things go, the Airsoft experience is remarkably cheap.

And as it is not a real firearm, I could cut this barrel to 10.5 inches and re-thread it for a flash hider. As for other uses, there are Airsoft equivalents to the paintball competitions, where competitors or teams of competitors engage each other in tactical environments. Since the pellets can bruise exposed skin, or damage eyes, you would not be allowed anywhere near the engagement area without face protection. You may view trouser protection as optional, but I would not.

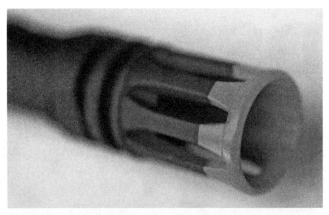

The flash hider is painted orange, a good thing, and required by law. Leave it alone.

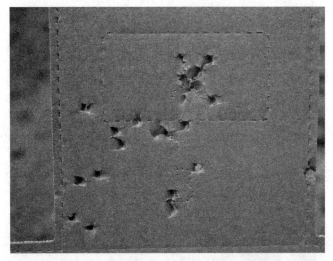

The result of quick presentations at 10 yards, trying to come up and get a hit under a second. Very good practice, and the cost is practically nothing.

Two bursts, at 10 yards, aiming at the paster. (Ignore the pistol-caliber holes.) If we can just figure out how to time shots, we can have one heck of a match indoors.

CHAPTER 21

DS Arms

Left side of the S16B.

Based in Barrington, Illinois, DS Arms is perhaps better-known for making FAL rifles. Starting by importing parts and building on receivers they machined, DS Arms has, due to both parts drying up, and import laws being more restrictive, been making more and more of their own parts. They now make everything that goes into or on an FAL. DS arms also imports firearms goodies of mouth-watering rarity and quality. They are the importers of the almost sinfully high-quality Brügger & Thomet tactical accessories. Tactical forearms for every military firearm known, B&T tactical forearms are Swiss quality and tougher than hell. DS Arms also brings in police-only select-fire firearms, and handles a whole slew of other tactical goodies.

But we're interested in ARs, which they make a number of, and they're all good. Since they have the machining stations making FALs, making an AR is a matter of programming the cutter paths, rolling the correct cutter tray up to the machine,

and feeding it the right materials. (Well not exactly that easy, and people spend a lot of time in classes learning how to perform just such a conversion, but it is a whole lot easier than it was in the "medium old days.") Once the machines are programmed, it is easy enough that DS Arms is making ARs, lots of them, and good ones.

The DS Arms AR they sent is a bit different from the slew of M-4geries, or full-size rifles filling my photo studio. The basics are all there, and well done. The upper and lower are cleanly finished 7075-T6 forgings in a dark matte black, but lack forge marks. (No problem, not all rifles have forge marks.) The lower is rollmarked and stamped with the name, serial number, model designation, and had "Safe" and "Fire" on both sides. The flat-top upper has the ejector lump and forward assist (And now that I think of it, I didn't get a single rifle that was in a "slickside" configuration. Hmm.) and everything back of the delta ring is just what you'd expect on an AR. The upper and lower had a tiny bit of wobble between them, but the front and rear pins were tight and we needed a booster rod to get them pressed for disassembly.

The stock is a standard A2, as this rifle shipped pre-sunset, but you can now get rifles with telestocks if you so wish. The pistol grip is a Hogue, softer than the standard, and with molded-in finger grooves. I like the softer grip, even though the finger grooves don't correspond to my fingers. No big deal, I've never found a grip yet that did. The trigger is a two-stage unit, and nicely tuned. The trigger has a spring-powered takeup, and then breaks cleanly at just over 4 pounds. Unlike a lot of military triggers, the reset doesn't feel like your trigger finger is being shoved out of the way by the trigger spring. The trigger had a lot to do with the shootability of the DS Arms, and the test crew remarked on it and how much they liked it.

The big difference was out front. The DS Arms AR shipped, the S-16B, is a handy, compact varmint model that can double as a compact police marksman rifle, too. The barrel is a stainless 1/8 twist tube that measures .923 inches in diameter. The forearm is an aluminum free-float tube, knurled in the middle for a non-slip grip, and it has the barrel nut built into it. The gas block is an aluminum block held on with a pair of set screws. The gas block has a picatinny rail on it, so you could mount iron sights on the S16B if you wanted, but why would you want to? The barrel is fluted both under the handguard and from the gas block forward almost to the muzzle, to bring down the weight a bit, which is listed as 7.75 pounds empty. Hmm, my scale shows this one an ounce under 8 pounds. Add a scope and base and rings combo, a loaded magazine and a sling or bipod, and you've got an 11-pound rifle. But not an unwieldy beast, instead a handy 11-pound rifle. With the weight up front in a stiff, short barrel, you don't feel like you're trying to swing a railroad tie up on the target. The S16B balances well between the hands, and you don't begin to notice the weight until you've been practicing your offhand shooting for a while.

As an easy-to-carry varmint gun, it would be no big deal

A thick, stubby barrel is very stiff, and should shoot well. This one does.

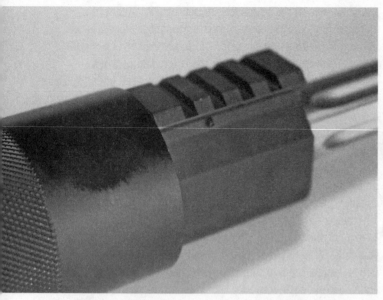

If you want to mount iron sights, the gas block has a rail.

to pack where you needed it. As a police marksman rifle, it would be very handy to carry up on a roof, or to a window. The weight dampens recoil without having your shooting buddies or marksman observer blasted by a comp. Which explained the rapid consumption of ammo at the test session where the DS Arms rifle was present. The clean trigger, nice hang weight and tack-driving accuracy caused ammo to evaporate. I had to hide the carton of Mk 262 Mod 1 ammo to keep it from all going downrange. For that was the load the S-16B loved. Later accuracy testing outside the usual feeding frenzy that some testfire sessions turn into, I found that the S-16B shot spectacularly well with the Black Hills Mk 262 Mod 1 and the 60-grain V-Max loaded by Black Hills. Single-hole groups that could be covered with a single paster were the norm. As with all heavy-barrel and aluminum tube handguard combos, the DS Arms S-16B is slow to heat up. You can do a good deal of shooting before the tube starts to get warm, and a bunch more before it becomes uncomfortable. The

Troopers on patrol in Iraq have no need for a heavy-barreled varmint rifle.

The heavy barrel is fluted, to relieve some of the burden without reducing stiffness too much.

With any optics the DS Arms was accurate. With the EOTech it was also fast

The DS̲ ̲_____-liked by the test crew. When at the range it was rarely out of the rotation.

...es a longer time to cool off. (You can't
...ng.) However, as I said, you can do a
...gets too hot to handle.
...g rifle, this is superb. As a
...SA/IPSC 3-gun shooting, this is
...t. The unthreaded barrel means
...be a hassle. But if you have need

of a rifle that is handy to carry, easy to pack, and delivers
stellar accuracy from a fixed position, the S-16B is the rifle
to have. If you need something more suited to Patrol Rifle or
a lightweight car gun, then I'm sure DS Arms can build you
one. The rifle they sent is superb, but there isn't much call for
an easy-packing varmint gun here in the Great Lakes, so I will
reluctantly send it back when I'm done.

The tube is knurled for a non-slip grip.

Everything you'd expect from a flat-top, and properly done.

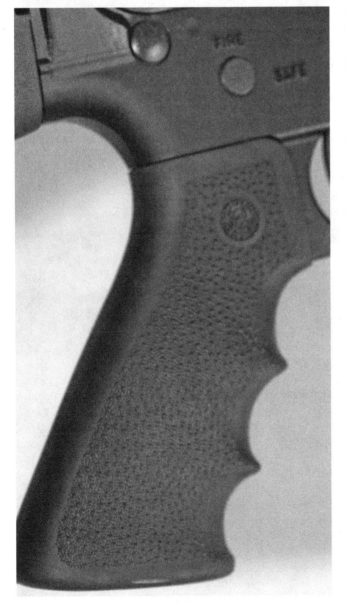

The Hogue grip is a non-slip pistol grip.

Well made, well marked, and a nice shade of black.

With the sunset of the AWB/94, you can now get t... on your DS Arms rifles if you wish.

Fulton Armory

Fulton Armory is Clint McKee, based in Savage, Maryland. In addition to building first-class ARs, Clint also builds semi-auto only M-14 rifles, commonly referred to as the M-1A. I contacted Walt Kuleck at Fulton on the first day I was rounding up rifles for the book, and the boxes from Fulton were the first to arrive, a week before any other rifles showed up on my doorstep. Fulton sent three, two tactical/duty rifles, and one full-house NRA High Power Match rifle.

FAR-15

The standard flat-top arrived as a plain-looking rifle that you wouldn't give a second glance to. And having passed it up, you'd have passed up a gem. The barrel, marked "FA MP 5.56MM MATCH 1/9" is a correct-profile M-4 barrel with a step for the M-203. The front sight housing is the correct, taller, size for use with a clamp-on back-up iron sights. The flash hider is a neat bit of engineering. Externally, it looks like a regular flash hider. But it isn't. (Of course, with the sunset

All Fulton rifles are up to date unless you order a classic slickside, which this isn't.

...ll shot extremely well. The FAR-15 was a real joy.

elestocks

Short stocks are easier to get used to than long ones.

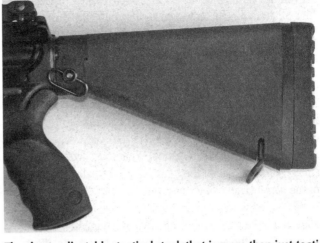

The short, adjustable, tactical stock that is more than just tactical.

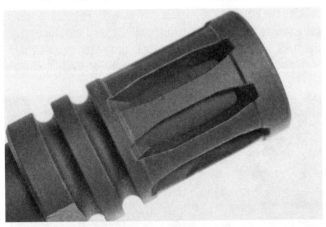

The Fulton Armory faux flash hider is neat, and passes muster where threaded barrels are verboten.

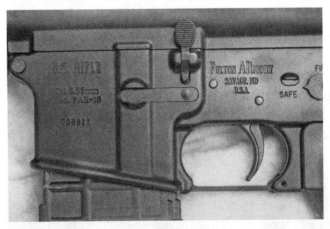

All Fulton rifles are nicely marked.

of the AWB, all this cosmetic effort is obsolete) The faux flash hider was simply a sleeve over the end of the bare muzzle, offering a degree of protection for the crown, while appearing to be a flash hider.

The handguards are standard, with a few edges here and there from flashing from the molds. While noticeable, the edges were so slight that simply handling the rifle wore them off, and by the second range session they were gone. The stock on this rifle is a standard A2 stock. Fulton offers standard, tele-stocks, and shortened "entry" stocks for those with short arms or who will be bundled up in warm clothing or body armor.

The upper and lower are standard AR, with full and correct fencing around the magazine button. The machining is smooth and even, and the finish is an even matte and a dead-black color. If you want to mix and match uppers and lowers by Fulton with other makers, and the colors don't match, don't blame Fulton. Theirs are correct. The fit is snug, with no rattle, and you'll need something to press the takedown pins with. Inside, the fire control parts are all AR, nothing modified M-16 in the bottom. The carrier is an M-16 with the auto sear shoulder machined back, unmarked. The bolt and extractor

are unmarked, and the extractor spring has a blue buffer in it. The upper is a flat-top, correct height, with the slots numbered as per military use. Why numbered slots? That is so if a GI takes a scope off, he can get it back where it was, and increase the likelihood of the scope returning to zero. As with the lower, the upper was beautifully matted and a dead black color. It has a forward assist (although Fulton offers a retro model that is a flat-side M16A1 clone) and has the ejector lump favored by left-handed shooters.

The FAR-15 handled well, balanced well, and had a lack of sharp edges and abrasion points, except for one: and I was the only one to notice. I have a peculiar grip on ARs: I choke up on the pistol grip a great deal, and have the web of my hand pressed tightly up against the top rear of the pistol grip curve. (No one else I've seen has a grip this radical.) The edge of the forging, above the pistol grip at the rear, is something I notice when I'm handling the rifle to write about it. I never noticed it while shooting it, so it can't be much of a problem (and one that a lot of other rifles exhibit) and it certainly was not something the testers mentioned. So mark it down to the writers peculiar grip, and don't worry about it.

Shooting the FAR-15 was fun. It is superbly accurate,

delivering a number of sub-MOA groups, both with Black Hills 52-grain match, and Hornady 75-grain match ammo. It never stumbled in all the testing, with various brands and bullet weights of ammunition. We did not test it with Wolf ammo or reloads. Fulton Armory specifically advises customers not to use steel-cased ammunition in their rifles, and feels strongly that reloaded ammunition can be hazardous. As it is their rifle (as much as I'd like to hang onto it) I respected their wishes.

The flash hider was interesting. What looks like a super-small clearance hole in the front baffle is actually the crown of the barrel. The look for postban guns was that it appeared to be a barrel with a flash hider. The pinned-in-place sleeve appeared to be a flash hider, and also made the rifle a tad shorter. Since the faux hider slid over the barrel, the effect was to make the rifle almost an inch shorter, while still using a barrel longer than 16 inches. I'm sure they can still do if for states where you have to be AWB-compliant, but the rest of us will get barrels threaded and with normal flash hiders on them.

Tactical FAR-15

The tac gun arrived with a tube handguard and a shorty stock. The barrel is another superb Fulton Armory barrel, M-4 profile and with the same markings as the other rifle. The faux flash hider gives the same, "is that a comp?" appearance. The upper and lower are just as gorgeous in their matte and black finish, although the tactical FAR arrived with the markings highlighted with white paint. The rest is different. The stock is a shorty tactical stock, for use by those with short arms (or barrel chests) or laden with web gear, body armor and who-knows-what else. The result is to make it a good 2 inches shorter than an A2 stock, more if you took off the adjustable buttplate. Yes, a tactical rifle with a target-style adjustable buttplate. Laden with the previously mentioned gear, you can't always get the buttstock down to where it should be for a proper hold. By making the buttplate adjustable downwards, Fulton lets you get a proper stock contact point, and still keep your face on the stock to aim. The shorter stock is almost too short for me with just a shirt or jacket on, but not quite. The effect, while

The faux flash hider looks right, and is legal length even though it looks like it isn't. The front sight is held in place by four set screws.

The Yankee Hill Machine logo on the forend.

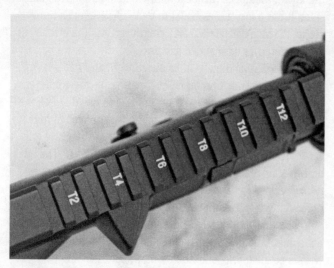

Top rails are numbered, as per mil spec.

Left side of the Tactical FAR-15.

odd-looking, is a stock that allows you to shoot well despite a range of clothing, or in the hands of radically different-height shooters. The stock uses a spacer between stock and receiver, which is drilled and tapped for a single-point sling attachment. Inside, the stock uses a carbine buffer weight and spring.

The forend is something else. Made by Yankee Hill Machine, the free-float tube handguard has four rails to attach equipment to. Machined from a single piece, then attached to a barrel nut, the tube handguard is almost small enough to be perfect. It is not as large and bulky as some, and did not receive the negative comments the largest tubes got, but the test crew were uniform in their assessment: it was just short of great. Made a bit smaller in inner tube diameter, it would have been their first choice of tactical handguards. As it was, many would opt for something else.

The adjustable buttplate of the FAR shorty stocks.

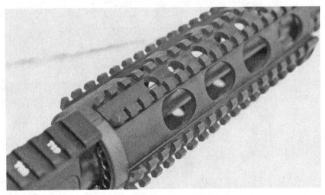

The Yankee Hill Machine forend does not lack for rail space.

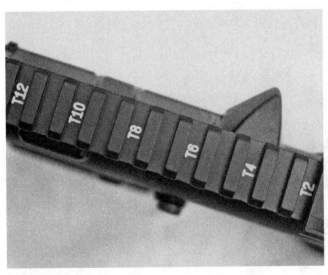

Again, numbered top rail.

The Yankee Hill Machine sight folds regardless of which aperture you've selected.

The single-point sling attachment.

Front sling attachment on the Yankee Hill Machine tube.

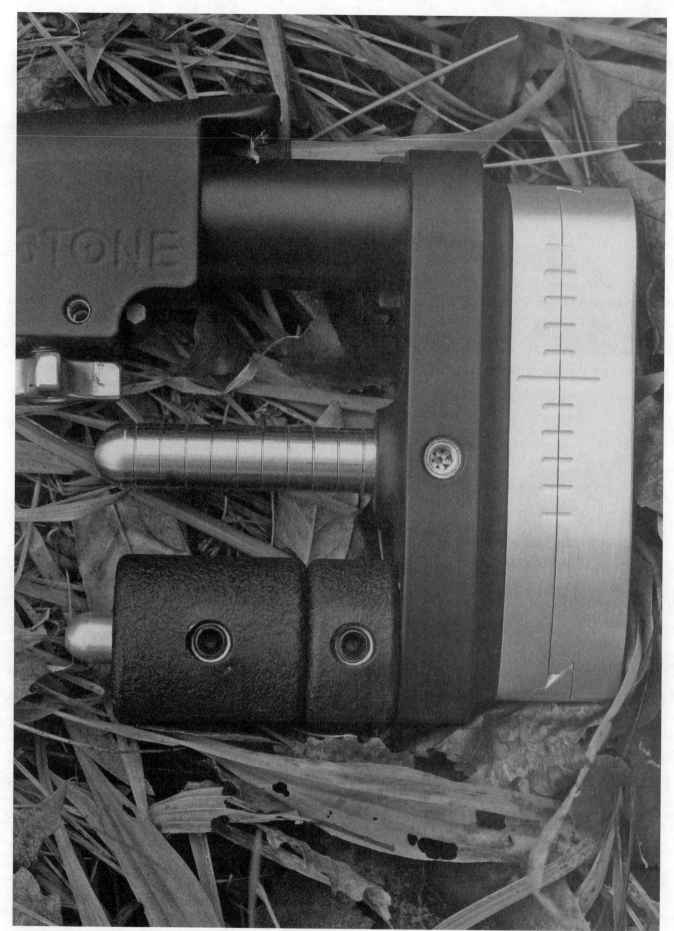

The buttplate adjusts up and down, you can tilt it, you can adjust the cheekpiece, you can change the weights or remove them.

The flat-top allows many types of scope bases.

The Ironstone stock is adjustable enough for anyone.

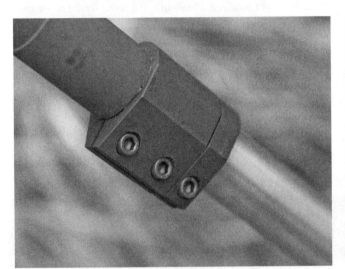

The clamping screws for the bloop tube.

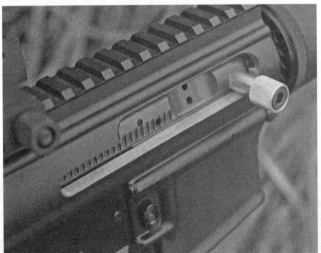

The operating handle is attached to the carrier, to allow working the bolt. Otherwise, there is no way to chamber a round.

Me, I didn't find the handguard that large, but I have somewhat large hands. I didn't have any problems with it, except for it getting a bit warm in extended testing. But any aluminum tube handguard is going to give heating problems, at least until someone figures out a way to either reflect the heat or install a fan.

The really slick part of the upper were the sights. Yankee Hill Machine front and rear folding sights, they locked up so you don't have to worry about your sights being knocked down while getting into position. The front comes on its own four-rail tactical gas block, so you can mount things there if you wanted to. Well-designed and beautifully machined, the YHM sights have one big advantage, and one small shortcoming. The advantage is that the rear sight is designed to fold regardless of which aperture is up. On many other sights, you can only fold the sight down when you have the large aperture in the firing position. That means you have no choice, when you go to irons you'll always get the

large aperture. If you need the small, then you have to do a double-select, get the irons up and then switch to the small aperture. With the YHM, you can set it on the small aperture, then fold. When you pop the sights up you'll get the small aperture. You can even switch from one to the other with the sight folded. The one detail about the sights I didn't like was the front post location. The front post, once zeroed, was screwed up out of the housing, such that the front sight post threads were in view. At least in the front. The rear of the housing covers the threads, and the plunger and spring are on the side of the sight. I looks like it was done to provide a smooth, level profile to the sight, but I would rather have a slightly bulkier sight, and protected threads.

The trigger in this rifle was spectacular. A two-stage trigger, it broke clean and crisp at 3 pounds. After firing the other rifles, with service-type trigger pulls, it took a bit of getting used to in order to shoot this one without the occasional early shot. It is a beautiful competition and varmint trigger, but

The long bolt catch bar allows you to close the bolt without getting unslung.

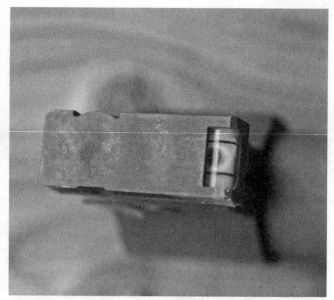

The front sight base has a built-in spirit level. Important when shooting at 600 yards.

The Accutron buffer spring comes gooped with grease, to cut down on buffer spring boing.

too light for duty use. Were I in the position of drawing up a departmental policy, or ordering duty rifles for a department, I would specifically not allow such a trigger. As much as I would want it in competition, it is just too good for the street, and officers who received only the departmental training and qualification probably would have trouble with it. (Think about it, an officer who is using the departmental Glock, Beretta or Sig, with a heavy DA trigger pull, then transitioning to this trigger. An inadvertent discharge is hardly going to be a surprise to us, now is it?) The trigger was helped by the Ergo Grip. With the Ergo Grip, it was easy to get a consistent grasp on the pistol grip, and with the hand properly positioned, my testers found it easy to produce a straight-back trigger pull.

I don't know if it was the free-float handguard, the light trigger, or some combination of both, but this rifle is a tack-driver. I had more sub-MOA groups out of this rifle than any other M-4gery I shot. Despite the short stock, shooting good groups was easy. With a scope mounted (and what a sight it was, with a big scope that cost more than the rifle!) I had no problem shooting at least one sub-MOA groups with every batch of ammo. Some, like the Hornady 75-grain match, delivered nothing but sub-MOA groups. The testers loved the trigger, loved the accuracy, liked the sights, and were only lukewarm about the tubular handguard. And wanted to take it home. With the rails on the gas block, most felt they'd rather have standard handguards, and then mount whatever they needed on the gas block.

Fulton Accutron Match Rifle

NRA High Power shooting, bullseye competition to 600 yards, has two general Divisions: Service and Match. A service rifle must look externally like and M-16-A2, while a match rifle can be anything the shooter can hold in his or her two hands and shoot. The Fulton Accutron Match rifle is one incredible shooting machine. How do you go about building a match rifle? Well, if you have an existing rifle, you basically take everything off the lower receiver (and most out of it) and throw the parts away. Lets start inside: the Match rifle has a two-stage trigger, set at a rules-compliant 3.5 pounds. There is only the spring-loaded takeup, and then no movement, before the hammer falls. The pistol grip is a Sierra match, a handful. The stock? Well, the stock is from Ironstone, and I can see where they got the name. The stock weighs almost as much as some of the rifles I tested. It has a modified buffer tube, containing a shorty/tele-stock weight and spring, heavily lubed. (High Power shooters love to goop lube into the buffer tube, to cut down on spring boing.) The tube has a moveable cheekpiece, so you can place it exactly where you need it for prone shooting. Turn the knob to loosen, slide, and lock. You can also rotate the cheekpiece, to fit it exactly to your face. It also has an allen wrench, and a holder for it on the rifle, to adjust the buttplate. The buttplate is adjustable up and down, to get it flat on your shoulder even though the bore line is several inches above your shoulder. You can adjust or remove the extra weights included. The buttplate is also adjustable for tilt, so if you happen to be a barrel-chested shooter you can get the plate to ride at an angle, across your manly chest.

Going forward, you'll notice the large, flat bar on the left side. That is the bolt hold-open lever. Shooting prone, a competitor is strapped in, lashed to the rifle with a sling. He or she can't use the left hand for anything, so to close the bolt (slow fire is shot one round at a time) you poke your trigger finger through and press the end of the bar.

And the sling? It attaches to the adjustable sling stop. Sculptured to take your shooting glove, the stop can be positioned anywhere along the 8-inch slot and act as a positive

The Accutron is meant for long-range, precision shooting competition. It excels at it.

The gas block, no way to mount a front sight. Where, then?

The right side of the FAR-15.

locator for your left hand. (Assuming you're a right-handed shooter.) The tube is aluminum and just under 2 inches in diameter, covering a bull barrel. At the gas block the barrel is .936 inches, forward of that it is .915 inches. At 26 inches in length, the barrel is going to deliver all the velocity any .223/5.56 load is capable of producing. Out front of that, the "bloop tube" adds another 5.75 inches. Why a bloop tube? To get the front sight farther out. With the tube on the long barrel, the sight radius is 36 inches, compared to the 20 inches of a standard rifle. Longer means more precise aiming, and a greater distance forward puts the front sight at an easier distance for comfortable focusing by your eye.

Coming back to the upper, the upper is a flat-top, but lacks a forward assist and ejector lump. The bolt has an operating handle attached to the carrier, with a clearance slot milled in the upper. The upper is also a thick-walled unit, not thin like a standard one. Why the carrier-mounted handle? Again, a prone shooter is strapped in. He or she can't get enough clearance behind (nor dislocate his right arm) to pull back and release the standard charging handle. All the manipulations and loading have to be done with the right hand, with as little movement as possible, to prevent changing the prone position.

The most specialized rifle of the bunch, the Fulton is a prime example of what it takes to do well in NRA High Power Match rifle competition. How does it shoot? Better than I can. Better than anyone I had try it. A rifle like this is built for iron sights, what with the built-in front rail and its spirit level, and the flat-top rear. Could I lay hands on a proper Match sight? Not a one. Which is not a big deal, as I'll be the first to tell you that there are a whole bunch of people who can shoot a rifle with irons better than I can. And recording groups fired with irons by me would not be a fair evaluation of the rifle. So, I clamped the Leupold long-range scope, the 3.5-10X40 on it, and proceeded to shoot groups. Boy, did I shoot groups. Fed what it liked, the Fulton match shot spectacularly. You can have your choice of a Krieger or a Fulton barrel. I opted for the Fulton barrel. Holy cow, if a Krieger shoots better than this, I have a lot of practicing to do to live up to one of them. Fed the Federal Gold Label 69-grain Matchkings, or the Black Hills 77-grain Mk 262 Mod 1, or the Hornady 75-grain match bullet, the Accutron simply delivered one-hole groups. Viewed through the Leupold scope, I could see the first hole simply get chewed larger with each shot. Once I figured out how well the rifle shot, it was a test of nerves: could I fire five clean breaks in a row, seeing the group form, without yanking one out? Well, the trigger and barrel helped me a lot, as even my yanked shots were often in the one-hole group.

Fed plain old 55-grain full metal jacket ammo, the Accutron still shot just under one MOA. Were I going to use this rifle in NRA competition, I'd load a bucketful of 55-grain fmj, and practice at 100 yards until I could shoot as best I could. Then I'd re-zero with heavier, match, bullets, and go to town.

After trying a few groups offhand, I have a whole lot more respect for NRA High Power shooters. Anyone who can hold that iron monster and shoot small groups with it obviously knows something about sight alignment and trigger control.

Fulton Armory

Offering more than just AR builds, the Fulton Armory web page with a ton of useful information. Clint has a great deal of experience, and you can find many answers on barrel cleaning, the use of steel-cased ammo and reloads, barrel twist, and a host of other subjects. And, you will have an overwhelming array of AR options from which to select.

After shooting the Accutron offhand, I have a lot more respect for those who do it.

JP Enterprises

Most shooters do not go to JP for an M-4gery. Formed in 1978, John Paul decided that ARs needed something besides more variants of military parts assembled into another black rifle package. With extensive firearms and machineshop experience, John has gone another path: the custom competition rifle as a production product, good for both competition and duty/defense.

Starting with billets of 7075, he machines them into uppers and lowers that use standard internals, but don't look like standard ARs. One of my test crew, seeing a JP for the first time, commented: "It looks like the AR Darth Vader would be packing."

The one John sent me was a model of his new CTR-02. Done in black, it is the basic rifle. You can have yours in a variety of colors, up to an including eye-searing shades seen

The author, running through a field course with the JP, shooting fast and looking good.

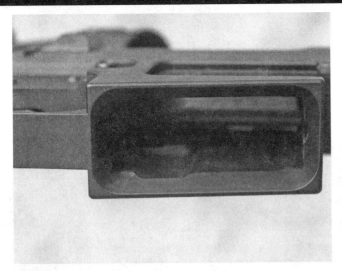

The integral mag well funnel.

The octagonal JP, with Trijicon ACOG on top.

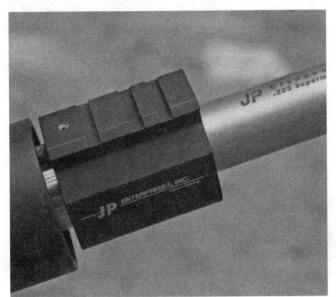

The adjustable gas block.

The top rail, and the Thermo-fit barrel collar up front of the receiver.

only in California. Milled from billets, the JP has a slab-sided, octagonal appearance that gives those who must decorate their firearms lots of space for personal expression. The upper and lower are thick-walled, but the top rail is located properly for clamping a scope, red-dot or the Acog from Trijicon. The stock on the sample rifle is the dual-rail with mag-holder competition stock. You simply stash a spare loaded magazine there, and if you need a reload in a match you snatch the extra from the stock instead of your belt. The foam padding makes for a soft, temperature insensitive resting place and insulates your face from buffer spring boing.

The receivers are machined with the lower having a large magazine funnel built-in, and the upper lacks a dust cover or forward assist. Sometimes useful in a military environment, a forward assist has no use in a match. Ditto the dust cover, unless you shoot in a dust-bowl environment. The ejection

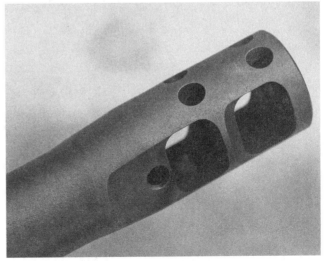

The Bennie Cooley comp, which dampens the recoil of the .223.

The drop-in trigger package, new from JP.

The JP tactical sight, for close-range high-speed shooting.

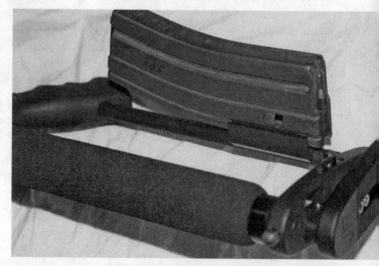

The stock holds a spare magazine, which can be pivoted to the exact angle you need or feel comfortable with.

My friend Andy Orians, working over the computer poppers with the JP at the National Guard base.

deflector lump is bolted on, which makes the machining a whole lot easier.

The handguard is a free-float tube using JPs own Thermo-fit™ barrel collar, the gas block is shaved and adjustable, and the barrel, a 416 stainless, is a cryogenically stress-relieved match barrel, with a Bennie Cooley comp on the end. The barrels come with either 1/8 or 1/9 twist, and .223 or 5.56 chambers, your choice.

Inside, the JP can be had with stainless carrier, or the low-mass competition carrier. Stainless is simply an easier-to-clean version of the standard carrier. The low-mass carrier is a means of reducing the recoil impulse, combined with the adjustable gas block and the comp. Let's take a moment here to discuss comps and recoil for those who feel that "manly men don't notice the recoil of the wimpy .223." No, no one ever said the recoil of the .223/5.56 was all that difficult to deal with. But in a competition environment, where not just seconds, but hundredths of a second, matter, recoil matters. In a fast target engagement, say leaning around a barricade and shooting two targets twice each, the "manly man" with his bone-stock M-4gery will be able to get good hits at good speed. If he tries to speed up too much, he starts getting sloppy hits, and wondering if the sights were where he thought they were. The competition shooter, using a JP CTR-02 tuned to the load being used, saw the crosshairs or dot on each target, and got the fourth hit before the first empty hit the ground. On a tuned competition gun, you can see the puff of lead of the bullet strike on steel, at 100 yards, through the scope. If you want that level of performance, you can get it with a JP.

Just turn the JP slightly, and the tactical sight rolls into view.

The trigger sent was not a stock trigger, nor was it a hand-fitted two-stage trigger. It was JPs new drop-in trigger unit. Rather than having a set of parts to be installed in the rifle, the JP unit is a single assembly that you drop into the lower and use the cross pins to hold in place. By making the whole thing a unit, JP can control the dimensions of the pivots, sear hooks and engagement. Rather than making the hammer hooks twenty thousandths oversize to accommodate any and every lower made, he can make it precisely what he wants ands customers need, and then permanently assemble it. The approach obviously works, as the trigger was superb and never failed.

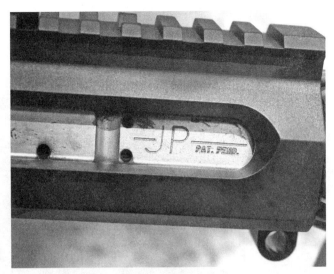

The JP rifles all lack dust covers. No big deal on a competition gun, or one well cared for.

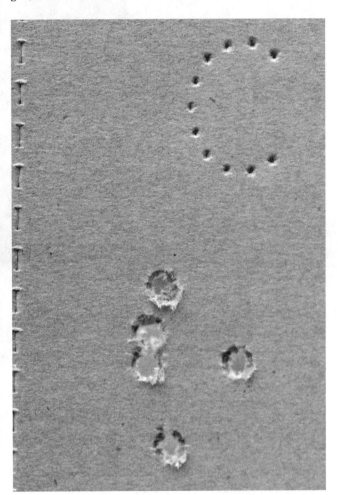

Not bad, a group around an inch in size. From 200 yards out.

The CTR-02 came with an Acog on it, using the JP reticle that Trijicon makes just for JP, already zeroed. With the rear flat-top, and the rail on the gas block, you can fit iron sights to the JP if you wanted to. Me, I just left it as-is, and shot it. Boy, did I shoot it. The accuracy was superb, so much so that I used it to verify the bullet drop charts we had been using for years in law enforcement: using a 100-yard zero, you have a 2.23 inch drop at 200 yards and 11 inches at 300. I did a basic 25-yard zero, verified at 100, and then took it off to a law enforcement class where I knew I'd have a chance to shoot at 200 and 300. Using a Nikon laser rangefinder to verify, I set up targets at 200 and 300, and fired for groups.

Your view of the tactical sight, with the JP tilted.

The 1-inch cluster two and a quarter inches low at 200 yards was all I needed. The charts we use are correct. At 100 yards, the maximum distance our club has, the JP would shoot sub-MOA all day long. Even with various surplus it shot very well, and only went over one-MOA with the one group of Wolf I subjected it to. What the JP really liked was PMC. I've never found a rifle that didn't just purr along with PMC, but they never seemed to shoot to their potential with it. And it was often noticeably slower than other loads. Where I'd get 3,200 fps out of a 55-grain bullet from Federal XM-193, PMC would often be posting velocities in the low to mid 3,000 range: 3,025 to 3,050 fps. Still plenty fast enough to make USPSA Minor with velocity to spare, but for those shooting at longer ranges the velocity loss can change trajectory. (If your matches call for shots past 300 yards, you should be using a 69-grain match bullet, and not 55-grain fmj ammo.) For long-range shooting, Federal Gold 69-grain match ammo turned in several one-hole groups, which for me and a low-power scope at 100 yards is spectacular

shooting. At closer distances, you can use the JP Short-Range Tactical sight. Mounted on the handguard, at the 2'oclock position, you use the back up irons at close ranges where the magnification of the Acog might slow you down. To use it is simple: you rotate the butt of the stock out, while keeping it against your shoulder. The optics rotate to the left, the irons come up, and you are already lined up behind them to shoot. For close targets it is blazing fast.

What would you use the JP CTR-02 for? Well, USPSA Three-gun competition comes to mind, which is a subject John is very familiar with. He's done quite well at the USPSA Three-Gun Nationals, the DPMS Tri-Gun Challenge and the World Championship Three-Gun Tactical, the successor to the old SOF match, to name a few recent matches. And his rifles are used by many big competitors, including Taran Butler and Tony Holmes.

If competition isn't your thing, but you want an absolutely dependable, tack-driving AR, and are not wedded to the A2/M-4gery look, then JP can build you just what you need.

Cloud Mountain Armory

Located in Utah, Cloud Mountain is one of those small shops with an idea, something that is so common in America, and so difficult to explain to the rest of the world. Robyn Church had an idea: make a big-bore AR that functioned, held together, and shot accurately. Not having a shop full of CNC machines, Robyn doesn't machine receivers, but obtains them from a vendor. (You'd be surprised at the number of big names, names you'd recognize, who do the same. Robyn is not alone in buying what she can't make.)

The heart of the 502 Thunder Sabre is a 416 stainless barrel in .50 caliber. The rifle I received came with a barrel made by Pac-Nor Barreling, a company I've had very good luck with when it comes to accurate tubes. Soon after Robyn sent me this rifle, she told me that future barrels would be coming

The left side of the Cloud Mountain Armory 502 Thunder Sabre.

A silver finish on the logo.

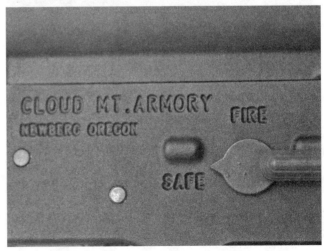

All firearms have to be marked with the location of the manufacturer.

The ejection port is opened slightly to accommodate the fat cartridge.

You can see the extra size of the rim and case, over a from .223/5.56.

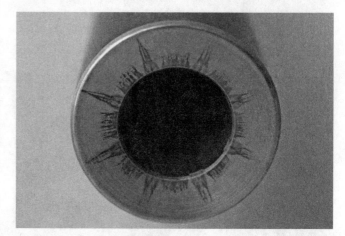

The barrel is huge, the bore huge, the crown well-cut, as you can tell by the fouling pattern.

The bolt is opened to accommodate the rebated rim.

from Lothar Walther. I'd be hard-pressed to believe that someone made better barrels than Pac-Nor, but if anyone can do it, I wouldn't bet against Walther.

The Cloud Mountain Armory receivers are nicely-made, with a dull matte finish, and markings that are machined into the surface before the anodizing is applied. On the left are the logo, the model "CM 1500," the serial number and the address and Safe and Fire. On the right, the lower has "502 Thunder Sabre" etched, anodized or laser-highlighted (I'm not

The custom-machined front sight housing, to fit the huge barrel.

Left side of the 502 Thunder Sabre.

Just in case you have some other .50 rounds, the brass is custom-headstamped.

sure which, but it works) on the magazine well wall. The upper is an A2, with Anchor Harvey forge mark, and the rear sight is a standard A2 with large and small apertures, with "8/3" elevation wheel. So far, nothing out of the ordinary. The ejection port of the upper has been machined to a larger opening, for the rounds and brass to clear. The dust cover door still latches, and works as expected, but the opening is larger. The deflector lump and forward assist are as normal. The forearm is an aluminum tube, knurled for a non-slip grip. If you wanted something else, the upper threads appear to be

You can see the size of the 502, compared to .223 and 5.56 rounds.

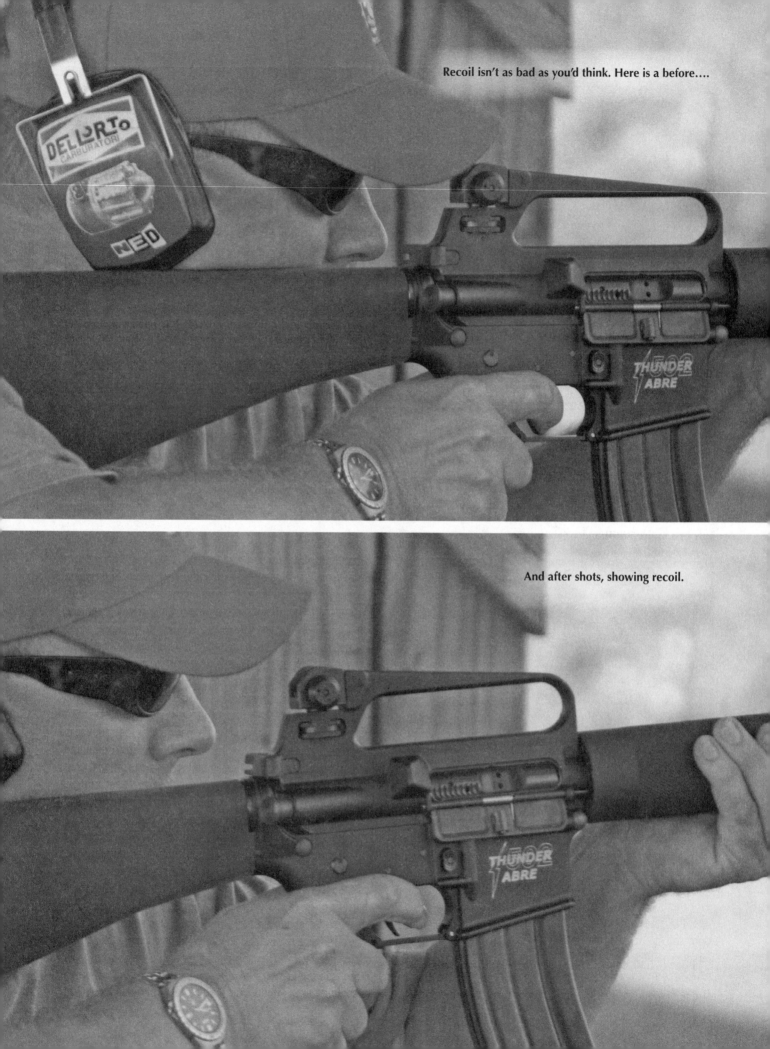

Recoil isn't as bad as you'd think. Here is a before....

And after shots, showing recoil.

standard, so you could remove and install whatever else you wanted, provided you could get it over the barrel. Yow! In order to hold the .50-caliber bullet, the barrel has a diameter of .925 inches. There are other barrels that get that big (but not many) but they have much smaller bores. In order to have iron sights, Cloud Mountain custom-machines their own front sight housings from a casting. The front sight housing is held on with a pair of lock screws, tightened up against a pair of flats machined onto the bottom of the barrel to give them purchase and indexing.

Inside, the Thunder Sabre is not as modified as you might think. One of the design targets of the conversion was to keep the modifications to a minimum, and they succeeded. Except for the markings, the lower is a standard lower. I tested it by taking the 502 upper off, and installing one of my own spare uppers in 5.56. With appropriate magazines it ran along just fine. If you wanted a dual-caliber rifle, you'd only need to swap the 502 off and install your own upper. The conversion works on the standard lower by using a gas port proportioned to work on a standard lower, and a modified bolt and barrel extension. Oh, and magazines, but we all expect to change magazines when we change calibers.

The bolt is opened up to hold the .444-inch rim of the 502, and the barrel extension feed ramps have been altered to allow the fat (.538-inch) short (1.680 inches overall, 1.280-inch case length) round to feed. That's right, the case is rebated. I know, rebated rims are supposed to be the invention of the devil, causing feeding failures and all kinds of malfunctions. Well, it never happened with the 502. The feed ramps are not so much enlarged, as the "hump" of the locking lug in-between the ramps has been shaved and turned into a ramp. The result is a rifle that feeds what it was never intended to feed: a brass cigar butt of a cartridge.

The ballistics of the 502 Thunder Sabre are impressive: a listed 335-grain jacketed hollow-point at 1,725 fps. When first looking at it, the test crew expected to get thumped really hard. After all, when you're looking at a cartridge the size of your thumb (OK, a short thumb) you expect some recoil. To sum it up: it isn't bad. The ballistics would lead you to believe that you're going to be shooting a 20-gauge slug gun. Indeed, the high-velocity 20-gauge load of a ¾-ounce slug (327-grains) at 1,600 fps is a good standard to keep in mind. Over the chrono, the 502 delivered 1,710 fps on a hot, sunny day, and 1,690 on a cold, damp day. The recoil is not difficult to deal with, as the straight-line bore to stock relationship of the AR system was designed to eliminate muzzle climb in recoil. The 502 comes back, but it isn't something you can't deal with.

The magazines are modified AR 5.56 mags, turned into single-stack loading and feeding. (How else are you going to get a .538-inch diameter case to feed?) For those planning to use the 502 Thunder Sabre for hunting (and it would make a great gun for that, in the proper application) Cloud Mountain offers a four-shot magazine. For those living in some People's Democratic Republics, you can get nine or 10-round versions.

Is this accurate enough for you? Blame the flyer on me, and not the rifle.

The aluminum tube handguard is knurled for a non-slip grip.

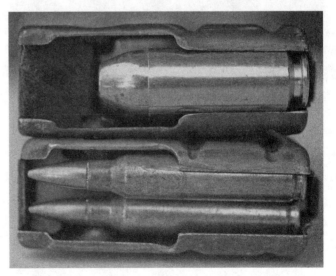

Magazines are modified to be single-stack, single-feed, and have an internal ramp.

And for the rest of us, 14 shots is the full-up capacity of a modified 30-round tube.

How does the 502 perform? Well, as I did not have a chance to shoot it on animate objects (testing was over and done, and ammo gone, before hunting season began) I can only tell you how it did on targets and ballistic gelatin. Off the bench, I managed a number of groups that were four shots in a cluster and one out. The one out was never the same one of the string, so it obviously wasn't something to do with accuracy differences due to first shot chambered or anything like that. It was simply that shooting from the bench, the 502 was more work than shooting it offhand. And more work than other calibers. If I mounted a scope (and fitted a cheekpiece) I'm sure I could bring those flyers into the group. But with irons on a shorty and 502 recoil, 2 MOA is my limit. If you are recoil-sensitive, Cloud Mountain can fit a muzzle brake for you.

In ballistic gelatin, the 335-grain jacketed hollow-points sliced through 36 inches of gelatin, not to be seen again. The wound track was opening up in the second block, so the bullet was obviously expanding, but it was going too fast to slow down in the gelatin we could fit on the stand. This load will punch a .50-caliber hole clean through any deer to walk North America since the Pleistocene. It would do a similar job on larger game, and judging from the enthusiasm with which it struck the backstop behind the gelatin, it would probably exit an Elk on a side or lung shot. You have no need to fear that your cartridge is not up to the task.

Yes, the ammo is going to seem pricey. At a suggested $31.50 for 30 cartridges the price is more than what you'd pay for surplus 5.56. But they are reloadable, the 502 uses standard .50-caliber handgun bullets, and loading data is available from Cloud Mountain. For someone who wants a hunting rifle, where .223 on deer is prohibited, there's a rifle for you.

The 502 Thunder Sabre is about to perforate two blocks of ballistic gelatin.

Wilson Combat Tactical Model

Bill Wilson was there in the early days of IPSC. And when the rest of us were grumbling about parts and gunsmithing work that was less than good, he was doing something about it. Today, Bill presides over a manufacturing and gunsmithing operation that any would be envious of. A few years ago Bill decided to branch out from 1911 work, and bought the tools, machinery and companies he'd need to build and work on shotguns and AR-15s.

The result is the Wilson Tactical Custom AR, an out-of-the-box rifle that has everything you'd need if you went the custom route. What the crew at Wilson sent me was a UT-15 Urban Tactical Rifle, post-ban configuration. (As I've mentioned before, many rifles arrived before the sunset, thus I have a mix of post- and after-ban guns.)

The base rifle as sent was a fixed-stock M-4gery, sort of a Colt Lightweight Sporter rifle of a decade ago. (With the AWB gone, there are more options now.) You could, as of the week after the AWB sunset, get Wilson rifles with tele-stocks and threaded barrels. And, even bayonet lugs, for those who have to have 'em.

Left side of the Wilson.

Up front, the Wilson sports a combo flash-hider compensator. The big secret, that couldn't be told during the AWB, was that despite being a compensator, it also acted as a flash hider. If you happen to live in a state that still has AWB constraints, sshhh! We won't say anything to them. But the comp, unlike a lot of other compensators, does diminish the flash.

The Wilson barrel is M-4 profile, but unmarked. Made to Wilson specs, it is 1/9, and a very nice barrel. The front sight is a short sight, machined as a fixed-sight front housing. The front sight is a casting that has been machined cleaner on the front and back, and not left blanked as many are. It is secured to the barrel with a pair of cross pins. The stock on the rifle sent is a standard A2 stock, but as mentioned, you can get tele-stocks now. The pistol grip is an Ergo Grip, very comfortable and it positions the hand well.

The Wilson upper and lower are the current profile, with full fences and reinforcements. The texture of the matte finish is a little coarser than others, and the color is a bit odd. On top of whatever anodizing is on the upper and lower, Wilson Combat applies their Armor Tuff finish. It is an epoxy-based baked-on resin finish, adding durability to the anodizing. It appears sort of gray, sort of green, depending on the light levels, light temperature, and time of day. It is dark, and interesting, and even attractive. But it is not mil-spec in color, and if you swap uppers and lowers with other rifles the color differences will show. The color is too subtle to show in a black and white reproduction, and went without notice

The Wilson rifle is heavily and cleanly marked.

by some of my test crew. Those who saw it on a sunny day noticed it, but one test session was a heavy overcast day, and the color was not commented on.

The lower has Tactical Custom on the right side, along with Safe and Fire, and on the left side are the serial number, and Wilson Combat and the required address. The curious thing about the markings is that they are not rollmarks. They have the appearance of being machined into the receiver before it was anodized, using a CNC machine and some type of publishing/page layout software. The appearance is markedly different from, and in many cases a step above, the typical rollmarked logo and markings. Inside the lower we have a two-stage trigger made by JP Enterprise, installed and tuned by the Wilson Combat gunsmiths. The trigger is set up beautifully, and is easily the best trigger of the entire batch of rifles sent to me. As a target and precision-shooting trigger, it is superb. Were I shooting this rifle in competition, or using it as a precision marksman rifle (i.e., sniper) in a law enforcement or military capacity, I would love this trigger. If I were in charge of training a group of street cops in Patrol Rifle, and/or in charge of a shift full of these rifles, I'd change them. I'd insist that Wilson find a way to make them at least 4.5, or better yet 5 pounds, in pull weight. They're just too light for the street. Lest you think I'm being harsh on street cops, or overly worrisome, I've seen, and fired early shots in training classes with just such triggers. Wilson is justifiably proud of this trigger, and their ability to fine-tune it to such brilliant results. God, this trigger is beautiful, but not every street cop needs to be driving a Ferrari as a patrol car.

The upper is a standard flat-top, with forward assist and ejector lump on the outside. Inside, the carrier is an M-16 with the auto sear shoulder milled back, and no markings. The bolt and extractor also lack markings, and the extractor spring does not have a synthetic insert. But it does have a rubber "o" ring around it as an extraction boost.

On top of the lower is the Wilson back-up iron sight. As with the trigger, this is one heck of a piece of machinery. The sight clamps to the upper with two bolts, tightened by hex nuts. I think you could get enough torque on those nuts to pinch the receiver, they are that stout. The sight is windage and elevation click-adjustable. It locks up, so it won't be pushed out of position by an inadvertent impact. To pop it up, you press either one of the bars that stick out right and left. Spring-loaded, the sight jumps up and lock in place. You have one choice in aperture size, no big deal if you're using it as a back-up. To fold it, press either bar, and pivot the sight down until it is in place. It locks down, too.

The handguards on the Tactical Custom brought the most comment. Almost to a man, the test crew felt the handguard was too big. Machined from a single piece, and attached to a steel machined barrel nut, the aluminum tactical handguard has four rails, each at the cardinal points. The base tube is machined to a nominal 2 inches (2.006" as best I can get an average) but the rails cause the problem: each rail is

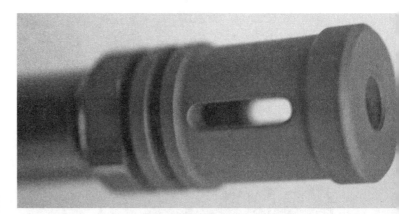

The comp that is also a flash hider. Sssh, it's a secret in some states.

The front of the tactical handguard.

The excellent Ergo grip, and Wilson's back-up iron sight.

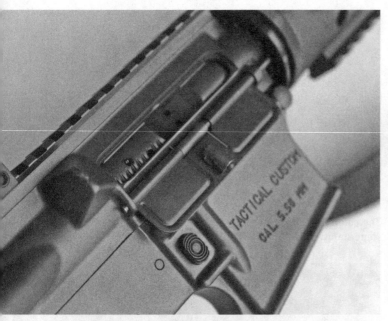

The flat top gives room for optics, in front of the Wilson back-up sight.

The back-up sight folds flat, out of the way. The Armor-Tuff finish is very tough, indeed.

Notice the hammer is not at all a military part.

The excellent trigger, with the Wilson-installed yellow-coat springs.

machined as if it rested on a base, adding thickness to the final diameter. We didn't even try putting rail covers on it, as it was large when bare. Adding thickness with the rail covers would have been too much. The test crew concluded that were they to buy their own Wilson, they'd get it with the standard handguards. If they felt the need for rails, they'd find something smaller in diameter.

The handguards (and the too-light trigger for duty/defensive use) are the only faults we could find. In the accuracy department, the Wilson was superb. While I did not shoot the smallest group of the test series with it, the barrel was so forgiving that there was nothing it didn't shoot well. It even

produced decent groups with the Wolf test ammo we put through it. There was nothing we could do to make it malfunction, short of abuse. (Which I'm up for, but because Bill Wilson was kind enough to loan me this rifle, and I didn't feel like taking advantage of his good nature.) It didn't matter what ammo we fed it, nor what magazines we used, the rifle kept working. On the subject of Wolf ammo, unlike using it in 1911s, which Bill and the crew are very much against, they don't have a problem with rifle ammo. They aren't keen on it, as they have run into production lots that were mildly corrosive. If you shoot corrosive ammo in your rifle, and don't scrub every trace of firing residue out, you'll rust your

The Wilson sight is adjustable for elevation and windage.

UP

rifle. (Even stainless barrels rust.) Wilson can't (nor can any manufacturer) warranty a rifle rusted into malfunction or failure to work. And, they aren't too optimistic about the extra wear the steel cases can create, but they won't tell you using it turns your rifle into a jam-a-matic, nor voids the warranty. Just, if you use it you may be on your own and find your Wilson rifle used up too soon.

So, I of course had to test it. As my previous attempts had been short-term and inconclusive, I set up a longer session for this test. I set aside a range session for the Wilson rifle alone. I first got it hot with regular ammo, putting 200 rounds through it in a little less than half an hour. The shooting pace is one we would spend days doing, at Second Chance, firing the Light Rifle Pop and Flop. There, every couple of hundred

rounds we'd run a wet patch and brush down the bore, and sit out for a rotation through the course. That would give the rifle time to cool a bit. Then, dry patches and a few rounds of "practice" ammo, and we'd get back into the match. The "practice" ammo was solely to burn up any traces of cleaning solvent in the bore or gas tube. I put 200 rounds of Black Hills 55-grain fmj through it, practicing on the steel plates. I then chambered a round of Wolf and racked it, letting the round soak up heat, and then letting the whole thing cool off. With the rifle a bit dirty, and the chamber heating up a round, we'd see if lacquer came off. I then spent the rest of the day practicing on the plates, using just over 700 rounds of Wolf ammo, and the Second Chance routine. The bore got swabbed, just because I'm not a barbarian and I keep my rifle

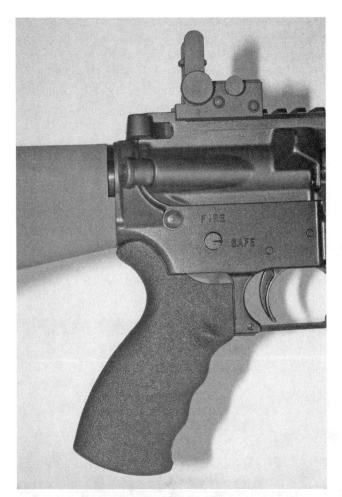

The Ergo grip fills the receiver above and behind the pistol grip, giving a better grip for many shooters.

In case you had any doubts as to who made it, the sight is marked.

The back-up sight is spring-loaded, and pops up when you press one of the big bolts.

(U.S. Air Force Photo by Tech. Sgt. Mike Buytas)

In combat rifles might get really hot, but we couldn't get ours hot enough to cause problems with Wolf ammo.

bores relatively clean. The chamber never saw a chamber brush, and I used a bore guide to keep from getting solvent into the chamber when cleaning the bore.

The handguard got warm, but never too hot to hold. I got very used to the light, clean trigger. I got the sights dialed in like you wouldn't believe. And I never had a problem with the rifle or ammo. Each time I needed a break, or had to paint the steel, I'd chamber a round, sling the rifle, and walk down to tend to the targets. Again, I was trying to get lacquer to come off the case and onto the chamber. Never happened. All I can think of, is that those who complain about lacquer deposits are a lot more willing to heat up a rifle than I am, and I'm not much of a softy when it comes to rifle use. I've shot rifles hot enough in matches to need a glove to protect my left hand. I've gotten rifles in this test series that hot. And I haven't had a problem.

I'm told that the issue of laquer on the Wolf ammo is now a moot point, as the company as gone to a polymer coating on all their steel-cased rifle ammo. You might still find some old Wolf with laquer if it has been sitting on the shelf for a while, but all their new production has been polymer-coated for some time.

As for ammo tastes, the Wilson had the most elevated and the most common tastes. It shot my various batches of Federal XM-193 like you wouldn't believe, with many sub-MOA groups and some single-hole groups. It also loved the exotic Mk 262 Mod 1 ammo from Black Hills, shooting it all into sub-MOA groups. I couldn't find anything that it didn't at least shoot very well. Far from being picky, the Wilson was a dependable performer with anything I fed it.

Bill Wilson and crew make superb firearms. If you want one set up the way Bill makes his, then there is no point in screwing around building, experimenting, customizing and still-more experimenting. If you want to go straight to "Go", and want a rifle that is ready without fussing, then you have to get a Wilson Combat Tactical. If I didn't already have a safe full of rifles on which I've already done the building, experimenting, customizing and fussing, I'd hang onto this one. But, back to Wilson it goes. If you want a deal on a rifle with a lot of life left in the barrel (even after all my shooting) call or e-mail Wilson Combat and see if they still have, and will part with, # WCR 1040. It's a damn fine rifle. If it is gone, they can make you one every bit as good.

Ejection was forward, safe for left-handed shooters.

The back-up sight proved to be more than just a backup, it works fine as a main sight, too.

When things "heat up" everyone wants a reliable rifle. You would have a hard time finding one better than Wilson.

(U.S. Air Force photo by Staff Sgt. Suzanne M. Day)

Clark Custom Gator

For those who haven't been paying attention, the name Clark, as in Clark Custom is an old and honored one.

Jim Clark, Sr. was a bull's-eye competitor back in the 1950s and early 1960s, who won just about everything. As a matter of fact, he not only won just about everything, he won just about everything he entered, setting records as he went. When he could not get what he wanted in guns, he figured out how to build them himself. What made him famous was his conversion that turned a Colt (they were the only ones making them then) .38 Super into a .38 Special wadcutter gun. Supers then were inaccurate but common, as Colt made slews of them for export to Mexico. The wadcutter gun was accurate, expensive and hard to obtain. If you sent Jim a Super and a check, he'd return your gun built to fire .38 special wadcutters, and as accurate as you wanted, depending on the size of the check you sent.

Jim Clark, Jr. inherited both his father's shooting skills, and his gunsmithing skills. But by the time Jim Jr. was shooting, bull's-eye was passé and IPSC and bowling pins were the hot game. After that, Jim was one of the first into the new outgrowth of USPSA/IPSC, Three-gun matches. When not going to Second Chance, he was off to the SOF match, which he won five times. The USPSA 3-Gun Nationals have been held at the Clark range and gunshop, in Princeton, Louisiana.

If you want an accurate, reliable, soft-shooting rifle that you would use to win matches (and even build into a police

The Clark Gator logo, on the right side.

marksman or military SPR) then you have to look long and hard at the Clark Gator. The upper and lower are made to Jim's specifications. The lower is marked on the left with Clark Custom Guns, address, Safe and Fire, the model and the serial number. The markings all look machined. On the right are the Safe and Fire markings, and the Clark Gator logo on the magazine well in laser etching or some other treatment that leaves the logo bright. The buttstock and pistol grip are both A2. You can easily change them if you need to, but as standard equipment they are hard to beat. The uppers and lowers are forgings, coated as per mil-A 8625-A and Teflon coated.

A subtle touch, the Clark Gator name somehow put into the stock itself.

Inside the lower, things get tricky. The hammer is an M-16 hammer with the autosear hook ground off, standard stuff. A lot of AR makers and builders use such hammers, as they are common, inexpensive, easy to find, and durable to a fault. Jim combines it with a JP Enterprises adjustable trigger. The result is a trigger that is so nice you have to try it to believe it. There really isn't any takeup. You simply apply enough force to fire it, and the hammer drops. Very nice, indeed. The carrier is a chromed AR carrier, with a large "D" stamped on the left side. The bolt is unmarked, as is the extractor, which has a blue buffer inside its spring.

The flat-top upper has the expected picatinny rail, the correct height, but forward of that you see the intent of the rifle: a competition-beating machine. First, the handguard. Made of carbon fiber, it is tough, relatively non heat-transferring, and is not as slick as it might look. When the carbon fiber handguards first came out, I asked the inventor at the exhibitors tent at one of the Nationals how tough they were. His reply was to pick it up and proceed to enthusiastically whack the aluminum tent pole with it. The pole, 7 inches in diameter and 20 feet high, rang like a bell. (That explained the marks on the pole, and the grimaces of his neighbors.) They are tough. You won't break it by mis-handling the rifle. The carbon fiber handguard is a $90 option over the aluminum handguard. Do yourself a favor, and opt for the carbon fiber. It is lighter, tougher, won't burn your hand on a sunny day after a lot of shooting, and won't scar as ugly if you take a spill and fall on it in the gravel. Inside the handguard is a Green Mountain barrel. A lot of makers are coy about who makes their barrels. Jim Clark, Jr. isn't. Green Mountain has been making barrels since 1976, and judging from the number of matches won by Branch Meanly, the owner, he knows something about making barrels. He must, or Jim Clark, Jr. wouldn't be buying them. With a 1/9 twist, you can expect it to shoot just about any bullet weight you'll need, accurately.

Barrel makers have strange ideas about how to "break in" barrels. The instruction card from Clark offers the advice to shoot and clean for each round for the first 25. Then clean after each 10 to 100 rounds. Had I done that for each rifle I received for the book, I'd still be at it, instead of you now reading this book. I swabbed the bore, shot to zero, and

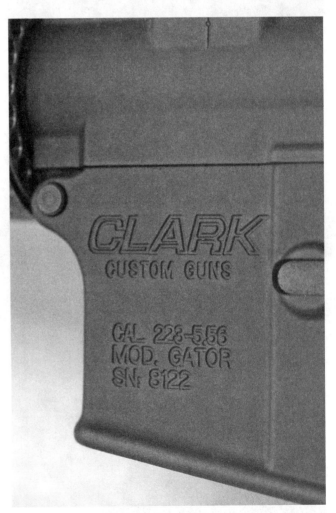

Clark Custom, machined into the receiver.

proceeded to shoot for groups. I cleaned it, then we shot it for reliability and handling. As you'll read, the rifle is a tack-driver, despite my failure to follow instructions. Perhaps, 15,000 rounds from now I'll regret the decision, when accuracy drops off sooner than it otherwise would. I'll bet not. If you have the time or patience, break-in the barrel as instructed. Or, follow my break-in process in the Barrel chapter.

Out in front of the handguard is the gas block, a JP adjustable. As a competition gun, the Gator might get fed reloads from softy 55-grain bullets at 2,800 fps to 75-grain Hornady Match loads. In order to make sure the rifle works reliably, and the shooters aim doesn't get disturbed by recoil any more than avoidable, the gas system can be tuned to deliver just enough gas and no more. At the muzzle, a Miculek comp. Damping both recoil and muzzle rise, the Miculek comp makes shooting the Gator a breeze. And shoot, it does. I tested it with the Leupold long-range scope on board, and with the scope cranked up to its full 10X I was able to

Inside, there is a JP adjustable trigger tuned to make the pull brilliant.

Jim Clark, Jr. putting a Gator through its paces at a USPSA Three-Gun match. He knows how to build them, and shoot them.

The left side of the Gator.

The Miculek comp, soft and flat-shooting.

Jim Clark, Jr. makes an M-16 hammer cut to AR specs work as a part of a superb match trigger pull.

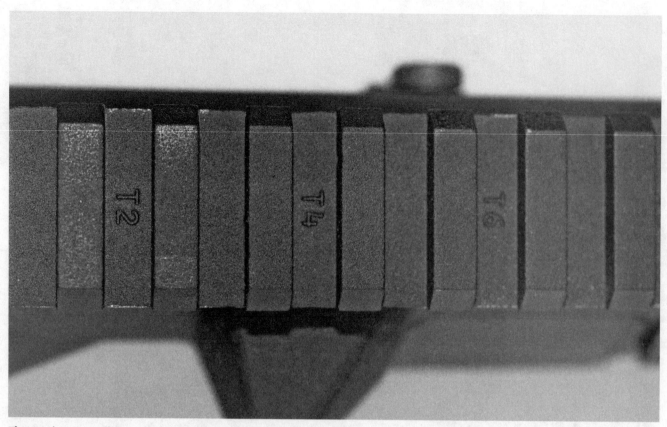

The receiver top rails are numbered, so if you take your optics off (say for airline transport) you can get them back where they were.

The JP adjustable gas block, allowing you to tune your Gator for the softest possible recoil while still being 100 percent reliable.

My test crew really liked putting the Gator through its paces.

punch sub-MOA groups with any ammo I had except the Wolf. (I had to try one group. It was a nearly 2-MOA cluster. Plenty good. I quit.) Based on marginally smaller groups (How much difference, statistically, is there between .650-inch and .750-inch groups?) I'd have to say that it shoots best with Black Hills red-box ammo loaded with V-Max 60-grain bullets. Right behind it was the Hornady 75-grain Match loads. But even plain, old XM-193 Federal posted more sub-MOA groups than not. Once I'd shot it for groups, I took the Leupold off and installed the C-More rail sight. It looked a little strange, what with the C-More sight having a rear sight, but no front iron on the Gator, but competition shooters aren't bothered by "strange." With the comp and the red-dot, the Gator was blazing fast on any kind of a field course. Our club only has 100 yards as the maximum range, but at that distance I was able to do head shots (oops, "B-zone engagements") if I remembered to slow down and let the trigger work for me.

Up close, the speed of the Gator was scary. I could engage a three-target array around the edge of a barricade, and have the last shot fired before the first empty hit the ground. Showing off like that, it helps if the rifle has vigorous ejection, which the Gator did at the gas port setting it came with.

If the basic Gator isn't what you need, you can put on whatever options fit your competition shooting situation. You can go with several different iron sights, a bunch of bipods, or other options, right from Clark. Or, mix and match with iron sights from someone else. With the basics of a dependable, accurate, superbly-triggered rifle to start with, you would have to work hard to go wrong with options.

The Gator isn't a patrol rifle. You won't see it in a patrol car, with the beat cop. But, as a police marksman's rifle, the Gator would be very hard to beat. Nestled onto a rooftop a block away, with a bipod, a spotter and a good scope, you would be set for administering the law.

Vulcan Arms

Vulcan is a relatively new manufacturer, and in some circles not well thought of. I figured I would see about borrowing a rifle, run some ammo through it, and probably end up dropping their loaner from the book. After all, who wants to read about bad stuff? Well those who slow down to gawk at traffic accidents, I suppose. As it turns out, I was pleasantly surprised. The Vulcan was not "bad stuff."

Vulcan sent me two rifles, a .223/5.56 made of their synthetic receivers, and a 9mm conversion complete rifle, out of forged upper and lower. To maximize the information, I asked for the 5.56 in a tactical forend configuration, and the 9mm in a standard. Both came with detachable front sights, mounted on a four-sided picatinny gas block. Both came in Doskocil hard cases, and the 9mm came with a Sten gun magazine. One of the things "everyone knows" on the internet (Hey, if its there, it must be true, right? Not!) is that Vulcan rifles are made on cast receivers. Short of turning it over to a metallurgy lab for destructive testing I can't be sure. But the receivers I got were not cast. They didn't look like it, the finish didn't appear to be, and the sound of the receivers being tapped didn't sound cast. I know, I have some on hand that I know to be cast, and these aren't them. Maybe in the past, something someone said was Vulcan was cast, but not the items they sent me.

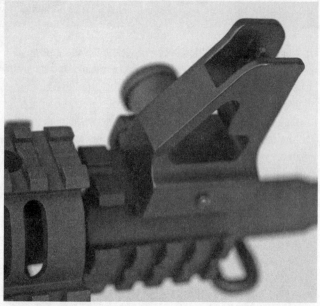

The gas block clamps on with a pair of allen-head screws.

The front of the tactical handguard, and the railed front sight /gas block housing.

The polymer lower has the serial number in a metal plate embedded in the casting.

The Vulcan 223 felt a bit odd in recoil, but shot accurately and reliably until we inadvertently unscrewed the handguard.

The 5.56 is interesting. The telescoping stock is from Rock River Arms. Being the modern, plastic design with no sling loop on top it cries out for a side sling attachment like the GG&G. The barrel is M-4 profile, threaded and with a flash hider on the muzzle. The gas block is four-sided with picatinny rails and a sling swivel. The gas block is held to the barrel with a pair of allen-head cap screws that do not appear to engage the barrel itself, and clamp the sight to the barrel. Some don't like that approach, but if it works for Armalite (to name a competitor that uses the same system) then it can't be too bad. The sling swivel is held in with a roll pin, and there are locations front and rear for the sling swivel. The

The Vulcan rear sight, with its high accessory rail.

The rear sight has space to store a battery for your optics.

The polymer upper lacked a dust cover door, and the ejector lump is oddly fluted. But it works.

The gas key got banged up when the forend loosened. Curiosly, the gas tube was not damaged.

front sight clamps on using a short rail and knob identical to that of the rear sight. The handguard on the tactical version is an aluminum tube with picatinny rails top, bottom and both sides. The tube appears to be either machined from thick-walled aluminum tube, or extruded. It is then bead-blasted for a matte finish and anodized. At the rear it threads onto

The rear sight had the correct elevation wheel, 6/3.

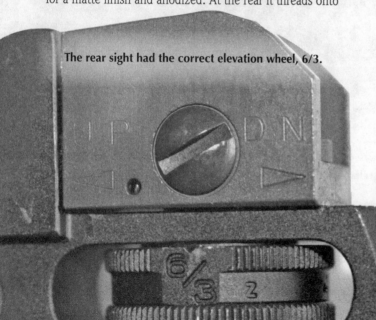

a barrel nut, which serves both to capture the barrel and provide a place for the handguard. The rifle as shipped came with a vertical foregrip.

The rear sight is a clamp-on system, like the standard M-4, but has an included picatinny rail on it. So instead of simply being a sight and handle, it is a sight and mounting place for red-dot optics. However, as the rail is elevated, you'll need a very low mounting system, with a red-dot with a shallow bottom, to work. Something like the EOTech Holosight sits high enough to block the iron sights from a proper sight picture. If that rail were half as high, it would have potential as a great system. The rear sight is an A2, but the rear housing is rather lightly stamped with the "UP" and "DOWN" markings and arrows. As most of us only use them to adjust zero when changing ammo brands or lots, it doesn't really matter. But it does look different. I was surprised to see that the Armalite M-4gery had an identical rear sight housing, complete with light markings. My guess would be that Vulcan got this batch of sights from Armalite, as I saw Armalite making their own on my visit there. One curious aspect of the rear sight is a large, threaded recess on the right side. Turns out it is a storage compartment for a red-dot scope battery. Interesting. And an explanation

You can have the current cool gear accessories on your Vulcan.

for the height of the rear sight assembly rail.

The real difference is in the receivers. They are made of a glass-filled polymer. The lower is almost indistinguishable from a forged lower, except for the slight difference in sheen in the polymer. The serial number is etched on a metal plate set into the mould that created the receiver, while the markings are part of the mold. Everything that attaches to, or goes inside of the lower is completely standard. You need not have a proprietary anything to assemble a Vulcan polymer lower.

The upper would not pass as a forging. First, the ejector block is fluted. Why? I can think of a number of reasons besides to look different. To give them enough flex to withstand the impact of brass, the impact of dropping, as a place to provide mold release are a few. The upper lacks an ejection port cover, or any means of attaching one. I would guess that a molded dust cover door hinge recess proved fragile, or that it was a significant expense in adding one that wasn't fragile. For most shooters the door is superfluous anyway. The upper also lacks a forward assist, another superfluous part. And one that might actually keep some of you out of trouble. My experience with forward assists is kind of like my experience with four-wheel-drive: it just gets you deeper in the mud, deeper in the woods. That is, if a particular cartridge doesn't want to chamber, and you aren't in the wilds of Afghanistan where dust is a part of life, food, water and clothing, then you don't want to force that cartridge. Extract it and find out what the problem is. Reluctant cartridges that have been hammered with a forward assist usually need tools to extract.

The vertical handle gave my testers enough leverage to loosen the tactical handguard.

The internals of the Vulcan V-15 were a modified M-16 hammer, AR trigger, disconnector and safety, and an AR-15 carrier. The carrier, bolt and extractor are not marked. The extractor spring has a black synthetic buffer inside of it.

The trigger has some creep, but fell to a reasonable weight of pull. The re-set was quite early, early enough that I was worried it might cause hammer fall on trigger release, but it didn't. Still, as a gunsmith I'm somewhat sensitive to such things, and were this my rifle I'd delay the timing of the hammer release to allow for more sear engagement.

The right side of the 9mm.

The aluminum lower is lightly marked.

Shooting

The Vulcan was a study in contrasts. First, several of the test crew remarked on the handguard, and how "edgy" it seemed. Not that it was sharp, but that it just wasn't something they could get a good hold of and feel comfortable with. It wasn't the largest, nor the one with the sharpest edges or anything like that. Just enough off to be noticeable. If the exact shape of a tactical handguard matters to you, get your hands on and try this one before buying it. Or, just get the standard setup and install your own handguard. But the rifle overall was light, well-balanced, and handled well.

The shooting was another contrast. This rifle was plenty accurate. Off the bench it produced military-acceptance sized groups or smaller. It was easy to shoot a qualifying score with it on the NEMRT course. But the recoil was reported to be "odd." When I shot it, I knew what it was, the receiver was flexing. Once you get used to it, it is just another bit of "what's happening" with the rifle. And lest you think that a flexing synthetic receiver is the sign of a cheap build, I have noticed the same thing (and to a greater degree) with some H-K rifles, notably the G-36 in 5.56, and the UMP in .40. No, it is simply what happens when you build with synthetics. Our left-handed shooters had no problem with it, and the empties mostly bounced out at a 30-degree forward angle, a good sign for a tele-stocked shorty.

The problems began when we used the V-15 in the Wolf steel-cased ammo tests. On the first test, the V-15 started to not lock open when empty, and at the end of the test was short-stroking. Hmm. The failure to lock open could be a magazine problem, but short-stroking, that's a rifle problem. Once cool, I tossed it back in its case and took it home. I dragged it back a few days later for the follow-up testing, and the bolt would not go forward. It stopped short. I took it

The Sten magazines fit and locked by use of an adapter block.

The 9mm has its forward assist plugged, and lacks a dust cover door.

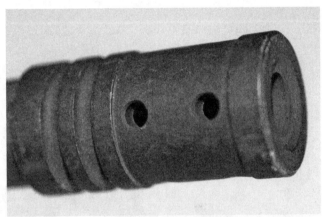

The Vulcan 9mm came with a comp, but how well a comp can work on any 9mm is a another question.

apart, and found the gas key on the carrier was crashing into the gas tube. It had hit so hard that the tip of the gas key was damaged, and the rifle refused to work. I called up Vulcan, got a return authorization, and sent it off on a Monday. That Friday it was back. What had caused the problem? The vertical forend gave my test crew enough leverage that they could start to unscrew the tactical forend. The twisting forend flexed the gas tube, and put it out of line with the carrier key. To solve the problem, Vulcan replaced the key (the gas tube appeared undamaged, much to my surprise) and used Loctite to secure the forend. Once back, I took it off to the range, where it worked without fail, although the forend still had some play in it.

Off the bench, using the big Leupold Mark 4 (a $1,200 scope on a $600 dollar rifle? Yes, if you want to test properly) the Vulcan shot well. It didn't shoot spectacularly, and it didn't matter what ammo I fed it. Ball ammo hovered just under 2 inches at 100 yards, and the priciest match ammo went down by half an inch. I've read of others complaining that the Vulcan failed them this way or that. I haven't put enough ammo through this one to provide a definitive answer as to how long it would work, or if anything would break, but this one has worked well once we solved the gas key problem. The accuracy was good enough to win a three-gun match that didn't involve long-range shooting, which is many matches held each year. I have no doubt that I could shoot clean on the military computer qualification course, out to 300 meters, with any rifle that holds 2 MOA or less.

So, what place is there for the Vulcan? One of my testers put his finger on it: If you want to get into shooting and not break the bank, and you feel comfortable doing your own work to fine-tune and smooth out the rough spots, the Vulcan would make a suitable competition gun. And the rough spots

were present, even if only minor: the loose handguard, the early timing of the disconnector, and the cotter pin in the carrier. (It was tight, and bent. One tester went to remove it with a knifepoint, and slipped and almost cut himself.) None of my test crew would have selected it as a defensive gun unless all the others were off the table as choices. But all remarked that it had worked without fail before the gas key problem, and also after it had been solved. If the tactical handguard were removed and a standard barrel nut and handguard installed in its place, we no-doubt would not have had the handguard/gas key problem. With standard handguards it would be reliable enough, and certainly accurate enough, for a competition shooter to do as well as his or her skills would allow.

The question comes down to this: Does a more expensive rifle offer refinements you need, or performance you can take advantage of? If so, spend more money. If you want to build and learn, or you have to save the money, then the Vulcan can prove a dependable rifle for you. Let's put it this way: you

Right side of the 223 as sent.

can buy a Vulcan and 6,000 rounds of ammo, for the cost of one $1,600 rifle. If all you did was put the ammo through the Vulcan, learned to shoot and gunsmith your own AR, and then rebuilt the rifle with the exact configuration parts you wanted next year, you'd be a heck of a lot better shooter than the guy who spent that $1,600 on a rifle, no ammo and no practice.

9mm

What place is there for a 9mm carbine? It doesn't kick less than a .223/5.56. It has more incidental pentration than a .223 does indoors, so it isn't safer to bystanders in case of an errant shot. It is a bit less expensive to run, especially if you load your own 9mm ammo. But the big one is, you can use it on indoor ranges that allow handgun calibers and not rifle

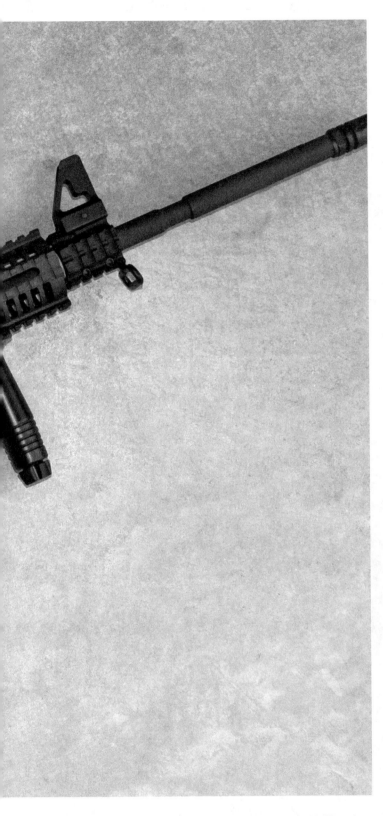

that because that's the first firearm I ever saw converted to 9mm) the method Olympic uses, which the Vulcan system comes close to, is to install a new bolt in a carrier. Colt designed the carrier to be the bolt, with the breechface in the front of the carrier. But you can only do that when you both machine your own carriers, and you have enough physical plant to have the machines to do so. (CNC makes that less of a problem, but then there is the design work.)

The problem is, the Vulcan system is not very refined. Starting from the inside out, we have the bolt. The carrier and bolt appear to be one piece. Further, the carrier is not a modified AR carrier, but a new piece turned from bar stock. The bolt is attached, and the "pickup rail" the rail that strips a round out of the magazine, is either welded in place or built up by welding. The ejector is pinned to the magazine well adapter block, which fills the magazine well for the Sten gun magazine.

The rest of the rifle is straightforward AR: the stock came from Rock River, the upper and lower are forged and the handguards are standard shorty handguards. The upper and lower don't match in color, although they come close. The upper lacks the dust cover door, the forward assist is plugged, and wouldn't work anyway, as the carrier is a "slickside" lacking the forward assist notches. The flat-top is some .030 inches taller than standard. The gas block is four-sided with picatinny rails clamped on with a pair of allen-head screws.

At first glance, the shallow markings of the model, maker and caliber would seem to indicate a casting, But the serial number is marked the same, and you can't cast that and change it each time. In all, the 9mm does not inspire confidence. In operation, it was irregular. Some days it ran fine. Others it failed to fire now and then. I thought it might be the lower, so I took the Vulcan apart, pulled out the magazine adapter, and put one of my own 5.56 uppers on the Vulcan. It worked fine. The 9mm upper worked on two different lowers I tried, but I only went through a couple of magazines each. Putting the two Vulcan halves together, it worked fine for a while, then failed to fire again. Which was frustrating, for when it was firing I was having no problem hitting the 100-yard gong at the club.

My frustrations were compounded by testing the Vulcan 9mm last, when I had no time to spend puzzling out the problem, or sending it back. Based on the quick turnaround of the 5.56 rifle, and the quick solution to its problems, the 9mm would probably be fixed as quickly. But I didn't have time to find out, which will remain a mystery for Volume 2.

The aluminum upper and lower inspire more confidence than the synthetic ones do, so if you were going to get a Vulcan, here's the formula: get a 5.56 rifle, with aluminum upper and lower, standard handguards, and a chrome-moly or stainless barrel. And then practice, modify and learn about your AR.

calibers. And there are USPSA/IPSC clubs that hold "Pistol Caliber Carbine" matches or have it as a division in handgun matches. Since the 9mm out of a carbine won't damage steel targets (it isn't even as fast as many Major handgun loads in .38 Super, for instance) you can shoot a handgun course and not get in trouble for cratering the pepper poppers.

The Vulcan 9mm uses the "Olympic" approach (I call it

Stag Arms

The logo. If you don't like a deer on your rifle, fine. More fine ARs for the rest of us.

Stag Arms is a new manufacturer in the universe of AR manufacturers. The guns are built on uppers and lowers made to their exacting specifications by a sister company with over 30 years experience in the aerospace and DoD manufacturing arena. I was greatly impressed with the sample sent to me. So far they do not offer a large number of models. When I started the book you could only get one: a left-handed upper, M-4gery. Before I was finished, the head

The left side of the Stag Arms carbine.

The ejector port cover and upper.

The dust cover door hinges up, not down.

Shooting a left-handed rifle for a right-handed shooter is an experience.

honcho at Stag e-mailed me to let me know they'd be making a right-handed version shortly (out by the time you read this) and you can get uppers or lowers. If you want a rifle built right, call Stag Arms. I've had some mall ninja types (people who were "so elite you wouldn't believe it") tell me that they can't bring themselves to own a rifle made by "Stag Arms." "C'mon, a picture of a deer? Who wants that?" Well, you too-elite snobs, whose scores never get posted because you're

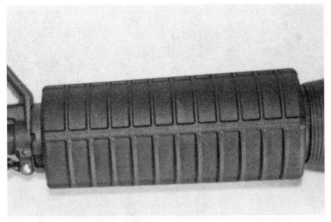
The full-size current mil-spec handguards.

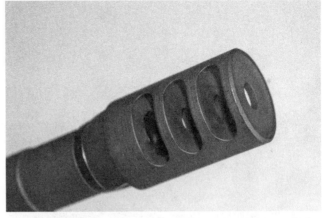
The comp on the Stag is a good one. Don't swap it for a flash hider unless you have to.

The current military-style tele-stock slider, lacking the upper sling loop.

Markings both sides, proper for a left-handed rifle.

too busy "training" to show up at any practical or tactical matches, you don't know what you're missing. And that leaves more for the rest of us.

One maker I know of makes everything that goes into or on their rifles. Even some of the big names buy a large percentage of the parts from subcontractors. What makes the difference is attention to detail, and accepting only the best parts. The result of proper attention is a quality product. In the course of looking over the rifles sent for the book, and seeing many, many other rifles through the years, I can tell you that Stag Arms is a quality product. One thing to demonstrate the point: on tele-stock ARs of the M-4 type, the retaining nut and retaining plate on the stock each have slots cut into them. On only two rifles, have I seen the slots staked as per military specifications: Colt and Stag Arms. The rest are tightened down, or tightened and have some thread-locking goo squirted into the threads before tightening.

As soon as I saw the web page, I knew I had to include

The forge marks.

Just be sure you right-handed shooters keep your fingers out of the way.

At first glance, there is something "wrong" with the Stag Arms. But there is nothing wrong with the way it worked, or how well it shot.

a Stag Arms rifle in the test. There are other left-handed rifles out there, but what you see in others are "last-bench" modifications. On the last bench before shipping, some guy turns right-handed whatevers into left-handed whatevers. Not the Stag Arms left-handed AR. First, they flipped the drawings for a die set from right to left. Then they had a die sinker make left-handed dies. Then, they provided those dies to their forger, to produce left-handed platters and blanked receiver lumps. And then, the critical part, they had a programmer re-program the cutter paths to produce a

left-handed set of upper parts for their AR. As if all this wasn't enough, they also designed and produced a left-handed carrier and bolt. Complete with forward assist notches cut into the carrier. All this cost money, but money invested in doing the engineering correctly is almost never wasted. And paying a good programmer to plan the cutter paths is also money not

wasted. Badly engineered gear never works right. And a poor programmer can make any operation into a money-losing proposition. One look at the Stag Arms rifle, and you know it was done right.

When I first looked it over, I noticed that the ejection port cover hinges up, instead of down. At first I puzzled over this,

then I realized that you can't hinge it down on the left side, the bolt hold-open is in the way. Yes, that's the best part of all, the left-handed upper fits on a perfectly normal lower. If you add an ambidextrous safety (which Stag puts on) and a Norgon Ambi-catch for the magazine release (A $75 option), you have a totally left-handed rifle.

Walk Around, Kick The Tires

The Stag rifle has a comp on it. (Yes, another pre-sunset rifle) but a very effective one. It looks a lot like the Colt comp, but during the ban so many rifle makers made basic comps to put on their rifles, it's a wonder any of them look different. (For all I know, Colt bought them from Stag, or they both bought them from a guy in my home town.) It is effective, and if you were looking for a comp for competition, this one would do nicely. The M-4 profile barrel has the M-203 mounting ring on it, and is marked "Stag Arms" just in front of the front sight housing. The barrel and chamber are chrome-lined, 1/9 twist, with a 5.56 chamber. The front sight is a forging, the correct height for a flat-top carbine, held on with two taper pins, and has the sling swivel riveted in place. The handguards are the correct, fat, M-4 double heat shield size for the look of the rifle.

The stock was a faux tele-stock, of non mil-spec diameter, as almost all but Colt are. Now, you can get sliding stocks and a threaded barrel, too. The stock is the modern, lacking a loop on top, synthetic, lacking a maker's mark. The pistol grip is A2, with the finger groove hook that I always find is in the wrong place. As mentioned before, the retaining nut on the faux tele-stock is staked in place, indicative of the attention to detail you'll find elsewhere on the rifle. The upper and lowers fit nicely, there is no wobble, but you don't have to get out a hammer to drift the disassembly pins out. The finish is correctly matted, there are no mars or blems on it, and it is dead black. The lower has the maker's logo, the serial number, and Safe and Fire on the left side. It also has the model and caliber. On the right, it simply has Safe and Fire, for the left-handed to read. The upper is a flat-top, with the ejection port on the left side. The door flips up until it hits the clamping rail of the carry handle, or whatever you have mounted up there. The upper has "AF" and "C" forging marks on it. The forward assist and ejector lump have also been moved to the left side, so the upper is a mirror image of the original.

Part of the engineering and changing of drawings also involved making a left-handed carry handle/sight. Instead of the tightening knobs being on the left, as they are on the originals, the Stag has them on the right, a nice touch. Despite the switch in knob side, the Stag Arms handle will fit on other rifles, and vice versa. The rear sight is an A2, with the elevation drum being the correct, "6/3" and not the common "8/3" you see on other carbines.

Internally, the Stag carrier is an M-16 lookalike (there were no left-handed M-16s, so this carrier was made from scratch for or by Stag) but the autosear shoulder has been shaved back. It is left-handed and unmarked. The fire control parts are all AR style. The bolt, unmarked, is left-handed and made correctly; the cam pin hole is correctly peened on the bottom so you can't inadvertently assemble the bolt right-handed, and create a malfunctioning rifle. The extractor is unmarked and has a blue synthetic buffer inside the extractor spring.

The trigger pull is within mil specs, and at first had a little bit of jerky creep to it. Once I'd shot it and dry-fired it a while, the creep turned into a simulacra of a two-stage trigger: the trigger creep would come out all in one "click" at about 4 pounds, and then the hammer would fall at a clean 7.25 pounds. I was able to easily shoot a 300/300 on the NEMRT Patrol Rifle class qualification course.

In function, the Stag was flawless. It gobbled everything I had, reloads as well as factory. I didn't try any of the Wolf in it simply because I had enough other rifles to use as test beds, and I didn't want to spread the steel-cased stuff too thin. The comp is quite effective. Effective enough for shooters next to the tester to notice the sideblast. As for accuracy, the Stag exceeded all expectations. It shot well with everything. What it shot best with were the Black Hills Mk 262 Mod 1 load, with the 77-grain open-tip match bullets, shot 1.0 to 1.5 MOA with iron sights. So, I took off the rear sight, and clamped the Leupold Mark 4 on it. (Yes, a 3.5-10X40 sniper scope, on a short-barreled carbine. It looked a bit strange, I'll admit.) Every single group I shot with that scope on the Stag Arms carbine, using the Mk 262 Mod 1, was sub-MOA. I then tried the other load it favored, the Black Hills red-box 60-grain V-Max bullet. The Hornady V-Max is a varmint bullet, and not one I'd want to be using for defense. But for target shooting, and varmint shooting, all I can say about this ammo in this rifle is: "Stand back, earth beings" because the Stag was spectacular with it. It was routine to have the rifle and ammo produce five-shot groups I could cover with a single paster. I shot several that were simply five shots in a single, ragged hole. Were I to go out varmint shooting, to work over a prairie dog town or something, I'd clamp the best scope I had on this rifle and take it. Let the other varmint shooters look down on my "tactical" rifle, I'd be too busy vaporizing long-range critters. This rifle, as a "sleeper" to win bets in an NRA High Power match, would certainly get you talked about. It shoots the Black Hills red-box V-max bullets so well I'm reluctant to use the ammo for any lesser purpose. I may just stash the remainder away until I can use this rifle someplace where the accuracy can produce big dividends, like the next USPSA Three-Gun Nationals.

What is it like, shooting a left-handed rifle? Probably the same feeling a left-handed shooter gets shooting a right-handed rifle. Once you get over how busy it all is, no big deal. At first, the noise, smoke and flying brass coming out of the rifle can be a bit disconcerting. But the ejector lump does its job, and you (at least I and my testers) don't get hit by brass. I'm sure with enough testing you could develop a load that ejected the brass oddly enough to have it land on you, but you could hardly blame the rifle for that, now could you?

Shooting it right-handed, the controls were all normal. With the Norgon ambi-catch, a left-handed shooter could use it without the usual gyrations needed to change magazines. And the ejection port cover flips up, out of the way of any dual-mount magazines like the Mag Cinch. You cannot, however, mount a Redi-Mag on it, as the housing will interfere with the ejection port cover. (I dropped the stag Arms upper onto another lower that had a Redi-mag on it, to check.) Considering the advantages, and accuracy and reliability, the inability to use a Redi-Mag is a small cost.

In the fullness of time, the AWB sunset. You can now get rifles with tele-stocks and threaded barrels. Were I bringing this rifle up to date, I'd probably swap the faux tele-stock out for the real thing. However, I would think long and hard about taking the comp off. It works very well, and if this was a competition-only rifle I'd leave it on. And if I left it on, I'd feel no need to thread the barrel. However, as a duty or defensive rifle, I'd want a flash hider, so this particular rifle would have the barrel pulled, threads lathe-cut, and a flash hider installed. Can I guarantee that every Stag Arms rifle will shoot as well as this one? No, I'm not sure anyone can. But based on the performance of this one, and the obvious quality that went into everything else on the rifle, I'd say your chances of getting a tack-driver of your own are pretty good.

And the rifle shoots so well, that even though I am not left-handed I'm tempted to tell Stag Arms they either have to accept my check for it, or as the British say, threaten legal action to get it back. This one stays with me.

CHAPTER 29

Gunsmithing

You need spare parts, but you also need to know how to install them. It is not always obvious how things go together.

In many ways AR is not like other rifles. In some ways the AR is JUST like many other rifles. To unscrew the barrel of a Mauser, for instance, you need a barrel vise and some sort of action wrench. If you lack these, you simply cannot remove the barrel. The AR requires special tools to keep from breaking things. If you lack a barrel clamp, or action clamp, you can't remove the barrel without breaking or seriously marring something.

If you do not have the correct drift punches, you will either mar the receiver, or worse, break a too-small drift punch off in a roll pin, creating a real headache. The good news is, the parts are easy to get.

For those of you who can't wait for Volume 2 and just have to get to work on your AR right now here are the basics of what you need:

Action Blocks

You have to have the action block, otherwise there is no way to hold the receiver. You can use the clamp-around-the-action type for barrel work. You can use the milling-machine type to do work on the upper. For the lower, you use blocks that fit in the magazine well, that allow you to clamp the lower without marring it, or having it slip and be damaged.

Bench Block

You'll be doing a lot of drifting pins on the AR. Get a blue or white bench block from Brownells, which allows you to brace and position the part. With it, you can move most anything. Without it, you'll have a tough time keeping the rifle steady while you go to hit the punch.

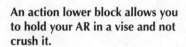

An action lower block allows you to hold your AR in a vise and not crush it.

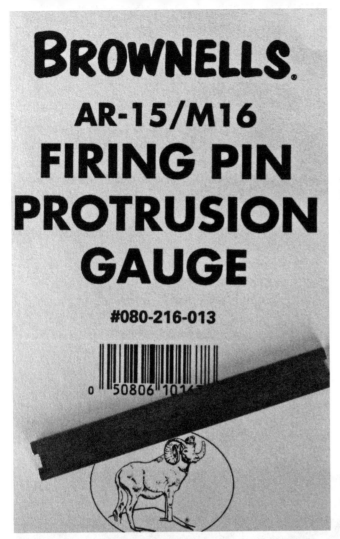

BROWNELLS.
AR-15/M16
FIRING PIN
PROTRUSION
GAUGE

#080-216-013

An armorer needs a firing pin protrusion gauge. You might own a bunch of ARs for a decade and never need it.

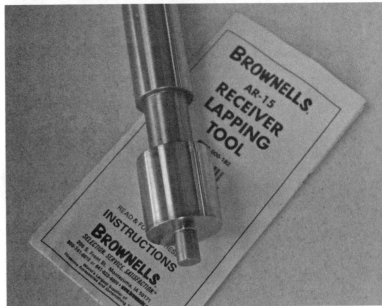

The receiver lapping tool is a specialized tool for advanced work. Impossible to do some things without it, but if you don't need it you don't need it.

If you're going to do any machine work on an AR upper, you must have this block. It also makes assembly a lot easier, as you can clamp the upper in a vise without crushing it. Get this one if you plan to do any assembly of sights or forward assists.

Barrel Nut Wrench

You cannot remove a barrel nut with a pipe wrench. Well, you can, but it will get real ugly, real fast. You need either the action blocks, or a barrel clamp, and a proper barrel nut wrench. Avoid the "surplus" ones that are a flat plate with three pins through it. Get a real wrench, one with a handle and many slots to contact many barrel nut splines.

Tele-Stock Wrench

If you plan to install or remove one, you need this wrench. When I started, I used a pipe wrench and a collar of PVC pipe slit to act as a cushion. All I can say is, it worked, and it didn't cost anything. As soon as I saw a real wrench that worked better, I put away the jury-rigged unit and didn't look back.

Headspace Gauges

If you plan to re-barrel, you'll need these. Get a set (don't mix brands) and keep them safely stored. I like Dave Manson Precision reamers and headspace gauges.

Drift Punches

You'll need a set. Look through the Brownells catalog and get a set for AR work. Get an extra of the smallest one, as you'll break it sooner or later.

Reading Material

This book is a start. Volume 2 will take you farther. But I am not the all-knowing OZ, I am still learning things about all firearms. Read, study, and don't take anything on the internet as gospel unless there is documentation to back it up.

Conclusion

So, what have we learned in creating this first volume? That the state of the art of AR making has advanced a great deal in the last decade. Based on what I saw from the early 1980s to the early 1990s, I was expecting to find receivers in a blizzard of grays and blacks. But the receivers were so uniformly black matte anodized that you'd think the same shop did them all.

I was also expecting accuracy to be all over the map. When I began shooting in practical shooting competitions, no one shot ARs if they could avoid it. Yes, there were some that were accurate, but most weren't. Colts were, but who wanted to spend twice as much for a Colt? And those that weren't, were not much more accurate than your basic surplus M-1 Carbine, never a tack-driver. When I began gunsmithing, and shooting at Second Chance, I quickly found ways to make an AR more accurate. But all the rifles tested were head and shoulders above the level of performance found on common guns when I started. And the best were breathtaking.

Which one should you choose? First, you don't have to choose just one. It is still a free country, and you can own more than one, and more than one brand, if you wish. You must decide for yourself if what you want is an ultra-durable duty and defense gun in harsh climates, a pampered competition gun, or the lightest possible gun to pack in your car or on your person. We just touched on sights, stocks, pistol grips, forends, and all the other options you can add or delete. Those will be in Volume 2, along with some rifles that arrived too late to make it in here.

Me, I found something to like on many of them. Most are rifles I could use in good conscience, in a class, on duty, for defense, or in competition. Few had shortcomings.

One other thing I learned was that when it comes to consuming ammunition at a fast pace, the test volunteers are even better at it when using ARs than they are when using 1911s. I never saw so much ammo go downrange so fast when there wasn't full-auto fire involved. And with one exception none of the rifles had a problem with that.

Twenty years ago this would have been a very different book. But the time has produced a much better, more mature, product than we had available to us then. Take advantage of the progress, and get yourself an AR.

These men count on the AR design every day. You can too.

(DoD photo)